HEALTH WARS

PHILLIP DAY

 Credence Publications

Table of Contents

The Mission

Hello. My name is Phillip Day. Thank you for taking the trouble to obtain a copy of this book and read it. May I start by saying how excited I am personally to share the following information with you, as the research I shall be reporting from the desks of some of the world's leading medical researchers connects with that most basic and worthwhile of human goals – to live a long and happy life, to prosper in circumstances, both in health and in quality of life and, most importantly of all, to help others.

For the past 17 years I have been researching and reporting on contentious health issues, publishing information that has been deliberately stymied or obfuscated by the political and medical establishments. My organisation is Credence Publications, a company dedicated to exposing quackery and hidden agendas within the health industry - be it the orthodox or alternative camp - which exist because of entrenched error, financial and strategic interests, quite a few of which we will examine later in this book.

As a reporter, I am interested in medical wars - situations where eminent scientists and doctors have done the unthinkable and directly challenged their own establishments over core issues of medical science. On the face of it, this seems to be a foolish move on their part, since to shut up and follow the party line would have guaranteed them the path of least resistance and a perpetuation of their enviable livelihoods and future prospects. But come out of the closet many honest men and women in the medical fraternity have done, to the great dismay of their peers, and there were those like myself ready to report the issues and agendas with which they felt compelled to unburden themselves.

I had no idea of the minefield I was about to enter at the time when, as a fledgling freelancer in Los Angeles all those years ago, I began uncovering both the good news and the bad from those individuals within the political and medical spectra, who had decided 'enough was enough' and were coming clean to the public about the gross sins of their establishments. In many cases, an immediate black-out of the facts they presented was implemented by the political/medical/chemical authorities they were exposing, and a campaign of intimidation and character-assassination against these men and women invariably followed. The work of these brave ones is condensed in the following pages, with notations and references, and makes compelling reading for those who have an open mind on the issues and a nose for the truth.

Truthful information in healthcare is only useful to those who decide to act upon it, and of course both the orthodox and alternative medical paradigms have much to bring to the table. But, while the following chapters may outrage and shock, and while the reader may form the conclusion at the final page that the measures described in this book 'make all the sense in the world', how many will actually act upon the information to improve their own circumstances? The sad reality in my experience is – tragically few. But why? Could it be because we have traditionally left our health and well-being for others to safeguard? Is it now so ingrained in our global socialist culture that Nanny Government is expected automatically to tend to us and nurse us when we are sick and counsel us over everything from what we use to brush our teeth to what sexual practices are best for us in order 'not to get a disease'?

I believe this to be our modern 'healthcare system', although, as the future pages will conclusively demonstrate, this is a brazen misnomer. I find it hard to discover any system at all operating in government-sanctioned 'healthcare' today that works to increase natural longevity in the individual and, perhaps even more significantly, to prevent diseases occurring in him or her in the first place. This is because illness IS the issue and the focus of big business in 'health' today. It's a sad but provable fact that the fundamental *raison d'être* for the medical establishment's existence in the form we find it today is to fight the war to cure disease and illness, not to prevent it from occurring in the first place. For this is where the profit is: in fighting the battle, not in avoiding it.

Yet if we commit a heresy and examine health from the diametrically opposite perspective to orthodox medicine today, *we find prevention is worth a ton of cure at a thousandth of the cost.* In some Eastern countries today, you fire your doctor if you become sick, the credo being that the job of doctors in these cultures is to prevent sickness as a first priority, rather than treat illness after it has arrived. It is no wonder prevention is not high on anyone's action sheet in Western corporate healthcare today because firstly prevention techniques cannot be patented and sold for great profit by drug companies, and secondly the very nature of preventative techniques ensures the reduction in need for medical drug intervention and profits slump as a result. Nowhere can this be more clearly seen than in the fact that doctors today receive almost no training at all in nutrition, the primary means of disease prevention. Inconceivable, isn't it? Why *wouldn't* they be trained in nutrition? Why indeed. Next time you visit a state-supported hospital at lunch-time, you'll see what I mean.

So it has been my job to collate statements and research put out by doctors and researchers on a variety of health issues, which all come together in this overview book, *Health Wars*. As always I extend a debt of gratitude and admiration to all who have helped in the crafting of this book, and especially the absent ones - those professionals operating both sides of the medical fence, who in many cases lost their livelihoods, their families and in certain cases their lives to bring you the information contained in these pages. Like them, I make no apologies for trying to convince you that the measures outlined in the following chapters, while very simple, are absolutely necessary and worth implementing in your life. Do you want to avoid huge expenses, family tragedy and misery, a premature and often agonising death, and a legacy where your hard-earned dollars end up in the bank accounts of the very individuals and institutions who may have contributed to your sorry demise in the first place? Then read on.

My task is also to convince you of the sense in taking back the responsibility for both your own and your family's health from your doctor and relegating the medical and political establishments to the role they were originally designed to play in this arena – namely to provide purposeful and effective medical intervention ONLY when absolutely necessary, and with your primary consent, based on ALL the evidence available. Most reading this won't feel the urgent compulsion

5

to change their attitudes in this way until they come to a well-informed understanding of the largely unreported health disasters, medical terrorism and drug quackery going on in their midst. This book offers a useful summary of the main disaster areas that are currently robbing you and your family members of many years of active, future life.

Can I convince you to change your views on your own health and how to manage it? I believe the following evidence will be as hugely persuasive and grounded in common sense for you as it was for me, backed up as it is by the highest levels of prevention science. But that won't necessarily mean readers will subsequently implement the prevention recommendations the following experts put forward. So consider the subject from another angle: If I could convince you that by doing a few simple things, as well as avoiding some pitfalls, you might conceivably add substantial years to your life, and good quality, healthy years at that, would you do them? What would, say, another 30 years on your score sheet really be worth to you? More importantly, what would another 30 years of your life be worth to mankind? What additional benefits, kindnesses and insights could you even offer your children, your friends and family with all those extra years? And how about teaching them how to qualify for extra mileage also?

So what is this all about? Well - before we look at the 'what', we'd better start with the 'why'. *Why has so much life-saving health information NOT made front-page news and banner headlines across the world?* The simplified answer is, because today is the Information Age. The real wars, as we shall discover, are not being fought with bombs and bullets, but with both information and the denial of it. Sometimes NOT reporting information is every bit as deadly as reporting it, and this is a game daily played by powers around the globe to control and direct the attitudes and opinions of the populations they govern. On the other hand, the people now find themselves equipped with a global weapon every bit as potent as those their governments possess. With the advent of the Internet and the ongoing globalisation agenda proceeding apace across our planet, there is now an immeasurable amount of information, both good and bad, readily accessible to the general public that simply wasn't there even five years ago. This apparent colossal benefit presents two problems for the general citizen in his/her quest to get educated: Information Overload and Information Apathy.

Information Overload is where too much information gets offered to the citizen, who simply cannot absorb it all and therefore chooses not to participate. After all, life's too complicated for many of us as it is and the mortgage has to be paid anyhow. Information Overload invariably leads to Information Apathy, where a citizen will, in blanket fashion, summarily reject almost all educative information without absorbing it, entering 'shutdown mode' whenever confronted with data on a particular subject that is outside the norm of their comfort zone and daily ritual. Never mind that this could be data of life-saving importance that is being firmly pushed away, to the eventual detriment of the citizen concerned. We shall see some examples of this tragic state of affairs in a later section, examples where accepted medical routines have lead, and continue to lead even the smart among us down the 'piper's path', resulting in us dying early and badly.

The first lesson I learned about reporting this strange new commodity called information was not to use a dump-truck, but to provide the public with simple, bite-sized chunks, working from the general premise of what I was trying to convey down towards the intricate detail, allowing the individual at all times control over how deep they wanted to dig. We see Ted Turner's CNN do this every day, with their 30-minute general news summaries expanded later with more in-depth studies. You can change the channels if it all gets too boring.

So, let's start from the outward premise of what *Health Wars* stands for and then work inward to the detail. In fact, none of this is rocket science, you'll be relieved to hear, but the picture IS hugely compelling and fascinating as it all comes together. Let's start with the initial pitch, which runs as follows:

ME: *If you knew that by changing a few simple things in your life, you stood a great chance of living to 100 in good health, able to enjoy an active lifestyle into your old age with your friends, family and grandchildren - would you?*

YOU: *Who wouldn't? What do I have to do anyway? How much will it cost? What buttons do I press?* etc. etc.

Only an imbecile would reply: "No, I'm perfectly happy hoping I'll balk the odds and survive to the national median age, spending the last years with my brain gradually destroyed by Alzheimer's, or eventually succumbing to cancer, heart disease or diabetes. I'm not interested."

What's strange in my experience is that none of us readily imagines the reality of what our old age holds for us in the future. When we wake up at 2am on occasions and lie there, contemplating the enormous questions of life, how many of us honestly face up to a future in a wheelchair in a home somewhere, health insurance payments being whipped out of our bank account, connected to strange machines, being filled with stranger drugs to combat the ravages of the drugs we have already been given, not even recognising our loved ones when they come to visit us, as we languish there, incontinent and drooling to the end? It's not a nice picture, but it is a true picture, according to current trends, of what faces most of us in old age at the moment, unless we resolve to do things a little differently. As the cliché goes, "If you keep doing what you're doing, you're going to keep getting what you're getting."

I think we need firstly to appreciate what we ARE getting, in terms of old age and associated poor quality of life, before we can expect to be fully motivated to make the few simple changes we touched on earlier. It's not that most of us kid ourselves imagining a life reaching to the venerable old age of 106, all our own teeth still stuck in our head, vibrant and cantankerous to the end when, all of a sudden, either on the golf course, in a nail salon, or in a bar somewhere, whammm! we're pole-axed with a mercifully quick stroke or heart attack.

No. The truth is, we mostly don't think about our end at all. But a report highlighted in Australia's *Herald Sun* shows that two-thirds of us are expected to contract a terminal illness, unless we do something about it. The Australian figures, not quite as bad as those from the UK, read as follows:

> ➢ One in five will suffer from a mental problem at some stage in their life
> ➢ One in three men and one in four women will develop cancer

- One in two men and one in three women will suffer from coronary heart disease
- One in four men and one in five women will have a stroke
- One in six will suffer from diabetes
- One in three will have asthma
- Eight in ten adults are physically inactive, have high blood pressure or smoke cigarettes[1]

From a harsh, statistical point of view, we're not going to make it, of course, at least to that golf course scene. Yet, while admittedly the death-rate is still one per person with a 100% hit-ratio, there is much we can do to avoid this sort of heartache. Psychologically however, we do very little proper health planning for our old age. We allow the final chapters of our lives to come upon us as they happen, and what little foresight and planning we do enter into is supposed to provide for the expected degeneration of our bodies - the pension, the medical plan and benevolent medical establishment, which we hope will care for us when old age and ill-health inevitably assault us. Well, in many cases, these institutions DO take care of us - permanently. In the coming chapters, we will learn that doctors and Western healthcare are now the third leading cause of death in the United States, next to heart disease and cancer, and the statistics of all three are rising.

In the UK you used to receive a telegram from the Queen upon your hundredth birthday. In the year 2000, we saw the amusing irony of the Queen sending the telegram to her own mum, the ever-mobile Elizabeth the Queen Mother, who had tipped the century to the delight of all. Well, in my book, that's fine for royalty – good luck to them - but what about us unwashed commoners? What are the chances of getting that telegram for myself? Could humans *routinely* survive to be a hundred in the rap, neon and jet exhaust of the 21st century?

---

[1] *Herald Sun*, "Two-Thirds Risk Terminal Illness", Australian Institute of Health and Wellness report, 27th November 1999

Getting the Queen's Telegram

Eric Storm was a young man in the 1920s who was planning to make it rich. Based in Java and working for Butterworth & Co as a commodities broker, Storm was in the profit vortex resulting from the massive commercial re-supplying of sugar, tea, coffee, rice and rubber to the Asian nations after the chronic shortages created by World War 1.

Eric Storm played and worked hard, becoming a partner in his firm – a frenetic lifestyle that was to have the tragic consequence of giving him a heart attack at the age of 34. Overweight at 238 lbs (110 kilos), a heavy smoker and drinker who indulged every culinary fantasy, Eric had an epiphany in his hospital bed about where his life was headed, if he didn't mend his ways and fast.

Eric's existence took a radical turn when he decided to make his life's work the study of longevity. He survived a further 69 years following his heart attack, dying peacefully in Sydney, Australia on 24th February 2000 at the age of 103. His legacy and life have come to symbolise the ability to change lifestyle and reap the immediate benefits, *no matter the severity of the current physical condition of the citizen.* Much of Eric's research centred on the so-called 'primitive' peoples who demonstrated a superb physical and mental health and in many cases, lived past 100 in full and active working order.

Storm's desire for longevity was of course nothing new. Longevity has captivated mankind for as long as history itself – and it's a subject that is growing ever more researched as time passes. Yet it is a fact that there are cultures on Earth today who routinely live beyond a hundred, who do not suffer from the frightening range of illnesses like cancer, heart disease and diabetes - diseases that are unknown to them - which are killing civilised mankind in the Western world.

Far from following in the tracks of the technologically advanced West, many members of these long-lived peoples, such as the Karakorum, the Abkhasians and Hunzas, move into the twilight of their years with firm and functioning bodies and a mind as sharp as a surgeon's scalpel, living off the land, eating their own produce and surviving to grand old ages, commonly 120-plus and in some instances reportedly up to 150. There is one thing though that these long-lived cultures do lack, which is a shortcoming of great concern to Western governments, anxious to civilise these tribal peoples and render modern 'aid' and 'healthcare' to them: they haven't yet started using Western doctors and their 'medicine'.

Like Eric Storm, it serves us to study these peoples in some depth to discover what it is about their lifestyles that enables them to survive to great ages almost completely unscathed by disease. After all, if you wish to live beyond a hundred, is it any good talking to doctors, whose average age is often below the median? Want to live to a hundred in a firm and healthy condition? Why get your medical advice from physicians and general practitioners who are generally among the most unhealthy professional group in our society, many of them dependent on the very drugs they themselves dispense?[2]

No, the answer, as Storm reasoned, is to research and take advice from those who, by being living, healthy examples of the lifestyles they pass on to their progeny, prove the validity of proper health concepts. Many reading this already know the handicap civilised societies have paid because of the dangers lurking in our toxin-loaded environments. But is that all there is to it?

Dr Samuel King Hutton remarked: *"Some diseases common in Europe have not come under my notice during a prolonged and careful survey of the health of the* [Labrador] *Eskimos. Of these diseases, the most striking is cancer."*[3]

Remarking on his interview with Joseph Herman Romig, dubbed 'Alaska's most famous doctor', Dr Weston A Price claims that *"...in his* [Romig's] *thirty-six years of contact with these people, he had never seen a case of malignant disease among the truly primitive Eskimos and Indians, although it frequently occurs when they are modernized."*[4]

---

[2] **Hammond, P & M Mosley** *Trust Me (I'm a Doctor)*, Metro Books, 1999. Dr Hammond's book created a sensation when it was released. It describes the real lives of doctors and nurses in marked contrast to the public's perception of them.

[3] **Hutton, Dr Samuel King** *Among the Eskimos of Labrador*, London and Philadelphia 1912

[4] **Price, Dr Weston A** *Nutrition and Physical Degeneration*, London and New York, 1939

These stories seem to be the same wherever non-westernised tribes are encountered. Lack of degenerative diseases in these indigenous tribes led famous explorer Roald Amundsen to comment in 1908:

"My sincerest wishes for our friends the Nechilli Eskimos is, that civilization may never reach them." [5]

The *Ecologist* reports: *"Sir Robert McCarrison, a surgeon in the Indian Health Service, observed "a total absence of all diseases during the time I spent in the Hunza valley [seven years]... During the period of my association with these peoples, I never saw a case of... cancer."* [6]

Dr Alexander Berglas sums up his own findings, in this case, about cancer and our polluted environment: *"Civilization is, in terms of cancer, a juggernaut that cannot be stopped... It is the nature and essence of industrial civilization to be toxic in every sense... We are faced with the grim prospect that the advance of cancer and of civilization parallel each other."* [7]

THE HUNZAS

Upon embarking on a study of longevity, you don't get very far into the project before you come into contact with the Hunzakuts. This isolated people of Northeastern Pakistan, located in the Himalayan foothill valleys, were not discovered until the 1920s, when the British Army traversed the mountain passes and came into contact with one of humankind's longevity miracles for the very first time. One practitioner who went with them was the aforementioned Dr Robert McCarrison (later Sir Robert McCarrison), who was able to document in some detail the astonishing culture he discovered.

The society the army engineers found was open, warm, friendly and religious and had a tremendous sense of community. One of the things McCarrison noticed immediately was the astonishing lack of diseases and the fine condition of the people. In their indigenous, isolated environment, the Hunzas exhibited near perfect physical and

---

[5] **Amundsen, Roald** *The Northwest Passage*, London and New York, 1908
[6] *The Ecologist*, vol. 28, No. 2, March/April 1998, p. 95
[7] *The Ecologist,* op. cit.

mental health. There was no sign of cancer, heart disease, diabetes, ulcers, colitis, diverticulosis, high blood pressure or childhood ailments. Neither was there any juvenile delinquency or crime. Respect for elders and age was ubiquitous and the tribe's sense of community made it clear to all members that if one was to succeed, all had to succeed. The teamwork with which the Hunzas executed their daily chores was very evident in their happiness, peace of mind and conspicuous lack of strife. The Hunzas had no police, no jails, no judges and no doctors or hospitals.

Their teeth were in the finest condition - perfect dental arches full of even, white teeth with no disfiguration, dental caries or other tarnishments common to the industrialised societies. Many of their population were later estimated to be older than 100, fathering children at 100-plus, with some of the most vital apparently surviving to 150 and beyond. Hunza womenfolk too were of the finest condition. No birth problems were observed and those ladies of 80 looked the equivalent of 40, with fresh and remarkably unblemished complexions.

McCarrison, later to become Director of Research on Nutrition in India and Chairman of the Post-Graduate Medical Education Committee at Oxford University, was so taken by these people that he spent years of his life uncovering the Hunzas' health secrets. He later wrote: *"These people are unsurpassed by any other race in perfection of physique. They are long-lived, vigorous in youth and age, capable of great endurance and enjoy remarkable freedom from disease in general."* [8]

Renee Taylor too studied the Hunzas and was told by their King, the Mir: *"The idleness of retirement is a much greater enemy in life than work. One must never retire from something, one must retire to something."* [9]

The Hunza workload was prodigious. It was common, researcher Roger French remarks, for a Hunza to walk the 200km return trip to Gilgit in neighbouring Pakistan, carrying a heavy load over mountain

[8] **French, Roger** *The Man Who Lived in Three Centuries*, Natural Health Society of Australia, 2000, p. 29
[9] **Taylor, Renee** *Hunza Health Secrets*, Keats Publishing, 1964

passes and dangerous terrain without any stops for rest other than meal breaks. The men regularly played vigorous games, including volleyball and polo. In a strenuous game of volleyball, the young men, aged 16 to 50, would play against the elders, who were well over 70 and, as observed in one game, included a man thought to be 125 years old. Hunza polo was ferocious and without rules and there were often teeth knocked out. As the Mir remarked: *"The men of 100 felt no more fatigue than the men of 20."* [10]

McCarrison got to the bottom of the Hunzas' success and roundly attributed it to super-nutrition and the absence of a toxic, industrially polluted environment. McCarrison set out to prove how diet was a major contributor to the Hunzas' success by taking rats and feeding them a staple Hunza diet – fresh fruits and vegetables, dried fruits, legumes, whole-grain foods and goat's cheese and butter. Meat was a rarity, and the meat and dairy components of their diet were low, in contrast to Westernised diets today.

Hunza water was later found to be highly mineralised, with a full spectrum of nutrients derived from fresh mountain streams and glaciers. The Hunzas also irrigated their crops with this mineral-rich mixture, greatly benefiting the crops that were subsequently harvested and eaten. McCarrison also noted that the Hunzas ate a high percentage of their foods raw and as close to nature as possible. Biochemist Ernst Krebs, along with other researchers, would also remark that the Hunzas, proud farmers of apricots, always consumed the seeds (kernels) of their fruits along with the pulp. This practice is widely condemned in Western societies today because of a supposed danger of cyanide poisoning (more details in a later chapter). McCarrison's Hunza rats were extremely long-lived and almost completely free of disease. Their condition was sleek. Their childbirth was easy and free of complications and the young ones were gentle, good-natured and healthy.

McCarrison then fed another sample of rats on the diet of the poor of the Bengal/Madras region: lots of pulses, rice, old vegetables, condiments and a little milk, together with city water. As described in his book, *Studies in Deficiency Diseases*, McCarrison's Bengal/Madras

---

[10] French, Roger, op. cit. p.30

rats were not happy rodents. The list of diseases afflicting them included diseases of the ear, nose and throat, lungs and upper respiratory tract, gastrointestinal diseases, skin diseases, reproductive problems, cancer of the blood and lymph, heart disease and edema.

Finally McCarrison fed a third sample of rats the same diet consumed by the working-class Englishman of the day: refined, white bread and sugar, margarine, sweetened tea, boiled vegetables, tinned meats and jams. The same rash of diseases as previously reported with the Bengal/Madras group broke out among the rats, this time with severe additional complications; namely nervous diseases and pronounced delinquency among the rodents, which bit their attendants constantly and finally, by the 16th day of the experiment, began turning upon their own, killing each other and cannibalising the weaker among them.[11] McCarrison's summary was succinct:

"I know of nothing so potent in producing ill-health as improperly constituted food. It may therefore be taken as a law of life, infringement of which shall surely bring its own penalties, that the single greatest factor in the acquisition of health is perfectly constituted food. Given the will, we have the power to build in every nation a people more fit, more vigorous and competent; a people with longer and more productive lives, and with more physical and mental stamina than the world has ever known." [12] [emphasis mine]

How much of a surprise is it to learn that McCarrison's advice and work went completely unheeded by the medical community of the day, fixated as ever on the expensive and patentable cure, to the inevitable cost of disease prevention? A careful study of what these and other indigenous, long-lived peoples do and don't do gives rise to six principles we are going to examine in detail throughout this book. I name them the Principles of Longevity. Here they are:

PRINCIPLES OF LONGEVITY
> ➢ Live in a non-toxic environment
> ➢ Work towards an alkalised body system

---

[11] For more information on the effect of diet on emotional and mental health, please see **Day, Phillip,** *The Mind Game,* Credence Publications 2002

[12] Quoted from French, Roger, op. cit. p.32

- ➢ Be well hydrated
- ➢ Be well mineralised and eat properly constituted food
- ➢ Be active
- ➢ Have a positive attitude and an optimism towards your future

The Hunzas of course are by no means the only ones to escape from disease almost completely unscathed.

THE GEORGIANS

The National Geographic featured, among many articles on longevity, an article on the Russian Georgians, among whom were estimated to be living 20,000 centenarians in the 1960s, according to the Soviet Institute of Gerontology and reported in *Nutritional Science & Health Education*.[13] Roger French reports that in one town alone, all the council members were over 100. Georgians were routinely fathering children over 100 and some were still working in the fields and leading active lives beyond age 120. The Georgian diet, like that of the Hunzas, consisted of whole, unadulterated raw foods in the main, supplemented with small amounts of goat and chicken meat, spiced with garlic, peppers and spices.

THE KARAKORUM

Another people, indigenous to the Himalayan foothills of Northeastern Pakistan are the Karakorum. I was interviewed by a lady working for a UK radio station who was originally from the Karakorum Mountains. She could confirm firsthand their extreme health and longevity and even what they ate. She expressed an amused interest in the British practice of retiring ladies at 60, knowing that where she was from, they were often still in the fields working past 110.

THE ABKASIANS AND AJERBAIJANIS

Two other tribes in the southern Russian republics with outstanding records for longevity are the Abkasians and Ajerbaijanis. The Russian central census noted around 20,000 centenarians in Ajerbaijan in the 1960s, with members of these peoples living beyond 120. One man was reported by the *Washington Post* as being officially 169 years old, a fact corroborated by the Academy of Science in the

---

[13] **Shears, C Curtis** *Nutritional Science & Health Education*, 1972

former USSR.[14] Interestingly, none of these peoples was pure vegetarian.

We see that elsewhere in the world, we have the Titicacas and Vilcabambans in South America, the Hopis in North America and the Aborigines in Australia. All these peoples have a great track record in longevity and health, and have, in their isolated states, shown a fine and virtually unblemished physique, great dental structure and a mild, non-warlike nature. And then along comes the white man....

So we see that it is possible to live to great ages with firm and functioning bodies and fulfil mankind's genetic potential discovered during the Biospheric experiments in the Arizona desert. This was later calculated by UCLA gerontologists to be between 120 and 140 years of age. Yet here we are today, not even fulfilling Nature's sevenfold potential in mammals[15], dying miserable deaths and lucky to make it to 75 with all our own marbles. The reasons why we are failing so spectacularly with our health and longevity have been some of the most awesomely researched topics in medicine – and also the most controversial. Because, to uncover the problems we are facing in health today, we have to admit that the current system is not working. That it has been set up DELIBERATELY NOT TO WORK with longevity. And then we have to confront that age-old beast of mankind – his own dark and greedy nature, which has shown a consistent propensity, down through the ages, to enslave and control his fellow human.

---

[14] *Washington Post*, 24th September 1972

[15] Invariably in the mammal kingdom, an animal's projected longevity is seven times its age of maturity.

Part 1

'the problems'

Population Wars
A Comparison of First and Third World Health Agendas

"It creates a very disagreeable impression to see people who are white, European, or of European origin, trying to sow the seeds of sterility in populations that are about to escape from under their domination." – Alfred Sauvy in "Le faux probleme de la population mondiale" (1949)

In this chapter we will start to examine the reasons why today's global and domestic medical, chemical and political infrastructures are perversely acting to shorten lives rather than extend them. This is some allegation, which is why I have devoted these next two chapters to the important issues involved. Firstly, let's discuss a little background to some of the forces operating in global healthcare today.

For many years I have studied strategic political and economic trends of governments and learned how these trends interact to dictate policy initiatives that affect us at the citizen level. On the street, few sane people would argue that a long, healthy and happy life is the most desirable. We ordinary decent citizens would therefore expect our politicians, corporations and medical establishment to be working tirelessly day and night to bring about this happy state of affairs for as many of us as possible. Sadly, as we shall see, this is almost the complete opposite of what is in fact occurring. More tragically, many in the upper echelons of power (power ironically given to them by their constituents) know their measures are deliberately shortening the lives of their voters, and yet these powerful ones *are deliberately signing off on the continuing slaughter of their own citizenry and even taking measures to ensure continuance of same.* Why? It might serve us to discover whether these startling allegations are true at all.

Governments, healthcare officials and drug companies are quick to advise the people that 'medicine has made fabulous strides forward in the 20th century, resulting in people living healthier and longer lives.' We often hear from cancer charities about the 'amazing progress' being made in defeating cancer. HIV-AIDS too is being battled with success, we are repeatedly told, with AZT and other AIDS drugs, known as

21

protease inhibitors, able to hold the fearsome HIV at bay. Currently, we learn from the news, the US government, the World Health Organization (WHO) and United Nations (UN) are working with drug companies to make these highly expensive drugs affordable to African nations, so these chemicals can bring much needed and life-saving relief to their beleaguered, suffering citizens.[16]

We hear about how government works day and night to pass regulations that will make our environment safer for us and our children to live in. We have organisations in America such as the US Food & Drug Administration (FDA), the American Medical Association (AMA), the Environmental Protection Agency (EPA), the National Institutes of Health (NIH) and the Centers for Disease Control (CDC) all beavering away to ensure that no harm befalls us through the food provided for us, the medicine or the water we are given to consume.

In the UK, we have a similar group of agencies watching out for us. The British public rest assured that the Medicines Control Agency (MCA), the Environment Agency, the British Medical Association (BMA) and the General Medical Council are overseeing the condition of the nation's health day and night. And elsewhere in the world, under the auspices of the United Nations, we are fortunate to have the World Health Organization and its myriad sub-divisions caring for the health and well-being of less developed countries (LDCs), who haven't yet the money or the technical expertise to set up similar watchdog agencies for themselves.

What organisation. Thank God for 21st century healthcare! What a relief that someone out there is watching over the planet.

Sad to say, everything mentioned in the above two paragraphs, with the exception of AIDS drugs being expensive, is a lie and the complete opposite of what is happening. In reality, as we shall see, these health agencies have been in possession of life-saving information for decades about cancer and heart disease, and have chosen not to use it. They have been in possession of life-saving information regarding HIV-AIDS, and have chosen to ignore it. They have been in possession of life-saving information concerning

---

[16] See section entitled *Entrenched Scientific Error*.

dangerous environmental contaminants and poisons used in everyday foods, water and products we use, but have chosen not only NOT to curtail their use and warn the public, but deliberately to promote their use, misleading the public about the dangers and ensuring their continued production.

And what about the massive aid the West is handing over to the developing nations? Surely that is making all the difference? Unfortunately once again, the exact opposite is happening. Most have no idea that the money extended to Third World nations in a supposedly benevolent fashion is always only given with the proviso that the receiving nation will agree to stringent population control and economic measures designed and formulated by the West.[17] The main cast of characters here are the World Bank, the UN, Western intelligence agencies, the IMF and certain Non-Governmental Organisations (NGOs) who are responsible for collating statistics, crafting the agendas, issuing and disbursing the funds, and implementing their stringent control policies. It has also been these loans for 'development and mechanisation', coupled with the forcing of modern technologies onto these developing nations which, more than any other factor, have been responsible for racking up the awesome debt beleaguering most Third World countries today.

Given the extraordinary budgets currently being ploughed into the developing nations under the guise of 'aid programs', it has been argued that this same money could have been used to eradicate world hunger and debt in these countries before now. In other words, instead of handing billions over to corrupt dictators, who used the money for waging war against their own and neighbouring populations, or who salted the cash away in Swiss accounts for their own retirements, why weren't the funds used to alleviate the real problems facing these developing countries? Why didn't the West supply the target nation with fresh, clean water to alleviate cholera, parasitic infections and dysentery? Three billion people on this planet do not have access to safe water and proper sewerage.[18] Why haven't proper sanitation facilities been purchased with the West's cash and plumbed into every

---

[17] For more information on Third World population control agendas, please see **Ransom S & P Day** *World Without* AIDS, Credence Publications, 2000

[18] WaterAid, Prince Consort House, 27-29 Albert Embankment, LONDON SE1 7YY UK Tel no: 020 7793 4526

village in Africa to prevent cholera, typhoid and other diseases? Why weren't proper agricultural programs installed to help the poor of these nations provide themselves with a sustainable food chain to avoid the malnutrition chronically afflicting the Third World today? In short, why wasn't the money used to help train these nations to develop themselves economically *so they could henceforth provide for themselves in these areas*?

These are the questions most people ask themselves whenever the issue of Third World poverty hits the headlines. Most citizens are baffled at the apparent complexity governments bring to bear on these issues when the simple answer seems to be staring them in the face: 'Give a man a fish and you feed him for a day. Teach a man to fish and you feed him for a lifetime.' What's the complication?

Helping developing nations with food and water and then educating them to become self-sufficient by assisting them with the development of their economy makes common sense. These are very achievable goals and in fact form the central agendas for many a well-intentioned Third World relief organisation. These organisations however become more than a little baffled by the strange lack of support they receive from national government or the UN in pursuing these matters. Why?[19]

The confusion facing the average citizen and aid organisation contemplating these matters arises because both are unaware that the UN and First World governments are desperately implementing an altogether different agenda. Namely, the systematic reduction (eradication) of burgeoning populations that are being viewed as a strategic threat to the First World. Put more simply, Western society and its associated power structures have ruled the world for five hundred years, and naturally wish to continue doing so, either through the Western-dominated UN or an eventual Western-influenced global government.

A Central Intelligence Agency document puts the perceived problem this way:

---

[19] **Mullins, E,** *Murder by Injection*, Iconoclast Books, Ketchum, ID, USA

"World population growth is likely to contribute, directly or indirectly, to domestic upheavals and international conflicts that could adversely affect US interests. Population growth will also reinforce the politicisation of international economic relations and intensify the drive [of less developed countries] for a redistribution of wealth and of authority in international affairs." [20]

However, as we shall learn, it was primarily not the *growth* of Third World populations that began to destabilise the world demographic picture, *but a marked decline in Western birth-rates*, which raised in the minds of strategists the spectre of the West's eventual marginalisation by new Third World economic and military superpowers. The need for the West to act to secure its continued survival as the world's dominant cultural and political power is succinctly if brutally put by political commentator Bertrand Russell:

"It cannot be expected that the most powerful military nations will sit still while other nations reverse the balance of power by the mere process of breeding." [21]

Pierre Lellouche, aide to French premier Jacques Chirac, reports the disparity of birth-rates between the First and Third Worlds thus:

"The African population is projected to triple within the next 30 years, reaching an estimated level of 1.6 billion. Moreover, the Middle East, Central Asia and the Indian sub-continent all have volatile admixtures of acute poverty, demographic explosion and political instability. Together these regions will have some 4 billion people within 30 years, while due north sit 500 million ageing Europeans already in a squall of demographic depression." [22]

Ben Wattenberg, an analyst with the influential American Enterprise Institute, is one of many scholars who believes that the First/Third World growth trends are probably now irreversible:

---

[20] **Central Intelligence Agency** *Political Perspectives on Key Global Issues*, March 1977 (declassified in part, January 1995). p.4

[21] **Russell, Bertrand** *Marriage and Morals*, London: 1985, p.161

[22] **Lellouche, Pierre** "France in Search of Security", *Foreign Affairs*, 72, no.2 (Spring 1993): pp.123-124

"Western culture was dominant forty-odd years ago after the end of World War 2, when the West made up 22% of the Earth's population. Today the West comprises 15% - and we are still dominant. [But] it is just about a sure thing that it will decline to under 9% by 2025 and probably down to about 5% by 2100 if present trends continue.

Even if Western fertility should climb back to the replacement level in the decades to come, the population of the Third World will be a much greater proportion of the world's population than it is now. Those Third World nations will also likely be richer and more powerful than they are now... Do we know enough about the Chinese, the Indians, the Indonesians, the Nigerians and the Brazilians? Do we know their languages? Do we know their cultures? We ought to. These are the demographic superpowers of the next century. "[23]

Does evidence unequivocally show the existence of Western-sponsored measures designed to curtail population in those developing nations deemed a national security threat to the strategic interests of the West? Do we see agendas underway to keep these burgeoning peoples in a state of perpetual emergency, either through the introduction of real or perceived threats to their national security, such as AIDS, famine and local conflicts, making the developing nation dependent on the West for relief and assistance? Have measures been crafted to reduce population rapidly without the target nation necessarily being aware of the full agenda being worked out under its nose?

It is not hard to discover, if you visit these developing countries, that the eradication of world hunger and disease is not only deliberately NOT being pursued, but is in fact the complete antithesis of what the Western hegemony wants for Africa, India and other developing nations, now deemed a strategic threat because of their populations. As we saw in *World Without AIDS*, when Africa cries out for simple agricultural tools and fresh water, the UN gives them condoms. When Africa asks for food for the children, the UN gives the kids safe-sex tee-shirts. When Rwandan women cry out to the UN to help bring an end to the deliberate mass-murder perpetrated by rival

---

[23] **Wattenberg, Ben** *The Birth Dearth*, New York: 1987: pp.97-98

tribes with machetes,[24] the UN responds by pulling out its peacekeepers and instructing the AID organisations to send in the condoms, bodybags and IUDs. [25]

As far as the First World is concerned, while it is true that life expectancy in these nations has increased during the technological gradient of the 20th century, birth-rates have markedly decreased. Despite the trumpeting of drug companies who like to take most of the credit for this extension in Western longevity, the increase has less to do with drugs conquering diseases as it has with vast improvements in nutrition and sanitation. In fact, the improvement in life expectancy during the 20th century, given the tremendous advances man has been able to make in technology of all kinds, can be viewed as somewhat disappointing. For instance, once men reach 50, they can only expect to survive about eight years longer than they would have in 1900.

LIFE EXPECTANCY IN AUSTRALIA
(total lifespan in years)

	AT BIRTH		FOR AGE 50	
	Men	**Women**	**Men**	**Women**
1901-1910	55.2	58.8	71.2	73.7
1996-1998	75.9	81.5	78.8	83.2
Increase in Lifespan	20.7	22.7	7.6	9.5

And so, birth-rates are declining in most First World nations today, many couples not even producing the two children necessary to replace and therefore sustain the existing population. One reason for this decline is family economics. It is costing more to live in the First World, especially as the direct and indirect tax burden increases. And while the ready availability of credit may give the false impression of a

---

[24] Disturbing CNN documentary footage shows besieged Rwandan Tutsi women and children, protected in UN-guarded compounds, begging the soldiers not to pull out and leave them, all the while machete-wielding Hutus circle the compounds and neighbourhoods in pick-up trucks waiting for the kill. The UN eventually pulls out and the expected massacres subsequently ensue. One million Tutsis are hacked to death by Hutus in just 100 days in 1994.

[25] Inter-uterine devices, a form of birth control.

family's wealth and social standing, real disposable income has been reducing, and with it the desire to add to a family's existing problems with even two or three additional children.

Such is our Western culture that our children almost never grow up to contribute in adulthood to their original family's day-to-day economic strength and survival. Our kids grow up, thank us for the education and the food, and then break away to form families of their own. By contrast, Third World families view offspring as an essential part of the family's work-force and earning potential *for life*, and so do not view multiple offspring in the same context economically as the West. A perspective study by the World Bank candidly points out:

"Few Africans are yet persuaded of the advantages of smaller families; they see land as abundant and labour as scarce." [26]

Declining birth-rates in the West also have much to do with the toxins with which a fully developed industrial society surrounds its citizens every day. This is an important subject which is given some detailed airing in this book.

Although at first sight, a First World family seems to have the optimum shot at longevity, the following general picture reveals the elements working for and against longevity for the Northern Hemisphere's industrialised populations:

FOR LONGEVITY	AGAINST LONGEVITY
- Better sanitation	- General environmental toxicity
- Better nutrition than developing nations	- Insufficient mineral content in food
- Non-toxic medical procedures	- Poisons in water supply and food
- Better law and order	- Dangerous medical procedures and the treating of metabolic deficiency diseases with chemicals

It is our mission to evaluate each of these factors as we proceed. Given what has already been revealed about Third World population

[26] **World Bank** *Sub-Saharan Africa, From Crisis to Sustainable Growth: A Long-Term Perspective Study*, Washington DC, 1989. p.41

growth, it should follow that the Western establishments should be doing all in their power to extend longevity in their subjects to increase population, and so begin to remedy their growing demographic inferiority to the developing nations. But this also is not the case. And it is here that we can start to put the truly sad picture of Western healthcare together.

Public Enemy No. 1

The indictment against Western Healthcare

"I know that most men, including those at ease with problems of the greatest complexity, can seldom accept even the simplest and most obvious truth if it would oblige them to admit the falsity of conclusions which they have delighted in explaining to colleagues, proudly taught to others, and which they have woven, thread by thread, into the fabric of their lives." - Leo Tolstoy

"You medical people will have more lives to answer for in the other world than even we generals." - Napoleon Bonaparte

Let our goal be to live to 100 in good physical and mental shape, enjoying a great quality of life. To have a reasonable chance of achieving this, we must implement a system which shows us things we must do, and things we must avoid, and we must know WHY we have to do and avoid these things. The system itself, as you will see, is simple, which is the key to its success. More importantly, the system is duplicatable, which enables us to pass the information on to others.

In these next chapters, we are going to examine why this book is called *Health Wars*, why it is that we have to fight a war in order to take hold of that which should be ours by inalienable right – a long and healthy life. A good place to start is to take a critical look at our current healthcare system in the West. Put simply – is it working?

Traditional medicine is failing very conspicuously to halt major killer syndromes such as heart disease, cancer and AIDS. That much is evident. It therefore serves us to study the fundamental flaw in the basic methodology followed by allopathic[27] medicine today that is at the root of this devastation. The flaw is simply this: our medical peers are treating our bodies with toxic drugs, radical surgeries and poisonous radiation treatments to combat diseases that are, in 90-95% of cases, either metabolic (nutritional) deficiency syndromes or... wait for it... diseases already caused by poisons (diseases of toxicity).

---

[27] allopathic – drug/technology based medicine, as practised by industrialised societies today

The virus and microbe do not dominate the causes of disease, yet these are the darlings of the drug and medical establishments, who routinely terrify the public witless with the possibilities of infectious epidemics and plagues, and who go on to patent expensive 'treatments' and 'vaccinations' to combat these 'fearsome predators' they have told us are in our midst.[28] The nutritional deficiency diseases, on the other hand – mankind's greatest killers by far - are not profitable diseases for the establishment to fight. Try making Mercedes payments out of telling the masses to eat more fresh fruit and vegetables. Toxin diseases are also not profitable for the establishment to fight. Try flying on holiday to Hawaii out of telling people not to use or consume the very toxins you, as the establishment, have a vested interest in promoting.[29] But the virus... now that's a different matter entirely. Later, we shall examine how medicine has, to the greatest cost to humanity, 'misinterpreted' past metabolic deficiency and toxicity diseases as infectious. And today, the error continues – most notably with Acquired Immune Deficiency Syndrome (AIDS).[30]

So, how successful has the establishment been in using the latest (patented) technologies to defeat illnesses that have entirely different and more simple underlying causes than those being promoted? Are these underlying causes being remedied in the headlong rush by the drug industry to foist their latest patented and money-spinning pills and potions on some poor hapless Joe (or Joeline)? How many of us have trusted our doctor and submitted to some of his most hideous chemicals and treatments with a childlike faith and perished as a result? We'll find out as we proceed.

Once again, let it be stressed that nutritional (metabolic) deficiency diseases and toxin-related sicknesses are the main killers of humanity today. They comprise 90 – 95% of the problems. Cancer, heart disease, osteoporosis, diabetes, which dominate the death statistics in the First World, are all chiefly metabolic in origin (although some also have a root toxicity cause, as described in more detail later). When our bodies

---

[28] **Ransom, S** *Plague, Pestilence & the Pursuit of Power*, Credence Publications, 2001 (available at www.credence.org)

[29] Her Majesty's Government in the UK is reported to have made an £8.7 billion revenue out of tobacco in 1999. Any chance that this factor could have influenced the reason why it took so long for the truth about tobacco officially to emerge?

[30] See section entitled *Entrenched Scientific Error.*

do not receive vital vitamins and minerals over a period of time, a nutritional deficiency disease results which, if not remedied, will lead to debilitation and eventual death.

TOXINS AND THE NATURE OF DISEASE

The problem the establishment has with dealing with mankind's greatest killers, such as heart disease and cancer, stems from its definition of 'disease' and the underlying causes of same. The Oxford Medical Dictionary defines the word as: *"A disorder with a specific cause and recognizable signs and symptoms; any bodily abnormality or failure to function properly, except that resulting from physical injury (the latter however may open the way to disease)."*[31]

As a result, allopathic medicine concentrates on bacteria, viruses, fungi, protozoa and other micro-organisms as being the predominant, suspicious causes for disease. Yes, diet and lifestyle are sometimes blamed. Environmental causations are only superficially entertained in relation to heart disease and cancer by the medical establishment, and toxaemia or nutritional deficiency problems are rarely discussed in relation to the major killers. So medical doctors are in a quandary; unable fully to appreciate the vital role nutrition and detoxification play in maintaining health, with their incomplete knowledge of nutritional science (they receive no formal training in nutrition), they concentrate on treating symptoms, destroying germs by squirting shots of penicillin and other antibiotics at them without appreciating why they became a nuisance in the first place. The science of Natural Hygiene, on the other hand, sees viral infection as a secondary causation, these microbes only able to gain a foothold in the body due to the primary malnutrition and toxicity causations.

These are two completely different views examining the same concept of disease. But which one makes sense and is correct?

In Natural Hygiene, colds and flu are viewed as the body's way of removing waste and toxins when required. Bronchitis removes waste from the bronchial tubes, pneumonia from the lungs; gastritis from the stomach, enteritis from the small intestine, and a runny nose and cold eject toxins via the mucus membranes. Psoriasis and eczema eject

---

[31] *Oxford Medical Dictionary*, Oxford University Press, 2000, p.188

toxins from the skin; pimples eject toxins from the skin; vomiting removes waste from the stomach more rapidly and is obviously not a disease either. It is a reactive causation to a deeper problem that is affecting the health of the human organism.

Making the important point that disease manifests in unhealthy, badly nourished bodies, researcher French explains a simple role for germs:

"Leading microbiologist Professor Rene Dubos stated that germs normally cannot and do not attack healthy tissue. They can only become viable, grow and multiply in a body that has some degree of internal pollution.

The best way to visualise the role of germs is with a simple analogy. Consider a garbage can. If the can is full of garbage, there will be rats and flies around it. We can shoot the rats with a rifle and spray the flies with poison, but as long as the garbage is there, rats and flies will keep coming. On the other hand, if we tip the garbage out and wash the can, there will be no rats or flies appearing and we won't need to fire a single shot or spray any pesticide to be free of them." [32]

Which means that if there are toxins and acidosis in our body, or our system is stuffed full of food waste and other detritus, germs will have a place to feed and the manifestation will be disease. Actually germs too have their role in breaking down and digesting toxins inside us and, through the diseases they create, urge the body to repel this harmful morass through saliva, nasal discharge, vomiting, faeces, etc. This is the reason why healthy people do not 'contract' colds and flu, whereas toxic persons do. This is the reason toxic, ill-fed cattle contract Foot and Mouth Disease (a heavy animal cold with fever blisters – that's all!) whereas healthy animals do not.[33] It's the reason a quarter of Europe died of the *yersinia pestis* (bubonic plague) in the medieval times <u>and three-quarters didn't</u>.

[32] **French R** *The Man Who Lived in Three Centuries*, Natural Health Society of Australia, High Street , Penrith NSW 2750, Australia
[33] Ransom, S *Plague, Pestilence....* Op. cit.

Healthy bodies have the ability to resist viruses and other diseases in ways which are as simple as they are ingenious. We are going to make a full study of these methods, taken from the practices of those peoples who successfully live long lifespans and live them almost completely disease-free. In summing up the difference between the two approaches to disease – conventional and complimentary – Roger French states:

"The difference between the two approaches is vast. Unfortunately the antibiotics destroy not only the pathogenic (disease-associated) bacteria, but also the beneficial or 'friendly' bacteria in the bowel that are of paramount importance to health. These 'friends' produce B Vitamins, digest dietary fibre and protect us against pathogens. Their partial destruction allows candida albicans to flourish, setting the stage for candidiasis and the symptom thrush. In addition, the antibiotic (meaning 'against life'), being itself toxic, contributes further to the toxaemia, which was the original cause of the illness in the first place. This is hardly the way to restore genuine health!" [34]

THE SURVIVAL DYNAMICS

Dynamic 1: Your body doesn't care if you are sick or healthy. It doesn't plan for the future. Your body doesn't think and it doesn't judge. It doesn't care if you are hurting or if you are happy.

Dynamic 2: Everything your body does, it does to survive. Your body makes thousands of perfect survival responses every instant of your life. You may like the results of these responses and call it 'health'. Or you may not like the results and call it 'ill-health'.

Dynamic 3: Survival of this instant is your body's only goal. Not survival later today, or next week, or next year. Survival now. Your body was designed to survive. It wasn't designed to be sick or well. What your body is, and how it looks and feels, is the accumulation of stresses that have been imposed upon it and the body's responses to those stresses.

---

34 French Roger, op. cit. p.55

Dynamic 4: For instance, osteoporosis, heart disease, cancer, arthritis, diabetes, flu, vomiting, diarrhoea and other conditions <u>are all the body's responses to survival situations</u>. They can also <u>all</u> be traced either to an inherent deficiency in the raw materials (vitamins and minerals) required by the body to get the survival job done, or to the assault of toxins.

Dynamic 5: If you don't like the body's response to a survival situation ('health' or 'disease'), don't put the body into a survival situation.

Dynamic 6: Stimuli are applied to the body when you:
> ➤ Eat
> ➤ Drink
> ➤ Breathe
> ➤ Absorb
> ➤ Exercise
> ➤ Rest
> ➤ Think (anger, emotion, laughter, love, etc.)

What kind of stimuli are you applying to your body in these areas? Are they compelling your body to issue a survival response?

Dynamic 7: The two areas in which disease is concentrated are:
> ➤ Metabolic
> ➤ Toxin-related

METABOLIC DISEASES

Metabolic diseases are simply illnesses (survival responses) that arise as a result of a nutritional deficiency. Once again, the disease itself is not about the symptoms primarily, but in what underlying factor (stressor) caused this survival response to manifest in the first place. It is important to stress that metabolic deficiency diseases do not have a cure, because a cure implies that the curative can be applied and then withdrawn as soon as the disease goes away. If this method is used with metabolic diseases, the disease returns as soon as the 'curative' is withdrawn. Metabolic diseases, such as cancer, scurvy, beriberi, pellagra, pernicious anaemia and many others (over 160 of them), must have the metabolic *preventative* (not curative) put back into the diet to correct the underlying deficiency until our need for oxygen ceases. Yes... for the rest of our lives. If this is not done, a recurrence of the metabolic problem will result.[35]

Metabolic deficiency diseases have certain noteworthy features to them, to which we shall be referring as we proceed:
- ➢ Metabolic diseases do not have a cure, they have a preventative which must remain in the diet for life. The disease (survival response or disease 'symptom') will generally disappear once the preventative is restored with its supplementary nutrition and the body recovers.
- ➢ If you don't want the metabolic disease, take the preventative in the diet. If you HAVE the metabolic disease, take the preventative in the diet!
- ➢ If you don't want the metabolic disease, take the preventative in the diet. If you HAVE the metabolic disease, <u>take as much of the preventative in the diet as the body can comfortably tolerate.</u>
- ➢ No metabolic disease (survival response) can be regressed by anything other than the metabolic preventative, which is always a food factor. *This means that drugs, which are not familiar to the biological experience of the human, while maybe treating the symptoms, will <u>fail</u> to correct the underlying cause of the problem, which is metabolic.*

These features describe the very nature of a metabolic problem, and also the sure remedy to see the back of it. Biochemist and cancer researcher Ernst T Krebs Jr. told the public the following in 1994 in relation to the last feature:

"Let me give you a categorical or axiomatic truth to take with you - one that is totally uncontradictable, scientifically, historically and in every other way. This is, that no chronic or metabolic disease in the history of medicines has ever been prevented or cured except by factors normal to the diet or normal to the animal economy. There have been many erstwhile fatal and devastating diseases that now have become virtually unknown. They have been prevented and cured

---

[35] **Griffin, G Edward** *World Without Cancer*, American Media, 1996 (available through www.credence.org).

by ingesting the dietary factors and thereby preventing the deficiencies which accounted for these diseases." [36]

So with that wisdom in mind, we can now see why it is that someone thought to be 'cured' of a particular metabolic disease like cancer by toxic drug treatments (chemotherapy) can get recurrences of that disease in spite of modern medicine's best (and highly expensive) efforts to combat it. The reason is *because the underlying deficiency or toxicity problem simply has not been addressed and taken care of by the drug and has not even been considered by the physician.* Yes, mind-boggling though it might be, we have many cases of 'terminally ill' cancer victims in remission because they had the deficiency elements for the disease put back into their bodies.[37] We have 'doomed' AIDS victims making full recoveries as a matter of routine.[38] We have arthritis victims, those suffering from diabetes, Alzheimer's, chronic fatigue - all manner of deficiency/toxicity diseases - now recovering once unhealthy bodies are given the simple (and natural) raw materials they require to rebuild and regain health and the toxins expelled. "It's a bloomin' miracle!" I hear many cry. Well, only if you regard putting gasoline into a completely fuel-drained car and then being amazed that it drives once again a life-changing, Lourdes experience. Otherwise, we can call it for what it is - plain common sense.

But, the so-often simple solutions sadly don't come into the public domain that simply, because we have a medical establishment today, which has, like a drunk who doesn't realise he has a serious alcohol problem, refused to allow the wife to take the car keys in everyone's best interests. Today, as previously mentioned, Western healthcare and its allopathic medical practices are the third leading cause of death in the United States. However, through the medical, chemical and political establishments' deliberate negligence in spreading life-saving information that could prevent killers Number 1 & 2 (heart disease and

---

[36] **Krebs, Ernst T** - Taken from a 1974 speech presented before the Second Annual Cancer Convention at the Ambassador Hotel in Los Angeles, California.

[37] **Day, Phillip** *Cancer: Why We're Still Dying to Know the Truth*, Credence Publications, 3rd ed. 2001. A comprehensive coverage of the medical establishment's chronic mishandling of the cancer crisis, the deadly toxicity of existing treatments that are not working, and the cover-up over the marked anti-cancer properties of Vitamin B17 (amygdalin/Laetrile) in its place within the treatment known as Metabolic Therapy.

[38] **Ransom, Steven and Phillip Day** *World Without AIDS*, Credence Publications, 2000. See also section entitled *Entrenched Scientific Error*.

cancer), it can be convincingly argued that, through the simple sin of omission, Western healthcare could be viewed as the world's Number 1 cause of death. Many doctors themselves, acutely aware that they have never been trained in nutrition, that most fundamental of medical sciences, are seeing this allopathic disaster occurring right before them in their work place, on the news and in the homes and medical centres they visit. And they have begun to speak out, as we shall see as we proceed.

That hospitals and clinics could, in themselves, be dangerous to our health is rarely considered by the average layman, whose respect for doctors and medicine borders on worship. Figures released in 1998 and published in *Environment and Health News* however make sobering reading:

"Australians may want to think twice before their next trip to the clinic. The chances of dying in hospital, or suffering some injury while there, stand at around 16% in Australia. Half this risk is due to doctor or hospital error – which means that 8% of hospital patients are accidentally killed or injured by the staff."[39]

In a recent emailed response to the *British Medical Journal* (BMJ), Ron Law, Executive Director of the NNFA in New Zealand and member of the New Zealand Ministry of Health Working Group advising on medical error, cites the following statistics and facts: Official Australian government reports reveal that preventable medical error in hospitals is responsible for 11% of all deaths in Australia,[40] [41] which is about 1 of every 9 deaths. *If deaths from properly researched, properly registered, properly prescribed and properly used drugs were added along with preventable deaths due to private practice it comes to a staggering 19%, which is almost 1 of every 5 deaths.*

New Zealand figures are very similar, according to Mr. Law. He states that the equivalent of New Zealand's second largest city

---

[39] *Environment and Health News*, Vol. 3, Jan 1998

[40] **www.mercola.com** *Iatrogenic Injury in Australia* - This is the executive summary of a 150-page official report revealing 14,000 preventable medical error deaths (only in hospitals - not private practice). (Full report on Dr Mercola's file).

[41] Australian Bureau of Statistics - Australian 1994 total deaths (1994) = 126,692, www.mercola.com, op. cit.

(Christchurch) has been killed by preventable medical error and deaths from properly researched, properly registered, properly prescribed and properly used drugs in Australasia in the past decade and its biggest city Auckland either killed or permanently maimed.

Dr Joseph Mercola, who hosts one of the most comprehensive health research sites on the Internet, has analysed Law's statistics:

"More than 5 million people have been killed by Western medical practice in the past decade (Europe, USA, Canada, Australia, and NZ) and 20 million killed or permanently maimed. Put another way, the economic impact of deaths due to preventable medical error and deaths from properly researched, properly registered, properly prescribed and properly used drugs is approximately $1 trillion over the past decade. Law notes that only 0.3% of these deaths are properly coded and classified in official statistics as being attributed to these causes." [42]

This mass quackery underway in traditional medicine is nothing new. But it was only quite recently brought to the public's horrified attention when consumer advocate Ralph Nader reported in the early 1990s that around 300,000 Americans were being killed by their doctors and hospitals *every year*. Health researcher Dr Joseph Mercola, as we will see in a moment, puts the figure conservatively today at around 225,000 a year in the US alone, according to current research. I would estimate that the real figure is closer to 2 million plus, which includes deaths that result from citizens not receiving life-saving information from their healthcare advisors. It must be understood that the *Journal of American Medical Association* figures, which Dr Mercola quotes below, do not take into consideration the number of cancer, AIDS and heart disease cases that could have been avoided if our medical establishment actually did what it was supposed to do, and promoted (unprofitable) prevention instead of hugely profitable and dubious 'cures'.

The JAMA data[43] is a follow-up of an Institute of Medicines report which hit the papers in December of last year. The problem was, this

---

[42] *British Medical Journal,* November 11, 2000; 321: 1178A (emailed response)
[43] *Journal American Medical Association,* Vol. 284, 26th July 2000

data was hard to reference as it was not in a peer-reviewed journal. Now it has been published in the world-renowned JAMA, one may be assured that the sources were verified. The author is Dr Barbara Starfield[44] of Baltimore's Johns Hopkins School of Hygiene and Public Health, and she describes how the US healthcare system is contributing to a shameful, iatrogenic or doctor-induced catastrophe.

UNITED STATES IATROGENIC DEATHS PER YEAR

Unnecessary surgery	**12,000**[45]
Medication errors in hospital	**7,000**[46]
Miscellaneous errors in hospitals	**20,000**[47]
Infections in hospitals	**80,000**[48]
Non-error, negative effects of drugs	**106,000**[49]
Total:	**225,000**

One key feature of the above statistics bears quick expansion. As a result of administering the *incorrect* drug or medication, 7,000 have died. As a result of administering the *correct* drug or medication, 106,000 have died. And this medical establishment is the one crying 'quackery?'

Dr Starfield offers several warnings in interpreting these numbers. Firstly, most of the data are derived from studies of hospitalised patients only. Secondly, these estimates are for deaths only and do not include negative effects that are associated with disability or discomfort. That the long-term fatal effects of some of these botched procedures are not included implies of course that the true figure is far higher. Dr Joseph Mercola advises:

---

[44] **Barbara Starfield** Department of Health Policy and Management, Johns Hopkins School of Hygiene and Public Health, 624 N Broadway, Room 452, Baltimore, MD 21205-1996 (e-mail: bstarfie@jhsph.edu)

[45] **Leape, L** "Unnecessary Surgery", *Annu Rev. Public Health*, 1992; 13:363-383

[46] **Phillips D, Christenfeld N & L Glynn** "Increase in US medication-error deaths between 1983 and 1993", *Lancet* 1998;351:643-644.

[47] **Lazarou J, Pomeranz B & P Corey** "Incidence of adverse drug reactions in hospitalized patients", JAMA 1998;279:1200-1205.

[48] Lazarou J, Pomeranz B, Corey P., op. cit.

[49] **Kohn L, ed, Corrigan J, ed, Donaldson M, ed.** "To Err Is Human: Building a Safer Health System", Washington, DC: National Academy Press; 1999.

"Another analysis[50] concluded that between 4% and 18% of patients experience negative effects in outpatient settings, [causing]:

> ➤ *116 million extra physician visits*
> ➤ *77 million extra prescriptions*
> ➤ *17 million emergency department visits*
> ➤ *8 million hospitalizations*
> ➤ *3 million long-term admissions*
> ➤ *199,000 additional deaths*
> ➤ *$77 billion in extra costs*

The high cost of the healthcare system is considered to be a deficit, but seems to be tolerated under the assumption that better health results from more expensive care. However, evidence from a few studies indicates that as many as 20% to 30% of patients receive inappropriate care. An estimated 44,000 to 98,000 among them die each year as a result of medical errors."[51]

Doctors Help Kill One in 10 Belgians
Reprinted from BBC News
24th November 2000

More than one in ten deaths in Belgium is due to euthanasia or drugs given by doctors to hasten death, experts believe. A survey of deaths registered during the first four months of 1998 revealed that thousands of deaths result from administration of lethal drugs "without the explicit request of the patient", despite the fact that euthanasia is illegal in Belgium.

Researchers from the Free University Brussels and Ghent University sent questionnaires to doctors who signed the death certificates and they received sufficient responses to allow them to consider 1,925 deaths in detail. They concluded that 705 deaths a year (1.3% of the total) could be attributed directly to euthanasia or "physician-assisted suicide". In as many as 3.2% of cases - 1,796 deaths - lethal drugs had been given without the request of the patient. And in 5.8% of cases - 3,261 deaths - treatment had been withheld with the express intention of ending the patient's life.

Additionally, some deaths could be attributed indirectly to the actions of medical staff, such as:

---

[50] **Weingart SN, Wilson RM, Gibberd RW, Harrison B.** "Epidemiology and Medical Error", *British Medical Journal*, 2000:320:774-777

[51] Kohn L, ed, Corrigan J, ed, Donaldson M, ed. *To Err Is Human: Building a Safer Health System*. Washington, DC, op. cit.

➢ Doses of opiod pain-killers like morphine, which can shorten life, had been given before deaths in almost 20% of cases.
➢ In 16.4% of cases overall doctors had made a decision not to carry out further treatment.
➢ The number of deaths which followed an "end of life decision" (ELD) was similar to that found in Holland, where euthanasia has not been a criminal offence since 1994.

The researchers also concluded that the "rate of administration of lethal drugs to patients without their explicit request is similar to Australia" - where the first act of legal euthanasia by administering a lethal injection was carried out in 1996.

The headline "230 a Day Who Need Not Die" appeared in the UK's *Daily Mail* on Monday 27th December 1999. The article stated that *"...at least 230 Britons die each day because the National Health Service is the sick man of Europe.... The deaths, from cancer, lung disease and heart disease amount to an astonishing 84,000 a year and stem from poor treatment in Britain's Third World wards compared with the best available in the rest of Europe."*

The mortality rate quoted by the *Daily Mail* incredibly approaches the average number of British civilian and military personnel who were being killed in combat during one of the past century's most devastating conflicts - World War 2. The study, commissioned by the Bow Group think tank and authored by researcher Chris Philp, also stated that these numbers may be on the low side because the study *"...did not look at all cancers and other diseases which claim lives within the NHS every day."* These figures do not cover medicine-assisted deaths as such, they just deal with deaths due to heart disease and the major cancers *which are considered preventable.*

Lois Rogers, a medical correspondent with the UK *Sunday Times*, submits the following report, which of course indicates that this healthcare catastrophe is occurring in other nations too:

BLUNDERS BY DOCTORS KILL 40,000 PEOPLE A YEAR IN BRITAIN - *Medical error is the third most frequent cause of death in Britain after cancer and heart disease, killing up to 40,000 people a year - about four times more than die from all other types of accident. Provisional research figures on hospital mistakes show that a further 280,000 people suffer from non-fatal drug-prescribing errors, overdoses and infections. The victims spend an average of six*

42

extra days recovering in hospital, at an annual cost of £730m in England alone.

A pilot study investigating the issue - the first attempt to measure the problem in Britain - shows that 1 in 14 patients suffers some kind of adverse event such as diagnostic error, operation mistake or drug reaction. Charles Vincent, head of the clinical risk unit at University College London, who is leading the study, has pioneered efforts to examine the extent of clinical errors in Britain. His team has so far concentrated on two London hospitals. The first data from one hospital showed that 32 out of 480 patients in four different departments were victims of hospital mistakes.

Vincent's estimate of 40,000 deaths comes from studies showing that 3-4% of patients in the developed world suffer some kind of harm in hospital. For 70% of them the resulting disability is short-lived, but 14% subsequently die. "It is a substantial problem," Vincent said. "There is a need to find out the true extent of error, what kind of things are going wrong and the cost." He believes the death rate may be even higher than indicated by the preliminary figures.

Britain's death rate is comparable to that in America, where recommendations in a report produced by the Kellogg Foundation... are likely to result in the creation of a new federal agency to protect patients from medical error. The report drew on studies that examined the records of 30,195 patients and found a 3.7% error rate. Of those injured, 14% died. Researchers concluded that 70% of the errors - and 155,000 deaths - were avoidable.

Department of Health officials are now examining a proposal for a £1.2m three-year national study of 20 hospitals and 10,000 medical records to establish exactly how these avoidable deaths occur and how to prevent them." [52]

The enormity of the United States JAMA statistics, along with those figures reported from Australasia and the UK, paint an astonishing picture and should be put into proper perspective. A conservative 200,000 – 300,000 people in the US are being killed by

---

[52]http://www.sunday-times.co.uk/news/pages/sti/1999/12/19/ stinwenws02011.html?1281951

botched medical procedures and inappropriate medication *every year*, according to Ralph Nader, the *Journal of the American Medical Association* and the *British Medical Journal*. This American death-rate represents up to 50 TIMES the number of that nation's servicemen and women who lost their lives annually in Vietnam on a field of battle dodging artillery and bullets (5,800 victims per annum).

Of course this death-rate of American soldiers, sailors and airmen in the Vietnam War resulted in massive social upheaval within America. As Dr Joel Wallach reminds us in his audio presentation, *Dead Doctors Don't Lie*, millions protested the war. A president was hounded from office. Demonstrating students at Kent State University, Ohio, were shot by National Guardsman. Worldwide outrage over incompetent military policies in Vietnam fuelled American public anger against its politicians and a backlash so severe that strategists in the Pentagon were compelled to seek an early resolution to the conflict. A memorial to the 58,000 dead was erected near the Lincoln Memorial in Washington DC.

Now a soldier, it can be argued, is trained in what to expect on a field of battle. But the average member of the public doesn't even know he or she is on a field of battle! But undeniably an immensely profitable slaughter is going on in medicine today that is conservatively estimated to be FIFTY TIMES as deadly to Americans as the Vietnam conflict. This new holocaust is a devastation which tragically includes, in military parlance, a high percentage of friendly fire against women, children and babies. I don't see any memorials to these people anywhere.

Some may speculate that in the war against global disease, a case could be argued that these deaths could be justified if we were getting on top of sickness in general; that the trillions of dollars spent by both the United States and the UK on healthcare were doing some good, albeit with some collateral damage occurring as a result. Unfortunately the only good this expenditure appears to be achieving, in the great majority of cases, is propping up the bio-tech share prices for the drug companies concerned. In fact what we have is extremely well-funded quackery on a scale which is nothing short of Herculean.

For all the money it spends on cutting-edge 'healthcare', of 13 countries in a recent comparison, the United States ranks an average of 12th (second from the bottom) for 16 available health indicators.[53] More specifically, the ranking of the US on several indicators was:

> 13th (last) for low-birth-weight percentages
> 13th for neonatal mortality and infant mortality overall[54]
> 11th for postneonatal mortality
> 13th for years of potential life lost (excluding external causes)
> 11th for life expectancy at 1 year for females, 12th for males
> 10th for life expectancy at 15 years for females, 12th for males
> 10th for life expectancy at 40 years for females, 9th for males
> 7th for life expectancy at 65 years for females, 7th for males
> 3rd for life expectancy at 80 years for females, 3rd for males
> 10th for age-adjusted mortality [55]

As US healthcare procedures are almost identical in many respects to those employed in UK and other First World nations, one can expect a similar pattern of iatrogenic death in these nations, and indeed this is, as we have seen, found to be the case. Dr Mercola again:

"The poor performance of the US [medically] was recently confirmed by a World Health Organization study, which used different data and ranked the United States as 15th among 25 industrialized countries in medical competence.

There is a perception that the American public "behaves badly" by smoking, drinking, and perpetrating violence. However the data does not support this assertion.

> *The proportion of females who smoke ranges from 14% in Japan to 41% in Denmark; in the United States, it is 24% (fifth best). For males, the range is from 26% in Sweden to 61% in Japan; it is 28% in the United States (third best).*

53 **Starfield B** *Primary Care: Balancing Health Needs, Services, and Technology*, New York, NY: Oxford University Press; 1998. Also *World Health Report 2000*, available at: http://www.who.int/whr/2000/en/report.htm.
54 **Guyer B, Hoyert D, Martin J, Ventura S, MacDorman M, Strobino D** "Annual Summary of Vital Statistics (1998)": *Pediatrics* 1999; 104:1229-1246
55 **Mercola, Dr Joseph** www.mercola.com

> The US ranks *fifth best* for alcoholic beverage consumption.
> The US has relatively low consumption of animal fats (*fifth lowest* in men aged 55-64 years in 20 industrialized countries) and the *third lowest* mean cholesterol concentrations among men aged 50 to 70 years among 13 industrialized countries.

These estimates of death due to error are lower than those in a recent Institutes of Medicine report, and if the higher estimates are used, the deaths due to iatrogenic causes would range from 230,000 to 284,000. Even at the lower estimate of 225,000 deaths per year, this constitutes the third leading cause of death in the US, following heart disease and cancer.

Lack of technology is certainly not a contributing factor to the US's low ranking.

> Among 29 countries, the United States is second only to Japan in the availability of magnetic resonance imaging units and computed tomography scanners per million population.[56]
> Japan, however, ranks highest on health, whereas the US ranks among the lowest.

It is possible that the high use of technology in Japan is limited to diagnostic technology not matched by high rates of treatment, whereas in the US, high use of diagnostic technology may be linked to more treatment. Supporting this possibility are data showing that the number of employees per bed (full-time equivalents) in the United States is highest among the countries ranked, whereas they are very low in Japan, far lower than can be accounted for by the common practice of having family members rather than hospital staff provide the amenities of hospital care."

Other scandals in healthcare are rife and they keep coming.

---

[56] **Anderson G, Poullier J-P** *Health Spending, Access, and Outcomes: Trends in Industrialized Countries,* New York, NY: The Commonwealth Fund; 1999.

"They laid 36 parts of my baby on a table. I put them into a bag and ran."[57] These were the anguished words of Paula O'Leary, whose son Andrew died at the age of 11 months from cot (crib) death. A post mortem had been duly carried out at UK's Alder Hey Children's Hospital in Liverpool. Unbeknown to Paula however, during the procedure, 36 different parts of Andrew's body were removed and put into glass jars. Andrew's body was given over for burial and Paula O'Leary thought that after her son had been laid to rest, the whole tragic episode of this part of her life could be laid to rest with him – given time.

But that time for healing was to be denied Paula. Later she was to discover she had buried only the shell of Andrew's body. Hospital administrative staff would later admit to Paula O'Leary that her son's liver, gall bladder, spleen, adrenal glands, thymus gland, kidneys, skull, brain and spinal cord had been removed and stored in glass blocks – the organs on the table before her now. His pancreas and thyroid gland had disappeared, Paula was told.

"Doctor had Child's Head in a Jar" states Britain's *Observer*,[58] recording how Dutch pathologist Dick Van Velzen decapitated a baby, which had supposedly died from 'Sudden Infant Death Syndrome' (SIDS), to preserve its head in a jar for later 'research'.

Later of course, the British public discovered that these scandals had not arisen from the actions of just one 'rogue pathologist', but formed part of an ongoing program to amass organs 'for medical research' that was to involve over 100,000 bodyparts stockpiled across 200 hospitals in the UK where, in many cases, the body's entire supply of organs had been removed from babies without their parents' consent.

"He was just three months old when he died," the *Daily Mail* reports.[59] *"His tiny body to be plundered of its parts by doctors. Over 10 years James had three funerals as his parents slowly learned the truth."* As more of James' organs were found to have been retained,

---

[57] *Daily Telegraph*, 31st January 2001, p.3

[58] *Observer*, 31st January 2001

[59] *Daily Mail*, 31st January 2001

Janet Dacombe would convene a funeral and bury them. Scott Woods of Kirkby died on October 31st 1989 aged just 12 hours. His retained organs were buried at a second funeral held ten years later on 5th November 1999. Now his family has learned that the hospital has wax blocks containing more organs belonging to Scott. A third funeral may be held.

Danielle Pitts of Winsford, Cheshire died after heart surgery on 18th November 1989. Her family had to hold a second funeral for her 10 years later on 24th November 1999 to bury her heart, brain, chest and abdominal organs. Now they face the prospect of a third funeral as it has recently transpired that a part of Danielle's brain has been retained in a different collection of organs.

Families were repeatedly given false information and some were offered body parts of their children to take home in cardboard boxes. Others had to reopen their children's graves three or four times to ensure they had buried the entire body.

Young Kayleigh Valentine died after a heart operation on 12th December 1990, aged four months. The hospital where she was treated removed all her organs, some ribs, her tongue and sex organs. Her parents held a second funeral on 9th November 1999, after which they discovered the hospital had not returned part of her brain. After the third funeral, they found out that Kayleigh's thymus gland may have been sold to a pharmaceutical company.

SUMMARY

As we proceed to examine the issues surrounding longevity, we will have to examine other medical agendas in more detail, such as the practice of First World pharmaceutical companies to peddle their 'failed' drugs to Third World nations under different guises to extend the 'legs' of a product's marketable life.[60] By contrast, we will also, by needs, scrutinise some of the more common and catastrophic treatments the orthodoxy is giving its patients in the First World.

Let us end this chapter therefore by concluding that there are, of course, fabulous men and women in medicine who devote their lives to

---

[60] Ransom, Steven & Phillip Day, *World Without AIDS*, op. cit.

making people well. But if the techniques and medicines they use are, by the admission of the medical authorities themselves, the third leading cause of death in the US (and by treatment association, in other First World countries also), and the medical establishment is also in possession of the provable answer and prevention to Killers 1 & 2 (heart disease and cancer), as we shall see, then the Western healthcare system can reasonably suffer the accusation of being the leading cause of death in the world today. The enormity of this is increased even further when we consider that many developing nations are basing their healthcare systems on US and UK medicine, and so are destined to suffer similar results.

This obviously begs the main conclusion: that, in general terms, the least you have to do with doctors and Western healthcare in your journey through life (barring some obvious exceptions), the longer you are likely to survive. This becomes ever more evident the further down the road we go on this fascinating and vital journey. For, to achieve a long and healthy life, expecting, as we might, a majority degree of success in our endeavours, there are certainly things we have to do, and then there are definitely the minefields we will need to avoid.

The Story of Hank and Jack Russell
Failure at the pump station

I poured myself some coffee and wandered with my cup onto the balcony which overlooked the apartment complex swimming pool. 'Twas a fine and beautiful morning in Southern California and I lazily watched the 747s lumbering into the air from nearby Los Angeles International Airport and thought that life could be worse. The great thing about California is that you always wake up with the feeling that you have a wonderfully clean slate on which to draw the coming day. Good weather has a habit of cheering the soul, despite life's trials, and I wondered fleetingly if it was still pouring down in England the way my mother had described over the phone the night before.

Evidently others in the apartment complex were coming out to peer curiously at the new day too. Rose, the manageress, bustled about, tidying up some litter from the previous night's revelry around the pool. Gemma was off to the gym, hair bound up and striding purposefully on athletic limbs towards her carport area. Old Hank shuffled onto his balcony across the triangle from me and leaned up against the railings, his grey hair an untidy muss. The heat was rising like a cauldron's mist so I turned and reached across to flip on the air-conditioning before returning to admire the morning once more.

Rose had gone indoors and old Hank was doing some impressively weird press-ups on his balcony. As I was idly trying to figure out his moves, he rolled onto his side and uttered a hoarse and agonised groan. Before I knew it, the coffee was stuffed onto a nearby table and I was sprinting like an Olympian out of the door and down the outside steps to the concourse.

I reached Hank about twenty seconds later and rotated him onto his back. His little white Jack Russell was all over him, yapping frantically. Part of me was observing the action at a distance. The heart attack had turned Hank's face a deep and shining purple and I remember being startled by the concept of the moment. His eyes bulged pitifully out at me as I tore open his flimsy shirt and began massaging his chest. He coughed explosively, phlegm and spittle flying into my face and onto my tee-shirt as I bellowed below to a startled

Rose to call a paramedic. The Jack Russell was doing better than I was. He was trying to lick old Hank back to life.

The old timer was definitely in a bad way. I've seen a few heart attacks and this one was a major leaguer. His rheumy eyes seemed to know I was trying to help him but then rolled in his skull as he fought for breath and failed to find it. Two minutes of intermittent CPR, blowing air between his slack lips in the macabre embrace of the living for the dying and then Hank's eyes glistened and gradually glazed over for the last time. Somewhere close by, a bird chirped happily.

"The medics say they'll be here in five minutes! Is Hank OK?" Rose querulously called up, brows knitted with fear. No Rose, he's a goner. I knew five minutes was an incredible response time, but I sensed deep within me that it might as well be five hours. I was looking down at a dead man. The Jack Russell was still trying to clean Hank's ears. Death at its most macabre, surrounded by normalcy. I diligently continued working on Hank the best I knew how right up until the first of the medics sprinted across the patio with his kit and hared up the stairs towards us. He checked the old man's vital signs and began CPR, intermittently pounding the chest of the old man with solid, hollow thumps. The paramedic's shirt smelled of the same stuff I washed my clothes with.

"He's outta here," the Texan drawled matter-of-factly as he watched his colleague roll a stretcher through the gates and across in front of the pool. He reached over to check the carotid artery in the fleshy jowls of Hank's old neck almost as an after-thought. "Nothing you could have done, fella," he reassured me.

God took Hank that morning. Left behind his mangy little Jack Russell and a funny smelling apartment with a man's lifetime of memories and modest treasures. Later I wandered down the street and onto the beach to let my mind roam for a while. Life the ultimate trip. And so apparently death.

* * * * *

The two leading causes of death in the Western world today are heart disease and cancer. Over 3,000 Americans die EVERY DAY from heart disease in its various forms. So, if we are interested in living to be

100, heart disease and cancer are two of the first hurdles we must overcome. Is that possible?

If you were able to remove heart disease and cancer from the general population, our world today would be radically different from what we see. How many relatives would still be with us? How much more money would there be available for proper research to conquer other, less well-known problems?

We are about to find out that both heart disease and cancer can end today based entirely on existing scientific knowledge. That is why I become increasingly tired of the whining British National Health Service and its government over cash shortages in Britain and how financially strapped the hospitals and health services are today. None of this would be happening if the population and its health services WOULD EXERCISE PREVENTION INSTEAD OF CURE. For who, in reality, is responsible for the soaring costs of healthcare today, if not we, the population, through not taking proper care of ourselves (our responsibility, not the government's)?

And how about the pharmaceutical industry, for overcharging for their dubious and dangerous 'cures' to fill the increased demand, all the while we become not only obstinate about changing our wicked ways, but ever more abandoned in our lifestyle and food habits as time moves on. Make no mistake out it. When you hear the financial creaking of a health service, like we hear sounding in Britain, what you are witnessing is a sickness dynamo that has succeeded in generating profits beyond its architects' wildest imaginations.

Hard to believe? Read on.

The medical/pharmaceutical industry is unlikely to gain an overnight morality and be the first to advise us to take proper care of ourselves to help prevent heart disease and cancer. Politicians on occasion however have attempted to redress the problem. The *Dietary Goals for the United* States, for instance, prepared by the Select Committee on Nutrition and Human Needs, declares:

"As a nation, we have come to believe that medicine and medical technology can solve our major health problems. The role of such

important factors as diet in cancer and heart disease has long been obscured by the emphasis on the conquest of these diseases through the miracles of modern medicine. Treatment, not prevention, has been the order of the day.

The problems can never be solved merely by more and more healthcare. The health of individuals and the health of the population is determined by the variety of biological, behavioural and environmental factors. <u>None of these is more important than the food we eat.</u>" [61]

Dr David Reuben puts it this way: *"There is a whole category of substances that have a far more intense effect on our patients than drugs. That category is food – and through no fault of our own, we have neglected that particular area of medicine. Our medical education neglected it, our internships neglected it, and our residencies neglected it.*

But now it is becoming obvious, with each successive issue of our most responsible medical journals, that many of these sick people are sick specifically because of what they are eating – or not eating. People of America, the greatest threat to the survival of you and your children is not some terrible nuclear weapon. It is what you are going to eat from your dinner plate tonight." [62]

As Hippocrates said: *"Let your food be your medicine and your medicine be your food."* Food today is apparently good enough to keep us alive, but not good enough to be used as medicine – an illogical argument. Yet imagine, if all of a sudden, large swathes of the population *did* begin eating correctly, cutting out harmful lifestyle peccadilloes and therefore became *less ill*. Panic would set in! The actuarial calculations of insurance companies would be hopelessly out, as people began to live longer. Biotech shares would teeter and health supremos would begin considering urgent ways in which the allopathic health industry could remain inside the profit loop. All that would be required to keep the cash flow intact would be to create *more* sickness.

---

[61] Quoted from **Diamond, Harvey & Marilyn** *Fit For Life,* Bantam Books, 1985 p.23-24
[62] **Reuben MD, David** *Everything You Always Wanted to Know About Nutrition,* St Martin's Press, 1985

An outrageous thought? Maybe. But, as we'll find out, creating more sickness is what is already happening, certainly in the realm of cancer and heart disease.[63]

Let's examine these two syndromes, beginning first with the heart, to see what can be done.

HAVING A HEART
The human heart beats around 100,000 times every 24 hours, pumping six quarts of blood through a freeway system of over 96,000 miles of blood vessels. This staggering feat is the equivalent of the heart moving 6,300 gallons a day, or shunting 115,000,000 gallons of blood by time you reach fifty. None too shabby, eh?

Then consider that those six quarts of blood each of us have are made up of over 24 trillion cells, seven million new ones of which are produced by our body every second, to replace worn-out cells and continue the work of transporting nutrients and removing waste and toxins. This amazing pump, responsible for all the action, has the capability to run maintenance- and service-free for decades without missing a beat. And no, it doesn't come with a warranty.

Coronary heart disease, heart attacks, angina pectoris, thrombosis, myocardial infarctions – trouble by any name – can be caused by certain types of drugs, as we shall see, and also by coronary arteries that have become progressively clogged by fatty material which prevents normal blood-flow (atherosclerosis). If you take your garden hose, which is supplying water to your lawn sprinkler (in countries which allow you to have one!), and bend the hose, the water flow ceases to the sprinkler. Likewise, if the arteries supplying blood to the heart become clogged with deposits, or blood clots brought on by sticky platelets, the same starving of liquid to the pump will occur.

PAULING AND RATH
But it's the underlying cause of almost all heart problems that is the most provocative and misunderstood issue in medicine today. Two

---

[63] In April 2002, the *British Medical Journal* published a report condemning 'disease-mongering' tactics used by some pharmaceutical companies, who attempted to sell hitherto non-life threatening diseases to the public as more serious than they are. Please see **Ransom, Steven** *Great News on Cancer in the 21st Century*, Credence Publications, 2002

doctors, Linus Pauling and Matthias Rath, popularised the scientific truth that had been whispered fearfully in medical corridors for decades, but which had failed to come out because of huge vested interests in the corporate profitability of heart disease – namely that heart disease was primarily only a fulminating deficiency of Vitamin C and the amino acids lysine and proline, which help form the collagen fibres that knit the artery walls together. Dr Matthias Rath sums up his findings:

"Animals don't get heart attacks because they produce Vitamin C in their bodies, which protects their blood vessel walls. In humans, unable to produce Vitamin C (a condition known as hypoascorbemia), dietary vitamin deficiency weakens these walls. Cardiovascular disease is an early form of scurvy. Clinical studies document that optimum daily intakes of vitamins and other essential nutrients halt and reverse coronary heart disease naturally."

The single most important difference between the metabolism of human beings and most other living species is the dramatic difference in the body pool of Vitamin C. The body reservoir of Vitamin C in people is on average 10 to 100 times lower than the Vitamin C levels in animals."[64]

What a revelation, eh?

SCURVY
French mariner Jacques Cartier was marooned when his ship became iced up in the St Lawrence River during the winter of 1534/5. It was not long before his men began dying from scurvy. Cartier's own words give a fascinating, if gruesome insight into what actually happened to his shipmates:

"Some did lose all their strength and could not stand on their feet... others also had all their skins spotted with spots of blood of a purple colour. Then did it ascend up to their ankles, knees, thighs, shoulders, arms and necks. Their mouths became stinking, their gums

---

[64] **Rath, Matthias** *Why Animals Don't Get Heart Attacks – But People Do!* MR Publishing, 2000, p.10

so rotten, that all the flesh did fall off, even to the roots of the teeth which did almost all fall out."

What Cartier was witnessing was the breaking down of the collagen and elastin in the bodies of his men. Their arteries and vessels literally sprang leaks as their bodies collapsed from the skin lesions and blood vessel fragility that is characteristic of scurvy. Later in 1753, John Lind, a Scottish naval surgeon, would discover that adding lime and lemon juice rich in Vitamin C to the provisions of sailors completely prevented and cured scurvy (hence the British becoming known as 'limeys'). Nevertheless, it was a further 48 years before his sound findings were adopted by the Royal Navy as official quartermaster policy. Another delay and countless more scurvy deaths resulted from the heel-dragging of the authorities of the day.

Which of course begs the question: *If heart disease is an early form of scurvy, then why didn't Cartier's men die of heart attacks before they died of scurvy?*

HEART DISEASE – MECHANICS AND REPAIRS
The answer appears to be the difference between how a chronic Vitamin C deficiency manifests (ongoing over a period of time as in the Western populations today) and the dramatic effects of sudden Vitamin C depletion (over a few weeks or months, as would have been experienced by Cartier's mariners), when this nutrient is completely removed from the diet. *It is how the body engineers its survival response to meet both these crises that gives rise to the noticeably different symptoms of heart disease and scurvy.*

For instance, Cartier noticed that:
> ➤ His sailors lost their strength and had difficulty actually standing
> ➤ They had purple spots of blood seeping from arteries and blood vessels
> ➤ The organs of his men began to deteriorate rapidly as the collagen broke down, literally leaking their own blood

With heart disease, the process is much slower, sometimes taking years to develop. As Rath reports, Vitamin C is essential for the production of collagen and elastin, the elastic, fibrous materials which knit the walls of arteries and blood vessels together. Collagen is a lot like the steel girders you see when builders are erecting a new skyscraper. Each collagen fibre has been calculated to be far tougher and stronger than an iron wire of comparable width. Collagen cells form the structure for arteries, and so a chronic Vitamin C deficiency causes the beginning of a collapse in the arterial walls, necessitating a healing process to commence, in the form of lipoprotein(a) fats which the body attempts to use to bond the thousands of tiny breaches in the arterial walls.

These lipoproteins are Nature's perfect Band-Aid. They are extremely sticky and form the atherosclerotic deposits associated with advanced forms of heart disease today. Cardiovascular medicine, unaware or willingly ignorant of the underlying nutritional deficiency cause of atherosclerosis, focuses its attention on vilifying the lipoproteins' LDL (low-density lipoprotein) cholesterol content as one of the primary *causes* of heart diseases, when it is in fact the healing (survival response) precursor, *brought on by a chronic Vitamin C deficiency*. Today the drug industry has mobilised a multi-billion-dollar business of anti-cholesterol drugs, which have wrought devastating results in cardiac patients, necessitating a further $20 billion drug program to combat all the side effects![65] Rath and Pauling discovered that

> ➢ Optimum Vitamin C intakes (600mg – 3g daily), along with supportive intakes of Vitamin E (800-1,000iu), the amino acids lysine and proline, the B vitamins, essential fatty acids (EFAs), minerals, trace minerals and amino acids, provide healthy arteries.
> ➢ A long-term Vitamin C deficiency will lead to atherosclerotic deposits in the arterial walls to cover the breaches caused by the disintegrating collagen, resulting eventually, with the heart, in coronary heart disease and, in the brain, to strokes.
> ➢ But Vitamin C depletion over a few months will lead to massive blood loss through leaky artery walls and death by scurvy.[66]

---

[65] Sellman, Sherrill, op. cit.
[66] Rath, Matthias, *Why Animals Don't Get Heart Attacks, but People Do*, op. cit. p.23

Vitamin C depletion (complete removal of the nutrient) in the industrial nations is almost an impossibility, even with the diets with which we feed ourselves today. However long-term Vitamin C deficiency is very common and occurs in almost all the population, hence the prevalence of heart disease in all its forms.

Coronary arteries sustain the most stress since they are the primary roadways for blood being pumped by the heart. The need for ongoing repairs of the leaky artery walls produces an overcompensation of repair materials, such as cholesterol, triglycerides and low-density lipoproteins (LDL), produced in the liver, which leads to infarctions as this plaque builds up. Other areas, such as arteries in the legs, are affected when varicose veins develop as a result of this ongoing healing process.

Collagen in our body is made up of proteins composed of amino acids, particularly lysine and proline. An optimum supply of Vitamin C, proline and lysine are decisive factors for the regeneration of connective tissue in the artery wall and thus for the reversal of cardiovascular disease. These factors are almost never prescribed by allopathic medicine, which is why, in spite of the most technical medicines and surgical procedures available, heart disease continues to be the main killer of industrialised, commercially fed, Vitamin-C-deficient humanity.

An interesting parallel can be seen in nature with hibernating animals which, during their extended sleep period, deplete their Vitamin C reserves, due to lack of incoming nutrition. As a result, fat molecules are deposited along their artery walls, which lead to a thickening of these vessels. In spring however, once these animals recover from their hibernation and begin consuming vegetation, their Vitamin C, amino acid and antioxidant intakes rise sharply, resulting in a reversal of these repair factors, leading to a restabilisation of their arterial walls and their normal function.

Lack of antioxidant material is also a major contributing factor. Current theories on this subject suggest that oxidative elements, known as free radicals, are brought into the body through smoking, car exhaust, pollution and smog, damaging the collagen in the artery walls, bringing on the need for further lipoprotein repairs. It is believed the damage is done because electron-hungry free radicals rob healthy cells to produce degradation in the cell and cell-death. These oxidative elements are now widely thought to be the leading cause of pre-ageing and cell degradation.

HEART DISEASE STUDIES WITH NUTRITION

So chronic vitamin deficiencies produce a breakdown of collagen in the arterial walls, leading to increased artery wall tension, narrowing of the artery diameter, thickening of artery walls and therefore high blood pressure. The result is heart attack, strokes (impairment of arterial flow to the brain), high blood pressure, irregular heartbeat (arrhythmia) and heart failure. Interestingly, as time marches forward, the public's ability to garner adequate supplies of Vitamin C from its diet through fruits and vegetables becomes progressively less as our food chain is corrupted further with processed, chemical foods and the public's penchant to move away from healthy, natural foods in favour of the more 'tasty' and better advertised artificial alternatives.

Ironically heart disease manifested itself less in medieval times since the predominantly vegetarian diet of the average working class citizen often provided well mineralised vegetables and fruits (at least in the spring, summer and autumn) *and no processed foods.* The killer was the more extreme of the Vitamin C deficiency ailments, scurvy, which resulted from sailors, for instance, dramatically halting their Vitamin C intake, due to the restriction of provisions available on board their ships.

Dr James Enstrom and colleagues from the University of California Los Angeles (UCLA) dramatically proved the heart disease link with Vitamin C when they studied the vitamin intake of 11,000 Americans over 10 years. Funded by the US Congress, their study demonstrated that citizens taking in at least 300mg per day of Vitamin C in their diet or through supplementation cut their risk of heart disease by up to 50% in males and 40% in females. This study alone should have made headline news. Who before could have claimed such a reduction in the number of deaths from the leading disease killer in the Western world? But nothing was mentioned! The study focussed primarily on Vitamin

C, but, as we will see, other nutrients also play a key role in the prevention or complete elimination of heart disease.[67]

Dr G C Willis demonstrated that Vitamin C could reverse atherosclerosis. Willis gave a sample of his patients 1.5 grams of Vitamin C a day and gave the remainder of the group no Vitamin C. After a year, the atherosclerotic deposits in the patients fed the Vitamin C had decreased in 30% of the cases. In contrast, no reduction in deposits was observed in the control group, which had even grown further. In spite of the clear evidence over 40 years ago of the benefits of Vitamin C through Willis' work, no follow-up study was ever commissioned.[68]

Professor Gey, from the University of Basel in Switzerland, conducted studies where he compared the Vitamin C, Vitamin A (beta carotene) and cholesterol intakes of citizens living in Northern Europe with those in the southern regions of the continent. His findings were recorded thus:

> ➤ Those living in the northern nations of Europe had the highest levels of cardiovascular disease and the lowest blood levels of vitamins.
> ➤ Southern European populations had the reverse statistics of their northern counterparts and so were more healthy.
> ➤ An optimum intake of Vitamins C, E and A had a far greater impact on decreasing risks of cardiovascular disease than the reduction of cholesterol, now becoming increasingly viewed as a secondary factor in heart disease risk (an inevitable result of the primary deficiency of nutrients leading to the breakdown of the arterial walls).

Gey's report also highlighted the preference for the Mediterranean diet, rich in wine and olive oil, abundant in bioflavonoids and Vitamin E, as a main prevention regimen for heart disease in almost all its forms.[69]

---

[67] **Enstrom, JE, Kanim, LE & MA Klein** "Vitamin C intake and mortality among a sample of the United States population", *Epidemiology* 3: pp.194-202

[68] **Willis GC, Light AW & WS Gow** "Serial arteriography in atherosclerosis", *Canadian Medical Association Journal* (1954) 71: pp.562-568

[69] **Gey KF, Puska P, Jordan P & UK Moser** "Inverse correlation between plasma vitamin E

Further studies showed that these nutrients <u>separately</u> produced impressive results for cardiac disease prevention:

> - Vitamin C intake lowers cardiovascular risk by 50%[70] [71]
> - Vitamin E intake lowers cardiovascular risk by one-third, documented in 87,000 study participants over six years[72]
> - Beta carotene (Vitamin A) intake lowers cardiovascular risk over 30%, documented in more than 87,000 study participants over six years
> - No prescription drug has ever come close to matching these figures in preventing heart disease[73]

However, when these nutrients were combined with other synergistic agents, such as Vitamin B3 (nicotinic acid), Vitamin B5 (pantothenate) and the amino acid carnitine, and levels of these maintained in the body over the long-term, near total prevention was expected, and in those already suffering from a variety of cardiac ailments, a clear record of efficacy in reversing these conditions was observed. [74] [75] [76] [77]

Autopsies of military personnel killed during the Korean and Vietnam wars showed that up to 75% of the victims had developed some form of atherosclerosis even at ages of 25 or younger. Victims of

and mortality from ischemic heart disease in cross-cultural epidemiology" *American Journal of Clinical Nutrition* (1991) 53: p.326, supplement

[70] **Ginter E** "Vitamin C deficiency cholesterol metabolism and atherosclerosis" *Journal of Orthomolecular Medicine* (1991) 6:pp.166-173; **Ginter E** "Marginal Vitamin C deficiency, lipid metabolism and atherosclerosis" *Lipid Research* (1978) 16: pp.216-220

[71] **Harwood HJ Jr, Greene YJ & PW Stacpoole** "Inhibition of human leucocyte 3-hydroxy-3-methylglutaryl coenzyme A reductase activity by ascorbic acid. An effect mediated by the free radical monodehydro-ascorbate" *Journal of Biological Chemistry* (1986) 261: pp.7127-7135

[72] **Beamish R** "Vitamin E – then and now" *Canadian Journal of Cardiology* (1993) 9: pp. 29-31

[73] Rath, Matthias, op. cit. p.53

[74] **Sokolov B, Hori M, Saelhof CC, Wrzolek T & T Imai** "Aging, atherosclerosis and ascorbic acid metabolism" *Journal of the American Gerontology Society* (1966) 14: 1239-1260

[75] **Opie LH** "Role of carnitine in fatty acid metabolism of normal and ischemic myocardium" *American Heart Journal* (1979) 97: pp.375-388

[76] **Avogaro P, Bon GB & M Fusello** "Effect of pantethine on lipids, lipoproteins and apolipoproteins in man" *Current Therapeutic Research* (1983) 33: pp. 488-493

[77] **Altschul R, Hoffer A & JD Stephen** "Influence of nicotinic acid on serum cholesterol in man" *Archives of Biochemistry and Biophysics* (1955) 54: pp. 558-559; **Carlson LA, Hamsten A & A Asplund** "Pronounced lowering of serum levels of lipoprotein Lp(a) in hyperlipidemic subjects treated with nicotinic acid" *Journal of Internal Medicine (England)* (1989) 226: 271-276

accidents are often found to have developed atherosclerotic deposits that would have become a problem for them, had they lived longer. Dr Rath comments:

"The main cause of atherosclerotic deposits is the biological weakness of the artery walls caused by chronic vitamin deficiency [malnutrition]. The atherosclerotic deposits are the consequence of this chronic weakness; they develop as a compensatory stabilizing cast of Nature to strengthen these weakened blood vessel walls." [78]

LEARNING FROM OUR ANIMALS

While the World Health Organization announces that more than 12 million people each year die from the consequences of heart disease and strokes, this death rate is just not occurring in the animal kingdom. When Vitamin C levels in animals were measured, procured as a result of their diets and own production of Vitamin C, they were found to have between 1g and 20g available a day, when compared with human bodyweight. Humans on the other hand, unable to produce their own Vitamin C, are now consuming less and less foods containing the essential nutrients available in fruits and vegetables, themselves now depleted of vital nutrients because of commercial and overfarming practices.[79] This dramatic paradigm shift in nutritional intake by the human over the past 150 years, from a diet almost completely vegetarian (5-10% animal protein intake) to one dominated by animal food sources, has manifested itself in the most disastrous death toll from cardiovascular disease, which can now be identified primarily as a nutritional deficiency disease.

LOW-DENSITY LIPOPROTEIN
(LDL – 'BAD CHOLESTEROL')

At the heart of the cardiovascular disease story is the misconception that arterial deposits are formed with LDL cholesterol. LDL is an ideal transport for fat molecules to our cells and is very abundant in our body. Studies by Rath and colleagues conclusively demonstrate that it is not LDL however that is the arterial problem, but an LDL molecule, with an additional sticky protein wall, known as lipoprotein(a), which is, as I term it, Nature's most ideal Band-Aid.

---

[78] Rath, Matthias, op. cit. p.57
[79] See section entitled *Why Are the Nations Dying?*

Amounts of this adhesive, globulous fatty molecule lipoprotein(a) increase as Vitamin C levels decrease and the need for Band-Aids to fix the corresponding deterioration of the arterial walls increases. As Rath himself states:

"In a vitamin-deficient body, lipoprotein(a) becomes the most important secondary risk factor for coronary heart disease and attacks, cerebrovascular disease and strokes, restenosis (clogging) after coronary angioplasty and the clogging of bypass grafts after coronary bypass surgery.

Moreover, none of the present lipid-lowering prescription drugs lower lipoprotein(a) concentrations. The only substances that have thus far been shown to lower lipoprotein(a) levels are vitamins. The therapeutic approaches to reduce the risk from lipoprotein(a) are thus:

> *Lowering of Lipoprotein(a) Blood Levels with Vitamin C*
> *Vitamin B3 (nicotinate)*
> *Decreasing Stickiness of Lipoprotein(a) with Lysine and Proline*

Lipoprotein(a) is a particularly interesting molecule because of its inverse relationship to Vitamin C. The following discovery triggered my interest in vitamin research: lipoprotein(a) molecules are primarily found in humans and a few animal species unable to produce Vitamin C. In contrast, animals able to produce optimum amounts of Vitamin C do not need lipoprotein(a) in any significant amount. Lipoprotein(a) molecules apparently compensate for many properties of Vitamin C, such as wound healing and blood-vessel repair. In 1990, I published the details of this important discovery in the Proceedings of the National Academy of Sciences *and invited Linus Pauling as co-author for this publication."*[80]

---

[80] **Rath M & L Pauling** "Hypothesis: Lipoprotein(a) is a surrogate for ascorbate" *Proceedings of the National Academy of Sciences* 87: pp.6204-7207; **Rath M & L Pauling** "Immunological evidence for the accumulation of lipoprotein(a) in the atherosclerotic lesion of the hypoascorbemic guinea-pig" *Proceedings of the National Academy of Sciences USA* 87: pp.9388-9390 ; quote from Rath M, *Why Animals Don't Get Heart Attacks...* pp.87-88

CHOLESTEROL-LOWERING DRUGS – THE FACTS

Many today have been prescribed cholesterol-lowering medications in the belief that these will steer the patient away from future heart complaints. Yet these drugs have a history of extreme damage to the consumer. In the 1970s, the World Health Organization (WHO) conducted studies with the drug Clofibrate in an effort to prove that drugs could lower cholesterol readings in the patients. The study was halted in the interests of the participants when extreme, life-threatening side-effects were reported.

In the early 1980s, a major study involving over 3,800 Americans tested the cholesterol-lowering drug Cholestyramine, to see whether the drug was effective in lowering the risk of heart attacks. One group took up to 24g a day of the drug in comparison to the control group which was given a placebo (a harmless control substance). The results conclusively showed that the drug-administered group suffered the same levels of death as the control group. Also, the Cholestyramine group reporting a number of accidents and suicides, which were thought to be a side-effect of the medication. Nevertheless, these death statistics were ignored, and the drug pronounced a success in reducing the number of heart attacks because it appeared that the number of heart attacks suffered by those under prescription were marginally less.

Other tests conducted during the late 1980s showed that a new range of cholesterol-lowering drugs also inhibited the production of essential nutrients in the body, such as ubiquinone (Coenzyme Q10). Professor Karl Folkers of the University of Texas raised the alarm in the Proceedings of the National Academy of Sciences when he reported that those taking cholesterol-lowering drugs risked life-threatening damage to their heart function.[81]

The final death knell to the credibility of cholesterol-lowering medications came on 6th January 1996, when the *Journal of the American Medical Association* (JAMA) reported: "Carcinogenicity of

---

[81] **Folkers K, Vadhanavikit S & SA Mortensen** "Biochemical rationale and myocardial tissue data on the effective therapy of cadiomyopathy with coenzyme Q10" *Proceedings of the National Academy of Sciences USA* (1985) 82: pp.901-904; later **Folkers K, Langsjoen P, Willis R, Richardson P, Xia LJ, Ye CQ & H Tamagawa** "Lovastatin decreases coenzyme Q10 levels in humans" *Proceedings of the National Academy of Sciences USA* (1990) 87: pp.8931-8934

Cholesterol-Lowering Drugs." Drs. Newman and Hulley of the San Francisco Medical School clearly demonstrated that the levels of these drugs currently prescribed to hundreds of thousands of people around the world were known to cause cancer in laboratory animals.[82] However, in spite of this, no ban on these drugs was ever implemented. Today cholesterol-lowering drugs are still prescribed with reckless abandon with scant regard for the long-term disastrous consequences to the health of those who blindly trust the drugs they are given as the answer to a chronic vitamin deficiency.

HIGH BLOOD PRESSURE AND ARRHYTHMIA

Modern medicine does not know the actual cause of high blood pressure in many of its cases, referring to these unknowns as "essential hypertension". Drugs prescribed can be diuretics, beta-blockers, blood thinners (including the rat poison, warfarin) and other medications. Yet studies again exist that have shown that Vitamin C[83], coenzyme Q10[84], Magnesium[85] and the amino acid arginine[86] are able to lower blood pressure very effectively without the attendant side-effects of prescription medications. Vitamin C also increases the production of prostacyclin, a small molecule hormone that relaxes the blood vessel walls and also keeps the blood viscosity at optimum levels.[87]

Arrhythmia, or inconsistent heartbeat, is also much misunderstood by conventional medicine. The term "paroxysmal arrhythmia", so often used, simply means "causes unknown". Beta-blockers, calcium antagonists and pacemakers are often prescribed in ignorance of the true underlying nutritional causes. Rath states: *"The most frequent cause of irregular heartbeat is a chronic deficiency in vitamins and other essential nutrients in millions of electrical heart muscle cells.*

---

[82] **Newman TB & SB Hulley** "Carcinogenicity of lipid-lowering drugs", *Journal of the American Medical Association* (1996) 275: 55-60

[83] **McCarron DA, Morris CD, Henry HJ & JL Stanton** "Blood pressure and nutrient intake in the United States" *Science* (1984) 224: 1392-1398

[84] **Digiesti V** "Mechanism of action of coenzyme Q10 in essential hypertension" *Current Therapeutic Research* (1992) 51: 668-672

[85] **Turlapaty PDMV & BM Altura** "Magnesium deficiency produces spasms of coronary arteries: relationship to etiology of sudden death ischemic heart disease" *Science* (1980) 208: 198-200

[86] **Korbut R** "Effect of L-arginine on plasminogen-activator inhibitor in hypertensive patients with hypercholesterolemia" *New England Journal of Medicine* (1993) 328 [4]: pp.287-288

[87] Rath M, *Why Animals Don't Get Heart Attacks...op. cit. p.102*

Long-term, these deficiencies of essential nutrients directly cause, or aggravate, disturbances in the creation or conduction of the electrical impulses triggering the heartbeat. Scientific research and clinical studies have already documented the value of magnesium, calcium, carnitine, coenzyme Q10 and other co-factors in helping to normalise different forms of irregular heartbeat, thereby improving the quality of life for the patients." [88]

This then is an overview of the nutritional side to heart disease. But what about lifestyle in general? How does that all contribute to the problem?

[88] Rath, Matthias, *Animals Don't Get Heart Attacks...* op. cit. pp. 123-124

Lifestyle Problems for the Heart

Today, diets are a serious problem in the Western world, after the advent of the fast-food concept of the 1950s. There is nothing we won't eat, so long as it can be lassoed, bludgeoned, fried and then wedged sideways into our mouths between two lifeless baps. We are what we eat... or to be more precise, we are what we absorb. Eat nothing but burgers for the next 15 years.... Become a burger.

Obesity in the Western industrialised nations is pandemic, with America leading the pack. In February 2001, the British government's National Audit Office (NAO) reported that one in five people in the UK is now considered medically obese. Under the *Daily Mail* headline of: *"A Deadly Warning as Heavyweights Triple in 20 Years"*, the British tabloid also advised that 58% of the British population are now considered to be overweight.[89]

Obesity caused more than 30,000 premature deaths in the UK in 1998 and cost the health service and country £2.6 billion in treatment bills and lost production. At least 18 million sick days can be laid at the door of obesity, the NAO report declares. Britain is due to equal the United States' staggering feat of 25% of the population medically obese by 2010, if nothing is done to curtail the current trend.

On my recent tour throughout the United States I was amazed at how much more obesity there was in evidence since I had lived in America in the early 1990s. During the 17,600-mile tour, which we drove, the only food available near the freeway was of the fast variety. The shape of the waiters and waitresses often reflected the food they served. We had to drive miles out of our way to find a salad-serving, vegetable-toting restaurant that could satisfy our modest needs.

In the UK things are admittedly a little better. The pub infrastructure usually gives one a choice of home-cooked, freshly prepared meals that are not as limiting as their US counterparts. But what we see of the food in Europe is one thing, what's inside it is entirely another. Aside from the obvious problems we share with our

---

[89] *Daily Mail*, 15th February 2001, p.17

American cousins concerning very high meat and dairy consumption, bad food combining, the incorrect consumption of fruit and the scarfing down of anything saturated in refined sugar and not nailed to our neighbour's placemat, we have other more insidious problems that have emerged over the past 40 years. Food additives, food irradiation, the use of chemicals as foodstuffs and the new science of food bioengineering (genetic modification of food products) are all now a reality at the dinner table, and their true cost in health is only just becoming recognised, as serious health problems are being progressively tracked back to the supermarket cart.[90]

Heart attacks kill hundreds of thousands like old Hank every year, without mercy, often without warning, any place, any time. And yet, experts correctly tell us that these types of problems, excluding congenital heart defects, are the result of lifestyle choices we have made and thus are entirely preventable. So whose court is the ball in now?

Getting to the heart of the cardiac problem is really not difficult when we examine how we abuse ourselves with lifestyle choices. Smoking, anger, irritability, sadness, trans-fatty foods and sugar products that tempt us, as well as prescription and recreational drugs are all part of the heart holocaust, as we have read countless times. Yes, we live in a fast-paced, stressful world today, where relaxation is often a luxury many of us cannot afford. Remember the fifties when we were being told that all this new technology would bring us more leisure time?

Now in hindsight, we can see what technology has brought us over the past five decades, aside from the contamination and health problems we'll examine later. We now have the technology to do more activity/work in a shorter space of time, resulting in greater productivity for our bosses and a drastically expanded global market-place which moves at a cracking pace barely imagined by our 1950s counterparts. Our forebears would be astonished to see how frenetic the world has become. Yes, technology has brought us some marvellous advances and new toys, but, in terms of the impact to

---

[90] See our section entitled *Supermarket Smarts*

health, all this increased comfort and convenience through technology has come with an awesome emotional and physical price-tag.

STRESS

Long-term mental and physical stress produces a chronic abundance of the hormone adrenaline. Every molecule of adrenaline produced requires a molecule of Vitamin C as the catalyst. These Vitamin C molecules are destroyed in these reactions, leading to a reduction in Vitamin C levels in the body. Couple this with smoking, releasing millions of free radicals into the bloodstream, requiring further Vitamin C to protect the blood freeway system of 96,000 miles from regional arterial damage (biological 'rusting' from ongoing oxidation of cells), and you have a sound reason why smoking-related atherosclerosis is often located at the body's periphery, resulting in the proverbial 'smoker's foot' and sometimes the need for peripheral amputations.

And did our technology and futurism buy us any more leisure time? How often do you hear the boss say: "Well, Miss Bentworthy, seeing as you have finished your day's allocation of work before 1pm... again! why not cut loose and go to the local park with the Management's blessing? Here's five pounds!" No, we go to work on more congested roads, or on trains that regularly break down (UK) only to work harder for longer for a wage that is increasingly reducing due to compounding direct and indirect taxation... which in turn creates more stress....

Stress undeniably plays a major role in heart disease and the risk of heart attacks, but it is diet and lifestyle that pave the way for pump action failure, as we move along life's great Interstate. I know that's not what anyone wants to hear, because no one likes to have their lifestyle judged deadly, unless they are a paid-up member of the Extreme Sports Club. The *British Medical Journal* reiterates this message in a report published in January 2000, which we can use as a summary of woes and remedies:

HEART DISEASE/ATTACKS

The Problem: The bottom line of the BMJ report's conclusion is that adult lifestyle choices account for the major portion of the risk associated with heart disease. Lifestyle concerns include as the major problem areas: smoking, bad diet, lack of exercise, excessive alcohol consumption, drug abuse, anger and irritability. Other research has shown that people with a domineering personality have a 47% higher risk of heart disease, and those with irritability traits have a 27% higher risk of heart disease compared with their more relaxed and easy-going counterparts.[91] The BMJ results are formulated from measuring the thickness of carotid artery walls among the 154 men and 193 women who took part in the study. Previous studies had linked thicker carotid artery walls with higher rates of atherosclerosis, high blood pressure, heart disease and stroke.[92]

Higher levels of uric acid in the blood are also indicative of a raised risk of heart disease.[93] Uric acid is a by-product of the continual process of old cells being broken down for elimination from the body as new ones are formed to replace them. Uric acid, which contains this detritus, as its name suggests, is eliminated from the body via the urine. Higher levels of uric acid in the blood indicate an inability of the body effectively to detoxify the blood of this dangerous waste product. Raised levels of uric acid are also related to meat-eating, increased alcohol consumption, obesity, diabetes, high blood pressure, high cholesterol and kidney disease. Later, we will see how this acid/alkali connection becomes relevant when applying the science of Natural Hygiene to our bodies to cleanse and detoxify them on an on-going basis in order to maintain health.

THE PILL
The contraceptive Pill has also long been linked to heart problems for chronic users. Researcher Sherrill Sellman:

"The Pill has been proclaimed as one of the most studied drugs in history. After three decades of experimentation (unfortunately on unsuspecting Pill-users), we are told that safe dosages are, at last, finally known. However as the thin veneer of advertising hype, cover-ups and sanitised clinic trials is peeled away, another picture emerges revealing the devastating consequences to women's health and well-

[91] *Psychosomatic Medicine 2000*; 62
[92] *British Medical Journal*, 29th January 2000; 320:273-278
[93] *Journal of the American Medical Association*, 10th May 2000; 283:2404-2410. The data is taken from 6,000 people aged 25 to 74 followed up and analysed over 16 years.

being from the use of steroid hormones found in the Pill, as well as in hormone replacement therapy (HRT) which uses the same steroid drugs." [94]

As the truth about using hormones for birth control came to light, it seemed that the sexual freedom women had fought so hard to attain had been won at a frightening cost to their health and well-being. Even though it was known as early as 1932 that abnormal levels of estrogen could cause cancer of the breast, womb, ovaries and pituitary glands in animals, in 1960 America's Food & Drug Administration approved Envoid, the first oral contraceptive, on the basis of a clinical trial involving 132 Puerto Rican women, who had taken the Pill for over a year - five of whom died during the study. In the rush to bring this revolutionary freedom to women around the world, the initial trials were flawed and inadequate, according to *Bad Medicine* author John Archer.[95]

It was also recognised early on that the Pill could cause blot clots, leading to thrombotic heart attacks and strokes. In the mid-1970s, an inordinate amount of young women began dying of these causes, bringing the problem into the news for the first time. Dr Ellen Grant, author of *The Bitter Pill* and *Sexual Chemistry*, declared back in the 1960s that she was shocked that synthetic hormones had not been taken off the market due to their then known serious and life-threatening side-effects. Later research has shown that the early users of the Pill were up to 11 times more likely to have thrombo-embolisms.[96]

Even today, marketing of the Pill continues to be deceptive and one-sided. Sherill Sellman believes that the early warnings by governments and the pharmaceutical companies were lies:

"A recent study for the Inspector General's Office of the Department of Health and Human Services disclosed that more than

---

[94] **Sellman, Sherill** *A Bitter Pill to Swallow – The Oral Contraceptives Betrayal*, Light Unlimited Productions, +61 (0)3 9249 9591, www.ssellman.com Published in *Nexus*, June–July 1997

[95] **Archer, John** *Bad Medicine*, Simon & Schuster, Australia, 1995

[96] *Australian Prescription Guide (APPG)*, Minulet monograph, 1995. 24th ed., p.1540. Also Sellman, Sherill, op. cit.

70% of oral contraceptive advertising to doctors is "misleading or unbalanced" – making contraceptives the most "deceptively advertised" category of prescription drug, with antibiotics in second place.

...The most notorious Pill side-effect reported in the 1960s was thrombosis, or simply, blood clot. Indeed blood clotting is still one of the most frequent and dangerous side-effects of the Pill. Clots can form either in arteries or veins, blocking the blood circulation. They can cause strokes, paralysis, heart attacks and severe abdominal pain."[97]

By 1980, many independent studies on the Pill were reviewed in total. The results published were that Pill-users had 1.5 to 11 times more risk of an embolism, 1 to 14 times more risk of a heart attack, and 2 to 26 times more risk of a stroke due either to thrombosis in a brain artery or to a haemorrhage in the membranes around the brain.[98]

New, low-dose Pills have been marketed during the 1990s, prompting glowing endorsements by men like Dr William C Andrews, President of the American College of Obstetrics and Gynecology (ACOG): *"The Pill is far safer today than it was in the early 1960s – when it had nearly four times the amount of estrogen and nearly 10 times the amount of progestin as it does now."* However, like so many other shifts in perspective, it sometimes goes forgotten that, back in the dangerous high-dose era, Dr William's ACOG defended the Pill's safety with a vengeance too. But even today, with much lower doses of estrogen being absorbed by the Pill-user, the potentially fatal effects of the Pill are still with us. The Sydney *Sun-Herald* ran the following lead story on 22nd October 1995:

"Warnings that low-dose contraceptive pills double the risk of women developing potentially fatal blood clots has caused panic around the world. The specific focus of these warnings pertained to the newer versions of the Pill – Fermoden, Trioden, Minulet, TriMinulet and Marvelon..."

---

[97] **Sellman, Sherill** *Hormone Heresy*, GetWell Int'l, Inc. 1998. Also **Seaman, Barbara** *The Doctors' Case Against the Pill*, Hunter House, USA, 1995, p.7
[98] **Grant MD, Ellen** *Sexual Chemistry*, Reed Consumer Books, UK, 1994, p.70

Sherill Sellman believes though, that like so much of the popular media coverage of this issue, the full perspective of the dangers remain unreported:

"What may have gone unnoticed amid the media coverage was the important point that a doubling of the risk which was reported was actually a doubling of the already existing three-to-four-fold risk associated with currently used... formulations of the Pill. The low-dose third generation Pill could elevate a woman's risk of blood clots six-to-eight fold when compared to the risk for a woman who has never taken the Pill. Some research places this figure even higher, making Pill-users up to 11 times more likely than non-users to have thrombo-embolism." [99]

Again, what must be noted is the purposeful inadequacy of the official warnings and the full implications of the Pill disaster being 'spun' in the press to minimise impact. Only now can we begin to get some idea of how the press selectively reports such issues, especially if there are powerful vested interests at stake, which stand to lose a lot if the Pill ever comes completely unstuck. After all, having the world's child-bearing-age females as a market, implicitly promising them 'no-strings-attached' sex, is a gravy train too good to lose without a fight.

The question is, is your health at stake in that war?

And what about HRT, the same steroid drugs sold to menopausal females in different dosages and packaging? A fuller study on Hormone Replacement Therapy and hysterectomy and their sorry histories of betrayal and lies is covered in a later section.[100] For what you don't know WILL hurt you.

PREVENTION OF HEART PROBLEMS
AND THE MAINTENANCE OF HEALTH
So what is the biochemical explanation for hormonal contraceptives, HRT and their connection to heart disease? In 1972, Dr M Briggs reported that women taking contraceptive pills over a period

---

[99] Sellman, Sherill, op. cit.
[100] See section entitled *Barking Up the Wrong Tree*

of time had significantly lower Vitamin C blood levels than normal.[101] Dr J Rivers confirmed these results and concluded that the Vitamin C pool depletion was primarily due to the estrogens used in the contraceptive drugs.[102] Thus, concludes Rath, it is not the birth control pills themselves that increase the risk for cardiovascular disease, but the associated depletion of the vitamin pool, leading to a weakening of the blood vessel wall.[103] Hormone stimulation will cause different stresses to the cardiovascular system, increased heartbeat and blood pressure, in turn producing more stress on the Vitamin C depleted collagen structure of the arteries. This leads to the body triggering lipoprotein(a) to fix the problem, resulting in atherosclerotic deposits coating the artery walls in the high blood volume areas - the heart muscle and the brain - leading to heart attacks and stroke.

The Answer: If we examine the three main areas for heart attack prevention therefore, we arrive at diet (and supplementation), exercise and lifestyle choices (rejecting smoking, alcohol, drugs and adverse character traits, such as anger, jealousy and irritability) as a means of normalising blood pressure, adrenal hormone secretions and even androgens (male hormones), which are linked to male pattern baldness and a higher risk of heart disease.[104]

The diet, exercise and lifestyle strategies relevant to avoiding heart disease are explained in a special section later. The dietary and supplement regimens are designed to optimise nutrition in a way that is very similar to the nutritional intake of those peoples who do not suffer these problems. Thus modified nutrition and an associated vitamin and mineral supplementation assure optimum nutritional protection against heart attack and stroke.

---

[101] **Briggs M** "Vitamin C requirements and oral contraceptives" *Nature* 238:277

[102] **Rivers JM** "Oral contraceptives and ascorbic acid" *American Journal of Clinical Nutrition* 28: 50-554

[103] Rath, Matthias, *Animals Don't Get Heart Attacks...*, op. cit. p.174

[104] Studies on male pattern baldness and its association with coronary heart disease (CHD) have shown that, from a test group of 22,071 male doctors aged 40 or older, studied over 11 years, those with some form of baldness faced the following increases in CHD risk when compared to men with no hair loss: 9% with frontal baldness only – 23% with mild vertex baldness – 32% with moderate vertex baldness and 36% with severe vertex baldness. These increased risks were increased further when compounded with other risk factors, such as high blood pressure or smoking (*Archives of Int. Med.* 24th January 2000; 160:165-171). These factors however can be effectively countered using the strategies explained later in this book.

THESE SIMPLE MEASURES ARE ALSO THE SAME FOR OTHER SERIOUS DISEASES, meaning, as we proceed, that we can develop a common lifestyle strategy that will work across the board for all the major problem areas. This strategy must be applied *consistently*. Those looking for a magic formula to repair a health condition need to know that the magic formula is *doing the right thing and doing it CONSISTENTLY*. Once again, there are things we must do, and there are things we must avoid.

Tossed Under the Bus
Cancer: The News the World Has Waited to Hear

Cancer, the second leading killer in most Western industrialised nations, is a disease which has crept from an incidence rate of around 1 in 500 in 1900 to between 1 in 2 to 3 today. Over 600,000 people are expected to die from cancer in America in 2001, and yet, in spite of supposedly the brightest and the best walking the corridors of our leading cancer research institutions, armed with the latest technology and limitless budgets, the incidence rates for cancer continue to rise.

Breast cancer serves as a poignant yardstick. This type of malignancy is now the leading cause of death in women between the ages of 35 and 54. In 1971, a woman's lifetime risk of contracting breast cancer was 1 in 14[105]. Today it is 1 in 8. *Rachel's Environment and Health Weekly*, No. 571 reports: *"More American women have died of breast cancer in the past two decades than all the Americans killed in World War 1, World War 2, the Korean War and Vietnam War combined."*

The amazing thing is, most physicians in the world today have absolutely no idea what cancer is, or even how it is contracted. Some believe cancer is virus-related. Others believe the cause is parasites. Others yet examine the environmental causal link.

Let's look at what society generally knows about cancer and see how it stacks up with the truth. Most believe that:

1) Cancer is a serious disease that kills those suffering from the life-threatening variants, such as lung, breast, bone, colorectal and liver.
2) Cancer can only be treated with chemotherapy, radiation treatments and radical surgeries to poison or break up tumours, or physically remove them altogether.
3) These cancer treatments sometimes work and sometimes don't. No one can be sure who will survive and who won't.

---

[105] **Epstein, Samuel S & David Steinman** *The Breast Cancer Prevention Program*, Macmillan, USA, 1997 ISBN 0025361929

4) Cancer is caused by genetics, smoking, and other less well-understood or –known environmental causes.
5) We still don't have the cure for cancer.
6) The cancer charities and famous pop and TV stars are doing a superb job raising money to help with the drug research to combat and defeat cancer.
7) Cancer appears to be a complex disturbance of cells in our bodies which mutate and then begin an uncontrollable proliferation. No one really knows what cancer is at the moment.

During the twelve years that I and my fellow researchers conducted our investigation into the cancer industry, what we found dispelled any illusions that cancer medicine was working in any way for the benefit of humanity. Here is what we found:

1) The proof behind what cancer actually is and how to combat it effectively has been known for almost a century.
2) Cancer is a healing process that simply hasn't stopped. Cancer cells are pre-embryonic stem cells that have been stimulated by estrogen in our bodies to form trophoblast healing cells. It is these trophoblast cells that may progress to form 'cancer' cells if the trophoblastic multiplication of these cells (the healing process) is not halted.
3) These rogue healing processes are started when our bodies become damaged in various ways. For instance, smoking damages the back of the throat and the lungs, resulting in site-specific healing processes that may or may not stop. In the event that a healing process is not terminated, healing trophoblast cells continue to proliferate to form a tumour.
4) All cancers can be traced to ENVIRONMENTAL- OR LIFESTYLE-RELATED CAUSATIONS that damage our bodies, initiating a healing process that may not stop. We can say 'ALL' because there are cultures alive today to whom cancer is entirely unknown.
5) There are at least 18 different peoples on Earth today who do not suffer from cancer. Many of these cannot record even one victim of the disease in their entire culture. By this definition, cancer can be deemed preventable.

6) The reasons why these peoples do not contract cancer are entirely known, yet this information, and the top researchers who discovered it, have been deliberately vilified by the medical establishment.

7) The methods for completely preventing cancer and treating ALL forms of the disease have been known for the last 50 years.

8) Orthodox medicine has waged an effective and relentless war against this life-saving knowledge to prevent its widespread dissemination and thus forestall an attack on the highly profitable cancer industry. There are more people today making a living out of cancer than are dying from it. The cancer industry turns over in excess of $200 billion annually.

9) Cancer charities are fund-raising institutions for the pharmaceutical combines whose livelihoods depend on the continuance of cancer. Thus we see all efforts made to *wage* the war on cancer, not win it. In the event that cancer were vanquished, millions around the world would need to retrain. Cancer charities have no interest in knowing the truth about cancer - my organisation can vouch for that. Their job is to raise as much money as possible through the emotional showcasing of the heart-rending consequences of cancer, thereby stimulating the public to give more money.

10) There is no evidence that chemotherapy and radiation treatments extend life in the major epithelial cancers, which are the majority of the cancers striking us today, *although these two treatments can and do sometimes effect a reduction in tumour size.* In a small minority of cases, as with some testicular and childhood cancers, efficacy with these treatments may be shown. Radiation and chemotherapy on the other hand have long been known to compromise the body's immune system, leading to the progressive degradation of the patient's health.

11) Chemotherapy drugs are cytotoxic, meaning that they indiscriminately poison the cells in our body that multiply the most rapidly (cancer cells). However, certain immune system cells, such as our T and B lymphocytes, are also targeted, as these multiply rapidly too, contributing to our body's inability to fight opportunistic diseases that may come upon us as a result of the treatment.

12) Radiations treatments harm the body, often leading to the production of more healing trophoblast. Radiation has been recognised to foster aggressive cell lines and in certain cases actually accelerate tumour growth.

13) Cancer is a chronic, metabolic deficiency disease that is exacerbated by general mineral depletion in the food chain and the missing dietary element, hydrocyanic acid. Cultures whose diets are rich in foods containing minerals and hydrocyanic acid suffer no cancer in their peoples, provided they are living in toxin-free environments.

THE POLITICS OF BIG CANCER
AND THE FAILURE OF CONVENTIONAL TREATMENTS

Let's review some startling comments made by insiders to illustrate the point that the shameful corporate story surrounding cancer has long been known and written about by honest physicians who see major mischief afoot. Also included in this section is the compelling truth that conventional cancer treatments are not extending life in the major cancers striking us.

One such leading critic of the cancer industry has been Dr Samuel S Epstein, chairman of the Cancer Prevention Coalition and a world-renowned toxicologist and Professor of Occupational and Environmental Medicine at the University of Illinois Medical Center in Chicago. Epstein's relentless attacks against corporate vested interests in the chemical and medical industries concerning the avoidable causes of cancer have led to the public gaining a far wider knowledge of these issues. Epstein has no hesitation in indicting 'Cancer Inc.', comprising the American Medical Association, the National Cancer Institute, the American Cancer Society (ACS), the cancer charities and the pharmaceutical industry, as well as other cancer administrative bodies elsewhere in the world, for losing the winnable war against cancer. Epstein contends:

"We are not winning the war against cancer, we are losing the war. The number of Americans getting cancer each year has escalated over recent decades, while our ability to treat and cure most common cancers has remained virtually unchanged.

The National Cancer Institute and the American Cancer Society have misled and confused the public and Congress by repeated false claims that we are winning the war against cancer – claims made to create public and Congressional support for massive increases in budgetary allocations."[106]

Quentin D Young, MD, president of the American Public Health Association, agrees with Epstein and highlights the chief environmental causes of cancer, which must be addressed if we are to turn the tide on the disease:

"Billions of public dollars are being misspent in an ill-conceived 'war on cancer' – a war we are losing because we are not addressing the increasingly carcinogenic environment that man has created. We have introduced these creations into our water and air, our food chain, our habitation, our workplace, and into the products produced there. In failing to allocate these resources for prevention, we are fighting the wrong war." [107]

John Cairns, professor of microbiology at Harvard University, recorded in his scathing 1985 critique in *Scientific American*: *"Aside from certain rare cancers, it is not possible to detect any sudden changes in the death rates for any of the major cancers that could be credited to chemotherapy. <u>Whether any of the common cancers can be cured by chemotherapy has yet to be established</u>."*

Making the point that chemotherapy is *not* curative, and actually has very little effect on the major cancers, Dr Martin F Shapiro stated in the *Los Angeles Times* that *"...while some oncologists inform their patients of the lack of evidence that treatments work... others may well be misled by scientific papers that express unwarranted optimism about chemotherapy. Still others respond to an economic incentive. <u>Physicians can earn much more money running active chemotherapy practices than they can providing solace and relief... to dying patients and their families</u>."* [108]

---

[106] **Epstein, Samuel** *The Politics of Cancer Revisited*, East Ridge Press, USA 1998
[107] Ibid.
[108] *Los Angeles Times*, 9th January 1991

Alan C Nixon, PhD, erstwhile president of the American Chemical Society, declares that *"...as a chemist trained to interpret data, it is incomprehensible to me that physicians can ignore the clear evidence that chemotherapy does much, much more harm than good."*

Oncologist Albert Braverman MD told the world in 1991 that *"...no disseminated neoplasm* (cancer) *incurable in 1975 is curable today... Many medical oncologists recommend chemotherapy for virtually any tumor, <u>with a hopefulness undiscouraged by almost invariable failure</u>."*

Christian Brothers, a retail organisation forcefully shut down by the American Food & Drug Administration (FDA) in 2000, states: *"In 1986, McGill Cancer Center scientists sent a questionnaire to 118 doctors who treated non-small-cell lung cancer. More than 3/4 of them recruited patients and carried out trials of toxic drugs for lung cancer. They were asked to imagine that they themselves had cancer, and were asked which of six current trials they themselves would choose. 64 of the 79 respondents would not consent to be in a trial containing cisplatin, a common chemotherapy drug. <u>Fifty-eight found all the trials unacceptable</u>. <u>Their reason?</u> <u>The ineffectiveness of chemotherapy and its unacceptable degree of toxicity</u>".* [109]

Dr Ralph Moss was the Assistant Director of Public Affairs at probably America's most famous cancer research institution, Memorial Sloan Kettering in Manhattan. He states: *"In the end, there is no proof that chemotherapy in the vast majority of cases actually extends life, and this is the GREAT LIE about chemotherapy, <u>that somehow there is a correlation between shrinking a tumor and extending the life of a patient</u>."* [110]

Walter Last, writing in *The Ecologist*, reports: *"After analysing cancer survival statistics for several decades, Dr Hardin Jones, Professor at the University of California, concluded in 1975 that "...patients are as well, <u>or better off untreated</u>."* Jones' disturbing

[109] Christian Brothers, www.christianbrothers.com. Site now suspended by US Department of Justice action
[110] Live on the Laurie Lee Radio Show, 1994

assessment has never been refuted. What's more, three studies by other researchers have upheld his theory."[111]

Professor Charles Mathe, French cancer specialist, makes this astonishing declaration: *"If I contracted cancer, I would never go to a standard cancer treatment centre. <u>Cancer victims who live far from such centres have a chance</u>."*[112]

From another angle, Dr John Gofman's mammoth research attacks 'preventative' measures, such as routine mammograms, for causing the very illness they are designed to prevent:

"Breast cancer is a largely PREVENTABLE disease, and we reach that good news because of our finding that a large share of recent and current breast cancer in the United States is CERTAINLY due to past medical irradiation of the breasts with x-rays - at all ages, including infancy and childhood. Much of today's radiation dosage is preventable, without any interference with necessary diagnostic radiology, and hence many future breast cancers need not occur."[113]

Epstein concurs with the risks mammograms and x-rays in general pose for the unknowing patient:

"X-rays are carcinogenic. The more X-rays you submit to and the greater the dose, the greater is your risk of cancer... Whatever you may be told, refuse routine mammograms to detect early breast cancer, especially if you are pre-menopausal. The X-rays may actually increase your chances of getting cancer.... Very few circumstances, if any, should persuade you to have X-rays taken if you are pregnant. The future risks of leukaemia to your unborn child, not to mention birth defects, are just not worth it."[114]

Breast cancer patients are certainly at risk of developing lung cancer after radiation. In one study of 31 patients who had received radiotherapy for breast cancer, 19 went on to develop a lung cancer, on

[111] *The Ecologist,* Vol 28, No. 2, March/April 1998, p. 120
[112] **Mathe, Prof. George** "Scientific Medicine Stymied", *Medicines Nouvelles* (Paris) 1989
[113] **Gofman, John W**, *Preventing Breast Cancer*:
www.ratical.com/radiation/ CNR/PBC/indexT.html
[114] Epstein, Samuel S, *The Politics...op. cit. p.304*

average, seventeen years later, mostly in the lung located on the same side as the breast that had been irradiated.[115] Some oncologists believe that the lung is especially sensitive to radiation damage, either scar tissue or inflammation – which would tend to argue against high-dose radiotherapy for lung cancer.[116] For Hodgkin's Disease, radiotherapy also poses a risk of breast cancer years later.[117] In rectal cancer, animal studies have demonstrated the descending colon may be especially susceptible to cancer caused by radiation, particularly after surgery, where blood vessels are joined up.[118] The current trend for health departments to promote routine and regular mammograms for early detection of breast cancers is also dangerous nonsense, given the evidence.[119]

The patent failure of modern medicine to halt cancer is now becoming obvious, as the strategies Big Cancer uses to cover up a disaster of its own making are unmasked and exposed for the sham they have become. For instance, in August 1998, the huge MD Anderson Comprehensive Cancer Center in Houston was sued for making the unsubstantiated claim that it cures "well over 50% of people with cancer." Leaflets were deposited in mailboxes throughout the Houston area by MD Anderson in an effort to solicit funds to continue their 'war against cancer.' Misrepresentations and conflicts of interests abound within the cancer industry. For example, the wretched performance of the world's largest 'non-profit' institution, the American Cancer Society (ACS), is examined in the appendix section entitled *Conflicts of Interest.*

Environmental causations are repeatedly downplayed by Big Cancer, which invariably follows a 'blame the patient' course in explaining the rising causes of cancer. It also partially explains the rise in cancer incidence by alleging that earlier and more accurate detection has inflated the numbers of cancer incidence that were in fact already existing. Another strategy is to state that more people are contracting cancer because they are living longer and therefore stand a statistically

---

[115] *Med. Onc.* 1994; 11:121-5

[116] *Strahl und Onk,* 1995; 171:490-8

[117] *1 Gyne, Ob. et Biol. Repro.* 1995; 24:9-12

[118] *Dis. Colon & Rec.* 1995; 38:152-8

[119] Epstein, Samuel S, *The Politics....* op. cit. pp. 290, 304, 313, 348-351, 353, etc.

higher risk of contracting the disease. Both these allegations are completely false. If age were a factor in cancer, then certainly the Hunzas and other long-lived cultures would be riddled with the disease. Clearly they are not. These strategies serve only to highlight clearly Cancer Inc's extreme reluctance to finger its cousins, Big Industry and Big Food, as the leading cancer felons worldwide today.

Cancer Inc. spares no effort in vilifying and pillorying alternative and non-toxic treatments which have shown a clinical track record of efficacy. Proponents of these treatments have been consistently harassed and defamed, and in certain cases jailed for the stand they have taken on this issue. The *unpatentable* treatment for cancer we will examine in a moment is not popular with an establishment that has shown itself eminently determined to keep its drug gravy train firmly on the rails.

CANCER - THE NEW APPROACH
In spite of the medical establishment's dictatorial attitude towards protecting their cancer income, huge inroads into conquering cancer were made at the turn of the 1900s by Professor John Beard of Edinburgh University. Beard was no exception in that he received harassment for what he subsequently found. But like many pioneers, he soldiered on nonetheless. John Beard can justifiably be praised for being the individual who broke the back of cancer's mystery and brought its demise forward by many decades.

Beard was an embryologist who was one of the first doctors to study embryonic stem cells, these enigmatic pre-embryonic cells that reside within our body. Beard had noticed that these cells had the ability to develop into the cell structure of any body part, and even into a new embryo, if given the right morphogenetic, hormonal stimulus.

He discovered that in pregnancy, the body uses the hormone estrogen to stimulate these stem cells into rapidly multiplying into a cell mass Beard called 'trophoblast', releasing quantities of human chorionic gonadotrophin (hCG), the hormone later to be detected with a pregnancy test. Beard's thesis stated that these trophoblastic cells have a job to do in pregnancy, namely to etch away part of the uterus wall so that the embryo can attach itself and start to develop.[120] Once this has been achieved, the trophoblastic cells are destroyed around the 56th day of pregnancy when the baby's pancreas comes online and emits its enzymes, which deconstruct the outer coating of the trophoblast, allowing the immune system to clear away the remainder of these cells. Beard had discovered that in the event that the baby's pancreas fails, both the mother and the child die of cancer. In fact, what they die from is an uncontrolled and unregulated proliferation of these trophoblast cells, which now have no pancreatic enzyme 'termination' agents to curtail them.

CANCER AS A ROGUE HEALING PROCESS

Beard found that these stem cells also exist in our body for healing. When we hurt ourselves, our bodies initiate an automatic healing process (survival response) – we know this, and have seen it happen a thousand times. But intriguingly, the healing process commences the same way as with pregnancy trophoblast, namely, the hormone estrogen stimulates our stem cells into producing a trophoblastic 'carpet' of cells which seals off the damaged area and repairs it with cells formed into the cell structure of the bodypart that is being fixed. This healing process is then terminated by pancreatic enzymes upon completion of the task. [121] In the event that we have low levels of these vital pancreatic enzymes, there is no termination agent for the trophoblast in our body and the trophoblast therefore continues to multiply and proliferate unopposed. The result is an ever expanding mass of trophoblastic cells in our body at the site specific to the original area of damage. Today we call this cell mass a tumour.

Beard discovered that our bodies become depleted of these vital pancreatic enzymes when we eat a diet rich in animal proteins. Without this protection, we become prone to developing cancer if the healing processes that initiate in our bodies are not terminated upon completion of their task. Beard began treating cancer patients to great effect using pancreatic enzymes trypsin and chymotrypsin, as well as other vital nutrients, up until his death around the beginning of World War 1. His theory, as expounded in his papers, was that, by introducing

---

[120] The abortion chemical RU486 is designed to prevent this from occurring, thus causing the body to reject the embryo.

[121] **Vialls, Joe** Laetrile: Another Suppression Story, www.livelinks.com/sumeria; Cancer Control Journal, Vol. 6. No.1-6

pancreatic enzymes into a cancer patient's body, the enzymes would continue with their job of digesting the outer protein coating of the trophoblast cells, allowing the body to clear away any dangerous trophoblastic proliferation.

We must remember that after Beard's career, medicine began treating cancer patients with Marie Curie's radium and other desperate remedies, causing further trauma, and no doubt generating more trophoblast as a survival response to counter the hurt being done to the body.[122] Beard's work was largely ignored until Ernst T Krebs Jr, a biochemist from Nevada, came across Beard's thesis during his work with enzymes and nutrition.

Krebs was studying those cultures on Earth who did not suffer from cancer. He was aware that men like Albert Schweitzer and explorer Roald Amundsen were coming back from remote areas of the globe reporting that cancer just didn't exist among the populations they had encountered. To the Labrador Eskimos, the Thlinglets, the tribes of Gabon, the Vilcabambans of Ecuador, the Georgian tribes of southern Russia, the Karakorum and Hunzas of eastern Pakistan and the Hopi Indians of Arizona, cancer was unknown – and Krebs was keen to find out why.

He discovered that these peoples differed from westernised populations because they were doing one or all of the following which Krebs believed resulted in their pronounced and healthy longevity:
> They lived in environments devoid of man-made toxins.
> They ate diets rich in minerals and raw whole foods.
> They ate the dietary compound hydrocyanic acid, a staple of the nitriloside food group, which had been largely eliminated from the diets of Western populations.

Krebs' work on hydrocyanic acid was especially controversial, even as it still is today. The biochemist found that this compound was contained within the apricot seeds of the Hunzas – indeed within all the seeds of the common fruits, excluding citrus, as well as other foods that had largely been cut out of Western diets. The Hunzas were

---

[122] Marie Curie herself was to die from the contamination effects of her own medicine in the 1930s

cracking open their apricot pits and consuming the soft seed within along with the pulp of the fruit. In addition, their womenfolk pressed the oil out of the kernels they collected and used it for cooking and cosmetics.

Krebs analysed hydrocyanic acid to discover its life-preserving qualities and reported that when this compound came into contact with trophoblast cells, it selectively killed them by manufacturing two poisons in minute quantities - hydrogen cyanide and benzaldehyde. Krebs also discovered that this reaction did not occur with healthy cells, thus preserving and even nourishing healthy tissue. Research demonstrated that the hydrocyanic acid compound could only be 'unlocked' by beta-glucosidase, a cellular enzyme which, although present throughout the body in minute quantities, was located in huge amounts at the site of trophoblast tumours. The beta-glucosidase contained in the trophoblast cells appeared to 'unlock' the hydrocyanic acid contained in the food to produce hydrogen cyanide and benzaldehyde at the cancer site. The two poisons combined synergistically to produce a super-poison many times more deadly than either substance in isolation. Thus the cancer cell met its chemical death at the hands of this unique compound's selective toxicity.

Krebs ran toxicity studies to determine whether hydrocyanic acid, or Laetrile/amygdalin/Vitamin B17, as the active principal would later become known, was dangerous to the organism if ingested in abnormal quantities. He reported that Vitamin B17 was harmless and chemically inert until stimulated by the beta-glucosidase available within cancer cells.

Later other researchers would replicate Krebs' work to confirm these findings. Sheep fed the equivalent of 8-10mg of HCN (hydrogen cyanide) per kilogram per day as linseed meal showed no toxic effects whatsoever. [123] Sheep weighing 66kg were intravenously administered a three-hour dose of 2.7 gms of B17 yielding 300mg of HCN. New Zealand researchers Coop and Blakely reported that *"...at no time during the experiment were even the slightest symptoms observed."* A total of 568mg of HCN was given to a 76kg sheep in the course of an hour. The only symptom the animal showed was *"a general sleepiness*

---

[123] **Franklin & Reid** *Australian Veterinary Journal*, 100:92, 1944

for an hour". [124]   Van der Walt failed to produce chronic poisoning in sheep even after administering 3.2mg HCN/kg daily *for two years.* [125] Worden showed that repeated dosing in rabbits does not produce a cumulative effect and the animal was capable of eliminating excess B17 within two and a half hours.

Other researchers, such as Dr Harold Manner, head of biology at Loyola University, Chicago, ever mindful of the extreme flak Krebs began receiving following the publication of his findings, put further pieces of the cancer puzzle together. Manner began combining Beard's pancreatic enzymes, trypsin and chymotrypsin, with Vitamin A emulsion and B17-Laetrile, and used this protocol with a radical change of diet supplemented with minerals and antioxidants such as Vitamin C and selenium to supercharge the cancer patient to halt the progression of rogue trophoblast and even eliminate it altogether. This procedure was later to form the basis of the nutritional Metabolic Therapy we see practised in the most successful cancer clinics today.

The public and press began showing a marked interest in this controversial research, especially in view of the fact that this new approach to cancer treatment did not involve the use of toxic or radical treatments that were now increasingly becoming viewed as largely useless and 'ethically questionable':

"When President Richard Nixon was deluged with tens of thousands of petitions from ordinary citizens everywhere demanding clinical trials for Laetrile, these demands were forwarded to his cancer advisor, Benno Schmidt... When Schmidt consulted all of his medical colleagues about Laetrile, he found them vehemently opposed to it. But, interestingly enough, as he told reporters later: "I couldn't get anybody to show me scientific proof that the stuff didn't work."" [126]

In 1973 a three-month trial at the Southern Research Institute in Birmingham, Alabama, intensively researched the therapeutic properties of Laetrile. The institute finally released its findings to the

[124] **Coop & Blakely** *New Zealand Journal of Science & technology,* 28th February 1949, page 277; op. cit, 31:(3)1; op. cit, February 1950, page 45)
[125] **Van der Walt** *Veterinary Records,* 52:857, 1940
[126] **Heinerman, Dr John** *An Encyclopedia of Nature's Vitamins and Minerals,* Prentice Hall, 1998 ISBN 0735200726

National Cancer Institute which proceeded to announce to the public that once again studies proved that B17-Laetrile had no effect whatsoever in the treatment of cancer. However not all was as it appeared. When the data and protocols from these experiments were subsequently studied in more detail by Dr Dean Burk, one of the National Cancer Institute's founders and head of its Department of Cytochemistry, inconsistencies in the trial protocols began to appear. [127] Researcher G Edward Griffin, whose controversial book *World Without Cancer* broke the Laetrile story to the public in the 1970s, explains:

"Every [Laetrile] study had been tarnished with the same kind of scientific ineptitude, bias, and outright deception as found in the 1953 MacDonald/Garland California report. Some of these studies openly admitted evidence of anti-cancer effect but hastened to attribute this effect to other causes. Some were toxicity studies only, which means that they weren't trying to see if Laetrile was effective, but merely to determine how much of it was required to kill the patient." [128]

Despite announcing to the world that Laetrile was useless, the National Cancer Institute, the American Medical Association and the drug cartels looked on with anger as a national grass-roots movement sprang up across America as a result of the many cancer recoveries being reported and attributed to Laetrile and supporting nutrition. It was the '70s and people were distrustful of their government as a result of Watergate and Vietnam. The Committee for Freedom-of-Choice in Cancer Therapy was formed, founding several hundred chapters across America which in turn held public meetings, press conferences and pressured state legislative committees into calling for the 'legalisation' of Vitamin B17.

The federal government eventually persuaded the cancer industry to test Laetrile, which they did – without the pancreatic enzymes and other supporting co-factors required to break down the cancer cell. Of

---

[127] Dean Burk, Ph.D, one of the National Cancer Institute's co-founders, endorsed B17's status as a true vitamin and offered this statement regarding Edward Griffin's *World Without Cancer: "A clear and revolutionary insight into both the science and politics of cancer therapy."* Dr Linus Pauling, the 'father' of Vitamin C and two-time Nobel Laureate, also supported the use of Laetrile (*The New England Journal of Medicine*, 8th July 1982)

[128] Griffin, G Edward *World Without Cancer*, op. cit.

course the trials failed and the results – or lack of them – were subsequently reported, the summary declaring that Laetrile has no anti-cancer benefit whatsoever. Meanwhile, other cancer industry-appointed scientists, such as Dr Kanematsu Sugiura, Dr Elizabeth Stockert and Dr Lloyd Schoen, were using the correct protocols at Memorial Sloan-Kettering and achieving startling results, as others would around the world in the years to come.

But even these results were misreported, and once again B17 was 'tossed under the bus' with Memorial Sloan-Kettering's incredible conclusion: *"These results allow no definite conclusion supporting the anti-cancer activity of Laetrile."*[129]

This did not stop many physicians across America and later the world from implementing this therapy into their treatments of cancer patients. Many of these professionals received constant harassment at the hand of the medical authorities, who accused them of practising quackery and treating their patients with an 'unappoved drug' which contained the dangerous 'cyanide'. Gradually, through persistent and at times downright paranoid propaganda, the little yellow apricot became a natural-born killer in the eyes of many. Interestingly, the establishment proved dismal in the consistency of its opposition, focusing on "cyanide – what are you crazy?!" but failing to pillory Vitamin B12 as a 'deadly agent', containing as it does the cyanide radical also (Vitamin B12 is known as <u>cyano</u>cobalamin).

Philip Binzel MD, a doctor who retrained to treat his cancer patients with this nutritional therapy, foregoing the dangers of toxic chemotherapy and radiation treatments, highlights in his book *Alive and Well* the problem many doctors were having with an inherent lack of knowledge on nutrition:

"Most of my first patients were those who had all of the surgery, radiation and chemotherapy they could tolerate and their tumors were still growing. I did for these patients the best I knew to do.

---

[129] Griffin, G Edward, op. cit.

My biggest problem at the time was understanding nutrition. In four years of medical school, one year of Family Practice residency, I had not had even one lecture on nutrition." [emphasis mine] [130]

Binzel's book catalogues the repeated harassment he received at the hands of the Ohio State Medical Board and the Food & Drug Administration over his use of Laetrile and nutritional co-factors for his cancer patients. Binzel's incredible story of amazing tumour regressions and eliminations amid the backdrop of draconian treatment at the hands of his peers is typical of the rollercoaster ride many courageous doctors underwent in order to bring the truth of wellness to their suffering patients.

Even the Food & Drug Administration had its defectors. June de Spain, one of its pharmacologists and toxicologists, wrote *The Little Cyanide Cookbook*, in which she dispels the 'deadly-cyanide-in-its-natural-form' myth and lays out hundreds of diets containing the essential nitriloside factor. De Spain sums up her own findings on the back cover of her book:

"Because of its unique molecular structure, this compound releases cyanide only at the cancer site, thus destroying cancer cells while nourishing non-cancer tissue. Those populations in the world which eat these vitamin-rich foods simply do not get cancer – and they live to be much older than those who subsist on the typical modern diet.

Cyanide in minute quantities and in the proper food forms, instead of being poisonous, actually is an essential component of normal body chemistry. Vitamin B12, for instance, contains cyanide in the form of cyanocobalamin." [131]

Other doctors around the world were doing their own research, such as Dr Hans Nieper, former Director of the Department of Medicine at Silbersee Hospital in Hanover, Germany: During a visit to

---

[130] **Binzel, P E** *Alive & Well*, American Media, 2000 (available through Credence at www.credence.org)

[131] **De Spain, June** *The Little Cyanide Cookbook*, American Media, 2000. For superb dietary ideas, see also **Day, Phillip** *Food For Thought*, Credence, 2000 (also available at the Credence web-site at www.credence.org)

the United States in 1972, Dr Nieper told reporters: *"After more than twenty years of such specialised work, I have found non-toxic nitrilosides – that is, Laetrile – far superior to any other known cancer treatment or preventative. In my opinion, it is the only existing possibility for the ultimate control of cancer."*

In Canada, Dr N R Bouziane, former Director of Research Laboratories at St Jeanne D'Arc Hospital in Montreal, published his repeated successes in treating cancers with nutrition, which were written up in the medical literature, including the *Cancer News Journal*, Jan/April 1971, p.20, under the article heading "The Laetrile Story".

In the Philippines, Dr Manuel Navarro, former Professor of Medicine and Surgery at the University of Santo Tomas, Manila, and an internationally recognised cancer researcher with over 100 major scientific papers to his credit, treated terminally ill cancer patients with Laetrile for over 25 years. He stated in the *Cancer News Journal*: *"It is my carefully considered clinical judgement, as a practising oncologist and researcher in this field, that I have obtained most significant and encouraging results with the use of Laetrile-amygdalin in the treatment of terminal cancer patients..."*[132]

In Mexico, Dr Ernesto Contreras, one of the country's leading medical specialists in nutritional treatment for cancer for over 30 years, remarks of B17-Laetrile's action with extreme terminal cancer cases: *"The palliative action* [the ability of a substance to improve the comfort of a patient] *is in about 60% of the cases. Frequently, enough to be significant, I see arrest of the disease or even regression in some 15% of the very advanced cases."*[133]

Ernesto's son Francisco Contreras continues the work today after his father's retirement. Francisco is author of *The Hope of Living*

---

[132] *Cancer News Journal*, Jan/April 1971, pp.19-21

[133] These are cases receiving a 100% death-rate prognosis, given up as hopeless by orthodox medicine. The fact that any of these survive *at all* is astonishing in itself. Dr Contreras' words were reported in the *Cancer News Journal*, Vol 9, No 3. Source: The Arlin J. Brown Inf. Center, Inc, PO Box 251, Fort Belvoir, VA 22060. 703 451 8638. Tel: 540 752 9511. E mail: cancerinfo@webtv.net

Cancer Free in which he lays out the protocols his clinic has used to marvellous success in treating thousands of patients since 1963.[134]

In Italy, Professor Etore Guidetti, of the University of Turin Medical School, announced startling results with Laetrile in successfully combating many types of cancer, including cervix, breast, uterus and rectum. After a speech, an American doctor rose in the audience, challenging the Italian professor that Laetrile had been found to be worthless in the United States. Dr Guidetti was abrupt and dismissive: *"I care not what was determined in the United States. I am merely reporting what I saw in my own clinic."*[135]

METABOLIC THERAPY
...as used by the clinics, may include:

> Full ionised colloidal mineral supplementation
> Vitamin C (up to 10 g a day)
> B-Complex of vitamins (B3, B5, B6, etc.)
> Calcium, Magnesium, Boron and Vitamin D supplementation
> Laetrile/amygdalin/Vitamin B17 (either in pharmaceutical or apricot kernel form). IV amygdalin is sometimes administered with the tissue-penetrating agent dimethylsulfoxide (DMSO).
> Pancreatic enzymes trypsin and chymotrypsin. Also calf thymus, pancreatin and lipase may be used in the enzyme formula, along with certain fruit enzymes, such as bromelain (pineapples) or papain (papayas), which mimic the demasking action of pancreatic enzymes.
> Vitamins A & E (emulsified). Regular carrot juice also.
> Antioxidants.

---

[134] **Contreras, Francisco** *The Hope of Living Cancer Free*, Siloam Press, 1999. A detailed overview of the nutritional therapy practised in many cancer clinics today. Contreras also examines the psychological and spiritual factors so important in assisting a patient in overcoming their illness and helping them through the healing process. (Available through Credence at www.credence.org).

[135] *Cancer News Journal*, op. cit.

- Other known anti-tumourals, such as Hawaiian Noni juice, hydrazine sulphate and the natural herb remedy, Essiac, popularised by Canadian nurse Rene Caisse.[136]
- Detoxification measures, including coffee enemas and Natural Hygiene procedures using properly combined foods and fruit consumption on an empty stomach before noon. The elimination of meat, sugar and dairy products from the patient's diet, and an ongoing juicing regimen and alkalising of the body system using a diet comprising 80-85% high-water-content, alkali-ash-generating, unrefined plant dietary (see chapter entitled *Eliminating the Pied Piper*).
- The removal of all toxins from the diet and personal environment and the avoidance of potentially harmful drugs and treatments.
- The replacing of household and personal care items, such as toothpastes, antiperspirants, shampoo and make-up, which contain potentially harmful ingredients, with non-toxic effective alternatives.

These measures are discussed in more detail in a later section. For a fuller and more dedicated treatment of the cancer topic and the information on Vitamin B17 Metabolic Therapy, please obtain a copy of my book *Cancer – Why We're Still Dying to Know the Truth*, available through Credence at www.credence.org.

OK. Let's move on....

---

[136] **Percival, J** *The Essiac Handbook*, Credence Publications, 2001

Water Under the Bridge

The Damning Case against Fluoridation

"During times of universal deceit, telling the truth becomes a revolutionary act." - George Orwell

The most pressing three battles we fight as citizens for our good health today are for the right to drink clean, uncontaminated water, to eat clean, uncontaminated food and to breathe clean, uncontaminated air. In our sophisticated Western world today, which allegedly focuses so much on the rights of its citizens, why are these three fundamental, 'unalienable' rights being wilfully trampled? Why, in a society which can do so much technologically for its citizens, can't we address these three fundamentals of life and progress *towards* good health and longevity, rather than racing *away* from them?

This chapter deals with the subject of water and fluoridation, and these two deserve their own chapter, simply because of the importance of the subject. Author Harvey Diamond puts it this way:

"As an absolute prerequisite to life, water is right up there with food and air. From the moment you are born until you leave this planet, your body instinctively craves food, air and water for your survival. You know what happens to a plant when it is deprived of water. It wilts and dies. The same would happen to your body if it were deprived of water. Its importance is clear." [137]

Bringing water to the public is a complicated and responsible business. If you get it wrong, and bacteria afflict the masses, you can definitely lose your pension. Some of the worst scourges mankind has faced have come about as a result of contaminated water supplies, infested with microbes that bring on the feared cholera, dysentery and other fatal syndromes that still afflict most Third World nations today. In the past, the bubonic *yersinia pestis* decimated over a quarter of Europe during the medieval ages with rat-borne contaminants that could easily be passed to others through touching, kissing and other close-quarters contact. Mankind though has largely forgotten the major health disasters it has suffered in the past. Much water, if you'll

---

[137] Diamond, Harvey & Marilyn, *Fit For* Life, op. cit. p.34

forgive the pun, has gone under the bridge, and we like to think that problems linked to matters so basic as those concerning water supply are simply those gremlins suffered by the less developed nations – not us. This false sense of security we enjoy in the First World though has not prevented governments and water authorities from rising to the challenge of delivering clean, fresh and bug-free water to the public as safely and as cheaply as possible, using some... well, shall we say, quite *unique* methods.

The halogen element chlorine is often added to the public drinking water to kill germs. When I am in the United States, waiters and waitresses will bring me a glass of iced water with my meal, which in many areas is quite undrinkable due to its high chlorine content. Most of the American public has become used to this type of water, and most are prepared to drink it, cook with it, shower with it and wallow around for half an hour in a bath with it. Prolonged chlorine exposure over the years though has been found to desiccate the skin, causing premature wrinkling, dandruff and baldness. Concerns over the long-term effects of bad-tasting chlorinated water fuelled a water filter boom in the early 1990s, which has never ended. For a few dollars, you can obtain a carbon filter that will screw onto the faucet and strip off the chlorine, delivering what the public believes is clean, uncontaminated H_2O.

But there's another halogen element, which some governments sanction to be put into water supplies, that has caused increasing fear over the past fifty years. Indeed very few public outcries have been as consistent and vigorous as the public's reaction to the fluoridation of water and toothpastes:

"Controversy surrounding the fluoridation experiment has persisted for half a century. Japan and all of continental Europe have rejected the idea for reasons of safety and medical ethics. Experiments in poor countries produced such harmful results that they were quickly halted. Why does fluoridation continue to receive vigorous government and professional backing in the English-speaking nations?" – Health Action Network [138]

---

[138] *Fluoridation – Why the Controversy?* Health Action Network briefing document, printed by the National Health Federation, PO Box 688, Monrovia, CA 91017 USA

Janet Nagel has authored several studies on the subject and explains how the idea of adding fluoride compounds to the public drinking water supply gained public support through the promotion of this controversial measure by industry and government over sixty years ago:

"In the 1940s and 50s, a vigorous corporate and government promotional campaign convinced large numbers of people that fluorides reduced susceptibility to tooth decay. In 1985, over 90% of all toothpastes sold in the US contained high concentrations of intentionally added fluorine compounds. Close to 60% of the US population consumed water containing 1.0 to 4.0 parts per million of fluoride compounds. Nearly all major US cities, and many smaller ones, intentionally add fluorine compounds to their water supplies."[139]

So what is 'fluoride' and why exactly is this chemical added to food, water and other products we consume on a daily basis?

The term 'fluoride' is often used to describe fluorine-based chemical additives that have been put into the public water supply or into toothpastes and foods. 'Fluoride' tablets are also prescribed to youngsters apparently to assist in the protection and development of their teeth. In repeatedly hearing the one term, 'fluoride', the public has been cleverly coerced into thinking that there is just one substance that has been made available to us by caring government and industry to maintain and promote healthy teeth and gums. The reality is, as we will see, the term 'fluoride' has been found to encompass everything from sodium, calcium and potassium fluorides through to the highly dangerous liquid toxic waste product hexa- (in the US - hydro) - fluorisilicic acid and the toxic powder sodium silicofluoride, both of which are dumped into the public water supply by industry with no detoxification procedures and refinement carried out beforehand.

Fluorine is an extremely reactive, electronegative element that is never found alone in nature. Thus there are many kinds of fluorides, such as calcium fluoride, which is found naturally in water, lead fluoride, aluminium fluoride, and so on. The solitary term 'fluoride', so

---

[139] **Nagel Ed. D, Janet** *Re-examination of Fluoridation Issues*, Health Action Network, op. cit. Statistics are from *Fluoridation Census 1985*, US Public Health Service, Centers for Disease Control (CDC)

often used, even by activists, is meaningless and misleading as it fails to describe other elements with which the promiscuous fluorine has combined. These other elements often make the difference in toxicity of the resulting compound.

Pure fluorine is gaseous and is described as *"a non-metallic halogen element that is isolated as a pale yellowish flammable irritating toxic diatomic gas"* (Webster's Ninth New Collegiate Dictionary, 1991). Fluorine was used to great effect as a battlefield gas by the militaries during World War 1. Fluoride compounds today are used in pesticides, aluminium smelting, etching metals and glass, aerosol propellants and refrigerants. Sodium fluoride, the same compound that is added to toothpastes under the admiring eye of the world's dental associations, is a chief component of Sarin nerve gas. It's also the main ingredient in rat poison, as any pest control expert will tell you.

The debate surrounding the pros and cons of fluoride additives has raged for half a century. The main areas of contention, which we will examine, are as follows:

1) Do fluoride compounds prevent dental caries (cavities) and assist in the development and health maintenance of teeth?
2) Are fluoride compounds dangerous to public health?
3) Are governments and industry mass-medicating their populations without consent?

DO FLUORIDE COMPOUNDS
REDUCE DENTAL CARIES (CAVITIES)?
The belief that fluoride compounds reduce the incidence of tooth decay is dental religion today, in spite of the fact that fluoride's original champion, H Trendley Dean, DDS, admitted under oath 40 years ago that his data purporting to prove the efficacy of fluoridation for dental health were not valid.[140]

In June 1993, New Jersey State Assemblyman John V Kelly publicised the disturbing fact that fluoride compounds used in

---

[140] *City of Oroville vs. Public Utilities Commission of the State of California* – H Trendley Dean Proceedings, Oroville, California, 20th –21st October 1955

toothpastes and the water supply have never received approval by the American Food & Drug Administration and are officially classified as 'an unapproved new drug'. Kelly's research also uncovered that neither the FDA nor the Institute of Dental Research (NIDR) nor the American Academy of Pediatric Dentistry could furnish any proof of fluoride compound safety or effectiveness, as required by law as part of the FDA drug approval process. Which means of course that in the US, almost every American is receiving treatment every day from a drug which is unapproved by the FDA.[141] This in turn means that doctors and dentists prescribing fluoride compounds to patients are committing an illegal act and that the fluoridation of public water supplies is medical experimentation without the target population's consent. If fluoride compounds are, as their proponents exhort, the greatest things to hit the teeth of humanity since fresh water, *then why hasn't the FDA approved these 'valuable' compounds?* We'll find out as we proceed.

THE GRAND RAPIDS/MUSKEGON FLUORIDE TRIALS

One of the first trials carried out in an attempt to prove fluoridation's effectiveness in reducing dental decay occurred in America in 1945 and involved the cities of Grand Rapids and Muskegon, Michigan. Grand Rapids' public water supply was fluoridated and Muskegon's was left alone to serve as the control. Within a couple of years, pro-fluoride advocates were clamouring that fluoridation was producing a 60% drop in dental caries in Grand Rapids when compared with those occurring in the city of Muskegon. The results were apparently so conclusive that this ten-year trial was halted after just five years when the authorities fluoridated Muskegon's water supplies.

Later however, the results of the trials were to reveal disturbing inconsistencies in the collection and reporting of the data. One graph shows that within one year, dental decay had declined 70.5% among six-year-olds in Grand Rapids, when studies were made of all 79 schools in the trial area. The reality is that the data used to start the trial included dental decay rates for all 79 schools, but from 1946 onwards, *only the children from 25 hand-selected schools in the trial area were examined*, giving rise to an apparent drop in decay rates.

---

[141] Trenton *Star Ledger*, "Kelly Seeks FDA Ban on Fluoride Supplement" by Guy Sterling, 4th July 1993; also Letter to US FDA Commissioner David Kessler by John V Kelly, 3rd June 1993

During the next three years, the dental decay rates actually rose by 65.2% among the 25 schools, indicating that fluoridation was having no effect in spite of the children (selectively chosen) having the apparent benefit of more years of fluoridation.[142] The only 'reduction' in decay rates had occurred during the year of the selection process.

THE KINGSTON/NEWBURGH TRIAL

A similar US study was conducted with the cities of Kingston and Newburgh, located in New York State along the Hudson River. Newburgh was to be the fluoridated township and Kingston the unfluoridated control. Within ten years of the study inception in 1945, Public Health fluoridation supporters were claiming a 60% decline in dental decay occurring in Newburgh. Not revealed however was the fact that Newburgh parents and their children received free consultations on dental hygiene, advice on the boycotting of sweets and dental visits to remove dental plaque. Someone somewhere wanted Newburgh to succeed. Kingston however was completely ignored and received no such advantages. Later it became apparent that not all the Newburgh children had been selected. Another bout of selective reporting had occurred.

After announcing their victory with fluoridation however, the Public Health Service proponents of fluoridation received a major slap in the face. For, during the tenth year of Newburgh's fluoridation, an independent study of the two townships had been underway, carried out by Dr John A Forst, Professor at the University of the State of New York and chief of the State Bureau of Health Services. He too studied both sets of school children and his results painted a disturbingly different picture:

	Kingston	**Newburgh**
Enrolled	5403	5119
Pupils Inspected	5303 (98%)	4959 (97%)
Pupils with Dental Defects	2209 (41.6%)	3139 (63.2%)
Pupils under Dental Treatment	1551 (29.2%)	2072 (41.7%)

These shocking results were too clear to be ignored. After ten years of fluoridation and when nearly all the children of both townships were examined, it was evident that Newburgh contained *more* children with

---

[142] National Research Council, publication #214

dental defects and *more* children undergoing dental treatment than in Kingston, a township left to its own water devices. To this day, Kingston remains unfluoridated, having vigorously rejected fluoridation at the conclusion of the trials. Later, a follow-up study in 1989 would show that after almost four decades of fluoridation, schoolchildren in Newburgh had no less dental decay than in unfluoridated Kingston.[143]

Research by the UK's Safe Water Society yielded similar research results:

1) A US trial studying 50,000 inhabitants across 68 US cities in 1986-7 showed that fluoride increased tooth decay.[144]
2) 400,000 children were studied in India and calcium and fluoride levels were measured. The study found that fluoride increases tooth decay while calcium reduces caries.[145]
3) 21,000 Japanese children were studied in 1972. Fluoride was found to increase tooth decay.[146]
4) After 20 years of water fluoridation in Seattle, Washington State, authorities reported an unprecedented dental crisis in the north-western American city.[147]
5) 22,000 children were studied in Tucson, Arizona. Fluoride was found to increase tooth decay.[148]
6) In 1987, Alan S Gray, DDS, FRCD(C), Director of the Division of Dental Health Services or the British Columbia Ministry of Health, called for a re-examination of the relevance of fluoride compounds in the Canadian public water supply when it was learned that tooth decay rates in British Columbia (where only 11% of the population use fluoridated water) were lower than those of other Canadian provinces with fluoridation rates of 40%-70%.[149]

---

[143] **Kumar JV, et al** *American Journal of Public Health*, 1989; 79:565-569
[144] **Yiamouyiannis, J** *Fluoride 23 #2*, April 1990
[145] **Teotia, SP** *Fluoride*, April 1994 pp.59-66
[146] **Imai, Y** *Japanese Journal of Dental Health*, 1972; 22:144-196
[147] **Porterfield, Elaine** *Tacoma Morning News Tribune*, "Demand Taxes Clinics Serving the Poor", 30th March 1992
[148] **Cornelius Steelinck** *Chemical and Engineering News*, 27th January 1992, p.2; also *Science News*, 5th March 1994, p.159
[149] **Gray, A S** *Journal of the Canadian Dental Association*, "Fluoridation – Time for New

7) In December 1993, a Canadian Dental Association committee, known as the Canadian Workshop on the Evaluation of Current Recommendations Concerning Fluorides, concluded that consuming fluoride does not prevent tooth decay or reduce its incidence. The panel also found that children exposed to fluoride compounds risked dental fluorosis.[150]

Leading fluoridation opponent John R Lee MD states that the trial results the dental and chemical industries invariably use are always misreported and techniques employed to give the public false impressions of fluoridation's supposed efficacy and harmlessness. These tactics include the 'percent reduction' method instead of 'rate of change of decay'. This data-manipulation strategy was exposed in the Rand Corporation report of 1981, in which author Craig B Foch states that fluoride studies *"suffer from poor experimental design and from analysis plans that largely ignore the possible effects of other factors in tooth decay."*

Lee reports that doctors and researchers are often in for a bumpy ride if they question fluoride's efficacy and challenge its alleged safety and cost-effectiveness:

"When one looks in the dental literature for evidence that fluoridation reduces dental costs, the results are equally dismal. In all studies in which selection bias is not evident [i.e. where the data hasn't been fudged], *no reduction in dental costs is found. When Dr Gray, a dental health officer in Vancouver, BC, Canada, examined* [the records of] *all schoolchildren in British Columbia, he found no dental benefit from fluoridation. Upon reporting this, he was demoted and obliged to desist in making any comment about it."*[151]

Delivering the target dose of 1.0mg fluoride compounds to each citizen every day costs money – and for what benefit, against what risk? Even supposing one believes in the efficacy of fluorides for dental health, against all reason and scientific evidence, why fluoridate the water supply? Why not just pass out the tablets? In other words, why

Baseline?" October 1987

[150] **Clark, Christopher** *Canadian Medical Association Journal,* 1993:149 (12), 15th December 1993

[151] **Lee, John R** *Fluoridation Follies,* a research paper, September 1995, p.13

deliberately spend more? According to one public water supply co-ordinator, the annual projected budget for fluoridating the water supply of Tacoma, Washington State was estimated to be $125,000 in 1991.[152] The cost of supplying fluoride tablets to the under 12s would be a mere $1.20 per thousand 1.0mg tablets in comparison. So why the fixation on medicating the water supplies? We will examine the reasons in the conclusion of this chapter.

In May 1992, Dr William Marcus, the senior science advisor and chief toxicologist with the United States Environmental Protection Agency, was fired from his post after publicly disclosing his frank comments concerning mass medicating the public without its consent and the appalling hazards of fluoridation. Marcus was concerned that the results of US Government studies on fluoridation, completed in 1984 and a second in 1987, were kept from the American public. After a long fight, Dr Marcus was reinstated on 28th February 1995. *"If this were any other chemical but fluoride,"* Marcus commented, *"there would be a call for the immediate cessation of its use. It shows potential for great harm."*[153]

ARE FLUORIDE COMPOUNDS
DANGEROUS TO PUBLIC HEALTH?

The evidence shows that fluoride compounds, especially those examined in this chapter, are harmful to humanity over the long-term. Undeniably fluorides used in the drinking water supplies are a toxic, non-biodegradable, environmental pollutant, officially classified as a contaminant by the US Environmental Protection Agency. The two main culprits, as mentioned, are hexa(hydro)fluorosilicic acid and sodium silicofluoride. Shocking though it may be to contemplate, the reality is, these chemicals are simply hazardous industrial waste - a by-product from the manufacture of phosphate fertilisers, gleaned from this industry's pollution scrubbers - which is largely disposed of in our public water supply.[154] Hexafluorosilicic acid, the most commonly used fluoridation additive, contains other toxic substances including lead,

---

[152] **Myrick, C R** Water Quality Co-Ordinator, City of Tacoma, in a telephone conversation with Wini Silko, Tacoma citizen, 15th November, 1991 (Health Action Network briefing document)

[153] **d'Raye, Tonita**, *The Facts About Fluoride*, PO Box 21075, Keizer, OR 97307 USA

[154] "AWWA Standard for Sodium Silicofluoride" and "AWWA Standard for Hydrofluorosilicic Acid", American Water Works Association, 1st July 1989; also "Fluoride: Commie Plot or Capitalistic Ploy?" **Griffiths, Joel** *Covert Action*, Fall 1992, pp.26-30+

beryllium, mercury, cadmium and arsenic.[155] Sodium fluoride, beloved of toothpaste manufacturers, is a hazardous waste compound from the aluminium smelting process, and is also used in water fluoridation schemes, although less frequently than the previously mentioned two compounds. Sodium fluoride is often given to children in tablet or liquid form and is almost always added to toothpastes in concentrations of between 500-1500 ppm.

Interestingly, Proctor and Gamble, the manufacturers of Crest toothpaste and an ardent supporter of sodium fluoride, were reported to have admitted that a family size tube of their world famous toothpaste contained enough sodium fluoride to kill a 20-30lb child if ingested.[156] Warning labels appear on American toothpaste packaging advising that in the event of ingestion, the victim should seek a poisons control centre immediately. This ridiculous notice is made more of a sham by the fact that you don't have to swallow poisons like this for them to become absorbed, IF THEY'RE EVEN UNDER THE TONGUE, THEY'RE IN THE BLOODSTREAM.

This author has met several elderly gentlemen in the UK who recalled one way conscripts used to attempt to dodge the National Service draft in the 1950s. They would consume half a tube of toothpaste, which subsequently made the recruit extremely ill and unfit to serve.

Government and industry have long denied that fluoride additives are toxic waste from industry, preferring to paint a picture of sanitised, benevolent chemicals guarding our teeth day and night administered through the 'safe' water we drink. The reality is, even those within government ranks have broken cover and confirmed the source of these chemicals. Tom Reeves, for example, a water engineer with America's Centers for Disease Control (CDC), controversially admitted in January 2001 that these fluoride additives were waste emissions from heavy industry:

[155] d'Raye, Tonita, *The Facts About Fluoride*, PO Box 21075, Keizer, OR 97307 USA
[156] *Spotlight*, 28th October 1996, p.8

"All of the fluoride chemicals used in the U.S. for water fluoridation - sodium fluoride, sodium fluorosilicate, and fluorosilicic acid - are by-products of the phosphate fertilizer industry.

The manufacturing process produces two by-products: (1) a solid, calcium sulphate (sheetrock, $CaSo_4$); and (2) the gases, hydrofluoric acid (HF) and silicon tetrafluoride (SiF_4). A simplified explanation of this manufacturing process follows: Apatite rock, a calcium mineral found in central Florida, is ground up and treated with sulfuric acid, producing phosphoric acid and the two by-products, calcium sulphate and the two gas emissions. Those gases are captured by product recovery units (scrubbers) and condensed into 23% fluorosilicic acid (H_2SiF_6). Sodium fluoride and sodium fluorosilicate are made from this acid."

Research highlighting the adverse effects of fluoride compounds on human beings is troublingly abundant. Fluoride's beastliness was summed up in a terse statement issued by Dr Dean Burk of the National Cancer Institute: *"Fluoride causes more human cancer death, and causes it faster than any other chemical."*[157] As far back as October of 1944, the *Journal of the American Medical Association* published an editorial stating: *"... that the use of drinking water containing as little as 1.2 to 3 parts per million of fluoride will cause such developmental disturbances in bones as osteosclerosis, spondylosis, and osteoporosis, as well as goitre."*[158] The Safe Water Foundation filed Freedom on Information Act requests to obtain the results of government studies. Dr John Yiamouyiannis (president of the Safe Water Foundation) said *"All tests came out positive."* (establishing a fluoride-cancer link) [159]

Dr John Lee, who was chairman of the Environmental Health Committee of his local medical association in Marin County, California, went head-to-head with authorities on the fluoride issue. According to Lee, the county had continually pushed water fluoridation on the local ballot until it passed by a slim margin of one per cent. Lee states:

---

[157] d'Raye, Tonita, op. cit

[158] *Journal of the American Medical Association*, "Health Damaging Effects of Fluoride", October 1944. A list of some thirty clinical trials demonstrating the adverse effects of fluoride compounds on bone are kept on file at Credence.

[159] http://www.whale.to/Dental/fluoride.html

"[Fluoride] *is a toxic waste product of many types of industry; for instance, glass production, phosphate fertilizer production and many others. They would have no way to dispose of the tons of fluoride waste they produce unless they could find some use for it, so they made up this story about it being good for dental health. Then they can pass it through everyone's bodies and into the sewer.*"[160]

Lee's comments on their own would be shocking and dismissive. The problem is, hundreds of specialists, doctors and biochemists have been saying the same thing for years. And sure enough, when the curtains were finally pulled back and the veil of secrecy lifted, federal research indeed discovered that fluoride caused cancer in humans and animals.[161] NCI's Dr Burk stated: "*It is concluded that artificial fluoridation appears to cause or induce about 20-30 excess cancer deaths for every 100,000 persons exposed per year after about 15-20 years.*"[162] Incredibly to this day, not only is fluoridation of the water supply and toothpaste still permitted, US federal goals require mandatory fluoridation of the water supply in 75% of all US cities by the close of the year 2000![163] Yet....

> ➤ Fluoride accumulates in the body like lead, inflicting its damage over long periods of time. Fluoride is more toxic than lead, and just slightly less toxic than arsenic. Lead is given a toxicity rating of 3, whereas fluoride's level is 4. Under US law, administered and enforced by the Environmental Protection Agency, the maximum allowable lead in drinking water is 0.015mg/litre. With fluoride however it is 4.0mg/litre, OVER 350 TIMES THE PERMITTED LEAD LEVEL. [164]
> ➤ Fluoride compounds initially cause dental fluorosis, a chalky mottling of the tooth enamel, leading to brittle and vulnerable teeth. Fluorosis is a permanent malformation of tooth enamel indicating an alteration in bone growth. Further symptoms of chronic fluoride poisoning may

---

[160] http://www.thewinds.org/archive/medical/fluoride01-98.html

[161] National Toxicology Program (NTP) 1990, National Cancer Institute, HHS Fluoride Report 2/91

[162] http://www.thewinds.org/archive/medical/fluoride01-98.html

[163] d'Raye, Tonita, op. cit

[164] Clinical Toxicology of Commercial Products, 5th Ed. 1984

include constipation, excess gas and other gastrointestinal disturbances, chronic boils or rashes, peeling, shrivelled skin between your toes or brittle, easy-to-break nails. Symptoms of extreme fluoride poisoning may include chronic fatigue syndrome, skin problems, bleeding gums, excess saliva, hair loss, edema swelling in the lower extremities, mental problems, kidney disease, cancer and death.[165]

➤ *"The fluoride dose prescribed by doctors and the dose administered without prescription to everyone in community drinking water is EXPECTED to cause dental fluorosis in 10% of children. Actual Public Health Service figures show that 30% of children in fluoridated localities have dental fluorosis, and 10% of children in non-fluoridated areas now have fluorosis."*[166] Even citizens living in non-fluoridated areas are expected to ingest amounts in excess of 1.0mg fluoride compounds per day through toothpaste use and consumption of food products manufactured with fluoridated water. Citizens living in fluoridated communities <u>may expect to be exposed to 5.0mg a day or more.</u>

➤ Medical research shows that hip fractures are 20-40% higher in fluoridated communities.[167]

➤ Fluorides are used in laboratory work to inhibit enzyme activity. Fluoride compounds have the same effect in the human body, accumulating in the skeleton structure over long periods of time. Fluoride poisoning is long-term and progressive.

➤ The chemicals injected into public water supplies to elevate fluoride levels are raw industrial waste. The two most commonly used additives are hexafluorosilicic acid and sodium silicofluoride, toxic by-products of aluminium smelting and phosphate fertiliser production.

---

[165] Dr Leo Spira's testimony before a US Senate investigative committee explained that the long-term effects of fluoride compound poisoning potentially implicated the chemical in a host of problems not readily identifiable as fluoride-causation, in view of the length of exposure.

[166] *Health Action Network* briefing document, op. cit. Also, *Review of Fluoride Benefits and Risks*, US Public Health Service, February 1991, p.53

[167] *The John R Lee MD Medical Letter*, February 1999

> Fluoridated water increases corrosion and leaching of lead from water mains and plumbing.
> About 1% of the fluoridated water used from public supplies is actually ingested by the public. The remainder is used for sewage, washing, industry and agriculture. This had led to the belief by industry that fluoridated industrial waste may be safely disposed of in this manner with little or no harm to the public. However, fluoride levels in the sewer effluent of fluoridated water systems are not monitored or controlled. Fish have been found to be poisoned by fluoride emissions at and below the 'acceptable' levels emitted by sewer effluent.[168]

The American Medical Association (AMA) issued a news release entitled "Study Links Fluoride to Rare Bone Cancer" on 8th December 1993. This study also showed that hip fractures were 27% higher in women, and 41% higher in men in the fluoridated city featured in the tests. Hip fractures (potentially fatal to the elderly) are linked to fluoridated water. [169]

In 1984, Japanese researchers began to close in on fluoride's ability to cause cellular damage, thus compelling the body to commence a healing process, possibly resulting in non-terminating stem-cell trophoblast, or cancer. Dr Takeki Tsutsui of the Nippon Dental College stated that *"fluoride caused not only genetic damage but was also capable of transforming normal cells into cancer cells."* Research journalist Val Valerian sums up the disturbing conclusions of Tsutsui's studies:

"In Dr Tsutsui's study, the level of fluoride used was the same level that the US National Cancer Institute (NCI) suggested should be used in a study to determine whether fluoridation of public water supplies causes cancer. The level of fluoride deemed 'safe' in the United States, 1 part per million (ppm), was found by Tsutsui to produce cancer in cells." [170]

---

[168] Health Action Network, op. cit.
[169] *Journal of the American Medical Association,* (JAMA) 3/8/95, 8/11-12/92, 7/25/91, 6/19/91, 7/25/90; *American Journal of Epidemiology,* 4/91; *American Journal of Public Health,* 7/90
[170] **Valerian, Val** *Perceptions,* "On The Toxic Nature of Fluorides", September/October 1995

Research completed in 1989 by the National Toxicology Program (NTP), an agency of the US Public Health Service, found a statistically significant dose-related increase of osteosarcoma (bone cancer) in male rats. Thyroid and liver cancers were also found.[171]

Amazingly, while the evidence of fluoride's ability to harm continued to mount, so too did the American Dental Association and the National Research Council's[172] continued endorsement of fluoride's overwhelming 'benefits' to society, the latter even denying that fluoride was carcinogenic to laboratory animals.[173] Four years later in 1992 however, the New Jersey State Department of Health published the results of a trial in which *six times the incidence of bone cancers were being found in fluoridated communities.*[174]

TROUBLE AT THE WELL

Notwithstanding the shiny, happy faces at the ADA and NIDR over fluoride's 'incalculable' contribution to humanity's health, malfunctions in the mechanics of city water fluoridation routinely cause predictable mayhem and tragedy. In 1992, fluoride feed machinery operating on one of two community wells failed in the township of Hooper Bay, Alaska, resulting in the death of one man and the poisoning of 296 other citizens.[175] On 16th July 1993, a water filter failed to remove the fluoride compounds in Chicago's drinking water before it was used in the treatment of three kidney dialysis patients at the University of Chicago Hospital. All three patients died. Six others suffered acute toxicity reactions after undergoing dialysis with fluoridated water.[176] On November 16th 1993, lethal levels of fluoride

---

[171] **Maurer, et al** *Journal of the National Cancer Institute*, vol. 82, 1990 pp.1118-26

[172] A National Academy of Sciences subcommittee dominated by fluoride proponents from the National Institute of Dental Research. Not one of the many researchers who had published adverse reports on fluoride was asked to be part of the committee.

[173] Press Release on Drinking Water Fluoridation from the National Academy of Sciences, 16th August 1993

[174] **Cohn, Perry D** "A Brief Report on the Association of Drinking Water Fluoridation and the Incidence of Osteosarcoma Among Young Males", Environmental Health Service, New Jersey Department of Health, 8th November, 1992

[175] **Alaska Department of Health and Social Services** "Hooper Bay Waterborne Outbreak – Fluoride, Final Report", 12th April 1993; **Hulen, David** *Tacoma Morning News Tribune*, 2nd July 1992

[176] **Wisby, Gary** *Chicago Sun-Times*, "Fluoride Blamed in 3 Deaths", 31st July 1993

compounds up to 70 ppm were found in the public water system of Middletown, Maryland.[177]

FLUORIDATION
MASS-MEDICATION WITHOUT CONSENT?

Water fluoridation has been described as the widest mass-medication program in the history of humanity. That this procedure is occurring without the informed consent of the citizenry is the chief ethical issue that has driven opposition to fluoridation since World War 2. Researcher Janet Nagel summarises:

"That nearly all physicians, dentists and other members of the dominant health professions have come to hold such uncritical faith in fluoride as a tooth decay remedy raises serious questions about the content and quality of their training as scientists and practitioners. That so many professional leaders and government officials have been willing to falsify or obscure scientific data in their zeal to maintain the fluoridation pretense raises concerns that are even more far-reaching." [178]

During the first four decades of the 1900s, global industrial output rose dramatically. During two world wars, industry raised its production profile many orders of magnitude in order to satisfy the unique demand for munitions, armaments, tanks and aircraft with heavy industrial production. Agriculture too was honed to a knife-edge. All available hands were put to the land in order to ensure the continuance of food output to beleaguered nations.

Both heavy manufacturing and the agro-chemical industries produce large quantities of fluoride compounds as toxic waste products. During the course of these activities, as early as the 1930s, fluoride in industrial emissions was increasingly regarded as a major pollutant. After the war, the major industrial nations began exporting fertilisers and heavy industrial goods to lesser-developed countries resulting in their gross national output expanding exponentially. By 1965, President Lyndon Johnson's Science Advisory Committee was

---

[177] *The Fluoride Report*, "Middletown, Maryland Halts Fluoridation After Toxic Spill in Water Supply", December 1993; **Eliassen, M** *The Frederick Post*, "Water Not For Drinking; Fluoride Levels Too High", 17th November 1993

[178] Health Action Network briefing document, op. cit.

naming fluoride compounds as one of America's four leading pollutants.[179]

Ironically, since water fluoridation was proposed in the 1940s, very little has been heard from the establishment regarding fluoride as an environmental pollutant. Clearly, the chemical and heavy manufacturing industries had a growing problem on their hands with raw toxic fluoride wastes, which also contained many metals harmful to human and animal health, such as cadmium, beryllium, lead, mercury and aluminium. Industry, faced with millions of dollars in operating costs to dispose of raw toxic waste in an acceptable manner, found themselves considering ways in which the problem could be dissolved, a little at a time, with little or no cost to their margins. Janet Nagel remarks:

"Laws controlling the disposal of toxic wastes do not permit the industries creating these fluorides to release them into the environment. However, the 'laundering' process of fluoridation allows these same toxins to be spread indiscriminately on lawns and gardens, incorporated into processed foods, and released by the ton into water and air, in sewer effluent and sludge.

The original promotion of fluoridation as a remedy for tooth decay was funded by the aluminum industry. Andrew Mellon, former Chairman of the Aluminum Corporation of America (ALCOA), was Secretary of the Treasury when the US Public Health Service was an agency of the Treasury Department. The research purporting to demonstrate fluoride effectiveness and safety was funded by ALCOA, Reynolds Metals, and other heavy fluoride emitters."[180]

The 1970s produced other quandaries for the fluoridation problem. Research was now clearly stating a long-term harmful link which few could deny. Water suppliers were becoming concerned at the high costs they would incur in having to remove fluorides from the water they supplied to the citizenry. Fluorides are not easily removed from water. Charcoal/carbon filters remove chlorine but not fluorides.

---

[179] **Jerard, Elise** "Total Fluoride Exposure", a report prepared for the Municipal Broadcasting System, September 1968

[180] Nagel, Janet, op. cit; also Griffiths, Joel, op. cit.

Reverse osmosis or distillation procedures are required effectively to strip the water of fluoride contaminants. To overcome this problem of cost facing suppliers, the US Environmental Protection Agency in 1988 actually made the decision to increase the Maximum Contaminant Level (MCL) for fluorides from 2.0ppm to 4.0ppm.

The charge of mass medication of the population can justifiably be made since fluoride is, by the admission of its proponents, pharmacologically active in supposedly preventing dental caries. Many of the trials quoted in this chapter demonstrate quite inarguably that fluoride compounds are also pharmacologically active in doing human and animal systems harm. Even the Food & Drug Administration wishes the whole fluoride embarrassment would quietly go away, having classified water fluoride compounds as 'unapproved new drugs' and obstinately left it at that. On the 16th March 1979, a surreptitious changing of the Federal Register occurred on page 16006. All paragraphs stating that fluoride compounds were 'essential or probably essential' were deleted by the FDA.

There are not many who will dispute the fact that fluoride compounds in amounts of 1.0 ppm (as advocated by fluoride proponents) do not produce changes in tooth enamel structure and bone formation. The point being made by fluoride opponents is that the citizens themselves should have the right to decide whether or not to take fluoride supplementation. At the present time, there is no regulation as to how much fluoride any given individual is taking in, due to varied water consumption, age, occupation, diet and lifestyle. This has led to obvious concerns over health risks which have failed to disperse over the last fifty years, which only serve to underline more forcibly the unassailable conclusion that there are no known essential uses for fluoride compounds in medicine or dentistry.

As one last example of how even experts in the field of chemistry and medicine have become divided on this issue over the years, the following Nobel Prize winners have either expressed reservations about fluoridation, or have outright opposed it. They are:

Adolf Butenandt (Chemistry, 1939)
Arvid Carlsson (Chemistry, 2000)
Hans von Euler-Chelpin (Chemistry, 1929)

Walter Rudolf Hess (Medicine, 1949)
Corneille Jean-François Heymans (Medicine, 1938)
Sir Cyril Norman Hinshelwood (Chemistry, 1956)
Joshua Lederberg (Medicine, 1958)
William P. Murphy (Medicine, 1934)
Giulio Natta (Chemistry 1963)
Sir Robert Robinson (Chemistry, 1947)
Nikolai Semenov (Chemistry, 1956)
James B. Sumner (Chemistry, 1946)
Hugo Theorell (Medicine, 1955)
Artturi Virtanen (Chemistry, 1945)[181]

NOTEPAD

Let us finish this chapter by listing the conclusions of one of fluoride's long-time antagonists, Dr John Lee:

FACT 1

Fluoridation is cancer-causing, cancer-promoting, and is linked to increased cancer rates in humans.[182]

FACT 2

Hip fracture rates are substantially higher in people residing in fluoridated communities.[183]

FACT 3

Dental fluorosis, the first visible sign of fluoride poisoning, affects from 8% to 51% of the children drinking fluoridated water.[184]

FACT 4

All of the recent large-scale studies on fluoridation and tooth decay show that fluoridation does not reduce tooth decay.[185]

---

[181] The International Fluoride Information Network www.fluoridealert.org

[182] *Carcinogenesis*, Vol. 9, 1988 pp.2279-2284; "Sodium Fluoride; Individual Animal Tumor Pathology Table [rats], Battelle Memorial Institute, 23rd February 1989; *Lancet* 36 1990, p.737; *Review of Fluoride: Benefits and Risks*, US Public Health Service, 1991, pp. F1-F7; *Fluoride*, Vol. 26, 1992, pp.83-96; *A Brief Report on the Association of Drinking Water Fluoridation and the Incidence of Osteosarcoma Among Young Males*, New Jersey Department of Health, November 1992; *Fluoride, the Aging Factor*, Health Action Press, 1993, pp.72-90

[183] *Journal of the American Medical Association (JAMA)*, Vol. 264, 1990, pp.500-502; *JAMA*, Vol. 266, 1991, pp.513-514; *JAMA*, Vol. 268, 1992, pp.746-748; *JAMA*, Vol. 273, 1995, pp. 775-776

[184] *Science*, Vol. 217, 1982, pp.26-30; *Journal of the American Dental Association*, Vol. 108, 1984, pp.56-59; *Journal of Public Health Dentistry*, Vol. 46, 1986, pp.184-187; *Health Effects of Ingested Fluoride*, National Research Council, 1993, p.37

[185] *Community Health Studies*, Vol. 11, 1987, pp.85-90; *Journal of the Canadian Dental Association*, Vol. 53, 1987, pp.763-765; *Fluoride*, Vol. 23, 1990, pp.55-67

FACT 5

Fluoride drops and tablets are not approved by the US Food & Drug Administration as safe and effective. On the contrary, fluoride tablets and drops have been shown to be ineffective in reducing tooth decay and to cause skin eruptions, gastric distress, headache and weakness, which disappear when fluoride use is discontinued. Dental fluorosis on the other hand, is a permanent disfigurement.[186]

WATER IS VITAL

An intake of lots of clean fresh water is vital. Yet drug-based medicine believes and teaches that water is nothing more than an inert solvent the body uses to transport the soluent (minerals, proteins, enzymes, etc.) around the body. But water is far from inert. The blood is made up of a large percentage of watery serum. Our cells literally owe their life to an adequate supply of fresh, clean water. When the body does not receive a constant, reliable supply of water, it has to ration what's available and cut back on certain functions in order to make the supply go round. Essential systems like the brain are prioritised, others are impaired or cut back until the brain has decided a reliable source of water has been garnered.

Here's the rub. Most citizens have become CHRONICALLY AND DANGEROUSLY DEHYDRATED (especially the elderly), since we decided water was too bland to drink and axed it in favour of beer, wine, sodas, flavoured water and other chemical-laced water alternatives. This has proven a disastrous and dangerous move for the body and society's health in general, and we have been reaping the whirlwind in terms of disease and death as a result. Many doctors today cannot readily identify the many water-deficient diseases and associated pains, and so the inevitable prescribing of drugs to treat the symptoms usually results.

The body needs in excess of four pints of water daily (2 litres). Water is used by the body for digestion, detoxifying cells, watering the lungs, keeping the body alkalised and a host of cleaning duties. Water

---

[186] Letter from Frank R Fazzari, Chief, Prescription Drug Compliance, US Food & Drug Administration to New Jersey Assemblyman John Kelly, 8th June 1993; *Preventing Tooth Decay: Results from a Four-Year National Study*, Robert Wood-Johnson Foundation, Special Report #2/1983, 18 pages; *Community Dentistry and Oral Epidemiology*, Vol. 19, 1991, pp.88-92; *1992 Physicians Desk Reference*, p.2273

expert Dr Fereydoon Batmanghelidj maintains that asthmas, allergies, diabetes, arthritis, angina, stomach upsets, chronic intestinal complaints and certain other degenerative illnesses are the body's many cries for water, complaints which are dramatically improved with a consistent and long-term intake of fresh, clean water.[187] Dr Batman's best-selling book has helped thousands quash long-term health problems effortlessly and inexpensively. Coffee, tea, diet sodas, beer and a host of other liquids do not qualify as 'clean, fresh water' for the body, and should not be consumed by the cancer patient. Many of these are diuretic (water expelling) in their effect because of their chemical compositions. Cancer patients especially should be consuming at least 4 pints of water a day[188] as part of their intake of vital nutrients, provided they do not have any renal (kidney) damage or disease that will cause complications with urine production resulting from the intake of additional water. Flushing the body with CONSISTENT, long-term water consumption is a superb way to assist with detoxification and hydration and is especially important for cancer patients. Drink a glass half an hour before a meal and then two glasses around two and a half hours afterwards for optimal digestive effects. The remainder of the day's intake of water can occur throughout the day. [189]

An indication of dehydration and acidosis in the body is if the urine is thick, dark yellow and rank (ammoniac) in smell. Here the body is cutting back on water usage throughout its various systems due to a chronic shortage.[190] The resultant urine the kidneys make is thus thick with waste consisting of less water than normal, giving rise to a more concentrated urine solution. The kidneys may also manufacture ammonia to raise the pH of acidic excreta before expelling the latter from the body.[191] The body can take several weeks to use water to full

---

[187] **Batmanghelidj, F** *Your Body's Many Cries For Water*, Tagman Press, 2000

[188] A carbon filter attached to a tap/faucet is adequate for producing chlorine- and soluent-free water to drink. This is preferable to plastic-bottled water which can be contaminated with chemicals from the plastic. Water in glass bottles is fine.

[189] Tap water filtered with one of the many carbon filters on the market today produces safe, good-tasting water in areas that do not have fluoridated water supplies. In fluoridated areas, reverse osmosis filters or bottled water is preferable. Ensure though that the bottles concerned are glass and not plastic, as the latter, especially in its pliable, 'squashy' format, contains estrogen-rich plasticisers.

[190] Note that B vitamin intakes can also darken the urine.

[191] See section entitled *Acid and Alkali Ashes*

effect, so ensure that this vital health bonus is used consistently and effectively. Dr Batman's book is a must for EVERYONE to find out about this incredible and FREE treatment and boon to their health.

The White, the Pink and the Blue
The Lethality of Sweeteners

"Let us go to the ignorant savage,
consider his way of eating, and be wise."
– Harvard Professor Ernest Hooten[192]

When it comes to identifying the most common poison we willingly use against ourselves, an amazing feat resulting in millions of deaths worldwide every year, there really is no contest. The perpetrator is as unlikely a candidate as any you might wish to name, and its unmasking is probably all the more horrifying because this substance has burrowed its way into our civilisation like a parasite, draped in the false colours of comfort and familiarity. It has an entire industry behind it as usual, hell-bent on marketing the stuff any way it can. It's whiter than heroin, sweeter than your fiancée, more soluble than the National Debt, and more pernicious than nicotine because, like a true demon, this little beauty comes in a million disguises and always dresses like a friend.

We grew up being brainwashed with all the sayings: " Sugar and spice and all things nice." "Sweetheart", "Sugar-plum" – all painting the white stuff in a great and cuddly light. But seeing as we are in the mood for some truth, let's take a hard look at the 's' word, and also its partners-in-crime, the 'sweeteners' aspartame and saccharin. Are you nervous about shattering some highly refined illusions?

Dr William Coda Martin was the first publicly to label sucrose a poison. Martin's definition came about after he determined the classical definition of a poison was *"...any substance applied to the body, which causes or may cause disease."* [193] So what is sucrose? Obviously the first task we must carry out is identifying exactly what sugar is. Once again, we have to do our homework and pre-empt the vocabulary – so let's define our terms. There are a number of 'sugars' around. Here are the main ones:

---

[192] **Hooten, Ernest A** *Apes, Men and Morons*, Putnam, New York: 1937
[193] **Martin, William Coda** *When is a Food a Food – and When a Poison?* Michigan Organic News, March 1957, p.3

Glucose – found with other sugars, but occurs naturally in fruits and vegetables. A number of core foods we consume are converted by our body into glucose, or blood sugar as it is sometimes called, which is the form in which this highly efficient energy source is made available to our life-systems. Glucose is always present in our bloodstream and is a key material in the metabolic functions of all plants and animals.

Dextrose - known as 'corn sugar', is manufactured from starches.
Fructose - natural sugar found in fruits.
Lactose – milk sugar
Maltose – malt sugar
Sucrose – refined sugar manufactured from sugar cane and beet.

The last, sucrose, is the white stuff that goes into the tea, coffee, soft drinks and sodas, and shows up in everything from tomato ketchup to Twinkies. There are few manufactured or processed foods today that do not contain either sucrose, aspartame or saccharin. Sugar's prevalence for 300 years has made the sweet-hearts in the sugar industry wealthy beyond most people's imaginations. Naturally, the sugar barons are willing to do or say just about anything to keep their products bathed in the safe and neighbourly light that has resulted in us scarfing the stuff down by the bushel-load without so much as a 'by-your-leave'. So let's firstly take a look at sugars, and see what the problems are.

Refined sugar, or sucrose, is manufactured from cane and beet extract, which has had its salts, fibres, proteins, vitamins and minerals removed to leave a white, crystalline substance devoid of any nutritional content, only offering empty calories. Sucrose is labelled 'a carbohydrate', that most generic of terms which describes a compound comprising carbon coupled with hydrogen and oxygen. Of course to label sugar 'a carbohydrate' gives manufacturers wide licence to lump this most popular of commodities in with other 'carbohydrates', refined or otherwise, which all show up on food packaging as... you guessed it, 'carbohydrates'! Thus the real content of sucrose in a product may be effectively concealed without technical fraud being perpetrated. In reality the different sugars listed above are composed of different chemical structures, which affect the body in radically different ways. Yet the well-meaning, 'think-no-evil' public has once again been snowed by a single word into accepting that one sugar is just about the same as another. Nothing could be further from the truth.

Sugars contained in natural, whole foods are easily metabolised by the body. Nature has ensured that fructose, for instance, obtained when we consume fruits, has the necessary vitamins and minerals accompanying it to allow this type of simple monosaccharide sugar to be converted efficiently into glucose (blood sugar), becoming fully metabolised by our bodies for energy. Vitamins and minerals, which accompany fructose, are essential for these complete assimilation and conversion processes to occur. Sucrose on the other hand, devoid of these vital minerals, becomes a vacuous, predatory, greedy starch, which cannot metabolise completely in our bodies, resulting in the formation of metabolites, such as pyruvic acid and abnormal, unstable sugars containing five carbon atoms.

These toxic by-products interfere with the respiration of cells, preventing the latter from acquiring sufficient oxygen to function correctly. These poisonous metabolites, in their free-radical or oxidation format, are constantly seeking to stabilise themselves by robbing our healthy cells of available electrons. This action in turn degrades the cell and the cell dies.[194]

A recent study conducted at the University of Buffalo involved 14 healthy men and women fasting for 12 hours before being given a drink containing 75 grams of glucose, approximately equivalent to the sugar content of two cans of soda. Six control patients were given a water and saccharin solution. Researchers collected blood samples from all the study subjects prior to the commencement of the trial and then at one, two and three hours after consuming the beverages. The purpose of the trial was not to highlight any irregularities with saccharin, but to demonstrate the oxidation capabilities of sugar. The results were as follows:

> ➢ Free-radical generation in the subjects who consumed the sugar water increased markedly at one hour and more than doubled at two hours.

---

[194] Martin, William Coda, op. cit.

> There was no change in free-radical generation in the control participants.
> In those who had consumed the sugar water, levels of alpha-tocopherol (Vitamin E), a powerful antioxidant, had dropped by 4% by the second hour and remained depressed at hour three.[195]

Researcher Dr Joseph Mercola remarks on these test results:

"Another reason to avoid sugar is to slow down the aging process. If you want to stay looking young, it is very important to limit sugar to the smallest amount possible. It is the most significant factor that accelerates aging. It is a negative fountain of youth. It does this by attaching itself to proteins in the body forming new sugar-protein substances called advanced glycation end-products (AGE). The higher the AGE levels, the faster you are aging. As this study points out, sugar also increases oxidation elements in the body (free radicals) which also accelerate the aging process." [196]

Advanced Glycation End-Products (AGEs) are readily seen as hard yellow-brown compounds that are, as Dr Mercola states, the results of blood sugar bonding with proteins in the body's tissue. This process is the precursor to degenerative disease, and may manifest itself initially as indicators associated with accelerated aging, such as premature wrinkles and grey hair.[197] We are oxidising and pre-aging our bodies towards an early death with sucrose as surely as the pick-up rusts its way to the scrap-heap if we leave it out in the yard throughout the winter. *Scientific American* puts it this way: *"After years of bread, noodles and cake, human tissues inevitably become rigid and yellow with pigmented AGE deposits."* [198]

---

[195] *Journal of Clinical Endocrinology and Metabolism*, August 2000

[196] **Mercola, Joseph** *Sugar Creates Free Radicals and Reduces Vitamin E Levels*, 27th August 2000, www.mercola.com/2000/aug/27/sugar_free_radicals.htm

[197] **Lee and Cerami** *Annals of the New York Academy of Science*, "The Role of Glycation in Aging", #663, pp.6370; also **D G Dyer et al** *Journal of Clinical Investigation*, "Accumulation of Maillard Reaction Products in Skin Collagen in Diabetes and Aging", Vol. 91, #6, June 1993, pp.421-422

[198] *Scientific American*, July 2000, p.16

All refined sugars are parasitic. They have no accompanying vitamins and minerals of their own and no nutritive value. They leach valuable minerals from the body when the latter frantically attempts to do something about them.[199] Sugar can cause copper deficiency, which reduces the elasticity of veins and arteries, leading to aneurism and stroke.[200] The body must digest, detoxify and then eliminate sucrose because it cannot make cell structure from it. A body suffering a daily intake of refined sugar can go into shock if it fails to get ahead of the game and render the sucrose harmless. Typically the body combats sucrose by mobilising elements such as sodium (from salt), potassium and magnesium (from vegetables) and calcium (from our bones) to form compounds with the invading sucrose in an attempt to transmute it chemically into a form the body can either store or eliminate.

As we will find out later, we sophisticated Westerners do not detoxify our bodies and take out the garbage, which means that the build-up of sucrose metabolites and partially detoxified sugars continues to accumulate as fat, rendering a toxic acid siege within us.[201] The body must then, as the onslaught continues, dig deeper to marshal more minerals, such as calcium, to rectify the acid/alkali imbalance this sugar bombardment is causing. More calcium is taken from our bones and teeth, resulting in an increased risk of osteoporosis.[202]

Excess sugar is initially stored in the liver in the form of glycogen. As more sugar is stuffed into our sagging bodies daily, the liver swells like a balloon to accommodate it[203], waiting in vain for the garbage truck to take it out of the body (detoxification/elimination). The truck almost never arrives because we do not detoxify our bodies (sugar has also been linked constipation[204]). Finally, reaching its limit, the liver has had enough and pours the sucrose toxins it has accumulated back into the bloodstream in the form of fatty acids, which are then taken to

---

[199] **Couizy, Keen, Gershwin and Mareschi** *Progressive Food and Nutrition Science,* "Nutritional Implications of the Interaction Between Minerals", No. 17, 1933, pp.65-87
[200] **M Fields et al** *Journal of Clinical Nutrition,* "Effect of Copper Deficiency on Metabolism and Mortality in Rats Fed Sucrose or Starch Diets", #113, 1983, pp.1335-1345
[201] **Dufty, W** *Sugar Blues,* Warner Books, New York: 1975
[202] **Appleton, Nancy** *Lick the Sugar Habit,* Avery Publishing Group, NY: 1989, pp.36-38
[203] **Goulart, F S** *American Fitness,* "Are You Sugar Smart?" March-April 1991, pp.34-38
[204] Ibid.

storage bins in the inactive areas of the body, namely the belly, thighs, hips, breasts and the backs of our upper arms (triceps area).

But still the sugar keeps a-comin': "Another doughnut, Officer?" "Thank you, ma'am. Don't mind if I do..." Once the inactive storage areas are filled to capacity, the body begins distributing the metabolite acids into the active organs, such as the heart and kidneys.[205] These fats accumulate as rapidly as the sucrose continues to pour in, impairing the functioning of vital organs, causing hormonal imbalance[206], creating lethargy, abnormal blood pressure as the circulatory and lymph systems are invaded, depleting vital Vitamin C reserves, threatening the cardiovascular system.[207] An overabundance of white cells occurs, leading to the slowing down of tissue formation. The system is nearing collapse at this point, and still the sugar keeps a-coming... "Do you want the one with extra icing, Officer?" (Naughty giggle). "Only if you insist, young lady..."

How about the cellulite, varicose veins and the rotten teeth?[208] [209] How about the kids bouncing off the walls with mineral depletion, ADD and ADHD because sucrose robs minerals, impairs brain function, resulting in increased emotional instability, concentration difficulties, hyperactivity and violence in the classroom[210] [211], ending up no doubt with black eyes, detention, lousy grades... and conceivably a school shooting or two...[212]

Glutamic acid, the key to proper brain function, is derived from a diet rich in unrefined plant dietary. Glutamic acid is broken down by B

---

[205] **Yudkin, Kang and Bruckdorfer** *British Journal of Medicine*, "Effects of High Dietary Sugar", #281, 1980, p.1396

[206] **Yudkin, J** *Nutrition and Health*, "Metabolic Changes Induced by Sugar in Relation to Coronary Heart Disease and Diabetes", Vol. 5, #1-2, 1987: pp.5-8

[207] **Pamplona, Bellmunt, Portero and Prat** *Medical Hypotheses,* "Mechanisms of Glycation in Atherogenesis", #40, 1990, pp.174-181

[208] **Cleave and Campbell** *Diabetes, Coronary Thrombosis and the Saccharine Disease*, John Wright and Sons, Bristol, UK: 1960

[209] **Glinsman, Irausquin and Youngmee** "Evaluation of Health Aspects of Sugars Contained in Carbohydrate Sweeteners", Report from FDA's Sugar Task Force, Center for Food Safety and Applied Nutrition, Washington DC: 1986, p.39

[210] **Schauss, Alexander** *Diet, Crime and Delinquency*, Parker House, Berkeley, CA: 1981

[211] **Goldman, J et al** "Behavioral Effects of Sucrose on Preschool Children", *Journal of Abnormal Child Psychology*, #14, 1986. pp.565-577

[212] *Journal of Abnormal Psychology*, #85, 1985

vitamins into compounds that regulate stop and go functions in the brain. B vitamins however are manufactured by symbiotic bacteria inhabiting our intestines. As the sucrose bombing continues, these bacteria are killed by the toxic sugar metabolites, resulting in a severe depletion of our B-vitamin production. This in turn impairs brain function. The results in adults can traverse the awesome spectrum from sleepiness and the inability to calculate or remember, through to dizziness[213], heightened PMS symptoms[214] and possibly finishing with those famous murderous impulses, resulting in your lawyer's "Twinkie Defence".[215]

And so, as the human becomes the sugar equivalent of the Frankenstein monster, pancreatic function may become inhibited by excess sucrose, resulting in the impairment of enzymes such as trypsin and chymotrypsin, vital for arresting healing processes and preventing cancer growths.[216] Sugar may lead to cancer of the breast, ovaries, prostate and rectum.[217] It has been implicated in colon cancer, with an increased risk in women[218], and is a risk factor in biliary tract cancer.[219] Sugar can cause appendicitis[220], increase the risk of Crohn's Disease and ulcerative colitis[221], and can exacerbate the symptoms of multiple

---

[213] *Journal of Advanced Medicine*, 1994 7(1): pp.51-58

[214] *The Edell Health Letter*, September 1991; 10:7(1)

[215] *"On 27 November 1978, Dan White, a former San Francisco city supervisor who had recently resigned his position, entered San Francisco's city hall by climbing through a basement window and then shot and killed both mayor George Moscone and supervisor Harvey Milk. After White's subsequent trial for the murders, a new term entered the American lexicon: "Twinkie defense." This phrase came to represent the efforts of criminals to avoid responsibility for their actions by claiming that some external force beyond their control had caused them to act the way they had, and it arose from the successful defense mounted by White's legal team that White's eating of Twinkies and other sugar-laden junk foods had diminished his mental capacity."* http://www.snopes.com/errata/twinkie.htm Author's note: The facts reveal that White's defence team argued that their client's junk-food diet was *evidence* of his depression, *not the cause of it*, as the papers subsequently reported.

[216] **Appleton, Nancy** *Healthy Bones*, Avery Publishing Group, NY: 1991

[217] *Health Express*, "Sugar and Prostate Cancer", October 1982, p.41

[218] **Bostick, Potter, Kushi, et al** "Sugar, Meat and Fat Intake, and Non-Dietary Risk Factors for Colon Cancer Incidence in Iowa Women", *Cancer Causes and Controls* #5, 1994, pp.38-52

[219] **Moerman, Clara et al** "Dietary Sugar Intake in the Etiology of Biliary Tract Cancer", *International Journal of Epidemiology*, Vol. 22, #2, 1993, pp.207-214

[220] **Cleave, T** *The Saccharine Disease*, Keats Publishing, New Canaan, CT: 1974, p.125

[221] **Cleave, T** *Sweet and Dangerous*, Bantam Books, New York: 1974, pp.28-43; also **Persson, B G et al** "Diet and Inflammatory Bowel Disease", *Epidemiology*, Vol. 3, #1, January 1992, pp. 47-51

sclerosis.[222] Excess sugar consumption has also been linked to Parkinson's and Alzheimer's Diseases.[223] Complete removal of sugar from the diet has seen stunning recoveries from cancer, diabetes and heart illnesses.

Sucrose has long been implicated in diabetes.[224] Type 2 diabetes usually occurs in adults and can be controlled with a combination of diet and exercise. People with the condition lose their sensitivity to insulin[225], which regulates the build-up of blood sugar, resulting in an overload of insulin, sugar, an increase in systolic blood pressure[226], fainting and coma. The 'Fight/Flight' survival response that accompanies these survival threats or stressors produces adrenalin, sugars in the blood and the accompanying insulin, manufactured in the pancreas, to ready the body's systems for instant physical action. In previous societies, notice how the Fight/Flight response would resolve itself *with explosive physical action* (either Fight or Flight!), which would in turn discharge the excess sugars and insulin.

Today however, the stressors do not tend to require an explosive physical response (although sometimes they do!). When we are stressed with money, relationships, hardships or work pressures, this Fight/Flight response may endure for days or weeks, but the body does not respond to these physically. Consequently, the amount of insulin produced by the pancreas in today's environment is substantially higher and does not tend to discharge itself through physical action. The results of this survival response can be diabetes.

Dr Joseph Mercola clarifies type 2 diabetes:

"The overall concept of insulin for Type 2 diabetes is absurd and makes absolutely no sense if one understands the way the body is

[222] **Erlander, S** *The Disease to End Disease*, "The Cause and Cure of Multiple Sclerosis", No. 3, 3rd March 1979, pp.59-63

[223] **Yudkin, J**, *Sweet and Dangerous*, Bantam Books, NY: 1974, p.141

[224] **Jenkins and Jenkins** *Diabetes Care*, "Nutrition Principles and Diabetes. A Role for Lente Carbohydrate?" Dept. of Nutritional Sciences, University of Toronto, Ont, Canada: Nov, 1995 18(11)pp/1491-8; also *Federal Protocol*, "Sucrose Induces Diabetes in Cats", Vol 6, #97, 1974

[225] **Beck-Nelson, Pederson and Schwarz** *Diabetes*, "Effects of Diet on the Cellular Insulin Binding and the Insulin Sensitivity in Young Healthy Subjects", #15, 1978, pp.289-296

[226] **Hodges and Rebello** *Annals of Internal Medicine*, "Carbohydrates and Blood Pressure", #98, 1983, pp.838-841

designed to work. However, since nearly all traditional physicians don't comprehend basic human physiology with respect to diet and health, it is not surprising that they could come up with the prescription for disaster of giving someone who is already overloaded with insulin more of what caused the problem.

The main reason most adult onset (type 2) diabetics have diabetes is that they have too much insulin. This is usually a result of having too many grains. The solution in nearly all of these individuals is to consume a proper low grain [gluten] diet and to exercise one hour per day." [227]

William Martin recounts some early observations with refined sugar: *"Sir Frederick Banting, the co-discoverer of insulin, noticed in 1929 in Panama that, among sugar plantation owners who ate large amounts of their refined stuff, diabetes was common. Among native cane-cutters, who only got to chew the raw cane, he saw no diabetes."*[228]

Sugar Inc. has designed a number of strategies to give long legs to their product and maximise revenues. "Sugar gives you energy..." and "Sugar was given to the troops before they went over the top of the trenches in WW1..." becomes "Sugar won WW1" in the minds of the laity. Yet sugar is NOT essential and humans cannot subsist on it.

"Later," Martin continues, *"the sugar pushers advertised that sugar was chemically pure, topping Ivory soap in that department, being 99.9% pure against Ivory's vaunted 99.44%. "No food of our everyday diet is purer!" we were assured. What was meant by purity, besides the unarguable fact that all vitamins, minerals, salts, fibers and proteins had been removed in the refining process? The sugar pushers came up with a new slant on purity: "You don't have to sort it like beans, wash it like rice. Every grain is like every other. No waste attends its use. No useless bones like in meat, no grounds like in coffee." 'Pure' is a favourite adjective of the sugar pushers because it*

---

[227] Mercola, J, www.mercola.com, op. cit.
[228] Martin, William Coda, op. cit.

means one thing to the chemists and another to the ordinary mortals."[229]

Sucrose addiction affects the vast majority of people today... and it IS an addiction. It must be shucked off *immediately*. We will examine the motives of the food industry in a later section. Suffice to say for now that cutting out all forms of refined sugar, sugar foods, sugar products such as chocolate, candies, jelly beans, twinkies and a million other products is *de rigeur* for a long and healthy future life. And don't think you can gallop away towards the hot and ready alternative either. Let's burst those two pink and blue bubbles while we're hot to trot and burning with vision.

SACCHARIN (THE PINK)

Saccharin has long been a traditional alternative for those on diets and those aware of the damage done to both teeth and general health by a chronic consumption of sugar. But saccharin itself, far from being the panacea for those addicted to the taste concepts of sucrose, has been dogged from the outset with its own health concerns.

Saccharin is a synthetic, white crystalline powder, which, in its pure state, is over 500 times as sweet as sugar cane. In its commercial state, it is 350 times as sweet, meaning of course that you need 350 times less of the stuff to approximate the same level of sweetness usually provided by commercial sucrose. Saccharin's compound is $C_6H_4CONHSO_2$, declaring itself to be, once again, that most deceitful of terms - a 'carbohydrate'. Yet it has no nutritive value and is not digested by the body. Dr Elizabeth M Whelan explains some of the problems saccharin has experienced:

"Saccharin, which has been in use as an alternative to sugar since the early 20th century, officially assumed the 'carcinogen' title in March 1977, when a rodent study in Canada produced an excess of bladder tumours in the male animals. This finding immediately triggered the threat of the so-called "Delaney Clause", a Congressionally mandated provision that requires the Food & Drug Administration to ban – literally 'at the drop of a rat' – any synthetic

---

229 Martin, William Coda, op. cit.

food chemical shown to cause cancer when ingested by laboratory animals.

When millions of weight-conscious Americans got the word that their only available low-calorie sweetener was going to be banned (cyclamates had been banned in 1970 for similar reasons), they were outraged – and immediately bought up almost every little pink packet in the land. Congress responded to this outrage by protecting saccharin from the Delaney Clause and allowing it back on the market with a health-warning label. Saccharin's reputation was further tarnished however when the US National Toxicology Program, referring again to the Canadian rat study, elected to put saccharin on its 'cancer-causing" list – formally declaring it an "anticipated human carcinogen."[230]

Evidence indicates that saccharin is a weak carcinogen in animals. Its potential for tumour mischief in humans however remains the subject of some heated debate. In May 2000, the upbeat United States National Institute for Environmental Health Services removed saccharin from its list of suspected carcinogens. Three years earlier though, a board of independent experts, which included the Center for Science in the Public Interest and the California Department of Health, had voted to err on the side of caution to keep saccharin 'a suspected carcinogen'.

The food industry has expended considerable resources attempting to get saccharin off the hook. Consumers appeared to have their own ideas. The food giants were encouraged by the many citizens who came forward to complain that every alternative to sugar was being systematically victimised as a carcinogen, as had been the case with cyclamate and aspartame. America's Food & Drug Administration, usually quick to follow its own policy of applying the Delaney Clause and banning even suspected carcinogens from public use, relented in the face of public pressure, but mandated that saccharin should carry a warning label.

---

[230] **Whelan, Elizabeth M** *The Sweet and the Sour News about Saccharin*, American Council on Science and Health, 17th May 2000

Dr Samuel Cohen, a pathologist at the University of Nebraska, is probably America's foremost authority on saccharin and its chemical ramifications. In answer to the investigative panel's queries on how exactly saccharin causes cancer, Cohen replied that when the sodium form of saccharin combines with rat urine, it creates crystal-like stones in the bladder of the creature. These stones in turn damaged the organs of the animal, leading to the potential for cancer.[231] Cohen however cast doubt on saccharin's danger to humans when he explained the significant differences between rat and human urine and how they would chemically react with the crystalline sweetener.

ASPARTAME (THE BLUE)

Today saccharin remains as controversial as ever, and the debate over whether or not it represents a cancer hazard to the public continues to rage. And yet, people who have turned to another alternative to saccharin and sugar over the past 20 years, have become equally dismayed at a parallel fur-fight over aspartame, decked out in the garb of a light blue sachet, which began adorning restaurant and diners the world over under the brand names Nutrasweet, Equal, Spoonful and Equal-Measure.

Aspartame was discovered by accident in 1965 by James Schlatter, a chemist working for G D Serle Company, who was testing anti-ulcer compounds for his employers. Aspartame's original approval as a sweetener for public consumption was blocked by neuroscientist Dr John W Olney and consumer attorney James Turner in August 1974 over concerns about both aspartame's safety and G D Serle's research practices. However, aspartame duly received its approval for dry goods in 1981 and its go-ahead as a sweetener for carbonated beverages was granted in 1983, despite growing concerns over its neurological effects.[232] In 1985, G D Serle was purchased by pharmaceutical giant

---

[231] Cohen's testimony is interesting as it dovetails with John Beard's findings that cancer is a healing process (survival response) that has not terminated. These healing processes are understood to be caused by damage done to the body by carcinogens. Therefore, a carcinogen can be deemed to be any material that causes cellular damage to the body, initiating a healing process carried out by stem-cell trophoblast.

[232] Two FDA scientists, Jacqueline Verrett and Adrian Gross, reviewed data from three studies which highlighted alleged irregularities in G D Serle's research procedures. The two government scientists declared that the irregularities they had uncovered were serious enough to warrant an immediate halt to aspartame's approval for use. *Food Magazine*, "Artificial Sweetener Suspicions", Vol. 1, No.9, April/June 1990.

Monsanto, and Serle Pharmaceuticals and The NutraSweet Company were created as separate corporate identities.

According to researcher Alex Constantine in his essay entitled "Sweet Poison", aspartame may account for up to 75% of the adverse food reactions reported to the US FDA, due primarily to its reported ability to affect neurological processes in humans. Dr Olney found that an excess of aspartate and glutamate, two chemicals used by the body as neurotransmitters to transmit information between brain neurons, could kill neurons in the brain by allowing too much calcium to collect in the neuron cells to neutralise acid. This neurological damage led Olney to label aspartate and glutamate 'excitotoxins', in that they, according to Olney, 'excite' or stimulate the neural cells to death.[233]

Side-effects laid at the door of aspartame include multiple sclerosis, Alzheimer's disease, ALS, memory loss, hormonal problems, hearing loss, epilepsy, Parkinson's disease, AIDS dementia, brain lesions and neuroendocrine disorders. Risks to infants, children and pregnant women from aspartame were also underscored by the Federation of American Societies for Experimental Biology, a research body that traditionally follows FDA policy and adopts a softly-softly approach to chemical problems. The Federation declared: *"It is prudent to avoid the use of dietary supplements of L-glutamic acid by pregnant women, infants and children. The existence of evidence for potential endocrine responses... would also suggest a neuroendocrine link and that... L-glutamic acid should be avoided by women of childbearing age and individuals with affective disorders."*[234]

Phenylalanine: The amino acid L-phenylalanine, used by the brain, comprises 50% of aspartame. People suffering from the genetic disorder phenylketonuria (PKU) cannot metabolise phenylalanine and so an excess of this amino acid builds up in parts of the brain, leading to a decrease of serotonin levels, bringing on emotional disorders and depression.

Methanol: Also known as wood alcohol, the poison methanol is a 10% ingredient of aspartame, which is created when aspartame is

---

[233] *The Guardian*, London, UK, 20th July, 1990
[234] *Food Magazine*, op. cit.

heated above 86°F (30°C) in, for example, the preparation of processed foods. Methanol oxidises in the body to produce formic acid and the deadly neurotoxin, formaldehyde, also used as a prime ingredient in many vaccinations. Methanol is considered by America's Environmental Protection Agency (EPA) as *"...a cumulative poison, due to the low rate of excretion once it is absorbed. In the body, methanol is oxidised to formaldehyde and formic acid; both of these metabolites are toxic."*[235]

A one litre carbonated beverage, sweetened with aspartame, contains around 56mg of methanol. Heavy consumers of soft drinks sweetened with aspartame can ingest up to 250mg of methanol daily, especially in the summer, amounting to 32 times the EPA warning limit.

Dr Woodrow C Monte, Director of the Food Science and Nutritional Laboratory at Arizona State University, was concerned that human response to methanol was probably much higher than with animals, due to humans lacking key enzymes that assist in the detoxification of methanol in other creatures. Monte stated: *"There are no human or mammalian studies to evaluate the possible mutagenic, teratogenic, or carcinogenic effects of chronic administration of methyl alcohol."* [236]

Monte's concern about aspartame was so great that he petitioned the FDA through the courts to address these issues. Monte requested that the FDA *"...slow down on this soft drink issue long enough to answer some of the important questions. It's not fair that you are leaving the full burden of proof on the few of us who are concerned and have such limited resources. You must remember that you are the American public's last defense. Once you allow usage* [of aspartame], *there is literally nothing I or my colleagues can do to reverse the course. Aspartame will then join saccharin, the sulfiting agents, and God knows how many other questionable compounds enjoined to insult the human constitution with government approval."*[237]

---

[235] *Extraordinary Science*, Vol. 7, No.1, Jan/Feb/Mar 1995, p.39
[236] *The Guardian*, "Laboratory Animals Back from the Dead in Faulty Safety Tests", April/June 1990
[237] Ibid.

Ironically, shortly after Dr Monte's impassioned plea, Arthur Hull Hayes, Jr., the Commissioner of the Food & Drug Administration, approved the use of aspartame in carbonated beverages. Shortly after, he left the FDA to take up a position with G D Serle's public relations company.[238] In 1993, the FDA further approved aspartame as a food ingredient in numerous process foods that would always be heated above 86°F, as part of their preparation.

Dr Joseph Mercola is no lover of aspartame. The well-known nutrition and health researcher itemises another catalogue of woes that have come to punctuate aspartame's hopeless legacy as a food additive:

"In 1991, the National Institutes of Health listed 167 symptoms and reasons to avoid the use of aspartame, but today it is a multi-million dollar business that contributes to the degeneration of the human population, as well as the deliberate suppression of overall intelligence, short-term memory[239] and the added contribution as a carcinogenic environmental co-factor.

The FDA and Centers for Disease Control continue to receive a stream of complaints from the population about aspartame. It is the only chemical warfare weapon available in mass quantities on the grocery shelf and promoted in the media. It has also been indicated that women with an intolerance for phenylalanine, one of the components of aspartame, may give birth to infants with as much as a 15% drop in intelligence level if they habitually consume products containing this dangerous substance." [240]

SUMMARY
Once again, world populations have been seduced into the habitual consumption of products, whose apparent benefits have been sold to us by some of the slickest marketers on the corporate payroll. And so you, the reader, have a choice to make. If it is your desire to continue

---

[238] Ibid.

[239] The FDA instigated hearings in 1985 on aspartame at the request of Senator Metzenbaum, when a sample case was heard, in which a woman's memory suffered almost complete collapse until she ceased taking aspartame-laced products.

[240] Mercola, Joseph, op. cit. See also: **Steinman, D** *Diet for a Poisoned Planet*, University of California study, p.190

consuming sugar, aspartame or saccharin, then this chapter has gone some way to discussing the very real concerns that scientists and researchers have with these products.

The watchword for *Health Wars* and the longevity it espouses must be to halt the influx of toxins into the body, expel those already there, and ensure a continued and prolonged life using whole foods that are clean, uncontaminated and nutritious, which provide the ideal, slightly alkali internal environment which the body craves. In my opinion, sugar, saccharin and aspartame have no place in a healthy body or a healthy world. It's going to mean restructuring our diets and desires to wean ourselves off the 'taste monster' and back to the food our bodies desire most. Sucrose, as mentioned, is an addiction. So, for that matter, is the desire to have sweeteners of any kind in food which does not naturally contain them in a form the body can break down and metabolise. In the final analysis, your body just wants to ask one question about what you feed it. "Can I use this material to build cells to replenish my systems?"

Sucrose, saccharin and aspartame are incompatible with this process and have been shown to work against the body. Thus, these materials are incompatible with life.

White Lies and Porky Pies
The Unsettling Reasons Why Excessive
Meat and Dairy Consumption Can Kill

Two other major food concerns are going to be discussed now – and a chapter for each of them: meat and dairy. If you are already blanching at what appears to be the systematic destruction of all you thought you knew to be true about food, then brace yourselves, because we aren't out of the woods yet! So fundamental to human health is a proper understanding of these vital issues that, like sucrose before them, we are going to examine where the problems lie with meat and dairy and why it is essential severely to modify our intake of these factors.

MILK - ARE YOU PREPARED TO LOSE YOUR BOTTLE?
Robert Kradjian MD, Chief of the Division of General Surgery at Seton Medical Center in Daly City, California, remarks as follows:

"Milk! Just the word itself sounds comforting. "How about a nice cup of hot milk?" The last time you heard that question, it was from someone who cared for you, and you appreciated their effort.

The entire matter of food and especially that of milk is surrounded with emotional and cultural importance. Milk was our first food. If we were fortunate, it was our mother's milk. A loving link, given and taken. It was the only path to survival. If not mother's milk, it was cow's milk or soy milk 'formula' – rarely it was goat, camel or water buffalo milk.

Now we are a nation of milk drinkers. Nearly all of us. Infants, the young, adolescents, adults, even the elderly. We drink dozens or even several hundred gallons a year each and add to that many pounds of 'dairy' products, such as cheese, butter and yoghurt.

Can there be anything wrong with this?" [241]

---

[241] **Kradjian, Robert M** *Don't Get Milk*, Seton Medical Center, #302, 1800 Sullivan Av, Daly City CA 94015 USA

133

Actually there is plenty wrong with it. Once again, the marketers of Big Milk have wooed us with their impressive campaigns of creamy moustaches and "Got Milk?" and "Milk – It Does a Body Good". There is one thing conspicuously missing in the logic of all this though – milk is actually for baby cows.

Many humans on Earth today do not consume milk because it makes them ill. Caucasians, on the other hand, lead the human pack as the only mammal weaned off its mom, only to spend the rest of its life stuck under the udders of a cow. No animal in the creature kingdom continues milk consumption past weaning and babyhood. Milk will take a little animal from birth to weaning, and after that it's time for big-boy/big-girl food. This is a law of nature. No one drinks milk once they are up and walking. Except.... Humans!

Harvey Diamond, author of the bestseller *Fit For Life*, sees milk as a politicised, but failing food experiment, now people are wising up to the truth:

"You can be absolutely certain of one thing: Milk is the most political food in America. According to the Los Angeles Times, *the dairy industry is subsidized (meaning the taxpayer foots the bill) to the tune of almost three billion dollars a year! That's 342,000 dollars every hour to buy hundreds of millions of dollars' worth of dairy products that will in all likelihood never be eaten... The demand for dairy products has declined substantially, as it is becoming more apparent that they are not the perfect foods they were once touted to be.*

But dairy production is continuous. Be assured that much of the publicity referring to the health benefits of dairy products is commercially motivated. In March 1984 the Los Angeles Times *reported that the Department of Agriculture decided to launch a $140-million advertising campaign to "promote milk-drinking and help reduce the multibillion-dollar surplus." Although the real reason for the advertising campaign is to reduce the surplus, the ads attempt to convince you to buy milk for its many so-called health benefits."*[242]

---

[242] Diamond, Harvey, *Fit For Life,* op. cit. pp.105-106

We've heard of milk lakes and butter mountains for years, demonstrating clearly that production of these dairy products completely outstrips the demand for them. And why is that? Thousands of articles exist in the scientific and medical literature with milk as the focus of these studies. The main thrust of these articles however, far from lauding milk as the perfect food we have been deceived into believing it is, deals with a horrific litany of ills with which milk has regaled humankind.

What do you find discussed in these studies? Do they tell us that milk makes strong bones, strong teeth and turns you into an Olympian athlete with the body of a Greek god? If we were to believe the piffle fed to us through the udders of the mass communications media, all the scientific journals would be telling us to go out and fill our swimming pools and baths with the stuff to ward off all those ills that milk is perfect in preventing. What complete tommyrot. What a dastardly whitewash. How could the public have been so completely creamed? The pro-milk pitch is of course not based in reality or science. It is the hype of the marketeer and the balance sheet.[243]

All you read about in these scientific journals is how milk brings on allergic reactions, asthma, intestinal irritation, intestinal bleeding, anaemia, diabetes, salmonella, and allergic reactions in children and infants. Toxicologists such as Dr Samuel Epstein have long been warning about other dangers, such as the chronic misuse of antibiotics and hormones in cattle farming, giving rise to a whole new smorgasbord of problems. Increased estrogen intake, brought on by farmers fattening their stock with estradiol, a hormonal anabolic with estrus activity, shows links in adults to breast and ovarian cancers, atherosclerosis and heart disease (Vitamin C depletion).[244] Notice all these conditions can be termed 'survival responses' to a specific, or series of threats. Leukemias and lymphomas, along with arthritis, accelerated sexual development in children and the potential for infection with bovine leukemia virus as well as childhood diabetes, are

---

[243] *Lancet 2*, "Beware of the Cow" (editorial), (1974): 30 4

[244] Epstein, Samuel S, *Politics....*, op. cit. Estradiol, Trenbolone, Zeranol and Melengesterol Acetate are all used as hormonal anabolics in rearing cattle. Residues of these drugs are passed into the food chain with the consumption of milk and beef products. Estrogen is used because it has the ability to promote the storage of energy in the body as fat, thus increasing the weight of the animal.

also discussed in the medical literature in connection with milk and meat consumption.[245] Contamination through the milk supply with pesticides and insecticides has also given rise to concerns with child health, including allergy, ear and tonsillar infections, bedwetting, asthma, intestinal bleeding and colic.[246]

Most of us milk moustachers don't realise that milk contains blood and white (pus) cells from the animal. USDA inspectors in America know this, and simply ask milk processing companies to keep the content of these white cells to a maximum of 1 to 1.5 million white cells per millilitre (1/30th of an ounce). The other pertinent point to consider before we suckle another of our favourite dairy dishes, is that fifty years ago, the average cow produced 20,000 pounds of milk every year. Today, the top gold-star bovines are churning out 50,000-plus pounds by comparison. Do you want to know how the cows are able to do this? Charles Atlas' Dynamic Tension Technique maybe? An LA sports club membership perhaps?

Antibiotics, drugs and recombinant Bovine Growth Hormone (rBGH) are the culprits. rBGH is a genetically engineered drug, produced by the Monsanto Corporation, which swears blind that the hormone does not affect the milk or meat of the animal.

Beef hormones are big business because they fatten cows, which means that farmers want to buy the hormones, since, in the case of estradiol, they can add significant weight to an animal during its 100-day fattening period prior to slaughter, resulting in at least an extra $80 in the farmer's wallet as a bonus. Dr Samuel Epstein, the cancer establishment's long-time antagonist and critic, describes a frightening legacy of non-regulation and governmental irresponsibility:

"As of 1990, more than 95% of American beef cattle were implanted with carcinogenic growth-promoting hormones. The European Economic Community banned hormone-treated meat in 1989, and does not allow US or other producers to export their meat

---

[245] *American Journal of Epidemiology*, "Epidemiologic Relationships of the Bovine Population and Human Leukemia in Iowa" 112 (1980): 80 2; *Science*, "Milk of Dairy Cows Frequently Contains a Leukemogenic Virus" 213 (1981): 1014 3

[246] *Pediatrics*, "Is Bovine Milk a Health Hazard?" Suppl. 75:182-186; 1985

into the EEC. This ban was recently (February 1998) upheld by a World Trade Organisation appellate body.

In the absence of effective federal regulation, the US meat industry uses hundreds of animal feed additives, including antibiotics, tranquilizers, pesticides, animal drugs, artificial flavours, industrial wastes, and growth-promoting hormones, with little or no concern about the carcinogenic and other toxic effects of dietary residues of these additives." [247]

And so the predictable cast of drug manufacturers, ever greedy for a fresh slice of the drug pie, prowl around this lucrative cattle-fattening profit-centre like fat cats around a milk churn. Of course, what the companies fail to tell you, in their headlong rush to bank their profits, is that what gets fed to the cows invariably comes out in the white-wash, so to speak. The milk produced by cows fed steroid-bolstered, antibiotic-laced, hormone-accelerated diets, which in certain cases can contain human excrement (France) and all these drug and bacterial elements, finds its way into the human food chain, bringing into our stomachs its Borgian poison-payload. "But that's what pasteurisation is for!" shrill the outraged white-moustachers. Wipe your faces, my friends, and please keep reading.... It all gets so horribly compelling in a minute.

rBGH causes a significant increase in mastitis (udder infection) in cows, which requires antibiotic treatment and salves. The residues of these drugs appear in the milk and survive pasteurisation, which is designed to kill off harmful bacteria. Even the US Government's General Accounting Office has stated that FDA and State legislation across America is failing to regulate the true extent of drug and hormone contamination in milk.[248] This contamination, taken in through meat and dairy products consumed by the human mother, shows up in her breast milk where these pesticides and drugs are then transmitted to the infant.[249]

---

[247] Epstein, Samuel S, *Politics...* op. cit. p.585

[248] Kradjian, Robert M, *Don't Get Milk*, op. cit. p.7

[249] *Lancet*, "Cow's Milk as a Cause of Infantile Colic With Breast Fed Infants" (1978):437 2; *J. Pediatr.* "Dietary Protein-Induced Colitis in Breast-Fed Infants", 101 (1982): 906 3; *J. Immunology*, "The Question of Elimination of Foreign Protein in Women's Milk" Vol. 19 (1930): 15

Dr Frank Oski, of the Upstate Medical Center Department of Pediatrics, has spoken out against the American Academy of Pediatrics' recommendation that whole bovine milk should be consumed by infants. Breaking ranks with his peers in the scientific journal *Pediatrics*, Oski states:

"It is my thesis that milk should not be fed to the infant in the first year of life because of its association with iron deficiency anaemia (cow's milk is so deficient in iron that an infant would have to consume an impossible 31 quarts a day to get the iron RDA of 15mg), occult gastrointestinal bleeding, and various manifestations of food allergy. I further suggest that unmodified whole bovine milk should not be consumed after infancy because of the problems of lactose intolerance, its contribution to the genesis of atherosclerosis, and its possible link to other diseases." [250]

So why do we drink cow's milk? Why don't we drink lion's milk to make us braver, or rat's milk to make us slyer or cat's milk so we can scratch up the furniture? The question is not as silly as it sounds. We drink cow's milk because that is culturally what we have always done. Also we can catch cows easily and they are docile when milked. You're not likely to have the same success if your penchant is for polar bear milk – and you probably won't live to get the Queen's telegram either.

No, we drink cow's milk because it is readily available and we have been conned into believing we cannot get by without it. And then along comes the breakfast cereal industry and hooks us on sucrose, gluten and milk, all mixed up together with some raisins sprinkled on the top for good measure, and persuades us to eat it during our morning elimination cycle. This then is our breakfast 'health food'. What is the difference between my getting out of the car and suckling a cow in the field to your evident horror, and Sainsbury's and Walmart obtaining it for me, packaging it and sticking it on their supermarket shelves for me to grab on the way to the till? The answer? Marketing. We'll drink it if it is provided for us. If it isn't, we won't go suckle the cow. Figure out the logic of that one when you've got a minute.

---

[250] *Pediatrics*, 1983: 72-253

But is cow's milk similar to human milk? Not in the least. Milk components vary widely according to species. Cow's milk, for instance, has three to four times more protein than human milk. Rat milk contains up to eleven times more protein than human milk.[251] Cow's milk is designed to assist baby cows in their development in very specific ways. It has five to seven times the mineral content but is markedly deficient in essential fatty acids when compared to human mothers' milk, which contains up to eleven times the essential fatty acid components, most specifically linoleic acid, essential for neurological development, which is completely absent in cow's milk when skimmed.[252] Cows, of course, are not famous for their mental gymnastics.

Harvey Diamond points out other problems with the consumption of the white stuff: *"The enzymes required to break down and digest milk are renin and lactase. They are all but gone by the age of three in most humans. There is a protein in all milk known as casein. There is three hundred times more casein in cow's milk than in human's milk. That's for the development of huge [cow] bones. Casein coagulates in the stomach and forms large, tough, dense, difficult-to-digest curds that are adapted to the four-stomach digestive apparatus of a cow.*

Once inside the human system, this thick mass of goo puts a tremendous burden on the body to get rid of it somehow. In other words, a huge amount of energy must be expended in dealing with it. Unfortunately some of this gooey substance hardens and adheres to the lining of the intestines and prevents the absorption of nutrients into the body. Also the by-products of milk digestion leave a great deal of toxic mucus in the body. It's very acidic, and it is stored in the body until it can be dealt with at a later time. The next time you are going to dust your home, smear some paste all over everything and see how easy it is to dust. Dairy products do the same inside your body. That translates into more weight instead of weight loss.

Casein, by the way, is the base of one of the strongest glues used in woodworking." [253]

---

[251] **Bell, G** *Textbook of Physiology and Biochemistry*, Baltimore: Williams & Wilkins, 1959
[252] Kradjian, Robert M, *Don't Get Milk*, op. cit.
[253] Diamond, Harvey, op. cit. pp.107-108

When I was a kid in school, we used to be given bottles of milk to drink in the playground. Of course, in those days, current political correctness and the Nanny State were but an embryo in the minds of the communist social architects of the 1960s, so milk got thrown everywhere, and so did the glass bottles that held it.

My early enduring memories of those days were the smell of decomposing milk, the thick mucus and taste of the stuff in my mouth, and most of all, the chronic runny noses and ear infections we all had, which weren't just because of the limb-snapping cold that often afflicts English kids in January. I know they were trying to kill us off before the age of seven, for who else but the terminally psychotic would ever send trusting kids out in Siberia temperatures IN SHORT TROUSERS to guzzle whole milk by the frozen (glass) bottle-load while we had sword fights with the icicles?

One kid's nose in particular used to gush like Niagara. Every time you saw the poor wretch, he had those glassy pearls coming out of his nostrils. I was fascinated with this phenomenon and fully believed my mates when they told me Farr's brains were coming out through his nose. Come to think about it, we all had runny Niagara noses and this thick, flobby gunk in our mouth after we had slogged the milk down our throats through those paper straws we later used as peashooters.

Dr William A Ellis, a retired osteopathic physician and surgeon, has researched and reported on milk and its health-related problems for over forty years. Dr Ellis' research shows conclusive links between high dairy products consumption and heart disease, arthritis, allergies and migraine headaches. He also, as a conclusion to his research, states that there is *"...overwhelming evidence that milk and milk products are a major factor in obesity."* He further states: *"Over my forty-two years of practice, I've performed more than 25,000 blood tests for my patients. These tests show, conclusively in my opinion, that adults who use milk products do not absorb nutrients as well as adults who don't. Of course, poor absorption in turn means chronic fatigue."* [254]

---

[254] **Biser, Samuel** *The HealthView Newsletter*, "The Truth About Milk", 14, Charlottesville, VA, USA. Spring, 1978: 1-5

Other studies have linked Type 1 diabetes to chronic milk consumption. On 30th July 1992 the *New England Journal of Medicine* wrote up a landmark report. In Finland there is *"... the world's highest rate of dairy product consumption and the world's highest rate of insulin-dependent diabetes. The disease strikes about 40 children out of every 1,000 there, contrasted with six to eight per 1,000 in the United States....*

Antibodies produced against the milk protein during the first year of life, the researchers speculate, also attack and destroy the pancreas in a so-called auto-immune reaction, producing diabetes in people whose genetic make-up leaves them vulnerable."[255]

These same researchers also studied 142 Finnish children with newly diagnosed diabetes and found that every one of them had at least eight times the level of antibodies against milk proteins than normal children. *"Clear evidence,"* as one of the researchers later stated, *"that these children had a raging auto-immune disorder."*

Another favourite marketing adage of Big Milk is that milk is pure, because of the pasteurisation, and besides, milk gives you calcium to assist in the development of healthy bones. This too is complete nonsense, bordering on the criminal. The pasteurisation technique of heating up the milk to kill the bugs is widely known also to kill off enzymes, destroy the germicidal properties of bovine milk and reduce the usable vitamin content by at least 50%. Calves fed pasteurised milk die within 60 days, as shown by numerous experiments, so why do humans drink it? Actually the benefits of pasteurisation revert to the farmer and the milk industry: pasteurised milk lasts longer on the supermarket shelves and farmers can get away with a lower standard of cleanliness around the farm.

And now the question of milk calcium. Calcium exists in the body to neutralise acid build-up and there is little question that milk contains calcium. However, the consumption of milk and dairy products greatly increases the acidity of the body requiring water and calcium to adjust the pH balance. The problem with milk calcium is that it is coarser than the calcium contained in human milk because it

---

[255] Also reported in the *Los Angeles Times*.

is bound up with the sticky protein casein we looked at earlier, making it more unavailable. The other problem is that most milk and dairy products have been pasteurised, skimmed, homogenised and otherwise processed and adulterated, further degrading the calcium, rendering it even more difficult for the body to absorb. Ingri Cassel remarks as follows:

"Our nutritional education in school (funded in part by the diary industry) taught us that dairy products are one of the four basic food groups we all need for proper nutrition. Largely as a result of this conditioning, the average American consumes 375 pounds of dairy products a year. One out of every seven dollars spent on groceries in the US goes to buy dairy products.

We have been told all of our lives to drink plenty of milk in order to build strong teeth and bones. Curiously, the US as a whole records one of the highest consumption of dairy products in the world and also boasts the highest incidence of bones fractures and osteoporosis.

In the January 1988 Journal of Clinical Endocrinology and Metabolism, scientists reported that calcium excretion and bone loss increase in proportion to the amount of animal protein ingested. Animal proteins, due to their high sulphur [acidic] content, alter the kidneys' reabsorption of calcium, so that more calcium is excreted on a diet based upon meats, eggs and dairy products. People on high protein diets excrete between 90-100mg of calcium a day." [256]

So here we have a picture of Westernised humans rendering their bodies acidic through the consumption of dairy and animal products which, by their very acid nature, compel the body to strip sodium, calcium and magnesium from its stores to alkalise the onslaught. Pause for a moment that hectic daily schedule of yours and consider where our society is, in terms of health, chomping and slurping all this endless 'healthy' dairy chow, with sicknesses endemic in our culture as a result of this wrong turn. With the evidence pointing to unweaned humans becoming sicker and more gummed up by the day, can we any

---

[256] **Cassel, Ingri,** *The Idaho Observer,* "Does Milk Really Look Good On You? Don't Drink It!" http://proliberty.com/observer/20000208.htm

longer maintain, with even a shred of credibility, that 'milk does a body good'?

In *Food For Thought*, the recipe tome that is a companion for *Health Wars*, we concentrate either on dishes with the meat and dairy component removed (for detoxification purposes) or those with a low meat and dairy component, which will again assist in detoxification and reversing the acidifying of the body's internal environment. More about all this in a later section.

Meating the Main Problem
The Dangers of Excessive Animal Protein Consumption

While we're machine-gunning the supermarket cart, let's examine the fables and myths surrounding meat. The first thing to appreciate is how much more meat protein we as a society are eating when compared with the average westernised diet munched before World War 2. In fact, culturally, chronic meat-eating by the Western populations is only a relatively recent fad. Back in the medieval times, meat was a luxury few could afford. The average peasant subsisted on a largely vegetarian diet. He didn't kill his cows because he wanted the milk. He didn't kill his chickens because he wanted the eggs. Straying into the King's parks to poach himself some venison or even a rabbit would, likely as not if he were caught, see him twisting in the wind by sunset.

Perhaps single-handedly though, the rise of the fast-food burger changed forever the topography of the modern diet when Ray Kroc and Richard McDonald's dream became everybody else's main-street food fixation. There is no doubt at all that meat features prominently in most people's diets in the First World today. But why do we think we eat it?

We think we eat meat because we love it, because it gives us protein and because it makes us strong. But once again, consumption of meat, especially on the scale we are currently witnessing, does go against logic, common sense and instinct, if you stop and think for a moment. My intention in this book is not to persuade you to give up meat, sugar, milk, cigarettes, and a host of other 'goodies', if you are determined to keep eating, drinking or smoking them. My intention is to give you the information you need to make an informed decision about your future dietary and lifestyle habits, if you are serious about adjusting a few things and achieving that healthy longevity. And with meat, this decision is probably as difficult and confusing a choice as any you are likely to contemplate, because not even the experts appear to agree on what is best. But it need not be so. Let's just use a little common sense.

Excessive meat-eating, according to researcher Ethel R Nelson MD, is at the root of many of the health woes that have damaged our families for years:

"For about the past twenty-five years, researchers in human nutrition have pointed to the unrefined plant dietary as a more ideal food than animal products. They have designated the Western world's high-fat animal product, fibre-poor, refined diet as the chief cause of so-called "Western diseases", e.g. coronary heart disease, diabetes, obesity, gallstones, appendicitis, diverticulosis of the bowel, hiatus hernia, hemorrhoids, osteoporosis, kidney disorders, varicose veins, cancer, and accelerated sexual development in children.

Some of today's most prevalent and devastating diseases in the United States have now been credited to excessive consumption of meat and animal products (milk, cheese, eggs) and insufficient ingestion of plant foods." [257]

The first thing to note are the words 'excessive consumption'. Humans, as Harvey Diamond explains, are not natural carnivores:

"A carnivore's teeth are long sharp and pointed – all of them! We have molars for crushing and grinding. A carnivore's jaws move up and down only, for tearing and biting. Ours can move from side to side for grinding. A carnivore's saliva is acid and geared to the digestion of animal protein; it lacks ptyalin, a chemical that digests starches. Our saliva is alkaline and contains ptyalin for the digestion of starch. A carnivore's stomach is a simple, round sack that secretes ten times more hydrochloric acid than that of a non-carnivore. Our stomachs are oblong in shape, complicated in structure, and convoluted with a duodenum.

A carnivore's intestines are three times the length of its trunk, designed for rapid expulsion of animal proteins, which quickly rot. Our intestines are twelve times the length of our trunks and designed to keep food in them until all nutrients are extracted. The liver of a carnivore is capable of eliminating ten to fifteen times more uric acid

---

[257] **Nelson, Ethel R** *The Eden Diet and Modern Nutritional Research*, the Twin Cities Creation Conference, Northwestern College, 1992

than the liver of a non-carnivore. Our livers have the capacity to eliminate only a small amount of uric acid. Uric acid is an extremely dangerous toxic substance that can wreak havoc in your body. All meat consumption releases large quantities of uric acid into the system. Unlike most carnivores and omnivores, humans do not have the enzyme uricase to break down uric acid.

A carnivore does not sweat through the skin and has no pores. We do sweat through the skin and have pores. A carnivore's urine is acid. Ours is alkaline. A carnivore's tongue is rough, ours is smooth. Our hands are perfectly designed for plucking fruit from a tree, not for tearing the guts out of the carcass of a dead animal as are a carnivore's claws.[258]

If the above doesn't convince you that humans are not natural carnivores, then trust to instinct. What do you think you are *psychologically* programmed to eat? Next time you pass over some road kill, screech the car to a halt, leap out with your juices flowing and go back and get stuck into the blood and guts. Tear that rabbit apart and delight and marvel as the blood flows down your throat. Feel the satisfying crunch of its bones and the slippery visceral sensation of its organs in your mouth. Well, why not? You're a meat-eater by instinct, aren't you? Any of your brothers and sisters-in-kin, like a fox or a crow or even a dog, would likely beat you to it. Don't be the runt of the pack! Get your muzzle in there, barge aside the competition, and chow on down.

And, while you're about it, leap over the fence when you're done and go and suckle a few of those Jerseys over there in the field to slake that rabid thirst. Don't worry about the cars that have pulled over on the side of the road, their occupants staring at you with ghastly fascination with their jaws on the floor. They're just a jealous bunch of failed meat- and milk-swillers wishing they had come along the road and got tuckered down a minute before you did. The point being made is that, even though they disapprove of your meat-garnering activities, your critics will be down at Safeways, Asda or Piggly Wiggly's at 4pm later *buying up their own supplies of meat and pints of milk.*

---

[258] Diamond, Harvey, op. cit. pp.97-98

Do you watch wildlife programs because you wish you were out there on the Serengeti, charging down the zebras yourself? Is your toddler crying in the kitchen? Maybe your little one is hungry. Try an experiment and give her a live hamster in one hand and a strawberry in the other. What will this child do by instinct? Eat the hamster alive and then toy with the strawberry?

Then imagine walking through a vineyard in summer time. You're hot, you're sweating from the heat that is only now burning off the dew and mist that cloaked the pasture in its morning glory. Above you, glistening in the sun, are bunches of ripe and tasty grapes, still with the dew on their skins. Now what are you instinctively going to do?

Meat is well known as 'a source of protein', but what kind of protein? Animal protein! Humans cannot use and create human protein directly from the consumption of animal protein. The human has to break down the animal protein into its constituent amino acids and then reconstruct human protein from these building blocks. Proteins are formed from chains that can range anywhere from 50 to 200,000 amino acid links. These chains have to be deconstructed and recombined into human links, a procedure that is extremely tiring to the human, and also an extremely inefficient form of manufacturing protein.

Flesh foods actually have very little going for them, in terms of their positive nutritive value, apart from Vitamins B9 and B12, which are essential for human health. Even if you are eating meat for protein, you aren't, because the meat is almost always cooked, charbroiled, fried, boiled or roasted, which destroys much of its enzyme and amino acid benefit, converting these protein components into an acidic toxic gunk which the body will later have to neutralise and eliminate.[259] Of course, if you were a true meat-eater, you'd be chomping your beef, chicken and duck <u>raw</u> to maximise the protection of the meat's amino acids, in the same way animals instinctively do in the wild. But you don't, do you?

---

[259] **Okitani, A et al** *The Journal of Food Science*, "Heat Induced Changes in Free Amino Acids on Manufactured Heated Pulps and Pastes from Tomatoes" 48 (1983): 1366-1367

Of course, the other deficit in logic centres around the question that is seldom asked: Where do the animals we eat, such as cows, sheep and chicken, get their protein from? From grass, vegetation and cereals! That's right, from the amino acids they derive, not from flesh foods, but from those occurring naturally in the plant kingdom. Carnivores will only attack and eat other carnivores in an emergency. In almost all other cases, true carnivores are happy to go for herbivores, attacking the stomach cavity in their victims first, to slop up the amino acid pool that has collected there, comprised as it is of pre-digested nitrilosidic grass and vegetation.

"But I eat my steaks to make me big and strong!" This also is a lie. All your tumultuous steaks are doing is giving you corpse-like breath, an overdose of protein your body has to neutralise and then eliminate, an inside track on bowel cancer and heart disease, and chronic indigestion problems eventually ending in appalling bowel actions. I worked with many bodybuilders when I was living in California, and the ones who were clued up weren't using meat to win their contests. Many of the top 230lb hulks at Gold's Gym, World's Gym and the Marina Athletic Club were mostly fruit and salad boys, consuming a minimum of flesh foods, but ingesting free amino acids. The vegetarian silverback gorilla, as Harvey Diamond points out, has no problems building its proteins. This animal is three times as large as a man, but over thirty times as strong.[260] Have an arm-wrestling match with one of those and I'll guarantee you two things off the bat. One, the gorilla won't have had a T-bone steak all day, and two, you'll lose.

In regard to energy, meat contains almost no carbohydrates. Yet carbs are where your fuel comes from. Meat also contains next to no fibre, is high in saturated fat, and can take days to pass through your gut. And it is here that the downside to flesh-food eating is massive and repellent. Meat, quite literally, rots in the stomach, especially when it is ill-combined with carbohydrates, such as rice, potatoes, chips and pasta. Meat proteins require the stomach to secrete acid to digest them, whereas carbohydrates require an alkali. Put the two together in the form of steak and fries, chicken tagliatelli, or eggs on toast, and the digestive juices cancel one another out. Later, as this gridlock continues to jam up our insides, the rotting and putrefaction

[260] Diamond, Harvey, op. cit. p.89

commence, resulting in horrible bear's breath, foul gas, rancid body odour, deposits of mucoid plaque along the insides of the colon, a frantic race against time to procure a ready supply of Tums, and ultimately 15 minutes reading the *Wall Street Journal* on the pan with the veins popping out of your forehead as you pull those ghastly faces at yourself in the mirror in the daunting lead-up to Beethoven's Last Movement.[261]

Dr Herbert Shelton wonders at the insanity of modern man's sick predicament: *"Why must we accept as normal what we find in a race of sick and weakened human beings? Must we always take it for granted that the present eating practices of civilized men are normal? ...Foul stools, loose stools, impacted stools, pebbly stools, much foul gas, colitis, hemorrhoids, bleeding with stools, the need for toilet paper are swept into the orbit of the normal."* [262]

Nutritionist Dr Dean Burkitt accuses the West's fibre-deficient, refined diet with too few plant foods, too little fresh water, as well as increased ingestion of animal foods, in accounting for the rash of modern Western diseases, such as coronary heart disease, cancer, kidney disease, osteoporosis, diabetes and liver disease.[263] Burkitt and colleague Alec Walker determined, by studying multiple bowel transit times, that meat-heavy, ill-combined meals were creating an aftermath of appendicitis, constipation, diverticulosis, varicose veins, hemorrhoids and colon cancer (the second leading cancer death). They found that the average time for passage for this putrefying detritus through the human alimentary tract was three to five days, and even as much as two weeks in the elderly. Rural Third World peoples, on the other hand, consuming diets fibre-rich in unrefined plant dietary, such

---

[261] Heartburn can be easily treated by simply increasing your daily intake of water to 4 pints a day. This extra water adequately hydrates the stomach and colon and the pain of heartburn will soon pass. Drink a glass of fresh water half an hour prior to eating, and then two and a half hours after eating a meal. Drink before you sleep. Drink when you wake up, and especially drink water during exercise. If you feel the heartburn sensation coming on, simply drink water. If you have any kidney complaints, please consult a health practitioner prior to increasing your intake of water. Your diet should also be amended to avoid acidic ash foods in favour of the alkali alternatives.

[262] **Shelton H M** *Food Combining Made Easy*, Shelton Health School, TX, 1951. p.32

[263] **Burkitt, D P** *Don't Forget Fibre in Your Diet*, London: Martin Dunitz Ltd., 1979

as yams, cassava, cereals, vegetables and fruits, with little animal products, passed easily propelled stools in 24 to 36 hours.[264]

William J Mayo, founder of the famous Mayo cancer clinic in the United States, addressed the American College of Surgeons with these words: *"Meat-eating has increased 400% in the last 100 years. Cancer of the stomach forms nearly one third of all cancers of the human body. If flesh foods are not fully broken up, decomposition results, and active poisons are thrown into an organ not intended for their reception."* [265]

Correct food-combining is one of the most important points dealt with in *Health Wars*, and we will cover this subject in our later section on The Science of Natural Hygiene. But it's important to see how all the pieces of the nutrition picture go together. For instance, as we learned in the section on cancer, according to research[266], a diet rich in proteins robs our body of its vital supplies of pancreatic enzymes, which are used by the body to terminate healing processes, which can otherwise go on to form tumours if they are not arrested upon completion.[267] These enzymes, such as trypsin and chymotrypsin, are employed during the complicated process the body undergoes as these foreign proteins are broken down into their constituent amino acids and reconstructed as human proteins – a process extremely taxing on the body's resources.

We also chomp meat because our society has bought into the fear of dying through lack of protein, most believing that unless we scarf down animal flesh by the rack-load, we are in serious danger of becoming protein-deficient. This myth originated from early trials conducted on rats. Later it would transpire that rats require up to eleven times more protein than humans, as evidenced by the commensurate increase in rat mothers' proteins in milk, as compared with the protein content of human milk. Today, it is recognised that human protein requirements are not nearly as great as formerly

[264] **Walker, A R P, Burkitt & Painter** *Lancet 2*, "Effect of Dietary Fibre on Stools and Transit-Times, and Its Role in the Causation of Disease", (1972): pp.1408-1412
[265] **Leonardo, Blanche** *Cancer and Other Diseases from Meat Consumption*, Santa Monica, CA: Leaves of Healing, 1979
[266] *Cancer Control Journal*, Vol. 6. No.1-6
[267] Binzel, P E, *Alive &* Well, op. cit.

assumed (between 20 – 40 g/day). Yet many are ingesting 100 – 200 g/day. It is this excess that is causing all the bother, especially in the realm of causing acidosis in the population that can eventually prove fatal. Nevertheless, the protein-scoffing trend has been hard to exorcise from the minds of the laity, which in turn has led to an overabundance of illnesses and scourges in the protein-gorging West.

These diseases, relatively rare in the 1930s, are now found in ever increasing abundance among our present-day, 'well-fed' populations, due to the massive increase protein advertising. Notice that the major food lobbies with limitless ad budgets are all pushing acid-forming foods, such as meat, grains, milk and sugar. But research shows that ancient peoples were also cursed with these diseases that came from heavy protein consumption, ironically a trait of all prosperous societies. In Exodus 15:26 of the Bible, God is addressing the Israelites:

"If you diligently heed the voice of the Lord your God and do what is right in His sight, give ear to His commandments and keep all His statutes, I will put none of the diseases on you which I have brought on the Egyptians."

What were these diseases of the Egyptians? For that answer, we go to Dr Marc Armand Ruffer, a paleopathologist who, along with his associates, has performed over 36,000 autopsies on Egyptian mummified remains of Pharaonic royals. Ruffer's research demonstrates that most of the diseases striking the Egyptian royalty bear an uncanny resemblance to those killing us today: atherosclerosis, various forms of heart disease, cancer, osteoporosis, stroke, obesity, tooth decay, arthritis, diverticulosis of the colon, and early sexual development in children.[268] [269]

Even back in 1992, heart disease alone was claiming 3,000 Americans *a day*. Colon and rectal cancers, now the second cause of cancer-death in America, for years have been associated with high-protein, low-fibre diets. Excessive bile acids are required to process

---

[268] Egyptians, Romans, Greeks and other heavy meat-consumers sometimes married young girls in their cultures who were under 10 years of age. Such actions demonstrate that these cultures recognised that these children were apparently ready for child-bearing.

[269] *Mysteries of the Mummies*, Loma Linda: Slide-tape program produced by Loma Linda University School of Health, 1984

proteins in the bowel *and bile acids are carcinogenic to humans.*[270] The transit time for foods through the alimentary tract is prolonged with low-fibre bowel content, allowing a longer period of time for bile acids to act on bowel mucosa. High pork, beef and chicken consumption correlates closely with the incidence of colon cancer.[271]

Interestingly, Americans have two and a half times the incidence of colon cancer deaths as the Chinese, and yet Chinese-American women who adopt the high-fat, high-meat dietary habits of the United States suffer *four times* the rate of colon cancer as their counterparts in China. In Chinese-American males, the colorectal cancer rate is *seven times* that of their Chinese counterparts. Colon and rectal cancers increase more than 400% among sedentary people, which also correlates with the increased incidence of constipation in this group.[272]

High protein diets have also been linked to breast cancer since high estrogen levels are a predominant factor in breast cancers. Meat-eating women have higher levels of estrogen in the urine than vegetarian women, according to research.[273]

The simple fact is, if you consume a balanced diet of fruits, vegetables, whole grains and nuts, you couldn't get a protein deficiency if you were hit over the back of the head with one, because your body will have access to all the amino acids required to construct human protein. There are twenty-three amino acids, fifteen of which can be produced by the body. The final eight however have to be procured through our diet, thus they have been labelled the 'essential amino acids'. Meat does not need to enter into the picture, so far as amino acids are concerned. The body makes use of a constant circulating bank of amino acids in the blood and lymph systems, known as the amino acid pool, which the liver and cells use to withdraw whatever material is required. The liver and cells are also capable of storing amino acids, which, in a balanced diet, are available in more than plentiful supply.

---

[270] **Galloway, D** "Experimental colorectal cancer: The relationship of diet and faecal bile acid concentration to tumour induction", *Br. J. Surg.* 73:233-237, 1986

[271] **Berg, J** Quoted in **Robbins, J** *Diet for a New America*, Stillpoint Publ. 1987. p.254

[272] **Whittemore, A** "Diet, physical activity and colorectal cancer among Chinese in North America and China", *J. Natl. Cancer Inst.* 82:915-926, 1990. Also Nelson, Ethel, op. cit.

[273] **Schultz, T** "Nutrient intake and hormonal status of premenopausal vegetarian Seventh Day Adventist and premenopausal non-vegetarians", *Nutr. Cancer,* 4:247-259, 1983

From this amino acid pool, the body is able to draw and chain aminos into protein blocks for use within the human body.

Once we understand how the body trades in amino acids, not proteins, either foreign or domestic, all the claptrap about protein deficiency can be tossed out and a new, healthier and leaner 'you' can break free of all turbulent, misleading myth. In fact, most of the ills of today's Western societies centre around the consumption of too much protein, protein poisoning and diseases arising as a result of the body's resultant acidosis and inability to rid itself of the toxic metabolites created as a result of chronic protein consumption. This links meat and dairy squarely with obesity.

The final problems with eating meat are in essence very similar to those with milk. As discussed briefly earlier, meats today can be, and are contaminated with recombinant Bovine Growth Hormone (rBGH), pesticides, insecticides, arsenic, antibiotics, hormone accelerators, steroids, ticks, parasites, viruses and pus cells. Feed additives, such as estradiol and DEA, synthetic estrogen mimics, are still added to the food chain. In spite of a clear record of carcinogenicity since its introduction in 1947, DEA, for example, has failed to be curtailed by the Food & Drug Administration, in spite of repeated attempts by researchers to have it scrapped.[274]

Meat is rarely unadulterated. Some meat receives chemical and dye treatments to turn it a 'healthy' red and not the usual grey of dead flesh. Some meat is treated with sodium sulphite to decrease the stench of decay. Farmers have been known to feed their cattle cement and concrete dust to increase weight for when their livestock comes up for sale.[275]

CONCLUSION
The plain fact is, meat and dairy are largely not required by the human body either for calcium, vitamins (apart from B9 & 12), minerals or proteins to maintain health and strength. In fact, in the case of calcium, meat can actually be a problem. Meat is generally high in phosphorous, an acid, which bonds with valuable alkalising calcium

---

[274] Epstein, Samuel S, *Politics...*op. cit. p.151
[275] *Nutrition Health,* Summer 1981

ions in our bodies to form apatite, which is then precipitated out of the body, causing a net calcium loss. The human body is not designed to consume human milk past infancy, and it is not designed for carnivorous meat intakes – humans are omnivores, which means that small amounts of organic meat are acceptable to the body. Interestingly, all nutrients the human body requires may be obtained from the plant kingdom with no downside, save that of a recent mineral deficiency problem, which has appeared through overfarming methods. This important point will be discussed in more detail as we proceed.

This is not to say that a human *can't* eat some meat and dairy products. A small amount of organic meat is desirable for nutrients such as the B9 & B12 we examined earlier, which are sometimes hard to obtain for vegans, who run the risk of these deficiencies if they are not diligent. In fact, a 5-10% component for organic meat/fish[276] and dairy balanced with the remainder of the diet consisting of properly constituted whole foods (salads, vegetables, nuts, legumes, etc.) seems to be ideal. But we just need to be aware of the problems with heavy meat and dairy consumption and simply side-step them.

Myths concerning meat and dairy, with which we have been regaled by various slick advertisers and vested interest promoters over the years, have resulted in a shameful legacy of disease, misery, shortened lives and chronic ill-health with their extreme over-consumption. So how do you feel now? Want to do something you haven't done before, lose some weight, feel some health, and extend those years of yours into the hazy mists of the 21st century? Then let's get busy. But before we do, there's a special chapter coming up for the ladies, which is important for the gentlemen to find out about too. It involves...

---

[276] Fish is a great component for getting essential fatty acids (EFA's) into the body. Persons suffering from motor neuron diseases or 'mental illnesses' should increase their intakes of fish, minerals and fresh, clean water. Ensure the fish is of the deep-sea variety. Lightly broiled fish makes an ideal substitute for a lot of meats currently consumed in the Western diet. For a full treatment on mental illnesses, please see **Day, Phillip** *The Mind Game*, Credence Publications 2002

Barking up the Wrong Tree
The Assault against Women by Healthcare

No book on longevity would ever be complete without an examination into the deliberate victimisation of women's health. In a previous chapter, we looked at the tragic implications of excess estrogen unwittingly absorbed into the female body through the use of the Pill and HRT. In this chapter, we will examine more fully the problems associated with much of what is put out in the name of 21st century healthcare for women. And yes, the same commercial characters sharpen their knives in the fight to corner a hugely profitable part of the pie for their shareholders. At stake is nothing less than a market comprising every adolescent, child-bearing, menopausal and elderly female on the planet.

Health Wars is very much about the extent to which our societies have become toxic with the exponential increase in the use of poisons in the materials we use, such as plastics, pesticides, medical drugs and the corruption of our food supply. As mentioned previously, there are things we can personally do to side-step this onslaught, and then there are things that are hard to avoid, which inevitably affect, as part of an industrialised society's toxic legacy, those who must be a part of it. The point to be made here is that we are succumbing to illness and death, *not so much from the things we can't do anything about*, but from needless exposure to drugs and toxins we are persuaded into taking and using – *a state of affairs absolutely within our sphere of control*.

The assault on womanhood begins with the drug industry promising the usual very lucrative benefits: unlimited, safe and unbridled sex with no biological accountability (and no apparent downside) through chemical birth control and surgical or chemical abortion; an end to those heavy, burdensome periods with all of their associated difficulties of stress, irregularity and mood-swings; a removal of our fears concerning osteoporosis and the menopause. In fact, so successful are the drug companies in talking us into this particular marketing bonanza, that husbands and boyfriends are often the ones persuading their ladies to get signed up for this promise of sexual freedom and social equality for the modern woman! Certainly, from its auspicious start with Envoid, the first contraceptive pill launched in the early 1960s, the estrogen industry ('Big Estrogen') has grown immeasurably to change the social and cultural fabric of our modern sexuality forever. In what has grown to become an all too depressingly familiar trait in modern scientific marketing today, the inevitable barrel full of rosy promises and guarantees of safety for future womanhood was made with tragically scant consideration for any downside.

The female body has been the saviour of many a healthcare professional – medically and financially speaking. As leading feminist Germaine Greer points out: *"The menopause is a dream speciality for the mediocre medic. It requires no surgical or diagnostic skill, it is not itself a life-threatening condition, there is no scope for malpractice action. Patients must return again and again for a battery of tests and check-ups."* [277]

With such a captive audience comprising half the population, and with so much myth and half-truth sown into this target demographic concerning how women's bodies work and what is and is not necessary for good health, women have been consistently lied to about their treatment options, and most insidiously, given the impression that, simply because they are female, they cannot do without the overarching arm of medicine to save them from the 'inevitable' health challenges womanhood has in store for them. Sandra Coney:

"The mid-life woman is oblivious to the deeply sexist ideology underlying the options she has laid down before her. Naively she may think these are offered simply for her own benefit. She is not cognizant of the others who benefit or may also be served by her decisions. She is unaware too that the options themselves may be incompletely tested, that there may be considerable controversy about them in the medical literature, and that doctors will differ in their views. What she is told – how much or how little – is mediated by her doctor. The end result is a woman poorly placed to decide for herself." [278]

---

[277] **Greer, Germaine** *The Change*, Hamish Hamilton, London: 1991
[278] **Coney, Sandra** *The Menopause Industry*, Spinnifex Press Pty Ltd., Australia, 1991. pp.164-165

No wonder the drug industry has focussed its most brilliant strategists on securing this lucrative market: hormones, implants, the Pill, drugs, medical tests, mammograms, diagnostic tests, more drugs and diagnostics to combat the side-effects of the previous drugs and surgical procedures. And then there are those interminable specialist visits. Researcher Sherrill Sellman remarks on one serious area of abuse:

"Hysterectomies are another big industry. The Pill has been a significant contributor to conditions that, later on, necessitate the removal of a woman's uterus and ovaries. To date, it has been estimated that 20 million Americans have had their uteruses removed. Close to one million American women have hysterectomies each year. Of those women, 42% will also have their ovaries removed. It's shocking to realize that presently 1 out of 3 women in the US will have a hysterectomy by 60 years of age... three quarters of them performed on women under the age of 49. Removal of the uterus as well as the ovaries will immediately catapult a woman into "surgical menopause", which necessitates hormones. What's more, an oophorectomy (removal of the ovaries), medically classified as castration, will also require more hormones." [279]

Sellman estimates the hysterectomy industry to be worth $4 billion in the US alone. Hormone drugs too rack up the turnover, she states, with the horse-derived estrogen product Premarin (pregnant mare's urine) on its own grossing a little under $1 billion a year. Find a market. Sell the need, and keep pitching into that market. There is little wonder, Sellman concludes, that the medical industry views women as an unlimited resource to be plundered. *"When it comes to profits, unbiased controlled studies, long-term trials and natural alternatives are all sacrificed for the insatiable hunger for profits,"* she states.

THE ORIGINS OF HORMONE REPLACEMENT

Researcher Rosalind Harrison reports on the controversial research of Dr Serge Voronoff, regarded by many as the father of HRT. In the 1920s-30s, Voronoff declared he had discovered the cure for ageing. Thousands of European men underwent an operation involving

---

[279] Sellman, Sherrill *Hormone Heresy*, op. cit. p.4

the surgical pairing of 'live' chimpanzee testicles with their own. Having no effect on longevity, this sort of research speaks volumes about limited intelligence in exalted positions. [280] Voronoff's work also led to the grafting of monkey's ovaries into women with the same dismal consequences. After failing with this line of enquiry, Voronoff's research switched to the possibilities of synthetic estrogen.

By the 1960s, books such as Dr Robert Wilson's *Feminine Forever* were loosening up the public to the 'potential' of synthetic estrogen as a means of 'empowering women'. Wilson was the chief architect in getting women to look at their biological cycles as a curse. Comments such as *"I have known cases where the resulting physical and mental anguish was so unbearable that the patient committed suicide..."* and *"I have seen untreated women who had shrivelled into caricatures of their former selves..."* and *"The transformation within a few years of a formerly pleasant, energetic woman into a dull-minded but sharp tongued caricature of her former self is one of the saddest of human spectacles..."* needed only the requisite public exposure, clad in the convincing garb of medical officialdom, for Wilson to be taken on trust as the voice of almost every expert. And in due time, as women's magazines everywhere gave tacit credence to his concepts, Wilson's pronouncements did become the voice of almost every 'expert'.

Wilson's foundation was given huge backing by Upjohn, Serle and Wyeth-Ayerst, the pharmaceutical giants manufacturing the products Wilson promoted. Wilson's 'unopposed estrogen' concept, namely that estrogen could usefully be prescribed, unopposed by its counter-weight, the sex hormone progesterone, became the rage of the day.

But by the mid 1970s, it became evident that excess amounts of estrogen, unbalanced by progesterone, were shortening the lives of many women with the onset of heart problems and cancer. Wilson's ideas soon fell out of favour with the medical establishment and the FDA, and the hunt was on for a safer, combined therapy that would use estrogen and progestin (synthetic progesterone) to ward off the ravages of menopause for women. Later this same 'safe concept' would even be

---

[280] Harrison, Rosalind *"Western Medicine as Contested Knowledge,"* Rethinking AIDS Homepage, 1999

touted as a preventative for osteoporosis, cardiovascular disease and Alzheimer's.

SYNTHETIC PROGESTINS

It is worth discussing briefly the role of synthetic progesterone. When it became obvious that estrogen by itself was causing serious health problems in females taking the Pill and early forms of HRT, drug companies began investigating ways of balancing the estrogens, not with natural progesterone produced by the body (which cannot be patented), but with a synthetic version that could become proprietary. Thus natural progesterone was chemically altered to give its resultant molecule patentability – a move which rendered these synthetic progestins dangerous because of their variance from the natural progesterone the body always uses.

Synthetic progestins come with many serious problems. Progestins mimic progesterone by binding to natural progesterone receptors in the cells within the female body, blocking out natural progesterone's ability to dock with these same cells to perform its usual tasks. Progesterone is also vital as it is the precursor hormone from which estrogens and testosterone are derived. So synthetic progestins not only shut out natural progesterone's ability to go about its regular business, but also, because they are not molecularly the same structure as natural progesterone, create a host of health problems by themselves. Couple progestins with synthetic estrogens in the form of HRT however, and you arrive at the hideous complications now witnessed in female healthcare today.

Provera, Duphaston, Primulut, Depo-Provera and Norplant are all synthetic progesterone analogues on today's market. Pharmaceutical companies have admitted to over 120 side-effects of progestins when coupled with estrogens in hormone replacement therapy.[281] Potential side-effects of Provera, for instance, are listed in the Physicians Desk Reference, and are as follows:

➢ Increase risk of birth defects such as heart and limb defects if taken during the first four months of pregnancy.

---

[281] **Beckham, Nancy** "Why Women should not take HRT" *WellBeing Magazine*, No. 67, p.70

- Beagle dogs given this drug developed malignant mammary nodules.
- Discontinue this drug if there is sudden or partial loss of vision.
- This drug passes into breast milk, consequences unknown.
- May contribute to thrombophlebitis, pulmonary embolism and cerebral thrombosis.

Then follows a lengthy list of contraindications in the Desk Reference, including cerebral apoplexy, liver dysfunction or disease, known or suspected malignancy of breast or genital organs and undiagnosed vaginal bleeding. Other side-effects include hirsutism (abnormal hair growth), cholastic jaundice, alopecia and cervical erosions.

HRT – THE SOBER STORY

It has been hard for HRT to maintain the pretence, even for a moment, that it is the cure it has been touted to be. Not even insiders pretended otherwise once the jury was in after the fanfare of HRT's launch. Dr Lynette J Dumble, Senior Research Fellow at the University of Melbourne in Australia, stated: *"...the sole basis of HRT is to create a commercial market that is highly profitable for the pharmaceutical companies and doctors. The supposed benefits of HRT are totally unproven."* [282] Dr Dumble's statement, surprising and medically treasonous at the time, was borne out later by the US National Institutes of Health's sponsored *Boston Nurses Questionnaire Study*, which painted a horrific picture of what IIRT was accomplishing in unsuspecting, trusting women across the US.

121,700 women were tracked for 18 years. The final report warned that women taking combined synthetic estrogens and progestins for over 10 years risked increasing their chances of breast cancer by 100%. The same study found that women using estrogen alone increased their cancer risk by 30-40%, when compared with a control group not taking post-menopausal HRT.[283]

The NIH study also showed that five years' worth of HRT posed significant health risks for its users. Cancer risk increased by 30-40%

---

[282] Sellman, Sherrill, *Hormone Heresy*, op. cit. p.9
[283] Ibid.

over just five years. In women aged 60-65, the risk compounded to 70% after five years of HRT. The study concluded that women who used HRT for more than five years were 45% more likely to die from breast cancer than those who either did not use it, or who used it for less than five years.

To understand the serious problems HRT causes, it is necessary to examine how the female body uses hormones during its reproductive cycle and what happens when women arrive at that much-publicised milestone....

THE MENOPAUSE

Menopause occurs when a woman no longer ovulates and has menstrual periods. This was widely believed to be when her lifetime's supply of eggs (ova) was used up during successive menstrual cycles. Scientists now believe that this may not be the case – that menopause, as well as puberty, may commence through hormone-driven events triggered by the brain.

A little girl is born with all the immature eggs in her ovaries, which will later develop and be released during her lifetime. Although the number of these egg 'follicles' within the ovaries may exceed 400,000 at puberty, only around 400 will actually develop and be released during the woman's lifetime.

The follicle, one of many such ovarian sacs containing its immature egg in a nurturing fluid, secretes estrogen as the egg grows up to its release time. Upon release of the egg, estrogen output from the follicle and other glands remains constant and then decreases during menstruation. In addition to continuing to produce estrogen, the egg-releasing follicle also manufactures progesterone during the second half of the cycle, providing the necessary safe hormonal balance for the estrogens estradiol, estrone and estriol, working away synergistically with their very intricately controlled hormonal ballet to prepare the female for her coming pregnancy.

One of the amazing features of a woman's inner workings is the way the follicle transforms itself, after releasing its egg, into an endocrine gland, known as the corpus luteum, which becomes the primary production plant for progesterone during the vital second half of the menstrual cycle. Remember this fact, as it becomes important in a moment. Contrary to popular belief, it is progesterone, not estrogen, which is responsible for preparing the uterus for pregnancy, heightening the sexual energy usually experienced by the woman during the time of ovulation, and maintaining the pregnancy after conception by preventing any further release of eggs from the ovaries. In the event that no fertilised egg implants itself in the uterus, the uterus lining, engorged with blood in preparation of an imminent pregnancy, sheds itself in the blood of menstruation, and the cycle then repeats itself, with another signal from the brain and glands, telling the body to begin ripening another egg for the next cycle.

So estrogen and progesterone are responsible for orchestrating regular menstruation in the female, and the primary production site of progesterone is the corpus luteum (egg follicle) once it has released its egg and taken the woman into the second half of her menstrual cycle. Around 40 years of age, this interaction between the two hormones usually alters, many doctors and scientists now believe, due to changes in the brain's interaction with the glandular output of the hypothalamus and pituitary glands, *not the ovaries*.[284] At the onset of menopause, estrogen levels drop to 40-60%, low enough to prevent the follicles from maturing and releasing further eggs. Gradually, as the female enters this new period of her life, known as menopause, menstruation becomes more erratic and sporadic before finally ceasing altogether.

Perhaps less well known, even among doctors, is the fact that during menopause, a woman's ovaries are far from 'shrivelled and useless', as is often pointed out to women, although there is some contraction in the 'theca' area of the ovaries where the eggs mature and are released. On the contrary, the inner part of the ovaries, the stoma, becomes active in a way not previously experienced in the female, enabling her to enter a new phase in her life, healthy and with new purpose. Hormones of course continue to be secreted, the brain

---

[284] Experiments with mice, where ovaries from young mice are implanted in older animals, have shown that the latter are incapable of reproduction. Contrariwise, old ovaries from animals no longer capable of reproducing, when implanted into younger mice, have enabled the latter to give birth after mating, giving rise to the belief that the brain and endocrine system have the majority part to play in triggering puberty, ovulation and menopause. Coney, Sandra, op. cit. Selman, Sherrill, op. cit.

playing the role of conductor between the ovaries and other gland sites, such as the pineal, adrenal as well as the skin, hair follicles, uterus and body fat to produce the required chemical messengers. The uterus too, far from being 'useless' and 'unwanted' once the female ceases menstruation, becomes the main production centre for prostacyclin, a hormone now believed to protect the woman from heart disease, thrombosis and unscheduled blood clotting.[285] In the event that doctors carry out a hysterectomy and remove the uterus, prostacyclin is no longer produced by the female, pushing her into a potential risk group indicating thrombosis, coronary spasms and other complications. Scientists at present cannot synthesise prostacyclin hormone in the laboratory, thus leaving the female without this valuable protector for the remainder of her life.[286]

HRT –MIRACLE OR ERROR?

This brief resumé of the wondrous inner workings of a woman's reproductive system is necessary in order to understand the ghastly state of affairs that will now be explained. Menopause is presented to women as being a deficiency of estrogen - a *disease* no less, requiring hormone supplementation with estrogen. Dr John R Lee, the noted authority of hormonal replacement therapy and its archest critic, explains that HRT violates that most precious of balances between estrogen and progesterone, <u>resulting in the female experiencing estrogen dominance</u> (unopposed estrogen). To supplement females with synthetic estrogen to disrupt and increase the estrogen dominance further is to invite a litany of symptoms all too depressingly familiar with women who have been down this particular path: heightened risk of cancer of the breast and endometrium (the inner lining of the uterus), ovarian cysts, uterine fibroids, anaerobic cell respiration (depletion of oxygen in cells – a cancer precursor), disrupted thyroid activity, breast fibrocysts, excessive blood clotting leading to thrombo-embolisms, and decreased sex drive. Then the doctor recommends a hysterectomy, with further catastrophic results potentially threatening the woman during the remainder of her life.

---

[285] Vitamin C also increases the production of prostacyclin, the small molecule hormone that relaxes the blood vessel walls and also keeps the blood viscosity at optimum levels.
[286] *Oxford Medical Dictionary*, 2000

Doctors are used to explaining to worried women that their child-bearing days are over; that their sex organs are no longer required; that, to prevent the risk of osteoporosis and the shopping list of menopausal blights to their health, HRT, a hysterectomy and complete removal of their ovaries are more often than not required. Women find themselves having to take the doctor's word for it all; they are aware that many of their friends have been down the same path and have had these procedures carried out; that female comedians joke about it all, rendering a depressing familiarity that states in effect 'that all women have to deal with this – doctor knows best - might as well get it over with'. This, as we will discover before this chapter is over, is about as far from the plain truth as you can get; a horrific betrayal of trust between a woman and her physician; a deliberate shortening of options that are never explained to the patient. Sherrill Sellman sums up the awful dilemma facing millions of women every year:

"With so many side-effects and dangerous complications, a woman must think very carefully about the HRT decision. Unfortunately, most doctors will say there is no other alternative and that it is relatively safe. While certainly most doctors are well-meaning and sincerely concerned about their patients, their primary source of education and product information comes directly from the pharmaceutical companies. Since most women also lack information and understanding about their options, menopause can be perceived as a rather frightening and perilous time. Women fear that if they don't follow their doctor's advice, then they may face the remaining years of their life with the threat of great suffering and physical deterioration. Women are often in for a rude awakening when they experience firsthand just how badly their health needs have been managed." [287]

THE MECHANICS OF ESTROGEN DOMINANCE

As previously mentioned, estrogen is a generic term to describe three main hormones that have estrus activity - that is, they stimulate cells in the inner lining (endometrium) of the uterus to bloat with blood in preparation for pregnancy. Excessive amounts of estrogens in a woman's body prior to menopause will cause the 'burn out' of her ovaries and jeopardise fertility. Excessive amounts of estrogens in a

---

[287] Sellman, Sherrill, op. cit. pp.23-24

male will bring on feminisation, resulting, in extreme cases, in the enlargement of his breasts (gynecomastia). Estradiol and estrone, two of the female's estrogen hormones, are known to stimulate stem cell growth, which can lead to trophoblast-cell proliferation in healing and pregnancies which, if not terminated by pancreatic enzymes, can result in cancer. Estriol, the third estrogen hormone, is actually cancer-inhibiting.

One of the functions of estradiol is that it stores energy obtained from food as fat in the body for future use. This is the reason estradiol is given to cattle during their 100-day fattening period. To maximise the weight-load of each animal is to maximise a farmer's profits at market-time. Excess amounts of the potentially harmful estradiol thus have been corrupting the food chain for years, not only through the population's prolific consumption of commercially fattened and slaughtered meats, but also through the water supply, when estrogen from contraceptive Pill-users survives the urine effluent treatment process and is passed back into the water supply with all its biochemical estrus capabilities surviving intact.

Excess levels of estradiol occurring in the body as a result of normal hormone production and HRT will thus cause the woman to put on weight. This is because menopausal females on HRT are suffering an estrogen dominance (unopposed by progesterone). Progesterone, in its natural form produced by the body (in marked contrast to the synthetic progestins used in HRT), works opposite to estradiol, and metabolises fat into energy, causing the female to lose weight. But doctors do not tell their patients about the amazing possibilities of natural progesterone supplementation, because natural progesterone is not a profit centre for the drug companies who educate doctors on the latest drugs available. Deceitfully too, doctors often refer to synthetic progestins as 'progesterone', thus muddying the waters further.

And so the female remains estrogen-dominant during hormone replacement therapy, loading on the pounds, bombarded by increased levels of estradiol and estrone in her body, not only from HRT steroid preparations, but from the estrogens now prevalent in the food chain and xeno-estrogens in the environment (estrogen mimics). Further compounding this estrogen/progesterone imbalance is the dwindling supply of progesterone in the female body after menopause commences, since the body is no longer producing progesterone from the corpus luteum follicles after they have released their eggs.

ANOVULATORY CYCLES

Another factor compounding the problem of estrogen dominance is when females do not ovulate during their menstrual period. This is known as an anovulatory cycle. The problem here is that the releasing follicle does not convert to the corpus luteum and generate progesterone. This in turn results in a month's worth of severe estrogen dominance for the female (from day 8 to day 26 of her cycle), with all the associated problems. Anovulatory cycles have traditionally occurred in females in their 40s onwards as they approach menopause. Today however, there is an alarming trend of these egg-free menstrual periods occurring commonly in females in their early thirties, and in some cases, even before this. The implications of this are potentially hazardous for the female in question, as fifteen years of unopposed estrogen dominance can easily occur before the output of estrogens eventually reduces with the onset of menopause.

ESTROGEN DOMINANCE AND OSTEOPOROSIS

Such an estrogen dominance and sharp progesterone deficiency over a protracted period of time will also have attendant side-effects with the depletion of bone mass in the female, giving rise to the fear of osteoporosis. Osteoblasts, the cells that build and replace bone mass in humans, have progesterone receptors. No progesterone, no osteoblasts, no osteoblasts, no new bone material created. Osteoclasts on the other hand, are multinucleate cells that dissolve old bone material in preparation for the osteoblasts, which move in to replace old calcified bone with fresh material. Osteoclasts have estrogen receptors. So, if there is an estrogen dominance, osteoclasts are hard at work breaking down calcified bone material, leaving bones scored and pitted in preparation for the bone-building osteoblasts, which fail to act because of the lack of progesterone docked at their receptors.

Put the two features together and you get bone murder. Estrogen dominance results in calcified (old) bone material being broken down. Couple that with a simultaneous progesterone deficiency and you do not have this calcified bone being replaced. The net result is, of course, a progressive bone loss in the female – osteoporosis – porous bones.

40-60% of females in the Western world today experience PMS symptoms, ranging from the noticeable to the severe. Many millions of women are guinea-pigs for Big Estrogen's onward march to its dividend payouts. The female public are warned about osteoporosis during menopause for good reason. Dominant estrogen bodies that are progesterone deficient will bring on a progressive bone loss for the reasons explained above. Now imagine the female's diet is also acidic with excessive meat and dairy consumption, requiring the body to bloat with water and mobilise calcium out of the bones to restore the pH balance. Then imagine the free-radical activity that results from the incomplete metabolism of refined sugars she has put into her body, resulting in the destruction of healthy cells as these unstable sugars attempt to complete themselves by robbing oxygen electrons out of healthy tissue cells. Now you begin to get an idea of what disasters lie in wait for women who follow the penchants for Western diets, Western healthcare, resulting in Western diseases. And chief among them are cancer, thrombosis and osteoporosis – all tied unimpeachably to the irresponsible expansion of the menopause-as-estrogen-deficiency mindset.

XENO-ESTROGENS IN THE ENVIRONMENT

Our petrochemically driven society, touted in the 1950s as being the future for our species, has engorged our bodies and environment with materials that mimic the activities of natural estrogens. From cling-film, polycarbonates and plasticised bottles used to store water and foodstuffs through to commercially used pesticides, insecticides, benzenes, DDT, organochlorines and organophosphates, these xeno-estrogens, as they are often known, are stored by the body in fat tissues where they become difficult to break down and remove. Environmental changes laid at the door of these chemicals include shrunken reproductive organs in animals affected, the loss of sex drive in birds and fish, and more disturbingly, the changing sex of fish found downstream of sewage treatment plants where these estrogen mimics have been ineffectively removed from the water supply prior to release.[288] On-going studies are now examining what the long-term effect on humans might be, given what is evidently occurring in the animal kingdom.

---

[288] **Archer, John** *The Water Your Drink – How Safe is it?* Pure Water Press, 1996, p.34

Naturally, these observed effects are trivialised and downplayed by the chemical industry which no doubt fears a major financial backlash if hard evidence of its involvement subsequently comes to light. Sellman reports that eagles in Florida were noted by ornithologists as far back as 1947 to have lost their sex drive and urge to mate. In the 1960s farm mink fed fish from Lake Michigan failed to mate and produce offspring. In 1977, female gulls in California were nesting with fellow females.[289]

The association between sexual changes and effects of estrogens in the environment was reported by Greenpeace, which announced: *"Exposure to hormonally active organochlorines early in life, especially in utero when hormonal feedback systems are being imprinted, can result in permanent alteration of systems that control estrogen and other sex hormones. Studies show increased rates of breast cancer among women born to mothers with indications of high estrogen levels during pregnancy. Thus the transfer of accumulated organochlorines from mother to daughter may indeed contribute to breast cancer."*[290]

SORTING THE PROBLEMS
Candida, endometriosis, thrush, fibromyalgia, certain allergies, osteoporosis, lupus, coronary spasm, Graves' Disease, thyroiditis and Sjirgren's Disease are implicated in estrogen dominance. Many occurrences of these distressing illnesses have been arrested with the introduction of natural progesterone to the suffering body. Yet the emphasis by the medical establishment is always on estrogen, serum tests conducted by physicians being interpreted by them as demonstrating a patient's estrogen deficiency. Many doctors do have serious reservations with the accuracy of such tests, since a very low level of active hormones is actually picked up by these indicators (up to 9%). The practitioner will then prescribe estrogen as he sees the need to raise the levels shown by the indicators, unaware that these dismal tests fail to detect up to 90% of active hormones in the patient's body. In fact, hormone levels cannot be pre-determined by yardsticks,

---

[289] Sellman, Sherrill, op. cit. p.56
[290] **Clorfene-Casten, Diane** *Breast Cancer, Poisons, Profits and Prevention*, Common Courage Press, Maine, 1996, pp.33-34

because of the many variables affecting hormone levels existing within the body of the female.

Further symptoms of estrogen dominance include migraines, hay fever, skin rashes, urinary tract infection, varicose veins, ectopic pregnancy and high blood pressure. Threats from these problems too have been averted by the regulation of natural progesterone in the body through the application of natural creams and lotions.

NATURAL PROGESTERONE

At the outbreak of World War 2, research into progesterone had discovered the properties of diosgenin contained in the Mexican wild yam. It was found that this substance could convert easily and inexpensively into the identical progesterone molecule used by the body. Dr John Lee, among many doctors, has been prescribing this natural substance with tremendous benefit for the female, even noting the average bone density of his patients increasing by 15% during the treatment. Lee unequivocally states that natural progesterone can alleviate many of the symptoms associated with menopause and associated complications, even allowing the patient to decrease their levels of estrogens along with diet and life-style changes to complete the transition.

Sellman too gives her seal of approval in encouraging women to consider the natural alternatives to chemical treatments for menopause: *"Supplementation with natural progesterone corrects the real problem – progesterone deficiency. It is not known to have any side-effects, nor have any toxic levels been found to date. Natural progesterone increases lop. cito, protects against fibrocystic breast disease, helps protect against and uterine cancer, maintains the lining of the uterus, hydrates and oxygenates the skin, reverses facial hair growth and thinning of the hair, acts as a natural diuretic, helps to eliminate depression and increases a sense of well-being, encourages fat burning and the use of stored energy. Even the two most prevalent menopausal symptoms, hot flashes and vaginal dryness, quickly disappear with applications of natural progesterone."*[291]

---

[291] Sellman, Sherrill, op. cit. p.86

With such a simple, natural alternative to the harsh chemical treatments so often fostered by the medical establishment today, what do women have to lose by doing their own research into this fascinating and life-changing subject? As with so many of the other subjects covered by *Health Wars*, often simple answers are so very before us and just waiting to be put into practice for a safer and more fulfilling life.

And lastly, consider the following:

> ➤ Percentage of US women who will have a hysterectomy in their lifetimes: 50%.
> ➤ Most common reason for hysterectomy – fibroids.
> ➤ Second most common reason for hysterectomy in the US – endometriosis
> ➤ Number of women with fibroids or endometriosis who are relieved of pain and heavy bleeding within three months of adopting a low-fat, high-fibre organic diet – the vast majority
> ➤ Percentage of American physicians who recommend dietary changes for fibroids and endometriosis – < 1% [292]
> ➤ Most widely prescribed drug in the US in 1992 – Premarin (used as 'estrogen replacement therapy').
> ➤ Primary reasons prescribed – hot flushes, osteoporosis and heart disease
> ➤ Percentage of women who obtained complete relief from hot flushes by taking 200mg of vitamin C and 200mg of bioflavanoids 6 times a day - 67%
> ➤ Percentage of menopausal women who obtained relief from hot flushes by taking two herbal capsules three times a day for three months in a double-blind, placebo-controlled study - 100%
> ➤ Percentage of US physicians discussing natural approaches with their menopausal patients - 2% [293]

[292] **West, Stanley** *The Hysterectomy Hoax*, Doubleday, New York: 1994, p.1,23
[293] *Pharmacy Times*, April 1993; **DeMarco, Caroline** *Take Charge of Your Body*, Winlaw, BC: 1994; **Hudson et al**, "A Pilot Study Using Botanical Medicines in the Treatment of Menopause Symptoms", Townsend Letter, 1994

The Pain in Your Arm

An Overview of the Question of Immunisation

"The whole aim of practical politics is to keep the populace alarmed - and hence clamorous to be led to safety - by menacing it with an endless series of hobgoblins, all of them imaginary." – H L Mencken

"I wish we had known sooner what an awful thing vaccination is," wrote Mrs A Kyles, in a letter to the editor of the *St. Louis Times,* in November 1926. Mrs Kyles was a grieving mother whose boy had recently died of lockjaw following vaccination. He was vaccinated on 15th October, lockjaw (tetanus) developed on 31st October, and her son died one week later on 8th November 1926.

On 7th October 1926, little Elmer Perry, four-year-old son of Mr and Mrs John Perry of Newark, New Jersey, was vaccinated by order of the United States health authorities. Fifteen days later he fell sick. He was admitted to hospital on 27th October suffering with lockjaw. A few hours later Elmer died. "They killed my boy! They killed him!" cried the horrified father.

On 20th June 1926 Geraldine Creamer, age 4, of Peekskill, New York, died of lockjaw, following vaccination during a smallpox scare – which turned out in Geraldine's case to be ivy poisoning misdiagnosed as smallpox.

Emotional scenes indeed. But over what? Just rare, freak accidents that should never have happened?

Another example of our faith in medical science can be found in immunisation. Every autumn in England, hundreds of thousands line up at the medical centres to get their flu jabs or other assorted needle cocktails. Much has been discussed about immunisation over the years, and once again, we see two extremely polarised positions on the subject. Yet it is an indication of how serious the health implications are with immunisation, that if we want to get the doorbell ringing and the royal telegram handed over, we need also to examine this subject in overview.

The use of vaccines to prevent and eradicate diseases like smallpox and tuberculosis is supposedly one of the great successes of modern medicine. But a tremendous amount of controversy has surrounded vaccinations from the start. The chief questions every parent should ask are listed below, and we will analyse them in this order. The answers to these questions and the implications thereof should convince every parent of the dangers of this practice and endue in them a firm resolve to educate others of the same.

> ➤ *Where and how did immunisation originate?*
> ➤ *How is immunisation supposed to work?*
> ➤ *What are the dangers involved with immunisation?*
> ➤ *What are my rights with immunisation?*

WHERE AND HOW DID IMMUNISATION ORIGINATE?

It is an interesting exercise to research the background to many of the practices we follow in our society today. Few however are more bizarre than the chequered history of immunisation. Dr Herbert Shelton writes:

"The practice is so mixed up with the religious superstitions of various peoples that its origin may be difficult for students of religious history to guess. In India, in Malaba and in other sections of the world, inoculation was mixed up with the worship of the smallpox goddess. Inoculation seems to have been nothing more than a superstitious rite designed to placate and appease the wrath of an irascible deity. People, who imagined all their sufferings were sent upon them because they had offended some of their gods or goddesses, originated the filthy rite to get the goddess into a good humor again." [294]

A Mr Porter, who was English Ambassador to Constantinople in 1755, explains the religious practice in his region: *"It is the tradition and opinion of the country that a certain angel presides over this disease. That it is to bespeak his favour and evidence their confidence that the Georgians take a small portion of variolous matter, and, by means of scarification, introduce it between the thumb and fore finger of a sound person. The operation is supposed never to miss its effect.*

---

[294] **Shelton, Herbert** *Vaccines and Serum Evils,* http://www.whale.to/vaccines/shelton1.html

To secure beyond all uncertainty the good will of the angel, they hang up scarlet clothes about the bed, that being the favourite colour of the celestial inhabitant they wish to propitiate." [295]

Immunisation is a term used to describe the cutting of the flesh and the introduction of foreign matter, usually diseased, into the body to give the patient immunity from disease. Quite when and where the practice originated is uncertain, although some believe it commenced in India, where so many of our superstitions were birthed, and spread from there to Africa and the West.

Dr Herbert Shelton continues: *"From time immemorial the Negroes and Arabs of Nubia practiced inoculation against smallpox. The Ashantees and the Moorish and Arab tribes in Northern Africa practiced arm-to-arm inoculation from ancient times. Savage tribes of the Upper Congo practiced it to prevent 'syphilis'. The Baris of Lado inoculated themselves over the left breast. The Negroes in Senegal inoculated their children on the arms. The Moors and Pouls of Senegambia practiced inoculation against pleuro-pneumonia. A practice of this kind was in vogue in Berne, Switzerland in the 18th century.*

The first record of smallpox seems to be in India, where also is the first record of inoculation, where the practice was in vogue over three thousand years ago. Dhanwantari, the Vedic father of medicine, and the earliest known Hindu physician, supposed to have lived around 1500 BC, is said to have been the first to practice inoculation and it is also stated that the Hindus employed a vaccine. For over a thousand years inoculation has been practiced in China." [296]

SMALLPOX AND EDWARD JENNER

The origins of inoculation in Europe appear to stem from the year 1774, when an English farmer, Benjamin Jesty, vaccinated his wife and three children with matter taken from sores on cows suffering with cowpox. He used a darning needle to cut into the flesh and transfer the pus from the sores of his diseased cows to his family. It was believed

---

[295] *Gentleman's Magazine*, October 1755
[296] Shelton Herbert, op. cit.

that those who were immune from cowpox would also be immune from the dreaded smallpox.

Notes of this bizarre experiment were taken by a doctor named Nash who subsequently died in 1785. Upon his demise, these notes passed to Mr Thomas Nash, who was acquainted with Edward Jenner, the man traditionally given the credit for having 'discovered' vaccination. In 1789 Jenner inoculated his eighteen-month-old son with pus from swinepox lesions. This experiment was followed with other inoculations of other children and vaccination thus was born (*vacca* is the Latin for 'cow').

An English writer, Arthur Wollaston Hutton MA, says of Jenner's qualifications: *"But his professional acquirements were but slender; his medical degree was the outcome of no examination or scientific work, but merely of a fee of fifteen guineas paid to the University of St. Andrews; while his other and more important distinction, his Fellowship in the Royal Society, was obtained by what even Dr Norman Moore, his latest biographer and apologist, is constrained to admit was little else than a fraud."*

Dr Joyce Marshall tells us: *"In England and Wales, free vaccination was provided for smallpox in 1840, made compulsory in 1853, and in 1867 orders were given to prosecute evaders, therefore, few escaped vaccination. Deaths from smallpox in England and Wales during 1857-59 were recorded at 14,244; in 1863-65, 20,059; and 1870-72, 44,840. Between the 1st and 2nd epidemic, there was only a 7% increase in population with an increase of smallpox deaths by 40.8%. During the 2nd and 3rd epidemic a 9% increase of population with an increase of smallpox deaths of 123% with an ever-multiplying number of vaccinations! Deaths per year from cancer in England and Wales between 1857-72 also began rapidly to increase."*[297]

In spite of the clear implications of severe contrary reactions, the fact that the vaccines were doing nothing to halt smallpox, and that the vaccinations themselves appeared to have been responsible for the very hideous explosion of disease they were designed to prevent, Edward

---

[297] Marshall, Joyce ND, Ph.D. drjhm@naturopathic-resources.com

Jenner became canonised as the saviour of the human race. Today immunisation rules supreme and has become medical and social lore to such a degree that even to question it raises the eyebrows of officialdom and even family at your presumed wretched mental predicament.

But let's look a little further and examine the claims made by medicine concerning immunisation.

HOW IS IMMUNISATION SUPPOSED TO WORK?

Immunisation is supposed to work by introducing a mild form of the microbe contaminant into the body to provoke the generation of antibodies, which will render the body immune from susceptibility to the disease. The Oxford Medical Dictionary definition of vaccination reads as follows:

"Means of producing immunity to a disease by using a vaccine or special preparation of antigenic material, to stimulate the formation of appropriate antibodies. The name was applied originally only to treatment with vaccinia (cowpox) virus." [298]

WHAT ARE THE DANGERS OF IMMUNISATION?

Dr. Joyce Marshall, who has studied the history of immunisation in great detail, explains how disease and danger have always historically dogged the practice: *"The Philippine Islands provide us with the most striking information on record that with much vaccination there is also much smallpox. Since the taking of the islands by the US, every attention had been paid to the perfecting of sanitation. But not content with this, their Public Health Service has seen to the thorough systematic vaccination of the population, adding thereto a considerable amount of serum inoculation.*

An American paper published in 1922 reported "The Philippines have experienced three smallpox epidemics since the US took over the Islands; the first in 1905-06, the second in 1907-08, and the third and worst of all in 1918-19. Before 1905 (with no general vaccination) the case-mortality was about 10%. In the 1905-06 epidemic, with vaccination well started, the case-mortality ranged from 25-50%.

---

[298] Oxford Medical Dictionary, op. cit. p.690

During the epidemic of 1918-19, with the Philippines supposedly almost universally immunized against smallpox by vaccination, the case-mortality averaged over 65%!"

These figures can be verified by reference to the Report of the Philippine Health Service. The statements are accompanied by the phrase, "The mortality is hardly explainable". To anyone but a Philippine Medical Health Commissioner, it is plainly the result of vaccination. The highest percentage of mortality, 65.3%, was in Manila, the most thoroughly vaccinated place in the Islands; the lowest percentage of mortality, 11.4%, was in Mindanao, where, owing to religious prejudices of the inhabitants, vaccination had not been practiced as much as in most other parts of the Islands. Vaccination had been forced on Mindanao since 1918 in the face of this direct proof that their people were safer without it, and with the result of a smallpox mortality increase to above 25% in 1920.

In view of the fact that sanitary engineers had probably done more in Manila to clean up the city and make it healthier than in any other part of the islands, <u>vaccination actually brought on the smallpox epidemic</u>, in spite of the sanitary measures taken to promote health. It is certain that over ten million vaccinations for smallpox were performed in the Philippines from 1905 to 1917." [299] [emphasis mine]

Closer to home, when Dr Herbert Shelton discovered that US authorities were blaming many tetanus (lockjaw) deaths on soil contamination, he challenged them to give him lockjaw by 'wounding me in a dozen places and rubbing the soil from the garden in every wound'. The US Commissioner of Health made a weak reply in the local paper, but ignored Shelton's challenge.

TETANUS AND ENCEPHALITIS

Tetanus and encephalitis have long been laid at the door of immunisation. The data on this is impressive. In 1923, 1924 and 1925 the British government spared no expense to have everybody vaccinated. Thousands of vaccinations were carried out. Immediately a

---

[299] Marshall, Joyce, op. cit.

huge increase in cases of encephalitis (lethargica) was observed.[300] In 1924, there were 6,296 cases of this illness and similar infections reported in England and Wales, with a population of 38,746,000 at the time; or 162 cases per million of population. Shelton records:

"In Liverpool, with a population of 836,000, there were reported 257 such cases; or 306 cases per million of population. Liverpool was fifty per cent better vaccinated than the average of England and Wales, <u>and had almost 100% more encephalitis</u>. In 1924 there were recorded in England and Wales 5,039 cases of encephalitis lethargica, 397 of cerebro-spinal fever, 777 acute poliomyelitis, 83 of polio-encephalitis—a total of 6,296 cases, with 2,200 deaths, 2,520 permanently injured brains (insane), and 1,575 complete recoveries. <u>The cases in 1924 were three times as great as the yearly average for the nine preceding years.</u>

In 1922-23-24 the physicians of England and Wales cooked up a number of smallpox scares, causing 288,000 revaccinations. Extra vaccination was followed by this extra crop of sleepy sickness. A case of post-vaccinal encephalitis was reported in Ireland in 1930 in a baby boy of 10 pounds. He was vaccinated on May 3 and became ill on May 10, "being cross and very restless with vomiting." Next day he was quiet and apathetic and on admission to the hospital his condition resembled tetanus.

In its report issued on 27th August 1928, the League of Nations covers 139 cases and 41 deaths in Holland. This resulted in Holland stopping compulsory vaccination during 1928-29. The total number of vaccinations in Holland in the first half of 1928 was less than one-third of those for the first half of 1927 and the deaths from encephalitis were reduced to less than one-third."[301]

US surgeon Charles Armstrong says in an article on post-vaccinal encephalitis: *"In so far as the age factor is concerned, the custom in this country of performing primary vaccinations at the sixth or seventh year would seem to predispose our population to the*

---

[300] encephalitis – *Inflammation of the brain. It may be caused by a viral or bacterial infection, or it may be part of an allergic response to a systemic viral illness or vaccination.* – Oxford Medical Dictionary, op. cit. p.213
[301] Shelton Herbert, op. cit.

complication. Cases have, moreover, occurred. Wilson and Ford, and Fulgham and Beykirk have reported 3 cases in this country which were confirmed by pathological studies. Other possible cases based on clinical and epidemiological grounds have been reported from Connecticut, Rhode Island, New York, Maryland, Illinois, California, Washington and the District of Columbia." [302]

'VACCINIA'

...was the name given to 'disease by vaccination', and also to cowpox. It is interesting to examine the pathology of this very common complaint:

Symptoms: Vaccinia begins after inoculation with slight *irritation* at the site of vaccination. On the third or fourth day the *eruption* appears in the form of a red papule, surrounded by a red areola. On the fifth or sixth day the papule becomes a vesicle, being filled with a watery substance or a clear substance, with a distinct central depression (umbilication).

By the eighth day the vesicle is perfected and is then surrounded by a wide reddened zone of *inflammatory edema,* which is the seat of *intense itching.* By the tenth day the contents are purulent (pus) and the vesicle has become a *pustule.* The surrounding skin is now much *inflamed* and *painful.* About this time the reddened areola begins to fade and *desiccation* sets in with the gradual formation of a thick brown *crust* or *scab,* which becomes detached and falls off about the twenty-first to twenty-fifth day, leaving an ugly *scar.*

The scar is at first red but gradually becomes paler than the surrounding skin having a *punched-out* appearance and is *pitted.* The evolution of this pathology is accompanied with *fever* and *constitutional symptoms, malaise,* and *enlargement of the adjacent lymph nodes or glands.*[303]

---

302 *Public Health Reports*, 23rd August 1929
303 Shelton, Herbert, op. cit.

WHOOPING COUGH

Whooping cough has also been a potentially lucrative market for vaccine manufacturers. However, the same problems also dogged the vaccine developers in the case of this 'disease':

SECRET TRIALS THAT CRIPPLED 55 BABIES
by Lucy Johnston

"Fifty-five babies died or were permanently brain-damaged during secret government trials to test a new vaccine for whooping cough, the Daily Express can reveal. The trials were conducted on thousands of pre-school children even though the drug was at a highly experimental stage.

Nobody told the parents that their babies could be at risk from the tests which also caused convulsions, and permanent disablement. Olivia Price from the Vaccine Victims Support Group said families now need proper compensation to help care for their loved ones.

She added: "This is unforgivable. The Government knew damage could be done - anyone with a baby should have the freedom of choice to decide whether or not they wanted their child to risk this. The fact that these parents were not told anything and their children were left so damaged is nothing short of abuse."

The trials, based in London, Bradford, Newcastle and Liverpool, were carried out by the Medical Research Council between 1948 and 1956. The victims are now in their 40s and 50s and still need round-the-clock care." [304]

MODERN IMMUNISATION PROGRAMS

Today immunisation is colossal business. There is hardly an illness that does not scare the pants off the public to the extent that they will sign on for just about any immunisation program for themselves and their newborn children. But in the Third World, a more sinister program has been underway. In one of the opening chapters of this book, and also in *World Without AIDS*, we have quoted industry's abuse of drug prescription, immunisation and 'aid distribution' in the

---

[304] *Daily Express*, 26th May 2000

developing nations and how these widespread and government-sanctioned programs are causing appalling attrition among the targeted populations. While none of us wishes to consider humanity's greed and desire for control at its worst, in summarily denying that such agendas are planned and underway, we choose to ignore the clear, unequivocal body of evidence.

'THE VACCINE AGAINST PREGNANCY'

On 21st January 1995, Sister Mary Pilar Verzosa RGS, of Pro-Life Philippines, Pandacan, Manila, wrote a letter to Judi Brown, President of the American Life League. The letter contained an alarm, which has since been sounded across the globe. Part of this letter reads as follows:

"At present we are doing research on the tetanus vaccines that were given last March 1994 by our Dept of Health to women of reproductive age. Many of the women complained of bleeding (miscarriages) and allergies. We got alarmed recently when we received communications from Magally Llaguno that the vaccine in Mexico contained hCG... if you have enough [research] papers, could your group do a press release via international press like Reuters so that all countries could be alerted?"[305]

The substance in question found in the vaccine was human Chorionic Gonadotrophin. Professional pharmacologist Judith Richter writes thus: *"hCG is released by the fertilised egg cell soon after fertilisation and continues to be produced by the placenta. It stimulates the corpus luteum in the ovary to continue to produce progesterone."*[306]

From this, most would be led to believe that the presence of hCG in a tetanus vaccine would actually have a beneficial effect on the overall health of the female recipient. However, such hCG is not that of a pregnant woman's own embryo and actually causes antibodies to be created that see the embryo or foetus as a foreign body and repel it through miscarriage. Thus hCG acts as a chemical abortion agent, and in the case of it being given to girls of reproductive age who are not

---

[305] Personal correspondence of the American Life League

[306] **Richter, Judith** *"Vaccination Against Pregnancy: Miracle or Menace?"* Catholic Family News, June 1995. In an earlier chapter we covered the role of the corpus luteum in becoming the primary production site for progesterone during the second half of the menstrual cycle.

pregnant, hCG likewise causes prevention of all fertilisations and therefore acts as a sterilising agent. Additionally, according to medical researchers Dr Judith Richter, Dr George Isajiuw and Robert Whelan[307], hCG suppresses the immune system and in certain cases may cause the onset of opportunistic diseases if malnutrition and mineral depletion are also in evidence.

Sister Pilar wrote a second letter three months later on 16th April 1995: *"We are in the midst of a court battle regarding the anti-tetanus vaccines used in the mass immunization of women of reproductive age.[308] The vials we tested proved positive for beta-hCG, while the women had antibodies against beta-hCG. This means their blood had built up antibodies against pregnancy. The women we tested had miscarriages, stillbirth or premature births. The government has all its forces against us - media is on their side and we don't know how the judge will turn..."*

Johns Hopkins University, long a major player in the field of eugenics[309], produced a report that as of 1990, 123 million women in developing countries had been surgically sterilised. Further, JHU was also under contract to the US Agency For International Development, according to the article *'Coming Attractions: Phantom Sterilizations'*,[310] which also cites a report prepared by the University on a proposed sterilisation program by vaccine.[311]

---

[307] **Whelan, Robert K** "Whose Choice: Population Controllers or Yours", *Human Life*, 1992 ISBN 0946680426. Robert Whelan's book cites India, *"which in 1952 became the proving ground for every technique for population control."* Referring to a 1992 British documentary, *Something Like War*, Whelan comments on the inexperience of many doctors hired to do sterilisations, who botched them, producing 4,000-5,000 ectopic pregnancies, many of which in rural areas resulted in the patient's death.

[308] Interesting that this mass immunisation program was only for women of reproductive age.

[309] Eugenics is the study of how to improve a race by judicious mating and/or destroying the undesirable genetic stock of the subject race. This racist philosophy was to reach a tragic climax with SS leader Heinrich Himmler's sanctioned eugenics program under Dr Ernst Rüdin and Josef Mengele in Auschwitz concentration camp during World War 2. Eugenic philosophies were not the sole prerogative of the Nazis however. Many British and American politicians, steeped in Darwinian evolution espousing 'survival of the fittest' sentiments, were active during the late 19th and early 20th centuries in supporting the idea of racially purifying human stock and doing away with the 'useless eaters'. For more information on this, please see **Day, Phillip** *The Mind Game*, Credence Publications, 2002

[310] *Coming Attractions: Phantom Sterilizations,* Baobab Press, Vol 3, #23, 1993

[311] For a fuller treatment of Third World population control policies applied by Western governments, please see *World Without AIDS*, available through Credence Publications

That these programs are also underway in our own industrial societies is all the more poignant and alarming when the human face of suffering is imprinted over the antiseptic starkness of the facts:

SUDDEN INFANT DEATH SYNDROME (SIDS)

The following excerpt comes from a statement made by a distraught grandmother testifying before the Committee on Labor and Human Resources (USA), regarding vaccination injury compensation:

"My name is Donna Gary. I am a constituent of Senator [Edward] *Kennedy's from Massachusetts. Our family should have celebrated our very first granddaughter's first birthday last month. Instead we will commemorate the anniversary of her death at the end of this month.*

Our granddaughter, Lee Ann, was just eight weeks old when her mother took her to the doctor for her routine check-up. This included of course her first DPT inoculation and oral polio vaccine. In all her entire eight weeks of life, this loveable, extremely alert baby had never produced such a blood-curdling scream as she did at the moment the shot was given. Neither had her mother ever before seen her back arch as it did while she screamed. She was inconsolable. Even her daddy could not understand Lee Ann's uncharacteristic screaming and crying.

Four hours later, Lee Ann was dead. "Crib Death," the doctors said. "SIDS" (Sudden Infant Death Syndrome). "Could it be connected to the shot?" her parents implored. "No." "But she just had her first DPT shot this afternoon. Could there possibly be a connection to it?" "No. No connection at all," the emergency room doctor had told them definitely.

"In the months before Lee Ann was born, I regularly checked with a friend as to the state of her grandchild's condition. He is nearly a year and a half older than Lee Ann. On his first DPT shot, he passed out cold for fifteen minutes, right in the paediatrician's office. "Normal reaction for some children," the paediatrician reassured. The parents were scared but knew what a fine doctor they had. They trusted his judgment.

When it was time for the second shot, they asked, "Are you sure it's all right?" Their paediatrician again reassured them. He told them how awful it was to experience, as he had, one of his infant patient's bout with whooping cough. That baby had died.

They gave him the second shot that day. He became brain-damaged."

In 1975, when Japan raised the age to receive vaccinations from 2 months to 2 years, the incidence of cot death (SIDS) virtually disappeared in that country.[312] In 1991, the Institute of Medicine released a report documenting a causal relationship between the rubella vaccine and acute arthritis in adult women. During that same year, links were found between this same vaccine and chronic fatigue syndrome. In 1992, the World Health Organization came under pressure and suspended use of a new measles vaccine when it was found that children in Third World countries had an increased risk of dying from other diseases in the years following administration of this vaccine, due to a suppressed immune system.

WHAT IS MY RIGHT WITH IMMUNISATION?
Each member of the public must investigate the question of immunisation thoroughly. This is so his undoubted later position *against* immunisation in all its forms can be maintained on the basis of facts and not the prevailing perceived wisdom of the highly profitable immunisation industry and its associated coercion and terrorism of the public.

Often mothers and fathers are put in extreme positions of coercion, the doctor or relative saying, "Well, Mrs Hawkins, if you do not get young Peter vaccinated, and he gets meningitis, on your head be it." Not having your child immunised because of concerns for safety is enough in some countries to have the parents put on a 'bad parents' register and their child denied access to schools and education ("Because your non-immunised child could cause other children to become ill and die, Mrs Hawkins.")

---

312 Scheibner, Viera, op. cit. p.49

On the 15ᵗʰ February 2001, US media network NBC aired an episode of the popular medical soap 'ER'. The television drama contained a storyline about a family who chose not to vaccinate their children, and one of the children contracts measles and dies from complications while the doctors on the show lash out at the mother and categorically deny any risks posed by the vaccine. The show provoked a rash of angry reactions from citizens, not least from the parents of those children who had been maimed or killed by adverse vaccination reactions. Leading vaccine critic Dr Joseph Mercola thinks there are other related storylines NBC might be interested in following up:

1. *Serious adverse reactions to vaccines (I have a Microsoft Excel data base of 25,000 adverse reactions to hepatitis B vaccine from the FDA and CDC Vaccine Adverse Event Reporting System, VAERS, available on request).*

2. *The money trail: state agencies or school districts that get money for forcing children to receive vaccines, and conflicts of interest that compromise the "experts" who testify for mandates.*

3. *CDC stonewalling on requests for safety data on hepatitis B and other vaccines.*

4. *Parents or other caregivers jailed for murder when their babies die, possibly from a vaccine reaction, when there is no direct evidence that they ever abused the child in any way. (Was a vaccine history taken in the English nanny case, by the way?)*

5. *Parents whose children are excluded from school and reported to Child Protective Services because they have exercised a legal and conscientious objection to a mandated vaccine (even against a disease such as hepatitis B that is very rare in children and not ordinarily transmitted in a school setting).*[313]

In the case of 'AIDS' of course, the dastardliness knows no bounds, as the pharmaceutical industry smacks its lips at the thought of immunising millions of 'vulnerable' Africans, Asians, Indonesians and Latin Americans from a range of diseases, not caused by any 'HIV', but because of poor sanitary conditions and malnutrition, bringing on cholera, dysentery, malaria and tuberculosis.

---

[313] www.mercola.com

Professor of the Athenian Faculty of Medicine, Leon Grigorski puts it this way: *"We are ourselves creating the diseases, and we are heading toward general cancerization and mental defectives through encephalitis, by the use of vaccines."* [314]

In Joyce Marshall's view: *"Upon limiting access to information the medical-industrial complex is able to maintain its authority mystique. Isolation is a well-known technique of brainwashing. Choices that challenge the position of the authority are limited and often times hidden. Because the intellect learns by comparison, when it is presented with only one point of view or other points of view are denigrated, it loses its capacity to discriminate and ultimately its capacity for fully rational thought."* [315]

Parents *do* have a choice, but often capitulate in the face of organised establishment outrage. Decades ago, the unsinkable Herbert Shelton was abrupt and dismissive of the public's continued flirtation with immunisation. With the fury felt by many of his day on the subject, Shelton sums up that *"...this criminal practice will end as soon as parents develop sufficient interest in the welfare of their children. At present parents offer up their children on the altars of the* [vaccination] *goddess, because commercial ghouls demand it, and hope that the children will not be greatly injured. If a child is invalided for life or is killed, the parents meekly accept the lying excuses of the scoundrels who maim and murder children for money, cry a little, and return to their movies and joy rides. Reader, do you know how Judas felt after he had sold his master for a few pieces of silver? If you have surrendered your child to be vaccinated and inoculated, after you learned the truth, you know how he felt. There is one great difference between you and him - Judas had decency enough to go out and hang himself."* [316]

To be fair, many parents wish to avoid immunisation for their children, but nevertheless go through with it to avoid the persecution that inevitably follows. Medical community and friends and family

[314] www.mercola.com
[315] Marshall, Joyce, op. cit.
[316] Shelton Herbert, op. cit.

alike make it very hard on mothers and fathers who declare that they do not want to immunise their children 'for the child's sake'. However today pressure groups have formed, to which dissenters may join, receiving a measure of comfort and security in the knowledge that, despite the trials, they made a correct and caring decision. The following piece comes from the Irish Republic:

MMR - WHY DO SOME IRISH PARENTS REFUSE TO HAVE THEIR CHILDREN VACCINATED?

Kathryn Holmquist looks at the growing resistance to immunisation: "Many of the parents who refuse to have their children vaccinated are informed, articulate and independent thinkers with a suspicion of the medical establishment. They do not want the State to dictate to them in the important matter of their children's health.

The State wants 95 per cent of children to be immunised against measles, but the growing anti-vaccination movement is going to make that near-impossible. In Britain, avid campaigners include the Allergy Induced Autism Group, Jabs, the Informed Parent Group and the International Vaccination Newsletter.

In the US, where vaccination is mandatory for school enrolment, websites disseminate information from vaccine dissenters. The Informed Parents Vaccination homepage claims that the US Food and Drug Administration's Vaccine Adverse Effects Reporting System receives about 11,000 reports of serious adverse reactions to vaccination annually, some one per cent (112 cases) of which are deaths from vaccine reactions. It alleges that "both national and international studies have shown vaccination to be a cause of sudden infant death syndrome (SIDS)". In the Republic, the Informed Immunisation Network was set up by parents who believe that they have a right to be fully informed about the pros and cons of vaccination. The network argues that the Department of Health gives only one point of view, in favour of vaccination, when it should be presenting a balanced picture.

"I am not an extremist but, based on the information I have, I am happy with my decision not to have my children immunised," says Anne Dunne, a member of the network." [317]

And in the United States:

HOUSE DEBATES VACCINE SAFETY 5th August 1999: *"We can no longer keep our heads buried in the sand like an ostrich pretending there is no problem," said Rep. Dan Burton, as he waved a sheath of documents he said showed thousands of casualties over the last year.* [318]

DOCTORS DO NOT PROPERLY EXPLAIN SIDE-EFFECTS RISKS PRIOR TO GIVING VACCINATIONS - *40% of US physicians did not mention risks of the vaccines they were administering, and 90% did not mention the National Vaccine Injury Compensation Program, according to a 2001 survey.* [319]

LEADING AMERICAN NUTRITIONIST SPEAKS OUT AGAINST MEASLES, MUMPS AND RUBELLA (MMR) VACCINE - Dr Joseph Mercola states: *"Children do NOT get sick and die from some bad, scary virus unless they have some predisposing factors. The major ones would be eating sugar and drinking soda and juice instead of water.*

I am absolutely certain that IF ANY child dies in the US from measles complications there are many more children who die from the disease who WERE vaccinated.

It is true that measles can be fatal. Perhaps 1 in 1,000 children who gets measles has complications, occasionally resulting in death. Measles is very rare these days, but vaccinated children can get it too. Of cases reported in Colorado between 1987 and 1998 (time interval probably chosen to include the epidemic of 1989-90), 45 were in "exemptors," but 137 were in vaccinated children (see JAMA of

---

[317] *Irish Times*, 30th August 1999
[318] *Salon Health and Body*. Vaccine Debate. www.salon.com
[319] *Pediatrics*, February 2001; 107(2):E17

12/27/00). In most cases, the source of the infection was not known or stated, but it was probably not indigenous to the U.S." [320]

And a remarkably candid front-page headline in the UK's *Mail on Sunday* reads as follows:

MEASLES JAB: NEW LINK TO BRAIN DAMAGE - *A Professor O'Leary, Director of Pathology at Coombe Women's Hospital in Dublin, provides compelling evidence of an association between infection by the measles virus and autism in children, many of whose parents said they developed the condition after they had been injected with Measles Mumps Rubella vaccine or MMR....* [321]

While the *Sunday Times* reports:

MORE MMR GRIEF IN BRITAIN - *One third of the members of a British government committee that has advised that the MMR vaccine against measles, mumps and rubella is safe have financial interests in drug companies that make the treatment.*

Twelve of the 36 members of the British Committee on Safety of Medicines have financial links with the MMR manufacturers, whose products they have given the all-clear on the basis of published research. Most members are academics or medical experts who specialize in pharmacology.

Five of them hold shares in the drug companies, or are paid consultants, while another seven have received grants or sponsorship from them to fund academic studies or clinical trials.

All members declare their financial interests in a register and before meetings. The chairman then decides whether they can participate in discussions.

Campaigners against the MMR vaccine, who fear it causes autism or bowel disease in children, claim the financial links between

---

[320] www.mercola.com
[321] *Mail on Sunday*, 9th April 2000

drug watchdogs and the pharmaceutical industry could lead to a conflict of interest.

While the government and most of the medical establishment argue that the vaccine is safe, research by Dr Andrew Wakefield, of the Royal Free Hospital, London, claimed the trials leading to the MMR vaccine's adoption in Britain were too brief to detect the feared complications. [322]

And in Japan:

WHY JAPAN BANNED MMR VACCINE - *Japan stopped using the MMR vaccine seven years ago. Japan is virtually the only developed nation to turn its back on the vaccine. Government health chiefs claim a four-year experiment with it has had serious financial and human costs.*

Of the 3,969 medical compensation claims relating to vaccines in the last 30 years, a quarter had been made by those badly affected by the combined measles, mumps and rubella vaccine, they say.

The MMR was banned in Japan in 1993 after 1.8 million children had been given two types of MMR and a record number developed non-viral meningitis and other adverse reactions were recorded. [323]

BUT WASN'T THE MMR VACCINE TESTED?

PROMINENT SCIENTISTS ASSERT MMR VACCINE SHOULD NOT HAVE BEEN LICENSED IN THE UK - *According to The London Sunday Herald, many prominent British researchers are now convinced that the controversial MMR shot should never have been licensed in the UK.*

This shocking assertion is to be made in an upcoming report to be published in the journal Adverse Drug Reactions, the paper reports.[324] *This is of course assuming that UK health officials are not successful*

---

[322] *Sunday Times*, 28th January 2001

[323] Female.co.uk, 6th February 2001

[324] *Adverse Drug Reactions*, November 2000, vol.19, #4

at preventing the publisher from printing the article, as they have reportedly attempted to do.

Several senior clinicians, including a former senior professional medical officer at the UK Department of Health, argue that the MMR should not have been licensed back in 1988 because there was insufficient evidence of its safety and the decision to license it was 'premature'. [325]

Dr Peter Fletcher, who was a senior professional medical officer for the UK Department of Health in the early 1980s, concurs with much of the criticism of MMR:

"Being extremely generous, evidence on safety was very thin, being realistic there were too few patients followed-up for sufficient time. Three weeks is not enough, neither is four weeks. On the basis that effective monovalent vaccines were available, the Committee on the Safety of Medicines could be confident that delay in granting a license would not result in a catastrophic epidemic of measles, mumps and rubella.

Caution should have ruled the day, answers to some important questions should have been demanded and encouragement should have been given to conduct a 12-month observational study on 10-15,000 patients and a prospective monitoring program set up with a computerized primary care database. The granting of a product license was definitely premature." [326]

The *Sunday Herald* reports that someone from the Adverse Drug Reactions journal said:

"All the reviewers conclude that something needs to be done about MMR and that there is a case to answer against the vaccine. The first thing this paper says is that the MMR vaccine should not have been licensed. There was not enough evidence of the safety to license it. The view is that the evidence was inadequate."

---

[325] *Sunday Herald*, 10th & 17th December 2000; www.mercola.com
[326] *Sunday Herald*, op. cit.

Dr John Griffin, editor of the *Adverse Drug Reactions* journal, is irate over a letter he received from a government health official, which he says tried to put him under pressure not to publish the potentially damaging MMR paper:

"I think this is an attempt to put pressure on me not to publish the article and I resent that. We are going to publish the article. We are not going to be deterred by threats. I think putting pressure on us not to publish is despicable." [327]

KNOW THE VACCINE'S CONTENTS

The plain fact is, vaccines kill and maim regularly, yet very little is publicly known about vaccine methodology or the substance of what is actually being injected into the human system during the inoculation. This is not altogether unsurprising. In the above case for example, Professor O'Leary was immediately instructed by his employers not to give any further information to the press.[328]

Hepatitis B vaccine contains mercury (thimerosal), aluminium and formaldehyde. The pertussus or whooping cough vaccine contains the same ingredients. Other components found in common vaccines include parts of aborted foetuses, dog and monkey kidneys, ethyl-glycol and carbolic acid (a full list of these fillers is contained in the end section of this book). These vaccines are then grown and strained through cultures. Cultures include monkey kidney, chicken embryo, embryonic guinea-pig cells and, in the case of rubella, Hepatitis A and chicken pox, dissected organs of aborted foetuses. Says one concerned vaccine researcher, *"Would you mix this and feed it to your child from a bottle? Yet the government requires it to be injected with a syringe directly into our children's bodies."* [329]

To date, the US National Vaccine Injury Compensation Program or NVICP, established in 1986, has paid out in excess of $1 billion in injury awards to Western vaccine-recipients. And there are quite literally thousands of cases pending. This despite the fact that the

---

[327] *Sunday Herald*, op. cit.

[328] *Mail on Sunday*, op. cit.

[329] Global Vaccine Awareness League. Toxic Chemicals in Vaccines. GVAL homepage. For a fuller list of potentially harmful vaccine components, please see section entitled *Vaccine Fillers*.

Health and Human Services Secretary Donna Shalala narrowed the definition of vaccine damage to such an extent that only immediate and severe reactions can now qualify. Seizures, disorders, brain damage, ataxia, paralysis, learning difficulties and deaths that occur many days or weeks following these vaccinations are now excluded. Added to this, doctors have little incentive to report themselves to the government's Vaccine Adverse Event Reporting System or VAERS, prompting former director of the FDA David Kessler to confess that *"...only 10% of vaccine injuries are ever reported."* [330] Lisa Jillani, of People Advocating Vaccine Education, has observed the growing number of children now suffering from 20th century behavioural disorders, and reports:

"So the injuries can even conservatively amount to tens of thousands of children, while doctors continue to diagnose and treat mysterious new illnesses and maintain the 'one in a million' adverse reaction myth taught in medical schools." [331]

A front-page article appeared in the UK *Sunday Observer*, dated 27th August 2000. *The Observer* obtained documents revealing that the UK government had attempted to cover up 11 deaths of children as a result of receiving the meningitis vaccine. The document also revealed that more than 16,000 adverse reactions to the meningitis jab had been reported by GPs, since the nationwide campaign began last year. With the UK Department of Health admitting that only between 10 and 15 percent of adverse reactions are reported, the actual number of children damaged as a result of this vaccine is probably far higher.

Notwithstanding the billions being made every year by the vaccine industry in the face of such damaging effects of their products, opposition to the mandatory use of vaccines is mounting, not least because *there has never been any impartial and empirical evidence that demonstrates even remotely that immunisation does any good whatsoever.* But in the short-term, while the political chess-game is played out, there is much we can do to avoid the misery and pitfalls of this errant arm of medicine. We can read up on the subject using the

---

[330] *Dayton Daily News*, 25th May 1993

[331] Boykin, Sam *A Shot in the Dark*, 1998 www.creativeloafing.com

many commendable books and organisations available. Then we can come to our own informed decision based on all the evidence.

This is a course of action tragically not followed by those heartbroken families who have had to endure so much, falsely secure in the lie that the immunisation system was there to improve their loved ones' health. We can avoid these mistakes.

"TRADE SECRETS":
THE LATEST IN A LONG LINE OF
CONSPIRACIES CHARGES

Press release – www.preventcancer.com
SAMUEL S. EPSTEIN, M.D.

Bill Moyers is to be warmly commended for his March 26 program "Trade Secrets". This PBS[332] Special will document the chemical industry's conspiracy in denying information on the grave cancer risks to hundreds of thousands of workers manufacturing the potent carcinogen vinyl chloride (VC) and its polyvinyl chloride (PVC) product.

As newsworthy is the fact that there is a decades-long track record of numerous such conspiracies involving a wide range of industries and chemicals, besides VC. These conspiracies have resulted in an escalation in the incidence and mortality of cancer, and chronic disease, among workers and the general public unknowingly exposed to toxics and carcinogens in the workplace, air, water and consumer products - food, household products, and cosmetics and toiletries.

This misconduct involves negligence, manipulation, suppression, distortion and destruction of health and environmental data by mainstream industries, their consultants and trade associations, notably the Chemical Manufacturers Association (CMA). These practices are so frequent as to preclude dismissal as exceptional aberrations and, in many instances, arguably rise to the level of criminality as illustrated below:

· Suppression of evidence from the early 1960's on the toxicity of VC by Dow Chemical, and on its carcinogenicity from 1970 by the VC/PVC industry and the CMA. Based on these findings, a blue ribbon

---

[332] American public broadcasting service

committee of the American Association for the Advancement of Science charged in 1976 that: "Because of the suppression of these data (by the CMA), tens of thousands of workers were exposed without warning - to toxic concentrations of VC".

· Suppression of evidence since the 1930's on the hazards of asbestos, asbestosis and lung cancer, by Johns-Manville and Raybestos-Manhattan, besides the Metropolitan Life Insurance Company. This information was detailed in industry documents dubbed the "Asbestos Pentagon Papers", released at 1978 Congressional Hearings.

· Suppression by Rohm and Haas of information, known since 1962 but not released until 1971, on the potent carcinogenicity of the resin bischloromethylether. This resulted in deaths from lung cancer of some 50 men, many non-smokers and under the age of 50.

· Suppression of carcinogenicity data on organochlorine pesticides: Aldrin/Dieldrin, by Shell Chemical Company since 1962; Chlordane/Heptachlor, by Velsicol Chemical Company since 1959; and Kepone, by Allied Chemical Company since the early 1960's.

· Falsification in the early 1970's of test data on the drug Aldactone and artificial sweetener aspartame by Hazleton Laboratories under contract to G.D. Searle Company.

· Falsification and manipulation by Monsanto since the 1960's of data on dioxin, and its contamination of products including the herbicide Agent Orange, designed to block occupational exposure claims and tightening of federal regulations. This evidence was detailed in 1990 by Environmental Protection Agency's Office of Criminal Investigation which charged Monsanto with a "long pattern of fraud" and with reporting "false information" to the Agency.

· Fraudulent claims by Monsanto since 1985 that genetically engineered (rBGH) milk is indistinguishable from natural milk. These claims persist despite contrary evidence.

· Monsanto's reckless marketing in 1976 of plastic Coke bottles made from acrylonitrile, a chemical closely related to VC, prior to its testing for carcinogenicity and migration into the Coke. The bottles were subsequently banned after acrylonitrile was found to be a potent carcinogen contaminating the Coke.

· Destruction of epidemiological data on ethyleneimine and other chemicals by Dow and DuPont. This was admitted at 1973 Department of Labor Advisory Committee meetings in response to challenges to produce data on whose basis industry had falsely claimed that these chemicals were not carcinogens.

· Destruction of test data on drugs, food additives, and pesticides as admitted in 1977 by Industrial Biotest Laboratories, under contract to major chemical industries.

· Failure of the mainstream cosmetics and toiletry industries to warn of the wide range of avoidable carcinogenic ingredients, contaminants and precursors in their products used by the great majority of the U.S. population over virtually their lifetimes.

(For supporting documentation of the above charges, see Dr Epstein's: Testimony on White Collar Crime, H.R. 4973, before the Subcommittee on Crime of the House Judiciary Committee, 12/13/79; The Politics of Cancer, 1979; and The Politics of Cancer, Revisited, 1998.)

Hopefully, the public and the media will be outraged by this longstanding evidence of recklessness and conspiracies, graphically reinforced by Moyers' program. The public and the media should finally hold industry accountable, and demand urgent investigation and radical reform of current industry practices besides governmental unresponsiveness. The Moyers' program has already galvanized formation of a coalition of grassroots citizen groups, "Coming Clean", to demand more responsible and open industry practices, including phasing out the use and manufacture of toxic chemicals.

Criticism should also be directed to the multibillion dollar cancer establishment - the National Cancer Institute and American Cancer Society - for their failure to warn Congress, regulatory agencies and the general public of the scientific evidence on the permeation of the totality of the environment with often persistent industrial carcinogens thus precluding corrective legislation and regulation, besides denying workers and the public of their inalienable right-to-know.

NOTE: PRNewswire, the nation's largest newswire service, which has released Cancer Prevention Coalition's numerous press releases for the last five years, refused to issue this release on 'legal grounds'.

DATE   March 23, 2001

SOURCE   Cancer Prevention Coalition

CONTACT: Samuel S. Epstein, M.D., Chairman of the Cancer Prevention Coalition and Professor environmental and occupational medicine, University of Illinois School of Public Health, Chicago, 312-996-2297;epstein@uic.edu; http://www.preventcancer.com

* * * *

EXAMINING BIG FOOD, BIG MEDICINE AND BIG CHEMICALS

And so another salvo is levelled against the chemical industry by world-renowned toxicologist Dr Samuel Epstein. The virulence of Epstein's attack is now being taken up by former sceptics around the world who are waking up to the pressing dangers our technological society is posing - dangers always trivialised by the manufacturers themselves who, with seeming impunity, pour thousands of new chemicals onto the commercial markets without adequate safeguards in place to advise the public of potential long-term health risks.

Environmental contaminants are one of the leading causes of chronic ill-health and death. Remember that 90-95% of the diseases killing us are metabolic and/or toxin-related and toxin-related diseases, including the newly diagnosed Multiple Chemical Sensitivity, are absolutely on the rise. In dealing with environmental contaminants, the first place we have to start examining is our own personal environment at home. And where do we go to stock our own environment? THE SUPERMARKET!

'Fresh'. This word is used in a variety of different ways, sometimes in combination with another word. Examples drawn to our attention are 'dew fresh', 'farm fresh', freshly harvested', 'garden

fresh', 'kitchen fresh', 'ocean fresh', 'oven fresh', 'sea fresh', 'sun fresh'. Whilst these phrases are intended to have an emotive effect, they have no real meaning.

UK Ministry of Agriculture, Foods and Fisheries (MAFF)
Food Standards Committee Second Report
On Claims and Misleading Descriptions, 1980

We have three industries stalking us for our dollars and pounds at the expense of our health and they are all found down at your local food-mart. They are BIG FOOD, BIG MEDICINE and BIG CHEMICALS. We've looked at the harrowing effects of Big Medicine as we've been progressing, but we have more on this colossal industry yet to come. This chapter is an overview of how these three industries interact and often take on each other's roles to produce massive profits for themselves, and chronic disease, ill-health and death for the unwary consumer. For instance, we have chemical medicines and chemical foods that produce a number of physiological reactions over both the long- and short-term, resulting in disease. But here's the thing – most members of the public honestly do not consider how their food is making them sick. The public has been taught how to trivialise the effects of Big Food, Big Medicine and Big Chemicals on their health through the comfort and non-threatening familiarity of the local supermarket where these products are made available. A concerned "You know those cheeseburgers are going to kill you..." is invariably met with a wry "Everything will eventually *kill* you, Bob." Yet the supermarket is where the death warrant is written for most of us, plus sales tax, of course.

Manchester Polytechnic's Food Policy Unit studied the dietary habits of a cross-section of low-income British citizens and produced their infamous *Jam Tomorrow?* report in 1984:

Meals of a 76-year-old Manchester man.
BREAKFAST: Corn flakes, sugar, milk, two slices white toast, butter, marmalade, cup of tea, sugar, milk
MID-MORNING: Cup of tea, sugar, milk
LUNCH: Heinz vegetable soup, cup of tea, sugar, milk, two digestive biscuits
AFTERNOON: Cup of tea, sugar, milk
EVENING: Fish fingers, peas, mash potatoes, cup cake, cup of tea, sugar, milk

BED-TIME: Horlicks, sugar

Meals of a two-year-old child from West Glamorgan, Wales
BREAKFAST: Cornflakes, milk, cup of tea
MID-MORNING: Cadbury Creme Egg, Milky Bar
LUNCH: Baked potato, slice white bread, butter
AFTERNOON: Ice cream, two slices Angel Cake, two digestive biscuits
EVENING: Chips (fries), two slices white bread and butter, cup of coffee

Meals of a 37-year-old unemployed man with a wife and two children
BREAKFAST: Cup of tea, sugar, milk
MID-MORNING: Two custard cream biscuits, cup of tea, sugar, milk
LUNCH: Nothing
AFTERNOON: Egg, chips, peas, two slices white bread, margarine, cup of tea, sugar, milk
EVENING: Cup of tea, sugar, milk
BED-TIME: Crisps, cup of tea, sugar, milk

Britain has been justifiably slammed for its appalling diet. Many citizens think this is grossly unfair, because we also sport a number of top chefs and culinary establishments. The point is, just because the furs are on the national cat-walk under the hot spotlights and popping flashbulbs, does not mean the average Joe is draped in ermine. As the above sample diets show, low-income Brits are having a tough time with a classic 'troubled interaction with nourishment' that is literally killing them.

Britain has had two things working against her from the start, not suffered by other countries around the world. She was the first industrialised nation. Suddenly, a tremendous shift in production went from the land and agriculture into the cities. In the 1800s, Britain became a world empire, controlling over a quarter of the globe – her unlikely rise to power due to her powerful army and navy, her massive new industrial output and ingenious innovation. Britain became the world centre for commercially produced sugar, biscuits and confectionary and the burgeoning companies overseeing this tremendous output were ever keen on the bottom line. Their work forces were fed the cheap, easily available diets predominant in the products they produced: lard, sugar, refined white bread and flour and salted meat. By the end of the 1800s, the health of the working class had been ruined, cancer and heart disease were on the up, and the condition and smell of rotting British teeth were making the Empire's camels wince as far away as Baghdad. By the 1930s, it was well known in scientific circles that bad food, lacking freshness and nutrients, was the major cause of wrecked health among the working classes in Britain.[333] And of course, Britain exported its errant diet to those nations within its sphere of control.

The second factor influencing Britain's appalling nutritional legacy was an outgrowth of World War 2. During the conflict years, special measures were drafted by the government to amend the British diet to bolster the health of her fighting men and women. Fears abounded of U-Boat blockades and the eventual starvation of the civilian population. Emergency measures were implemented to make Britain self-sufficient in agriculture and so the emphasis in diet fell back to fresh fruits and vegetables, which could be grown in plentiful supply throughout the country.[334]

The results were excellent. Fibre, nutritional intake and whole foods increased dramatically while processed foods, saturated fats and sugar decreased. The population gamely went for the war diet ("All hands to the wheel, chaps!") and everything was to be done to defeat the enemy. British health excelled during the war years.[335]

When victory came in 1945 however, people wanted an end to the austerity of the war years. The nations across the world were starved of rubber, sugar, gasoline, food and raw materials, and so industry switched from manufacturing tanks, ammunition and armaments to what they were producing at great profit during the 1920s and 1930s. The result was a return to refined flour and sugars, confectionary, margarine, lard and other cheap, convenience foods that eclipsed the sensible fruit and vegetable-based diets of the war years. Health immediately began to deteriorate. And then, in the 1960s, the fast food revolution began to sizzle....

---

[333] **Boyd Orr J** *Food, Health and Income,* A survey of adequacy of diet in relation to income. London: MacMillan, 1936

[334] **Acheson D** "Food policy, nutrition and government". Tenth Boyd Orr memorial Lecture. *Proc. Nutr. Soc.,* 1986; 45:131-138

[335] Ministry of Health. On the state of public health during the war years. Report of the Chief Medical Officer, London: HMSO, 1946

EXAMINING BIG FOOD

Many choose to level a Food Conspiracy charge at Big Food, but the food industry of course has more to gain by people living longer. Dead people don't eat food. The plain fact is, fresh food goes bad quickly because of the life in it. This presents problems for the food industry, whose bottom line depends on good commodities lasting longer. Big Food too has always enjoyed the mantle of Saviour and Philanthropist it rightfully earned during the war years, and has become exceptionally peeved at the direction in which its reputation has been headed since the public began waking up to the horrendous shortcomings of the present inadequate food supply. Geoffrey Cannon explains the dilemma that has traditionally faced Big Food and the reason why it processes our foods at all:

"Generally speaking the best commodities are the worst foods. Manufacturers will always tend to make foods from good commodities, simply because these good commodities are better for business. Saturated fats, processed starches and sugars, and salt have one quality in common: they are all good commodities.

Unsaturated oils are volatile and become rancid; turned into solid, unsaturated fats by the process of hydrogenation, they become stable. Wholegrain flour goes rancid because of the unsaturated oils in the germ of the grain discarded in the manufacture of white flour, which therefore keeps much longer. Contained in fruits, natural sugars come as part of a wet, fibrous package which rots quickly; processed sugars, stripped of all nourishment, are therefore the best commodity of all and, like salt, are themselves preservatives." [336]

Today, Big Food is under siege and it has begun to hit back, labelling its critics 'food terrorists', 'food Leninists', 'food zealots', 'food extremists' and 'food rapists'. Ken Livingstone, controversial Left Wing mayor of London, incurred the ire of Big Food when he funded the London Food Commission in April 1985. Dr Tim Lang, the Commission's Director, stated at that time:

"I want the debate, which properly has started with concern about health, to move to the production and distribution of food. In

---

[336] **Cannon, G** *The Politics of Food*, Century, London: 1987, pp.94-95

order to understand the effect of food and health, we need to understand everything that goes on in the food system before the food is eaten." [337]

Naturally this digested badly with Big Food, which in turn mobilised Big Sugar to get in on the 'Reds Under the Bread' act, with its "Putting Sugar In Perspective" news bulletin. Its release quoted 'top food writer' Digby Anderson hammering home the emotive "Food Leninist" moniker, saying:

"Health education about diet should not be confused with Food Leninism... A lobby has emerged demanding other policies. The Government should tax food products the Food Leninists decree unhealthy and ban their advertisement, and also ordain how food should be labelled and push propaganda to persuade people to eat differently. Neither Government nor Food Leninists have the knowledge to invoke such proposals." [338]

In other words, even though people are dropping dead left and right because of diet and it's common gossip on the street that the contents of our supermarket carts are doing us in, I, as a 'Food Leninist', do not have sufficient knowledge to enter into the democratic process to have these industries brought to account.

Big Biscuit also hit back at the Greens with a press conference organised by SNACMA – the Snack, Nut and Crisp Manufacturers Association - in March 1986. Their efforts inspired the wry headline of "CRISPS: THE APPLE OF A DIETICIAN'S EYE" in the *Sunday Times*.[339] The dietician concerned turned out to be Professor Donald Naismith, head of the Department of Nutrition at King's College, London University, and a consultant of SNACMA. Naismith declared in the press release:

"Others have resorted to the tactics of the terrorist, holding to ransom the minds of the British public by generating doubts and fears

---

[337] **Lang, T** Presentation at the launch of the London Food Commission, April 1985

[338] **The Sugar Bureau** "Food Leninists attacked at sugar conference" press release, October 1985

[339] *Sunday Times*, 9th March 1986

about food in the hope of forcing government and the food manufacturers to bend to their uninformed opinions and half-baked [sic] *hypotheses. Snack foods have been particularly maligned."* [340]

Yes, but rightly or wrongly?

Memory Lane Jam Tarts – "We Haven't Forgotten How A Good Cake Should Taste" –

Ingredients (most predominant first): Wheatflour, sugar, glucose syrup, animal and vegetable fats, apples, gelling agent (liquid pectin), apricots, raspberries, blackcurrants, salt, citric acid, acidity regulator E331, flavours, colours E102, E110, E122, E123, E124, E132

A banana flavoured milk shake drink, which comes in a banana-shaped package, strangely contains... no bananas:

Ingredients: Sugar, skim milk powder, flavouring, colours E102, E110; Vitamins C, B2, A, B1

Mandarin yoghurt flavour Angel Delight (containing no mandarins):

Ingredients: Sugar, hydrogenated vegetable oil, modified starch, emulsifiers E477, E322; flavourings, lactose, caseinate, fumaric acid; gelling agents E339, E450a; whey powder, stabiliser E440a; colours E110, E160a; antioxidant E320

"Whole Wheat" (big writing) breakfast cereal, whose small print declares:

Ingredients: Wheat, sugar, honey, glucose syrup, colours E102, E110

These last two colours are the controversial coal-tar dyes tartrazine and sunset yellow.

Or a famous brand of **oxtail soup** (1986):

Ingredients: Modified starch, dried glucose syrup, salt; flavour enhancers monosodium glutamate, sodium 5-ribonucleotide; dextrose, vegetable fat, tomato powder, hydrolysed vegetable protein, yeast extract, dried oxtail, onion powder, spices, flavouring; colours E150, E124, E102; casseinate, acidity regulator E460,; emulsifiers E471, E472(b); antioxidant E320

---

[340] SNACMA news release, March 1986

Geoffrey Cannon, whose extensive research into the food industry resulted in the monumental *Politics of Food*, examines the truth of meat processing:

"Meat is expensive. Meat plus water is more profitable. The process of adding water is one of 'adding value'. Consumers are sometimes confused by the term 'added value', imagining that it refers to a product made more valuable. In a way, that is exactly what it means, but it refers to value added from the manufacturer's point of view.

Reformed meat is not meat that has mended its ways, but bits and pieces from the tumbler and massager, from different animals, crushed together with moulds and bound together on cooking into an apparently solid shape. Another term for this process is 'restructuring'. The resultant product has the same relationship to meat as chipboard has to wood." [341]

'Mechanically recovered' meat is another process by which all those animal bits, not currently used, are assigned to a minced foodstuff. Meat and gristle left on the bone after butchering are crushed and pulverised before being pressed against a sieve with great force. Fish and poultry can also be rendered down in the same manner, sometimes having their remains put into a powerful centrifuge to isolate bone fragments. The following is a description of chicken mince, used in sausage, produced in this way:

"It in fact consisted of chicken necks and stripped chicken carcasses, which were then crushed and placed in a centrifuge. A quantity of water was then added and the resulting slurry was centrifuged to remove the bone. Further ingredients and even more water were then added. Not only did the end product contain 48% of added water, but the Public Analyst found 'very little muscle tissue present, a high proportion of connective tissue, and traces of feather fragments.'" [342]

---

[341] Cannon G, op. cit. p.80
[342] **Roberts D** "When is a sausage not what it seems?" *Municipal Journal*, 16th August 1985

With these tantalising insights into Big Food, with their use of potentially carcinogenic food additives, flavourings and colourings, one gets a sense in which the 'what is good food and what isn't' battle is always raging, but change itself, on a industry-wide basis, is painfully slow in coming. One way we can avoid the dangerous end-game of damage to the consumer (that's us), is to allow ourselves to restore control over the buying process, consciously blotting out the effects of surreptitious and cunning advertising, which will always seek to pull us back into the creamy, sugar-stuffed embrace of Big Food. To this end, if you examine the section entitled *Supermarket Smarts*, you can take a quick tour of the supermarket and appreciate to what extent Big Food has penetrated our chow supply and perverted it with processed, adulterated materials that have been palmed off on the public as 'food'.

Fruits and vegetables too have been messed with. The average apple sold off the supermarket shelf will have been contaminated with chlorpyrifos, captan, iprodione, vinclozolin and then sealed in wax for longer shelf life. These pesticides, when tested, have variously caused birth defects, cancer, impaired immune response, fungal growth, genetic damage and disruption to the endocrine system.

The average vitamin-depleted white bread roll can be tested positive for pesticides such as chlorpyrifos-methyl, endosulfasulphate, chlorothalonil, dothiocarbamates, iprodione, procymidone and vinclozolin. [343]

One of the first tasks we should accomplish is to seek out a proper source of organic fruits and vegetables, and support that supplier with our business. These foods will comprise the majority of our future diets, so it serves us to get it right. Although much is made of the additional expense of organically grown produce, the point is moot, since, by eating *good, nutritious, natural, whole foods*, we will, mostly without even realising it, begin to consume less of the processed variety. The good food will quite literally satisfy us.

BIG CHEMICALS
In *Cancer: Why We're Still Dying to Know the Truth*, we devote an entire chapter to potential and actual carcinogens in the personal

---

[343] *The New Zealand Total Diet Survey*, 1990/1

care and household products marketplace which have seriously affected health for decades. The problems stem from governments' inability financially to test and effectively regulate these chemicals with the limited budgets they have available. Compounding this problem are the conflicts of interest that exist between chemical manufacturers and the government regulatory agencies themselves, making independent, objective adjudication of these drugs and chemicals a near impossibility.

Agencies, such as Britain's Environment Agency and America's Environmental Protection Agency exist, so far as the public is concerned, for no other reason than to ensure that we can raise our families and work at our jobs in, as far as possible, a contamination-free environment. All technologically advanced nations have such environmental agencies, and yet every year, people still die by the hundreds of thousands, polluted and poisoned by these substances. So what has gone so very wrong?

The major problem stems from the rate at which new chemicals and chemical products are pouring onto the world's markets. Government agencies, already so tightly controlled financially with annual budget constraints, simply do not have the resources to test more than a dozen or so each year. Therefore they must rely heavily on industry-sponsored reports on product safety *from the manufacturers themselves*, which naturally opens up a wide arena for abuse. Agencies such as the EPA threaten dire fines on pharmaceutical and chemical companies found indulging in any foul play in order to ram potentially unsafe products through regulation. But prosecution of such cases by government on a realistic scale is rare since litigation consumes prodigious amounts of taxpayers' money.

Worse, the very government regulatory agencies themselves, such as the US Food & Drug Administration and Britain's Medicines Control Agency (MCA), which are supposed to protect the public from potentially dangerous products coming onto the market, are horribly compromised because of personal investments or ties with the chemical/drug industries. A USA TODAY analysis of financial conflicts at 159 FDA advisory committee meetings from 1st January to 30th June 2000 finds that:

- ➤ At 92% of the meetings, at least one member had a financial conflict of interest.
- ➤ At 55% of meetings, half or more of the FDA advisers had conflicts of interest.
- ➤ Conflicts were most frequent at the 57 meetings when broader issues were discussed: 92% of members had conflicts.
- ➤ At the 102 meetings dealing with the fate of a specific drug, 33% of the experts had a financial conflict.[344]

"The best experts for the FDA are often the best experts to consult with industry," says FDA senior associate commissioner Linda Suydam, who is in charge of waiving conflict-of-interest restrictions. But Larry Sasich of Public Citizen, an advocacy group, says, *"The industry has more influence on the process than people realize."*

Britain's Medicines Control Agency fares little better with its track record for impartiality when it comes to regulating the drug industry. According to a *Daily Express* investigation, key members of the Committee on Safety of Medicines and the Medicines Commission themselves have heavy personal investments in the drug industry. Yet these committees are the ones which decide which drugs are allowed onto the market and which are rejected!

According to the report, two thirds of the 248 experts sitting on the Medicines Commission have financial ties to the pharmaceutical industry. Drug regulators such as Dr Richard Auty have £110,000 worth of holdings with AstraZeneca. Dr Michael Denham owns £115,000 worth of shares in SmithKline Beecham. Dr Richard Logan has up to £30,000 shares in AstraZeneca, SmithKline Beecham and Glaxo Wellcome (now GlaxoSmithKline). Logan's role with the committee involves examining cases where a drug might have to be withdrawn from the market for safety reasons.

David Ganderton was an advisor for nine years with the CSM panel who used to work for AstraZeneca. His current shareholding with this drug company is worth £91,000. Other members of the committees

---

344 *USA Today* article by Dennis Cauchon, *FDA Advisers Tied to Industry*, 25th September 2000, http://www.usatoday.com/news/washdc/ncssun06.htm

with substantial holdings for example include Dr Colin Forfar, with £22,000 with Glaxo Wellcome and Dr Brian Evans owning £28,000 worth of shares with Glaxo Wellcome.[345]

The Daily Express report goes on to tell us: *"Tom Moore, a former senior executive with AstraZeneca, told the Sunday Express that the drug companies go out of their way to build strong links. He said, "Their objective is to get as close as possible. They are an extremely powerful lobby group because they have unlimited resources."*

The [drug] *companies provide* [members of CSM and other regulatory committees] *trips abroad to conferences, large research grants that can keep a university department employed for years, and consultancies that can boost an academic's humble income."*

Many of these government regulators will eventually leave their posts to take up positions with the companies they once regulated. This makes excellent strategic sense for the chemical industry, which can use the expertise of such talent to smooth the way through their products' regulation and approval procedures.

PERSONAL CARE AND HOUSEHOLD PRODUCTS
Poor regulation, self-regulation and a blizzard of confusing and contrary scientific data has resulted in a tragically large number of chemicals making it into our personal lives with little or no warnings attached. Most people have no idea, for example, what the personal care products they use every day are doing to them. As an example, in 1990, 38,000 cosmetic injuries were reported in the US that required medical attention.[346] Health concerns are continuously being raised about ingredients in shampoos, toothpastes, skin creams, and other personal care products. In fact, researchers in Japan, Germany, Switzerland, and the US say many ingredients in personal care products may be related to premature baldness, cataract formation, environmental cancers, contact dermatitis and possible eye damage in young children. We'll find out what some of these substances actually

---

[345] *Daily Express,* micro edition, 6th August 2000

[346] **Steinman, D & Samuel S Epstein** *The Safe Shopper's Bible,* pp. 182-183, ISBN 0020820852; also Consumer Product Safety Commission (CPSC), Product summary report: Washington DC, 1990

are in a moment and why these researchers have every reason to be concerned.

The National Institute of Occupational Safety and Health has found that 884 chemicals available for use in cosmetics have been reported to the US Government as toxic substances.[347] So why are these potentially harmful ingredients allowed in personal care products?

In 1938 the US Government created a legal definition for cosmetics by passing The Federal Food, Drug and Cosmetic Act. Cosmetics were defined as products for *"cleansing, beautifying, promoting attractiveness, or altering the appearance."* In this definition, a cosmetic is defined *"in terms of its intended purpose rather than in terms of the ingredients with which it is formulated."*[348] Although the Food and Drug Administration classifies cosmetics, incredibly it does not regulate them. According to a document posted on the agency's World Wide Web homepage, *"a cosmetic manufacturer may use any ingredient or raw material and market the final products without government approval."*[349]

On 10th September 1997, Senator Edward M. Kennedy of Massachusetts, while discussing an FDA reform bill, stated, *"The cosmetic industry has borrowed a page from the playbook of the tobacco industry, by putting profits ahead of public health."* Kennedy further stated, *"Cosmetics can be dangerous to your health. Yet this greedy industry wants Congress to prevent the American people from learning that truth. Every woman who uses face cream, or hair spray, or lipstick, or shampoo, or mascara, or powder should demand that this arrogant and irresponsible power-play by the industry be rejected. A study by the respected, non-partisan General Accounting Office reported that more than 125 ingredients available for use in cosmetics are suspected of causing cancer. Other cosmetics may cause adverse effects on the nervous system, including convulsions. Still other ingredients are suspected of causing birth defects. A carefully*

---

347 Steinman, D & S Epstein, *Safe Shopper's Bible*, op. cit.
348 Consumer Health and Product Hazards/Cosmetic Drugs, Pesticides, Food Additives, Volume 2 of The Legislation of Product Safety, edited by Samuel S Epstein and Richard D Grundy, MIT Press, 1974
349 http://vm.cfsan.fda.gov/~dms/cos-hdb1.html

209

controlled study found that one in sixty users suffered a cosmetic related injury identified by a physician."[350]

In 1998 Peter Phillips and *Project Censored* listed the year's top 25 censored stories. The number 2 censored story (as detailed in his book) was titled "Personal Care and Cosmetic Products May Be Carcinogenic."[351]

Shocking news indeed. Let's take a brief look at a few of the ingredients that top the list of potentially harmful compounds that are present in products we use every day.

Sodium Lauryl Sulphate (SLS)

SLS is a very harsh detergent found in almost all shampoos and more than a few toothpastes. Pick up a cross-section of these products next time you visit the supermarket and you will find SLS or SLES in pride of place under the ingredients label. SLS started its career as an industrial degreasant and garage floor cleaner. When applied to human skin it has the effect of stripping off the oil layer and then irritating and eroding the skin, leaving it rough and pitted. Studies[352] have shown that:

> ➢ Shampoos with SLS could retard healing and keep children's eyes from developing properly. Children under six years old are especially vulnerable to improper eye development (Summary of Report of Research to Prevent Blindness, Inc. conference)
> ➢ SLS can cause cataracts in adults and delays the healing of wounds in the surface of the cornea.
> ➢ SLS has a low molecular weight and so is easily absorbed by the body. It builds up in the heart, liver, lungs and brain and can cause major problems in these areas.
> ➢ SLS causes skin to flake and to separate and causes substantial roughness on the skin.

---

[350] This statement is quoted from Senator Kennedy's office on http://www.senate.gov/~kennedy/statements /970910fda.html
[351] **Phillips, Peter** *Censored 1998: The News That Didn't Make the News*, Project Censored, 1998 ISBN 1888363649
[352] **Vance, Judi** *Beauty to Die For*, Promotion Publishing, 1998

> SLS causes dysfunction of the biological systems of the skin.
> SLS is such a caustic cleanser that it actually corrodes the hair follicle and impairs its ability to grow hair.
> SLS is routinely used in clinical studies deliberately to irritate the skin so that the effects of other substances can be tested. [353]

Ethoxylation

Ethoxylation is the process that makes degreasing agents such as sodium lauryl sulphate (SLS) less abrasive and gives them enhanced foaming properties. When SLS is ethoxylated, it forms sodium laureth sulphate (SLES), a compound used in many shampoos, toothpastes, bath gels, bubble baths, and industrial degreasants. The problem is, the extremely harmful compound 1,4-dioxane may be created during the ethoxylation process, contaminating the product. 1,4-dioxane was one of the principal components of the chemical defoliant Agent Orange, used to great effect by the Americans during the Vietnam War to strip off the jungle canopy to reveal their enemy. 1,4-dioxane is a hormonal disrupter believed to be the chief agent implicated in the host of cancers suffered by Vietnam military personnel after the war. It is also an estrogen mimic thought to increase the chances of breast and endometrial cancers, stress-related illnesses and lower sperm counts.

Dr Samuel Epstein reports: *"The best way to protect yourself is to recognize ingredients most likely to be contaminated with 1,4-dioxane. These include ingredients with the prefix word, or syllable PEG, Polyethylene, Polyethylene Glycol, Polyoxyethylene, eth (as in sodium laureth sulphate), or oxynol. Both polysorbate 60 and polysorbate 80 may also be contaminated with 1,4-dioxane."* [354]

Propylene Glycol

Propylene glycol is a common ingredient used extensively in industry as a component of brake fluids, paint, varnishes and anti-freeze compounds. It also appears in many beauty creams, cleansers, makeup and children's personal care products. Judi Vance writes:

---

[353] Study cited by *The Wall Street Journal*, 1st November 1988
[354] Epstein, Dr Samuel *Safe Shopper's Bible*, p. 190-191

"If you were to purchase a drum of this chemical from a manufacturer, he is required to furnish you with a material safety data sheet (MSDS) and it may alarm you to find that this common, widely used humectant has a cautionary warning in its MSDS that reads: "If on skin: thoroughly wash with soap and water."[355]

The American Academy of Dermatologists published a clinical review in January 1991 that showed propylene glycol caused a significant number of reactions and was a primary irritant to the skin even in low levels of concentration (around 5%). However propylene glycol routinely appears in the top three ingredients of a given product, indicating that it is present in high concentration. [356] It has been shown that propylene glycol:

> ➤ Has severe adverse health effects and has been found to cause kidney damage, and liver abnormalities.
> ➤ Damages cell membranes causing rashes, dry skin, contact dermatitis and surface damage to the skin.
> ➤ Is toxic to human cells in cultures.

Diethanolamine (DEA)
Cocamide DEA
Lauramide DEA

A colourless liquid or crystalline alcohol that is used as a solvent, emulsifier, and detergent (wetting agent). DEA works as an emollient in skin-softening lotions or as a humectant in other personal care products. When found in products containing nitrates, it reacts chemically with the nitrates to form potentially carcinogenic nitrosamines. Although earlier studies seemed to indicate that DEA itself was not a carcinogen, more recent studies show that DEA has the capacity unequivocally to cause cancer, even in formulations that exclude nitrates.[357] DEA may also irritate the skin and mucous

---

[355] Vance, Judy, *Beauty to Die For*, op. cit.

[356] The first two or three ingredients listed on a product label usually constitute over half of a formulation. In some products, the first two or three ingredients can constitute 70-90% of the formulation. Ingredients are listed in descending order, going down to 1% concentration. Below 1%, ingredients may be listed in any order.

[357] **Epstein, Samuel S** *The Politics of Cancer Revisited*, East Ridge Press, 1998. p.479

membranes.[358] Other ethanolamines to watch out for are: triethanolamine (TEA) and monethanolamine (MEA).

Fluorides (Sodium Fluoride and Hexafluorosilicic Acid)

As previously discussed, fluorides used in the drinking water supplies are a toxic, non-biodegradable, environmental pollutant, officially classified as a contaminant by the US Environmental Protection Agency. Shocking though it may be to contemplate, the reality is, these chemicals are simply hazardous industrial waste - a by-product from the manufacture of phosphate fertilisers, gleaned from this industry's pollution scrubbers - which is largely disposed of in our public water supply.

Alcohol

A colourless, volatile, flammable liquid produced by the fermentation of yeast and carbohydrates. Alcohol is used frequently as a solvent and is also found in beverages and medicine. As an ingredient in ingestible products, alcohol may cause body tissues to be more vulnerable to carcinogens. Mouthwashes with an alcohol content of 25 percent or more have been implicated in mouth, tongue and throat cancers, according to a 1991 study released by the National Cancer Institute. Also a disturbing trend in accidental poisonings has been attributed to alcohol consumption from mouthwashes. After the NCI figures were published, Warner Lambert, manufacturers of the mouthwash Listerine (26.9% alcohol), announced a new version of their product with significantly less alcohol.[359]

Alpha Hydroxy Acid (AHA)

An organic acid produced by anaerobic respiration. Skin care products containing AHA exfoliate not only destroy skin cells, but the skin's protective barrier as well. Long-term skin damage may result from its use.

---

[358] Many nitrosamines have been determined to cause cancer in laboratory animals. Nitrosamine contamination of cosmetics became an issue in early 1977. The Food & Drug Administration expressed its concern about the contamination of cosmetics in a Federal Register notice dated 10th April 1979, which stated that cosmetics containing nitrosamines may be considered adulterated and subject to enforcement action.

[359] *Wall Street Journal*, 23rd April 1991 p.B1, Ron Winslow

Alumin(i)um

A metallic element used extensively in the manufacture of aircraft components, prosthetic devices, and as an ingredient in antiperspirants, antacids, and antiseptics. Aluminium has long been linked to Alzheimer's Disease, which is currently afflicting 1 in 2 persons over the age of 70. Use of aluminium pots and pans to cook food and the use of aluminium cans for soda, as well as the unnecessary cultural penchant for spraying aluminium directly into our lymph nodes as underarm antiperspirant all give grave causes for concern.

Animal Fat (Tallow)

A type of animal tissue made up of oily solids or semisolids that are water-insoluble esters of glycerol and fatty acids. Animal fats and lye are the chief ingredients in bar soap, a cleaning and emulsifying product that may act as a breeding ground for bacteria.

Bentonite

A porous clay that expands to many times its dry volume as it absorbs water. Bentonite is commonly found in many cosmetic foundations and may clog pores and suffocate the skin. Bentonite is used by fire fighters to suffocate forest fires by eliminating the oxygen available.

Butane

Aerosol propellant. Flammable and in high doses may be narcotic or cause asphyxiation.

Animal Collagen

An insoluble fibrous protein that is too large to penetrate the skin. The collagen found in most skin care products is derived from animal carcasses and ground up chicken feet. This ingredient forms a layer of film that may suffocate the skin.

Dioxin (see also Ethoxylation and 1,4-Dioxane)

A potentially carcinogenic by-product that results from the process used to increase foam levels in cleansers such as shampoos, tooth pastes, etc., and to bleach paper at paper mills. Dioxin-treated containers (and some plastic bottles) sometimes transfer dioxins to the products themselves. It has been shown that dioxin's carcinogenicity is up to 500,000 times more potent than that of DDT. [360]

Elastin of High-Molecular Weight

A protein similar to collagen that is the main component of elastic fibres. Elastin is also derived from animal sources. Its effect on the skin is similar to collagen.

Fluorocarbons

A colourless, non-flammable gas or liquid that can produce mild upper respiratory tract irritation. Fluorocarbons are commonly used as a propellant in hairsprays.

Formaldehyde

A toxic, colourless gas that is an irritant and a carcinogen. When combined with water, formaldehyde is used as a disinfectant, fixative, or preservative. Formaldehyde is found in many cosmetic products and conventional nail care systems.

Glycerin

A syrupy liquid that is chemically produced by combining water and fat. Glycerin is used as a solvent and plasticiser. Unless the humidity of air is over 65%, glycerin draws moisture from the lower layers of the skin and holds it on the surface, which dries the skin from the inside out.

Kaolin

Commonly used in foundations, face powders and dusting powders, kaolin is a fine white clay used in making porcelain. Like bentonite, kaolin smothers and weakens the skin.

Lanolin

A fatty substance extracted from wool, which is frequently found in cosmetics and lotions. Lanolin is a common sensitiser that can cause allergic reactions, such as skin rashes, sometimes due to toxic pesticides present in the sheep's wool. Some sixteen pesticides were identified in lanolin sampled in 1988. [361]

---

[360] Epstein, Samuel, *Safe Shopper's Bible*, p. 342
[361] National Academy of Sciences' concern over lanolin contamination: NRC, 1993, p. 313

Mineral Oil
A derivative of crude oil (petroleum) that is used industrially as a cutting fluid and lubricating oil. Mineral oil forms an oily film over skin to lock in moisture, toxins, and wastes, but hinders normal skin respiration by keeping oxygen out. Used in baby oils.

Petrolatum
A petroleum-based grease that is used industrially as a grease component. Petrolatum exhibits many of the same potentially harmful properties as mineral oil.

Propane
Aerosol propellant. Is flammable and in high doses may be narcotic.

Salt
Very drying, irritating, and corrosive.

Talc
A soft grey-green mineral used in some personal hygiene and cosmetics products. Inhaling talc may be harmful as this substance is recognised as a potential carcinogen. Talc is widely recognised to be one of the leading causes of ovarian cancer. [362] It is used by many around the genital area and can also be found on condoms.

So what do you do? Where can you go to get hold of safe personal care products that are effective and of high quality?

Samuel Epstein MD, the world-renowned authority on the causes and prevention of cancer we met earlier, was named the 1998 winner of the Right Livelihood Award (also known as the 'Alternative Nobel Prize'). Dr Epstein has devoted the greater part of his life to studying and fighting the causes of cancer. He is Professor of Occupational and Environmental Medicine at the School of Public Health, University of Illinois Medical Center at Chicago, and the chairman of the Cancer Prevention Coalition.

---

[362] Steinman, D & Samuel S Epstein *The Safe Shopper's Bible*, p.259

As the author of *The Politics of Cancer* and *The Breast Cancer Prevention Program*, he advocates the use of cosmetics and other products that are free from suspected carcinogens. Based on Dr Epstein's research and recommendations, he has awarded one company the 'Seal of Safety' from the Cancer Prevention Coalition. This company, Neways International, manufacturers and distributes its own personal care products, which are free of potentially harmful ingredients. Dr Epstein is enthusiastic about the groundbreaking work Neways has done in this area: *"Neways has pioneered and succeeded in providing consumers with cosmetics and toiletries free of cancer-causing and harmful ingredients and contaminants. I warmly congratulate them on their accomplishments."*

During the course of our work on this book, Credence researchers have had an opportunity to work with Neways technical personnel and examine the Neways product line. I myself have flown to Utah to examine their production plant at Salem and talk with their executives at length. As a result of Credence's investigations, like Dr Epstein, we do not hesitate, as an independent, non-affiliated organisation, to recommend Neways' carcinogen-free personal care products and nutritional supplements to all who are looking to make a change for the better.

Tom Mower, President of Neways, lays out the focus of his organisation: *"Neways is in the business of helping people detoxify their bodies. Knowing the chemical constituents of your personal care products and their effects on your body enables you to understand how toxic culprits can contaminate your body. Ingredients like sodium lauryl sulphate (SLS), diethanolamine (DEA), triethanolamine (TEA), propylene glycol, fluoride, and alcohol have been identified by experts as known or potential carcinogens that can be found in ordinary personal care products.*

So Neways provides shampoos without sodium lauryl sulphate. We have lotions without propylene glycol, bubble bath without DEA or TEA, toothpastes without saccharin or fluoride, and mouthwash without alcohol. We use toxin- and carcinogen-free products that give consumers something more than clean skin or fresh breath - they provide peace of mind."

See our *Contacts! Contacts! Contacts!* section for further information on how to obtain non-toxic substitutes for toothpastes, cosmetics, detergents, polishes, sprays and deodorants, or whole bathroom change-out kits. Don't use insecticides. Press for clean, non-fluoridated tap water. Most importantly, think 'clean' with your diet. The new lifestyle we must adopt must be a sensible, easy-to-follow regimen, and we must know why we are following it. Which now brings us to...

Part 2

'the solutions'

The Woman Who Ate Her Audience
Examining the Desire for Change

Are you willing to consider a whole lifestyle change for lasting health? We have, up to now, looked at some of the challenges and pitfalls that affect human longevity. However, as we start to assemble the complete picture of a future lifestyle that will give us the best shot at the Queen's telegram (or your face on an American jam jar, courtesy of Willard Scott), the road to successful longevity must inevitably commence with the question: *"ARE YOU WILLING TO DO WHAT IT TAKES?"* This raises the obvious question: *"Well, what do I have to do?"* And of course, the key to anyone sticking to a successful new program of nourishment for life will hinge on a) the results they enjoy, and of course b) desirability of the program itself.

Now, the choice to stay the same or do something different is of course an old marketing saw, but still needs to be spelled out: *"If you keep doing what you're doing, you're going to keep getting what you're getting."* Or, *"Insanity is doing the same thing and expecting different results."*

If you do change, and follow a new route consistently, you will get a different set of results from what you are currently getting. The key here is to change your eating and lifestyle habits for the better, <u>and then keep doing it</u>. These actions will then, down the road, translate into benefits you would not have otherwise enjoyed. The cleaner you eat, the cleaner you'll be. If you don't want to change, then that's fine too. You have a perfect First Amendment right to live the way you want, so long as it's legal, and you may expect all the attended benefits or downsides with which that lifestyle is endowed.

But if you've made it this far in the book, you are probably willing to make a change. The question is: *"How far are you prepared to go?"* The answer? *"That depends....!"* What if I told you that, for a moderate change in lifestyle (saving you a wad of money too, by the way), you could prepare yourself for the same potential benefits enjoyed by those peoples with pronounced health and longevity? What if you really didn't have to paint yourself blue and go back into the jungle to escape the health pitfalls we were examining earlier?

In a previous chapter, we looked at the obesity statistics in America and the UK, which can fairly be taken as a rough guide to what the standard 'westernised' lifestyle is doing for belt sizes and health elsewhere in the world, wherever these practices are adopted. See how the health paradigm has shifted! In the UK, we are now watching 26 hours of TV a week, twice as much as in the 1960s. Almost all of our youngsters between age 7 and 18 are now classified as 'inactive'. Why are we surprised that the statistics for heart disease, cancer and other serious illnesses continue to grow before our eyes?

If you're NOT worried about what your lifestyle is doing to your own health, then consider what it is doing to those you love. Children adore their parents as they grow through toddlerhood, and so they will usually follow the wisdom passed down to them by their family peers. But look at the legacy we are leaving them! One in ten of Britain's under-4s is now considered medically obese, with recent studies showing a doubling of children with weight problems.[363] In England, the adult trend is no less alarming. In 1980, 8% of women and 6% of men were obese. By 1998, these figures had grown to 21% and 17%, involving over 8 million adults. A further 32% of women and 46% of men are now classed as overweight in the United Kingdom.[364]

Interestingly the bill for treating Britain's obesity and associated maladies currently costs the National Health Service £500 million in drugs and other therapies. How much would it cost the NHS, and therefore the taxpayer, if prevention were exercised as the primary initiative, and these overweight people were simply thinned down through proper food education? Actually it isn't primarily the fault of our authorities. It's our own fault. Many overweight folks simply do not want to change their ways, or, through emotionally addictive ties to their food, cannot. They have what the psychiatrists describe as, 'a troubled interaction with nourishment'. They eat when they want, as opposed to *eating when their bodies are hungry*. And then there is all that advertising which teaches us to eat what supposedly tastes best, rather than what our bodies need most. Have you noticed how advertising concentrates on taste? Waitresses are now approaching the

---

363 *National Audit Office*, 14th February 2001
364 *Daily Mail*, 15th February 2001, p.17

table and asking: *"Does that taste good?"* Imagine them enquiring: *"Is that nourishing and alkalising your body systems adequately, valued customer?"*

Media advertising for food, the way it is specifically targeted and presented, is an incredibly powerful medium, even to declared sceptics. And yet, many of us refuse to believe we are not in control of the basic choices we make. This is where things can go so tragically wrong. I worked for a number of years in advertising, and know firsthand how the major media houses go about the business of mass-persuasion.

The public is actually told very little about how effective advertising is. A good example can be found with the well-known, raging debate over whether TV violence affects the actions of those who watch it. After being presented with five volumes of scientific data showing that sex and violence shown on TV and film had a significant effect on society, American ABC network executives issued a statement denying that televised imagery affected real-world behaviour in any way. Film critic Michael Medved was outraged: *"Now if ABC TV believes that, then it better start refunding billions of dollars in advertising revenues. Because if televised imagery does not affect real-world behaviour in any way, what is it doing selling ad time?"* [365]

We can clearly see that governments are not going out of their way to use the mass communications media to educate their populations AS A MATTER OF URGENCY on proper food consumption and good diet. That's not to say that good health programs do not appear – they do. The difference is, they are not usually sponsored by the taxpayer, which, in my humble opinion, would probably be one of the more worthwhile goals our taxes could achieve.

When we did get around to discussing overweight on British TV a while back, we were brought face-to-face with a large Vanessa Feltz, who told her doubtful congregation that 'you can be fat and sexy, fat and successful and fat and happy'. I remember seeing how Vanessa was failing even to convince herself with her own pitch. Evidently the TV

---

[365] **Medved, Michael** *Hollywood: License to Kill*, a video presentation, American Portrait Films, P.O. Box 19266 Cleveland, OH 44119 U.S.A. (800)736-4567

company wasn't taken in either. Shortly after coming out of the food closet, Ms Feltz's existing TV show contract was not renewed.

Today however, I am happy to report that Vanessa is a changed woman and back in the national spotlight. 84lbs lighter, trimmer in the stirrup and leaping buxomly ever forward, more enthusiastic than a Royal Navy frigate on Customs duty, she has shed her weight apologetics for a ministry of contrition and Thinity. She no longer makes excuses for having, or needing to be overweight:

"Lord knows, I know what it's like to be obese. I was size 24 and on television. A vast sitting target in a fuchsia-pink suit. I've been called everything from 'Mrs Blobby on reinforced stilettos' to 'the woman who ate her audience'. I know I now sound like an evangelical convert, but please let's stop and think about what we are doing to ourselves. Obesity levels have tripled in 20 years. Do we really want to breed another generation of fatties?

We don't have to accept fat as our fate. There's no need to slide into being a statistic. Weight loss isn't rocket science. Eat healthily. Don't diet. Diets don't work. <u>Simply find an eating program you can tolerate and be a grown-up.</u>" [366] [emphasis mine]

Sentiments forged in the fire of trials, I would say. Good on you, Vanessa. Like many, I too know what it is like to fight the fat demon, having fought my own weight problem in the past. A million diets have concentrated on what to eat, and almost all of these diets have failed spectacularly. WHY?

The 'why' is the key. A healthy longevity is completely governed by what we let into our bodies and what we keep out. But before we examine this, <u>the first move has to be for us to acknowledge we have a problem with the food we are currently eating.</u> DO WE WANT TO DO SOMETHING ABOUT IT? Want to stop being an alcoholic? Then admit you have a problem and resolve to do what it takes to get out of it. Want a new healthcare system that takes into consideration nutrition and the old Hippocratian adage, "First do no harm to the body"? Then we need to admit our current healthcare system is riven

---

[366] *Daily Mail*, 15th February 2001, p.13

with problems and most definitely IS doing harm to the body. In other words, we've got to admit the problem and then move to the solution.

How many times have you come across a stubborn relative or friend who just doesn't see things the way you do? Chances are, they don't see a problem, won't admit that there is a problem, and so remain unmoved with your passionate entreaties. I know folk who cough their guts up smoking 20-40 a day, and still blame it on the weather. The same with food. If we have a problem, we must be a man (or woman) and admit it. Then get down and do something about it.

We must also admit what our food actually is and what it contains. This goes against some especially powerful cultural programming in areas like meat, sugar and dairy. Are we convinced these foods are harming us? WHY then are we letting them into our bodies?

Every diet on the market concentrates on what to put into the body for the desired end-result. These diets will inevitably fail if they do not address the issue of lifestyle and detoxification. After all, if you cannot maintain the diet (and most people don't) then the diet fails and the weight gets loaded back on when the subject returns to his or her previous eating habits. Almost all diets that are here today and gone tomorrow never address the issue of detoxification, or the elimination of waste products; rather they fixate on particular (patented) dietary products or techniques which produce fast results before those of us with the attention-span of a laboratory amoeba get fed up and trot off in search of the Golden Arches.

Imagine driving your car down the road with a rag in the tailpipe, the wrong kind of gasoline in the tank, bald tyres, the engine badly tuned, the steering wonky and unadjusted, the radiator low on water and the oil light flickering on. Then a mechanic, who hasn't been trained in oil or gasoline, tells you that if you replace the tyres, all your problems will be solved. He tells you that, because replacing tyres is a quick fix that will render him a rapid and handsome profit. Modern drug medicine works the same way. Most doctors are not trained in nutrition, that most basic of body sciences, and so their recommendations on what are best for the health of your human machine are based on flawed assumptions to begin with – namely that drugs, surgical procedures and cutting-edge medical techniques, rather than nutrition, are the cures for the ills of mankind. Doctors were taught that in the institutions in which they were trained, funded by drug companies. And they are continually reminded of this by the drug company reps who come a-knocking to tell them of the latest drugs available to their surgeries.

Doctors aren't taught nutrition in the schools they attended because nutrition and its associated products are useless commercially in rewarding drug-company shareholders. Detoxification is, by its very nature, a prevention ethic, and so is not normally appreciated by doctors not trained in prevention procedures. Modern drug medicine, in its current form, is at best, if I'm kind, a temporary fix for a problem, which, ninety-nine times out of a hundred, you can fix for yourself anyway. At worst, medicine will aggravate your health problems, and even introduce new problems that weren't there to begin with.

You have heart disease. The doctor recommends a bypass. Why not attempt to clear out the gunk in your arteries with diet and nutrition BEFORE the problem gets that far? You have to have major dental surgery and you hate dentists. Fine. Ditch the sugar and fluoride and you will probably not need a dentist until you fall down the stairs one day and chew the carpet. You have cancer. The doctor wants to pump toxic drugs into your system and irradiate your body. Why did you end up with cancer in the first place, if not because you failed, either deliberately or through ignorance, TO AVOID THE PROBLEM IN THE FIRST PLACE?

Prevention, it has often been said, is the best cure. Modern medicine however doesn't practise prevention. Prevention just doesn't pay the bills. The Science of Natural Hygiene, however, which we shall examine in the next chapter, has prevention as its headline; it sings prevention to the tops of the clouds; and carries it out in such a way that disease is avoided years before it can ever become an issue and harm you and your family.

We mentioned earlier that 90-95% of all the diseases and health problems that are killing us today tend to be metabolic-, toxin- or healthcare-related in origin. Solve those problems and you solve 90-95% of what is going to kill you prematurely. The other 5-10% of the problems that are afflicting us, we will examine in our summary analysis. Let's do some quick revision and define our terms:

Metabolic diseases are diseases that are wedded to our utilisation of food. Metabolic diseases chiefly arise because a dietary element or nutrient is chronically missing from our food. Examples are scurvy, pellagra, beriberi, pernicious anaemia, rickets, and so on. Metabolic diseases cannot be solved by anything other than the missing metabolic preventative, which is always a food factor. Which means, in case you didn't pick up on it earlier, that drugs foreign to the biological experience of the human body will never cure a metabolic disease. What's currently being used by the establishment to halt metabolic diseases? Drugs.

Toxin-related diseases are diseases that arise because of poisoning from our food or environment. Often these diseases have a shared problem with metabolic nutritional deficiency. Examples are heart disease, cancer, osteoporosis, diverticulosis, multiple sclerosis, diabetes, lupus, ME (chronic fatigue syndrome), fibromyalgia, sciatica, psoriasis, Crohn's, arthritis, Bell's Palsy, and so on. Toxin-related problems are solved by removing the toxin antagonist(s), and then flushing the poisons out of the body, all the while nourishing the system with key nutritional factors, as well as full-spectrum nutrition. The underlying problems that generate toxin-related diseases can never be solved by introducing more toxins into the body in the form of drugs, which are foreign to the biological experience of the human body.

Healthcare-related problems include poisoning from prescription drugs, either wrongly or correctly prescribed, botched or unnecessary medical procedures that injure or kill the patient, and deaths arising from infections picked up in hospitals. Healthcare-related problems are solved by avoiding unnecessary healthcare situations where at all possible. Many illnesses and problems arising from healthcare are often treated with further healthcare (drugs and procedures), exacerbating the problem further. New diseases, such as AIDS and SMON, have also appeared, which are exclusively the result of pharmaceutical and recreational drug abuse and/or malnutrition.[367]

---

[367] **Ransom, Steven & Phillip Day** *World Without AIDS*, Credence Publications, 2000

You can see immediately that all three categories are completely preventable, so long as you understand *that there is the problem in the first place.* Often when we get a stubborn Uncle Joe, he does not appreciate the forces arrayed against him, and therefore drifts blindly into disease and a bad death, not understanding he is under attack in the first place. Uncle Joe has a healthy regard for food, because food has not always been plentiful in his life. Sugar and butter are an elixir for him, simply because these were denied him during the rationing of World War 2. Sugar and butter to Joe, even today, are luxuries he once was forced to do without. Joe is therefore likely to have a white-knuckle grip on the sugar-bowl and the butter pot and will not look kindly on your desire to help him understand the problems sugar and dairy are causing in his life. Likely as not, Uncle Joe will suffer what he must suffer, if he remains stubborn, and will inevitably become a statistic of those diseases, which will claim him for his lifestyle at the regular Western incidence.

Likewise, imagine telling Texans drastically to cut back their meat intake! Will they demur without a word, or will you have a beady eye fixed on you from under the Stetson, a spurt of tobacco hitting the end of your Nikes, and a dry: "You ain't from round here, are ya, boy?" before the rope is slung over the local beef ranch's T-bar? I jest of course, and am very fond of Texans, (and actually they're not like that at all, so sorry!), but the point is made. We are products of the marketing monster and the vagaries of our culture. When the oracles sound, we mostly drink it all down without so much as a hiccup.

Imagine persuading the good folk of Wisconsin that their over-consumption of dairy products is killing them and others by degrees, when they are the No.1 producers of the stuff everywhere west of the Canaries. Old habits die hard, but I'll tell you what. If we don't change the bad habits that plague our lifestyles, then we must be prepared to die hard.

One of the greatest things about the Science of Natural Hygiene is, that if we suspend our cultural programming and fall back on those valuable attributes we all have within us: instinct, common-sense, logic and reason, we find that, surprise surprise, it all makes perfect sense. After we appreciate a few things about what Natural Hygiene really is, and how this premier body science can help us to stay fit, healthy and primed for a long life, believe me when I tell you: you will have no more desire to stick a burning cow in your mouth than in your ear.

Eliminating the Pied Piper
The Science of Natural Hygiene

Dr Herbert M Shelton, one of Natural Hygiene's leading proponents, described the science as *"...that branch of biology which investigates and applies the conditions upon which life and health depend, and the means by which health is sustained in all its virtue and purity, and restored when it has been lost or impaired."*

Natural Hygiene recognises that the human body, with all of its wondrous workings, is an organism that is constantly striving for wellness. The words 'Natural Hygiene' imply a cleanliness of the body that is achieved through natural, non-contrived means. No patented potions. No weird rituals. No monopoly on hidden or arcane knowledge. Natural Hygiene is a way of eating and living practised under various different names and disguises by hundreds of thousands around the world who are enjoying long, disease-free lives as a result of applying some very simple but telling techniques. Harvey Diamond, whose *Fit for Life* series is a worldwide banner for Natural Hygiene, and whose own life was radically turned around with its application, gives his own summation:

"The underlying basis of Natural Hygiene is that the body is self-cleansing, self-healing, and self maintaining. Natural Hygiene is based on the idea that all the healing power of the universe is within the human body; that nature is always correct and cannot be improved upon. Therefore nature does not seek to thwart its own devices. We experience problems of ill-health (i.e. excess weight, pain, stress) only when we break the natural laws of life." [368]

The science of Natural Hygiene revolves around the following topics:
  ➤ Understanding The Body's Natural Digestive Cycles
  ➤ Correct Consumption of Fruit
  ➤ The Concept of High Water-Content Food
  ➤ Correct Food Combining
  ➤ Detoxification

---

[368] Diamond, Harvey, op. cit. p.19

THE BODY'S NATURAL DIGESTIVE CYCLES

The basis of Natural Hygiene teaches that the human body's digestive system goes through three eight-hour cycles every twenty-four hours:

Noon – 8pm: **Appropriation** of food (eating and digestion)
8pm – 4am: **Assimilation** of food (absorption and use)
4am – Noon: **Elimination** (excretion of waste products)

It is not hard to see these cycles in action. It is also uncomfortably clear when these cycles are thrown into confusion and turmoil by, for example, eating a pizza late at night or eating a big breakfast.

APPROPRIATION

The body prefers the Appropriation Cycle to happen on time, commencing at noon. Those who rise late in the morning can easily make it through to noon without any food, because the body is currently in the Elimination Cycle and isn't yet ready for food. After the commencement of the Appropriation Cycle however, once afternoon arrives, we become uncomfortable if we do not eat anything. Our body craves nourishment during Appropriation and will let us know of its needs in no uncertain terms if we are remiss in supplying it the necessary fodder. The most important rule during Appropriation is *to eat only when your body is hungry.*

ASSIMILATION

The Assimilation Cycle mostly occurs at night, and ideally must, like Britain's RailTrack, leave on time. Assimilation (nutrient extraction and use) at night makes all the sense in the world as the body is resting and the digestive system can crank into gear and do its thing with the minimum of interruption. Night-time is naturally not a good time for Appropriation (eating and digestion) because of the horizontal angles involved. During Assimilation at night however, the body extracts nutrients in our intestines, which are twelve times the length of our trunks, designed as they are to keep high-water-content, unrefined plant dietary food in their clutches until all the nutrients are withdrawn. If you leave three hours between your last meal and when you go to bed, a properly combined supper, along the lines we will be examining, will already have left the stomach and be well on its peaceful way through the alimentary tract for its squeezing and extracting by the time you lay your precious head down on your pillow.

During the night, your body is putting all those nutrients to work replenishing your systems, replacing damaged cells and allowing the blood and lymph systems to pick up waste and take it to the garbage collection points in preparation for the truck the following morning.

If however you commit the cardinal sin and wolf down your cheese and pineapple pizza (with the obligatory jalapenos) immediately prior to going to sleep, you will go to bed feeling like you have swallowed an anvil. Your body is horizontal which means that gravity is working against your stomach and everything therein, inevitably resulting in the desperate need to throw down half a bucket of antacids at 2:30am to douse the mighty conflagration, or else prop your head up on a pillow in a vain attempt to stop the resultant hydrochloric acid reflux bringing those jalapenos and cheese up for a chat.

ELIMINATION
At 4am, Elimination cuts in and the garbage truck arrives to take out the junk. Your body has sorted through the food it has processed, and has rejected the food debris that cannot be absorbed and satisfactorily metabolised into its constituent nutrients for further use. Elimination is simply the removal of waste matter from the body, be it from fibrous, non-metabolised food or other waste products the body generates, which we will examine in a minute. The human body has very efficient systems to accomplish the shedding of waste from the body, using the bowel and urine to excrete the junk the body no longer wants to be involved with. The body also eliminates metabolic toxins, which have accumulated in the body, shunting them out via the underarm, the bowel, the urine, glands at the backs of the knees, glands behind the ears, from the groin area, from the nose, the mouth, the ears and the skin.

Emergency elimination can be dramatic and is carried out by the body when time is of the essence in getting rid of dangerously toxic material before the body's internal systems and health are threatened. Examples of this are diarrhoea, a waterfall of a nose during colds, and of course, vomiting. Or even my favourite, which can often be seen outside The Pig and Whistle Pub in the Old Kent Road in London at 12:30 at night – projectile vomiting.

Elimination is the most thwarted digestive cycle of the three - an abuse that has led to chronic obesity in our populations and catastrophic ill-health. *The reason is because the Elimination Cycle is almost always sabotaged by us unwittingly eating big, badly combined breakfasts, preventing the body from executing its essential daily function of getting waste out of the body.* Thus the junk stays put and gets filed in all the parts of our bodies where it can do the least harm. We look at our naked bodies in the mirror with horror: *"Good grief, my bum DOES look big in this. I look like a beached whale."* Your body is naturally offended at the insult being aimed in its general direction, and caustically replies: *"Then unplug me, Einstein, and let's get rid of the whale..."*

WASTE PRODUCTS
It's a good idea to have a cursory knowledge of waste products with which our bodies have to get to grips on a daily basis. These include:
- ➤ Food detritus
- ➤ Toxic food metabolites and mucoid plaque
- ➤ Catabolic cellular debris
- ➤ Chemical toxins

Food Detritus
...we have already looked at. It's simply the fibrous waste the body cannot absorb to make cell structure. This fibre, as most know, is extremely beneficial in adding bulk to digestion, giving you that 'full' feeling and enabling the colon to move everything comfortably along. Fibre also scours the digestive tract of impacted faecal matter (mucoid plaque) and cleans everything it passes with its Brillo-pad action.

Toxic Food Metabolites and Mucoid Plaque
...are more dangerous compounds and include the mess of partially processed complex animal proteins, the acidic gunk resulting from bad food combining and uric acid from chronic meat-eating unable to be broken down because humans lack the enzyme uricase. The danger of toxic food metabolites is that, with a junk diet, these poisons can accumulate at a more rapid rate than the body can eliminate them. This condition is sometimes referred to as toxemia or acidosis. Toxic sucrose and milk metabolites are also created since the body lacks renin and lactase enzymes to break down milk proteins and the vitamins and minerals necessary to process the hopeless sucrose.

233

These toxins are of course also acidic and represent a danger to the body.

Clogged colons are one of the major causes of diseases today, not least because a clogged colon cannot efficiently absorb nutrients from the food it is processing. The other problem is that moisture is extracted from food as it is digested, and the resultant mass can become gluey and adhesive, coating the walls of the colon and intestines (mucoid plaque). Modern processed foods are the worst for accomplishing this.

It has been estimated that an adult consuming an average, animal protein-heavy Western-style diet during their life can have between 7 to 25 pounds or more (3 to 10 kilos) of layered, impacted faecal matter clogging their digestive system. The average Westerner consuming this diet faithfully holds eight full meals of undigested food and waste matter within their digestive system at any one time. The mucoid plaque can be rubbery or hardened material, unable to complete the journey through the intestines, that quickly begins to rot, producing foul odours and gases. This decomposing material is a haven for germs and bacteria, which quickly thrive, producing toxins that can enter the bloodstream and affect the entire body.

Curiously we as humans once again take the Biscuit of Distinction for being the only creature in nature almost always corrupting its natural food supply by processing, boiling, frying, irradiating, roasting and otherwise destroying its valuable nutrition prior to slamming it together in any combination and wolfing it down like Lassie at suppertime. This 'bad', nutritionally corrupted food produces its own acidic by-products, including unstable oxidation elements ('free radicals'), which can damage the colon, causing healing processes to commence, potentially resulting in irritable bowel, Crohn's and colorectal cancers. It is a measure of how serious this food-processing and -corrupting problem has become in the West that colorectal cancer is the second leading cause of cancer death for both males and females across the industrialised world.

Catabolic Cellular Debris
...is toxic waste and results from the ongoing replenishment of cells in your body as tissue is built up (anabolism) or broken down

(catabolism) as part of the body's usual life-preserving activities. There is a new 'you' being produced every seven years or so, and Your Inestimable You-Ness can only be manufactured from the nutrients with which you supply your body. If you want to have the body of Aphrodite or Zeus, then supply your body with first-class Olympian (raw material) nutrition and assist it in ridding itself of the old bricks and mortar. If however you don't want to make the effort, then expect to look like Bacchus (does the body of Mars come from eating same?). It has been estimated that old cells are being replaced by new cells at the rate of three hundred to eight hundred billion a day. I don't know. I didn't do the counting (*'Oh, heck. Missed one. Better start again.'*) Harvey Diamond explains metabolic imbalance:

"Old cells are toxic (poisonous) and must be removed from your system as soon as possible by one of four channels of elimination: bowels, bladder, lungs and skin. This is a normal, natural process of the body and is not something with which to concern yourself, unless for some reason this toxic waste material is not eliminated at the same rate that it is being produced. As long as there is a sufficient amount of energy at the body's disposal, this waste is eliminated properly.

The second way toxemia is produced in the system is from the by-products of foods that are not properly digested, assimilated and incorporated into cell structure. As far as your weight is concerned, common sense will tell you that if more of this toxic waste is built than is eliminated, there is going to be a build-up of the excess. This translates as 'overweight'. Adding to the problem, toxins are of an acid nature. When there is an acid build-up in the body, the system retains water to neutralize it, adding even more weight and bloat."[369]

Metabolic imbalance thus occurs when your body is producing more waste than it is eliminating. This waste is acid. The body tries to use retained water and minerals, such as sodium, magnesium, boron, calcium, iron and potassium, to render the system a harmless, slightly alkaline pH (7.4). Minerals, such as calcium and boron, are often leached from the skeleton, eventually resulting in weakened bone structure, poor teeth and a breakdown in cartilage and connective

---

369 Diamond, Harvey, op. cit. p.30

tissue. These problems will invariably lead to osteoporosis and the various forms of arthritis. As previously seen, a heavy animal products consumer can lose up to 90 – 100mg of calcium a day as the body tries to maintain a healthy alkali balance.

How do we know if we are toxic and acidic? Below are some of the indicators:

> A constant feeling of sluggishness and being 'off-colour'.
> Chronic tiredness or chronic fatigue syndrome
> A susceptibility to infections, colds and flu
> Stomach and digestive problems
> Bad breath unrelated to dental problems
> Body odour that persists after bathing
> A coated tongue in the morning
> Poor wound healing
> Aches and pains or the start of rheumatoid arthritis
> Suffering from a degenerative disease

ENVIRONMENTAL TOXINS

The last category of waste products that concerns us here are general environmental toxins we looked at earlier. These will include chemicals in personal care and household items that are absorbed through the skin and the mouth, which cumulatively collect in our tissues and organs. Other toxins will be tar, nicotine and other poisons from cigarettes, alcohol metabolites from social drinks, drug residues, both pharmaceutical and recreational, vaccination toxins such as formaldehyde, air pollutants, water pollutants, food pollutants such as chemicals, drugs and hormones fed to animals we later eat, cosmic radiation, terrestrial radiation, environmental radiation and chemical residues and hormonal anabolics absorbed through our skin by the man-made products we touch and use.

These toxins are naturally missing from the environments of those cultures traditionally living long lives. This does not mean we are doomed to die early because we live in a chemical junkyard of a society; it means we have to be ever mindful of ensuring that we rid toxins out of our environment, use safe products free of these chemical problems, and see that the garbage gets put on the Elimination Truck every day when it comes a-calling. At the moment, Garbage Elimination, Inc. for most of us isn't calling at all.

OPTIMISING THE ENERGY SYSTEM
The body expends a great deal of energy processing food and detoxifying compounds, so the human body is essentially an energy system that needs to be calibrated efficiently. You can give your body an easy time with digestion by properly combining foods (in which case you free up loads of energy for detoxification duties), or you can be a beast to it and slap together all manner of gut-warping culinary treasons. The body, you'll be pleased to hear, is self-calibrating, but this calibration can easily get thrown out of the window if we decide to write our own computer program on how the body should run.

Hopefully you are now beginning to appreciate how important a efficient, undisturbed Elimination (Detoxification) Cycle is, and why it is essential that the body conserves its energy for carrying out this life-saving and longevity-preserving function.

Your greatest weapon in assisting the body to cleanse itself centres around...

THE CORRECT CONSUMPTION OF FRUIT
At the heart of Natural Hygiene is the science of energy. The great news is that you can manipulate your body's energy usage very simply by the sort of food you consume, and you can start right now. As we have already seen, to assist the body in eliminating toxins and waste during its morning cycle EVERY DAY, the idea is not to introduce anything during the Elimination Cycle that will divert the body from doing its life-saving housework. No traditional breakfasts. No Aunt Lily's Arkansas Pancakes. No grits or muesli. No British Heart-Attack-on-a-Plate, with the fried eggs, fried bread, sausages, tomatoes, and bacon. The problem is, many folks are culturally prepared to eat a herd of wildebeest in the morning, since it was hammered into us by our obese grannies time and time again that a healthy, farm-fresh breakfast was essential to our optimum welfare. Unfortunately this dangerous rubbish which our grannies fervently believed and took to their eventually failing hearts, is why many of them remained the size they did, up until they died of a toxin-related food-abuse disease, such as coronary heart disease, stroke or cancer.

If you want the Queen's telegram, and wish to achieve a happy and healthy longevity, bouncing your great-granddaughter upon your firm and functioning knee, then you must admit you aren't going to make it with the West's current food *modus operandi*. The frightening legacy this dietary treachery will give you will be a heart attack, cancer, and the other nightmares we were examining in a previous section. If you want to live to be a healthy hundred, find those who routinely live to these ages, and do what they do.

Making the change means making a decision to avoid completely unnecessary tragedy, pain and heartache, both for your benefit and for those who love you and want you around for as long as possible. I remember having dinner with a preacher and his wife in America. His wife unfortunately had suffered a stroke and was wheelchair-bound. During the meal, the pastor was explaining how he believed his wife's condition was God's way of communicating a message to them both. I heartily agreed with him. God was certainly communicating a message. It was: *"My lovely children. You are killing yourselves with your troubled interaction with nourishment."* The meal we had that night consisted of a huge sidewalk of beef and an Everest of mashed potatoes slowly eroding into an Atlantic Ocean of gravy. Upon enquiry, I learned that this gastronomic profanation, together with some other close offshoots, was their regular evening munch.

Fruit is your man. Clean, light and more mobile than an SAS infiltration unit. Fruit digests in the intestinal tract, not the stomach, and charges through your system in 30 minutes like the 5:15pm from Paddington. Fruit contains the monosaccharide sugar fructose, which is completely metabolised and converted to blood glucose, the energy form the body uses to sustain its life-systems. Your brain runs on nothing but glucose, and fruit is your most efficient source of this essential blood sugar. Besides, blood sugar levels rise and normalise after adequate fruit consumption, meaning that your hunger switch is turned off and you scarf less food.

Fruit (uncontaminated with pesticides, of course), is rich in hard-working enzymes, vitamins, amino acids, minerals and fibre and is an extremely low-taxing amino acid source in the morning, which makes it ideal for breakfast. And what do amino acids build? That's right.

Proper human proteins. Fruit is alluring with its shapes and colours, has the most exotic tastes, and is loved by almost everybody. Those few who hate fruit are usually addicted to heavy, processed foods, which they indiscriminately combine with fruit into an apocalyptic jam-preserve, which will produce fermentation, putrefaction, acid residues and the resultant graveyard gas and corpse-like breath. If your breath smells like something has died... it has. And guess what sometimes gets the blame? Fruit! Naturally this is a no-no, and we'll have a look at why there are set rules for fruit consumption, which, if followed, clear up all the bad press in which fruit has been embroiled over the years.

Fruit can be described as the perfect food because humans have been found in the past to survive indefinitely on it, all the nutrients required for life being found in a diet of varied fruits which grow on six out of the seven continents on Earth (and who wants to live on Antarctica anyhow?). Within the past seventy years however, commercially grown fruit, cereals and vegetables have lost a significant part of their mineral content due to over-farming.[370] This deficiency can be easily and simply remedied using mineral and antioxidant supplementation, which shall be discussed later.

Here are the Ten Fruit Commandments. Tattoo them on your cookie jar:

> *Eat fruit <u>on an empty stomach</u> any time during the day*
> *Always leave 30 minutes after fruit consumption before eating foods other than fruit*
> *Leave at least 3 hours after a properly combined meal before consuming fruit. This allows the previous meal to leave the stomach and avoids putrefaction and fermentation*
> *Before noon, consume only fruit*
> *Never combine fruit with any other foods*
> *Never eat fruit AFTER a meal as a dessert*
> *Steer clear of bananas, avocados and dates in the morning. These can be eaten, properly combined, during the Appropriation Cycle, after noon*

---

[370] **McCance & Widdowson** "The chemical composition of foods", special report series no. 235/297, Medical Research Council, & MAFF, 1940, 1946, 1960, 1976 &1991

> *If you get hungry during the morning, eat another piece of fruit and keep munching until the blood sugar levels normalise and your hunger abates*
> *Eat organic fruit only where possible*
> *Do not eat processed, canned or cooked fruit, which normally contain sugars, e-additives and other aliens*

Fruit is the perfect food when eaten on its own. Although sometimes described as an acid, malic acid from apples, for example, actually yields an alkali ash in the body, unless it is combined with other foods, whereupon the usual acid gunk is produced. During the morning Elimination Cycle, fruit is invaluable in assisting in detoxification and the elimination of toxins. The fruit consumer, properly following the above rules, will experience a rapid return of energy, a steady and satisfying weight-loss, and an overall feeling of health and well-being, as these nutrients use the vital juices of fruit to gain instant access to the energy processes of the body. All these benefits just from consuming fruit the right way? YES!! And we haven't even got to the really good tools yet.

If fruit is eaten with, or even after other foods, problems will, more often than not, result. This is because the Fruit Express is trying to get through to its destination quickly, and its clear path is blocked by a Chicken Fried Rice Goods Train lumbering through the colon at walking speed. The resultant wincing collision causes the liquefied fruit juices to combine with China's finest and this fruity morass in your stomach will begin to spoil. Proteins in the chicken putrefy and the rice carbohydrates ferment, resulting in the usual problems. Culturally we have come to view fruit as a dessert, which is nutritional heresy, in that fruit will always charge down the tunnel before hitting the back end of the Beef Risotto you chose to wolf down half an hour earlier. Once again, fruit should always be consumed on an empty stomach for happy smiles and care-free miles.

The other important consideration is water. Lots of it. As previously mentioned in the chapter on water and fluoridation, the body needs in excess of four pints of water daily (2 litres). Water is used by the body for digestion, detoxifying cells, watering the lungs, keeping the body alkalised and a host of cleaning duties. Water expert Dr Fereydoon Batmanghelidj maintains that asthmas, allergies, diabetes, arthritis, angina, stomach upsets, chronic intestinal complaints and certain other degenerative illnesses are the body's many cries for water, complaints which are dramatically improved with a consistent and long-term intake of fresh, clean water.[371] Dr Batman's best-selling book has helped thousands quash long-term health problems effortlessly and inexpensively. Coffee, tea, diet sodas, beer and a host of other liquids do not qualify as 'clean, fresh water' for the body, and should not be consumed by the cancer patient. Many of these are diuretic (water expelling) in their effect because of their chemical compositions.

Cancer patients especially should be consuming 4 pints of water a day[372] as part of their intake of vital nutrients, provided they do not have any renal (kidney) damage or disease that will cause complications with urine production resulting from the intake of additional water. Flushing the body with CONSISTENT, long-term water consumption is a superb way to assist with detoxification and hydration and is especially important for cancer patients. Drink a glass half an hour before a meal and then two glasses around two and a half hours afterwards for optimal digestive effects. The remainder of the day's intake of water can occur throughout the day.

THE CONCEPT OF HIGH WATER-CONTENT FOOD
The greatest tool in Natural Hygiene is to rearrange your diet to include an extremely high percentage of high water-content food in addition to the water you drink. Items like vegetables and fruits contain very high levels of water. A water melon for instance is 98% water. In a perfect world, this fruit water would be bowing under the weight of minerals and vitamins from the soils in which it was grown, and also laced with other nutrients. As mentioned before however, a significant portion of this mineral content is now missing from the food chain because soils are not currently being replenished with the minerals stripped out of them by successively grown crops. And so supplementation of vitamins and minerals in their correct form must be carried out by us citizens in order to avoid a gradual and deadly mineral deficiency building up to strike us down with disease.

---

[371] Batmanghelidj, F, *Your Body's Many Cries For Water*, op. cit.

[372] A carbon filter attached to a tap/faucet is adequate for producing chlorine- and soluent-free water to drink. This is preferable to plastic-bottled water which can be contaminated with chemicals from the plastic. Water in glass bottles is fine.

Natural Hygiene is all about keeping the body in balance nutritionally, metabolically, and also constantly replenished with water. 70% of our planet's surface is water, our bodies are 70%-80% water, so it makes sense to eat a diet consisting of at least 80-85% water-based foods that have not been processed and had the water and much of the accompanying nutrients stripped out.

Water is essential to life. On a cellular level, water is used by the body to transport nutrients to the organs and remove the waste products we examined earlier. Our blood comprises a very high percentage of water (blood serum), which the body naturally wishes to replace regularly. The difference between drinking water and fruit and vegetable water is in the nutrient content. Naturally a body fed on a diet comprising 80-85% unrefined plant dietary (unadulterated, organic fruit and vegetables) is a body being saturated in water-borne nutrition that is instantly and highly bio-available. A body well-watered in this way is a body whose three digestion cycles, APPROPRIATION, ASSIMILATION and ELIMINATION work with consummate ease. A well-watered body is a body which can clean itself on the inside with more precision than a laser.

But we don't eat this way today. Our societies are sick, obese, acidic, feeble, oxygen-starved, dehydrated, disease-ridden, pharmaceutically poisoned havens for mischief. There we are, showering our external bits squeaky-clean every morning with the cheapest chemicals available at the most expensive salon prices, and yet no cleaning is ever done on the insides of our bodies. That is why we are dropping dead of cancer and a whole host of other problems. We don't allow the body to cleanse and properly nourish itself on the inside and even if we do, we don't give it the water it needs to carry out the job. Why? Because the average Western diet we will consume today primarily comprises concentrated and processed foods – *foods which have had the water content stripped out of them.* We eat these foods because we have had the mother-of-all-selling-jobs done on us by Big Food who have sold us on taste. Actually a human doesn't need much selling on taste, but *"...boy, we've got the taste for sugar, chocolate, and a range of refined foods now, baby!"* as Ted Turner would say. And these have led us, like the Pied Piper, away from sanity and health, and down the broad path that leads to destruction.

Acid and Alkali Ashes

Q: If we're so rich and smart, how come we're so sick and tired?
A: Because our bodies in the Western world are in a constant state of acid siege.

Dr Ted Morter Jr. has spent a lifetime analysing the effects different foods have on our internal environment. Morter states that the body responds perfectly to every stimulus that is applied to it and each of these body responses is geared towards one aim and one aim only - survival. Sometimes this response is termed 'disease', if it goes against our ideal of what 'health' should be. Morter confirms the fact that the human body likes to dwell in a slight alkali (around pH 7.4). When we acidify our internal environment with certain types of food, the body is forced to neutralise, or 'buffer' this acid using a number of ingenious systems, mostly comprising alkalising minerals, such as sodium, calcium, potassium, magnesium and iron. Urine pH is a great indicator of what is happening inside the body and varies according to how much excess protein is consumed and has to be 'buffered' (neutralised). Note that blood pH must ALWAYS be between 7.35 and 7.45, or else life ends abruptly within a matter of hours.[373]

Foods we eat leave an 'ash' in our system. Rather than the dry flaky stuff that gets all over the carpet when we blow on an old fire, food residues in the body can be solid or liquid, but the 'ash', or residue they leave can either be acid or alkali (and on the odd occasion, neutral). The main acid generators are proteins, whether derived from animal or other sources. The key problem of course is the high level of proteins humans have been persuaded to eat today.

THE DANGERS OF EXCESSIVE PROTEIN

There is nothing wrong with protein. The body needs it, and we'd all be in a disaster situation without it. But, once again, the human body does not need anywhere near the level most have been conned into consuming. By the way, notice that the main acid-ash-producing foods are all backed by tremendously powerful and wealthy food

---

[373] Natural (physiological) acid produced through normal cell respiration is easily expelled in the breath via the lungs. Our blood pH is normally 7.35 when it is carting this acid, in the form of carbon dioxide, to the lungs for elimination. Blood is pH 7.45 after it has been 'cleaned up', the CO_2 removed, and then oxygen is taken on to deliver to your heart and the rest of your body.

lobbies with huge advertising budgets – i.e. meat, sugar, grains, dairy... and yes, even orange juice! A quick survey of the TV content of one evening will give you a picture of how many advertising dollars go into persuading the public to become acidic. Where's the alkali lobby for fruits and veggies? There's no big money in these foods in comparison to the previous list, so there is no lobby.

The protein levels most of us eat today are many times greater than the body actually needs (between 20-40 g a day are the estimated requirements) and the excess we consume can quite literally kill us. Some of us are slogging down up to 10 times the body's protein requirements and more, in our efforts to consume a herd of wildebeest and drink a swimming pool full of milk with our grain 'cereals' laced with refined sugar every morning. How our systems eventually exhaust themselves and collapse with all the acid generated is a book all on its own. But for our purposes here, the key is in understanding the effects of excess protein consumption and how the body tries to deal with it. When the digestive system is hit with a storm of acid derived from excessive protein food metabolism, this acid is potentially lethal and our hard-working body needs to sort the problem in a hurry.

Firstly the brain mobilises mineral buffers to raise the acidic pH of our internal environment towards neutral in an effort to counteract the protein acids.[374] After scarfing down burgers, chicken, eggs, pasta, cheese, seafood, grains – all accompanied by the inevitable acid-producing coffee, tea, sodas and alcohol, the mineral buffers use alkalising minerals and water to combine with the acid generated by these food ashes to raise their pH, before escorting them out of the body via the kidneys. Notice the body loses these alkalising minerals when they are eliminated along with the acid.

THE AMMONIA BUFFER
More often than not, the mineral buffers alone are not strong enough to render the internal environment alkaline enough not to hurt or even damage the kidneys. Fortunately the body has several back-up systems. The one we're interested in is the ammonia buffer. The kidneys begin producing ammonia, a strong alkali (pH around 9.25),

---

[374] The pH (potential of hydrogen) scale runs between 0 for pure acid and 14 for pure alkali. 7 is neutral.

which dramatically raises the pH of the excreta, sometimes as high as pH 8.5. Some people will notice that their urine smells of ammonia, and urinating can even hurt, due to the caustic nature of the solution being squirted out. Hence the need for our old friend, cranberry juice – an acid – which will then normalise the solution and eliminate the pain (there must be an easier way than all this!).

A strong smell of ammonia in the urine may indicate that the body's reserves of alkalising minerals are severely depleted. The body of course can mobilise further supplies of alkalising minerals like calcium, boron, sodium and magnesium, but you won't be happy with where it takes them from (calcium from the bones, etc.). A chronically acidic environment over many years will cause a severe depletion of minerals from the body, resulting in dangers of kidney exhaustion (too much ammonia production and acid damage), osteoporosis, mineral deficiency diseases, and then the auto-immune problems brought on by excess acid lodged in the joints and cartilage, such as arthritis and a host of other complaints.[375] Notice that the body is amoral in this regard. Morter sums up the body's attitude very succinctly:

"Your body doesn't care if you are sick or healthy. It doesn't plan for the future. Your body doesn't think and it doesn't judge. It doesn't care if you are hurting or if you are happy. All it does is respond to survive. Your body makes thousands of perfect survival responses every instant of your life. You may like the results of these responses and call it 'health'. Or you may not like the results and call it 'ill-health'. Your body doesn't care whether you like the responses or not. Survival of this instant is your body's only goal. Not survival later today, or next week, or next year. Survival now. Your body was designed to survive. It wasn't designed to be sick or well. What it is will be the accumulation of stresses that have been imposed upon it."[376]

Osteoporosis, heart disease, cancer, arthritis, diabetes and other ailments <u>can all be traced to the body's attempts to survive</u>. They can also all be traced to an inherent deficiency in the raw materials

---

[375] Kidney dialysis is used when the kidneys can no longer filter out waste products from the body. Without dialysis for damaged kidneys, the body would become overwhelmed with acid and soon die.

[376] **Morter, M T** *An Apple a Day?* BEST Research, Inc. 1997

(vitamins and minerals) required to get the survival job done. In the context of this book, we've seen that cancer is a healing process that hasn't terminated upon completion of its task, due to malnutrition. External (or internal) damage done to the body will always provoke a survival response. When we detect the nature of that response, we may exclaim, "Ah, a symptom!" But as Morter declares, the body doesn't care whether you like the results of its survival efforts or not. When you eat, drink, breathe, exercise, rest and think, you elicit a response from your body. So 'health' and 'disease' can be termed effects of your body's responses. Diarrhoea, vomiting, colds, flu, arthritis, osteoporosis and diabetes may not be anyone's idea of a good time, but these dramatic conditions are the result of the body's response to a stimulus. As Morter says, if you don't like the body's response, change the stimulus.

ACIDOSIS
With this in mind, we can begin to join a few dots. If the body likes to be alkali, and we are eating extremely acidic (processed), malnourished diets because we are told to by our TV, our body's response will be to buffer the resultant acidic gunk and excrete it rapidly. There are many 'diseases', or body responses, that can be evident from the body accomplishing these actions. Heartburn (acid reflux), indigestion, diarrhoea, mineral loss, resulting in mineral deficiency diseases. Calcium loss diseases, magnesium loss diseases, and so on.

And then, because we are chronically dehydrated because we don't drink water and eat high-water content food any more (that's all gone out of fashion), we are plagued by water deficiency ailments, such as constipation, asthma, heartburn, colitis and more ailments than I've got time to write down for you. In addition, your cells really don't go a bundle on being chronically bathed in acid, either inside or outside the cell environment, so there is a potassium buffer response within your cells to raise the pH of your intercellular environment. Cells break down as part of the life and death processes going on in your body all the time, so they add their catabolic acid to the sludge of the fast food nightmare. Now your brain is forced to order the kidneys to excrete more ammonia to alkalise the excreta before the latter's acid begins burning up the delicate tissues of the kidneys, urethra and other components.

By this time, we've normally managed to scoot down to the doctor's waiting room where we can expect to get drugs, which will 'make us feel better' (they treat the symptoms – not cure the underlying cause). GPs are generally unaware of the alkali/acid struggle going on with many diseases, and they are certainly unaware of the nutrition causation, because most of them haven't been trained in nutrition. Drugs given to a patient will themselves elicit their own responses from the body (side-effects), almost all of which will be acidic. High sugar sodas will fool our body into producing acids in preparation to digest a meal that never arrives, so there is even more acid flying around.

Clinical urine analysis is always useful in providing an indicator of what is going on in the body. When I was living in Los Angeles, there was a big thing going on in the tabloids about how freelance reporters were going through the trash of the stars who lived in Beverly Hills and on Mulholland Drive in order to find material for a 'good' story. While I do not condone in the least this sort of parasitic behaviour, going through your body's own trash, using a urine analysis and pH test, yields a lot of useful information. You can learn a lot from the things your body throws away.

A lot of people like to get technical over these issues. They measure protein grams, they measure urine pH, they put themselves through all kinds of strictures, which to me destroy the fun of life. My take is this: simply recognise the signs your body provides that your internal environment is acidic and begin moving it towards alkali by consuming a diet that is 80% alkali-ash-producing foods and 20% of the other stuff. Notice from the lists at the back of the book that almost all fruits and veg are alkali-ash-producing, *and yet many are acidic going in.* Even a humble pear will register pH5.5, and yet pears, along with the malic acid in apples, *have an alkalising effect on the body.* Thus fruits and veggies are the best alkalising tools on the market, containing as they do all the essential minerals the body requires to set up its intricate buffer systems. If your tongue or mouth hurts when you consume fruit, this may be an indicator of how acidic your body is, *before* you begin to do something about it. Start to change your diet gradually using steamed vegetables and your body will appreciate you for your care and gradual education.

ALKALI BODIES ABSORB OXYGEN

Dr Otto Warburg, who received a Nobel Prize in the 1930s, noted that alkaline bodies absorbed up to 20 times more oxygen than acidic bodies. He found that diseased bodies were acidic bodies which repelled oxygen. Warburg worked with almost 50 species of animals and was able to induce cancer in animal tissue simply by acidifying the body and driving out the oxygen.

Warburg found that alkaline bodies are healthy bodies, with a high absorption of life-preserving oxygen. And today, those cultures living long life-spans all have alkalised body systems. The Okinawans, for instance, renowned for their longevity and health, live on their southern Japanese island, which is made predominantly of calcium compounds (coral reef). The water these Japanese citizens consume has been found to contain, per quart, 8,300 mg of dissolved (ionised) calcium and 9,700 mg of un-ionised, non-dissolved calcium for a total of 18 grams of calcium in its various forms. And the Okinawans drink 4/5 quarts a day, and then irrigate their farm soils with it! Researcher Robert Barefoot, who has made a study of the Okinawans, states that by the time he added it up, the Okinawans were getting over 100,000 mg (100g) of calcium in various forms a day and probably violating the RDA over hundredfold for every mineral and vitamin.[377] Yet we are told the RDA for calcium is a miserable 600-1000mg a day.

When Otto Warburg explained his exciting acid/alkali conclusions to his medical peers over half a century ago, they threatened to revoke his licence. Yet experiments with ulcerated breast mass and other tumour material show categorically that malignant cells grow prolifically in acid, anaerobic environments, but shrivel and die in calcium- and oxygen-rich alkalis.[378]

Dr Carl Reich, noted nutritional research pioneer, demonstrated that Vitamin D was crucial to the absorption of calcium, and that modern man, in addition to being chronically deficient in ionised calcium, also dwelt mostly under artificial light and was not getting

---

[377] **Barefoot, Robert R** *The Calcium Factor*, an audio briefing. Available at www.exxelaudio.com; also *The Calcium Factor*, published by Deonna Enterprises Publishing, PO Box 21270, Wickenburg, AZ, 85358, USA
[378] Barefoot, Robert, op. cit.

enough interaction of full-spectrum sunlight on the cholesterol in his skin to produce abundant Vitamin D through photosynthesis.

CELLULAR RESPIRATION

Researchers Carafoli and Penniston were studying the calcium ion in the 1980s, and determined that a common trigger exists that precipitates such diverse biochemical processes as the secretion of a hormone and the electrical contraction of a muscle. This trigger, they discovered, was a minute flux of calcium ions. Later research was to show that calcium ions played a far more fundamental role in how each of our cells 'breathes'. Hundreds of research papers today show how cells use an ingenious mechanism of rosette-shaped calcium proteins to open and close ion channels in each cell membrane like doors, which allow nutrients to be taken in and out of the cell.

As the nutrients inside the cell undergo chemical reactions freeing up their nutrient radicals for cell growth, calcium ions are liberated, reducing the pH of this intracellular fluid from 7.4 to around 6.6 and giving it a positive charge. The intracellular and extracellular fluids now have a potential difference, or voltage build-up, of around 70 millivolts. This is enough to bend the calcium rosette 'doors' in the cell membrane open to allow another influx of nutrients into the cell, which react and produce another voltage build-up. In this way, the cell 'breathes', and a continued electrochemical chain reaction ensures a continued production of nutrient raw materials to produce further cells. This entire procedure is completely dependent on ionised calcium being richly abundant in the body and properly absorbed into the bloodstream using the Vitamin D/sunlight catalyst.

Carl Reich, Otto Warburg and later Robert Barefoot understood that calcium has a three-fold effect on vital cell respiration and nutrition:

1. Calcium-bound protein rosettes regulate both the size and the opening and closing of ion 'breathing' channels in every cell wall
2. The calcium ion has the ability to stack nutrients electrically and draw them into the cell through these doors for potential difference (voltage) discharge and chemical reaction

3. Calcium combines with the phosphates in the extracellular and intracellular fluids to create a slightly alkaline, buffered and oxygen-rich medium necessary to sustain life[379]

Gregory R Mundy, Professor and Head of the Division of Endocrinology and Metabolism at the University of Texas, writes as follows:

"A number of important metabolic processes are influenced by small changes in extracellular ionised calcium concentration. These include:

> *The excitability of nerve function and neural transmission*
> *The secretion by cells of proteins and hormones, and other mediators, such as the neurotransmitter acetylcholine[380]*
> *The coupling of cell excitation with cell response (for example, contraction in the case of muscle cells, and secretion in the case of secretory cells)*
> *Cell proliferation*
> *Blood coagulation, by acting as a co-factor for the essential enzymes involved in the clotting crusade*
> *Maintenance of the stability and permeability of cell membranes*
> *The mineralisation of newly formed bone"* [381]

Low levels of organic meat (5-10% of the diet) are OK and a source of Vitamins B9 and B12. Meat-eating to excess, aside from causing unwanted and potentially harmful acid toxins, can result in a loss of ionised calcium from the human body. Meat is phosphorus-dominant (an acid), when compared with calcium, which results in calcium phosphates being produced (apatite), which are then precipitated out of the body.

---

[379] **Moolenaar WH, Defize LK & SW Delaat** "Calcium in the action of growth factors", *Calcium and the Cell*, Wiley, 1986

[380] Acetylcholine is a neurotransmitter hormone essential for memory. It is formed from the amino acids choline and serine with Vitamin B5, DMAE, pyroglutamate and manganese as co-factor nutrients. An acetylcholine deficiency is being partly blamed for causing Alzheimer's and other memory problem diseases. Key ingredients to mental health are zinc, B5, B6, C, iron and the minerals. In other words, A HEALTHY DIET!

[381] **Mundy, GR** "Calcium homeostasis: Hypercalcemia and hypocalcemia", University of Texas

Dr Reich found that when a patient has adequate levels of ionised calcium, his saliva pH range was slightly alkaline at 7.5 to 7.0 (neutral). Body excretions tended to be acidic as the body rids itself of toxins and waste in the ideal way. However, when the body was calcium-deficient, the saliva pH range tended to be acidic, from 6.4 to 4.6, and the body excretions were now alkaline, as the body attempted to mobilise calcium and water to rectify the acid/alkaline balance. Dr James K van Fleet states: *"When the body does not get enough calcium, it will withdraw what little calcium it has from the bones to make sure there is enough in the bloodstream, then the body does its best to bolster the sagging architecture by building bony deposits and spurs to reduce movement and limit activity."* [382] Notice that this is another survival response. Once again, your body does not care whether you hurt or not, it is simply exercising damage control due to an extreme threat situation.

Osteoporosis, arthritis, rheumatism, sclerosis and periodontal disease are all the body's way, not of exhibiting 'disease', but of discouraging and preventing unnecessary movement during a raging mineral deficiency. Calcium lactates, along with magnesium and Vitamin D, are the sure way to help these symptoms, together with a change of lifestyle and diet.

Alkalising the body in children can happen within days with food and supplements. Adults take much longer, sometimes months, and the elderly may take up to a year to start rendering an alkaline result on the saliva test. The good news is, they will be moving in the right direction if they make some dietary and lifestyle changes for the better.

Want to live to be a healthy hundred? Then find someone who is a healthy hundred, like the Hunzas, and do what they do. Diets low in meat and milk, but rich in 80-85% unrefined plant dietary and alkali ash foods, along with full trace mineral supplementation (including calcium/magnesium/ Vitamin D) are diets rich in mineral-saturated, high-water-content *alkalising* foods that will start combating unnecessary dietary acids and start shifting your body's pH values towards health and longevity – it's as simple as that.

---

[382] **Van Fleet, JK** *Magic of Catalytic Health Vitalizers*, Parker Publishing, 1980

It is interesting and poignant to note that the observations outlined in this chapter were encountered over 50 years ago and yet today, modern cancer research still refuses to make nutrition and body acid/alkali a firm priority. Notice the comments made in 1967 by Corinne H Robinson in *Normal and Therapeutic Nutrition*:

"Because the body makes [pH] *adjustments in the regulation of body neutrality, the reaction of the diet is of no practical significance in health.... Those who become concerned about the relative acid or alkalinity of foods have often been misled by false advertising claims of the food quack."* [383]

If I really had the time, I would find out what Ms Robinson's 'special interests' were when she wrote those words. Never mind. We can't straighten the world out all in one day. So let's press on to the next chapter and find out...

[383] **Robinson, C H** *Normal and Therapeutic Nutrition*, 13th ed. New York: MacMillan & Co., 1967, p.131

How Exercise Helps

Natural Hygiene also promotes exercise to get oxygen into the system to encourage a dynamic circulation, elimination and mobility for your marvellous human machine. Quite simply, if you are doing good for your body, you will feel so darned fine, you will quit your job and begin promoting the Natural Hygiene lifestyle full-time like the dedicated nutritional evangelical you have become, for the rest of your extended happy days.

I love exercise, having lived in California for a number of years. But before you can come to terms with the need for it (exercise, not California), you have to see, like swimming, how far you will sink without regular movement. I am hardly a zealot with exercise, as many are, but I do my part and have developed a discipline over the years that has served me well, and I have been disease-free for the last fifteen years, not only as a result of exercise, but also thanks to the other factors covered in this book.

I have to say though, the one thing that impressed me most about Californians who lived healthy outdoor lives down in those beach communities like Malibu, Santa Monica, Playa del Rey and Redondo Beach, was that they actually enjoyed themselves, looked great and were living life to the full. Months later, I too was part of that euphoria that is healthy Southern California.

I was amazed when, as a pale Englander, I had first arrived in Los Angeles to see tanned and fit octogenarian men sailing by on roller-blades and vital, pretty ladies in their seventies playing volleyball on the sandy beaches before picking up their bikes and cycling along the famous bike-path to one of the great restaurants along Santa Monica Bay for a scrumptious chow-down, consisting of - you guessed it - platefuls of high-water-content, unrefined plant dietary.

SUNLIGHT
And isn't it strange how we have all been taught to fear the sun? Most already know about the scare concerning the planet's supposed ozone (O_3) depletion. Tales abound about holes above the North and South Poles two and a half times the size of Europe.

Chlorofluorocarbons (CFCs) released through industrial activity supposedly rise into the atmosphere and are broken down into chlorine particles by the ultraviolet energy of the sun. These radical chlorines, we are told, in turn destroy ozone molecules at the rate of 1 Cl to 100,000 O_3. A thin layer of ozone in the stratosphere is responsible for shielding the earth from the sun's damaging radiation spectrum emissions. The shield is apparently now 5% depleted. Scientists estimate that at 17% depletion, we may as well forget about putting away for that pension. Did you know the US government actually spent $19 million of taxpayers' money to find out whether the belching and farting of cattle damaged the ozone layer?

Let's now learn a few things about ozone. O_3 is a poisonous gas that is a product of the chemical reaction of the sun's light meeting the earth's atmosphere. Ozone does indeed act as a barrier in the upper atmosphere, filtering out the sun's radiation and thus behaves as a shield, protecting us. The thing is, very little ozone is produced at the earth's poles simply due to the fact that the sun's light does not play on these regions directly but strikes at an angle without producing O_3. Which means, there have always been ozone holes at the poles and in surrounding areas.

There is no *global* ozone catastrophe. Indeed the facts such as they are indicate that man's ozonic depredations are extremely minor when compared with the damage caused by volcanoes and their aerosols. One eruption, such as Mount St Helen's, will do more to damage the ozone layer than 10,000 years of spraying stink pretty under our arms.

It is true that areas in proximity to the poles are not adequately protected by ozone for the foregoing reasons of sunlight-angle and so produce problems for humans and animals, if they are not adequately nourished and protected. In the extreme south of Chile, ranch cattle developing conjunctivitis to an abnormal degree have been reported staggering into one another. In southern Argentina, farm labourers become severely burned after spending just 20 minutes in the sun. Skin cancer in humans in the danger zones blanketing the poles and adjacent areas is also a recognised serious issue, and seems to be on the rise, but only because of the encroaching metabolic deficiencies in the humans concerned. Simply put, too much of anything is going to do you harm. Too much water and you'll drown. Is that a good reason for giving up water?

In recent years, when the ozone layer was measured across the planet (not just at the poles), it was found to be thicker than the first time we examined it! The pillorying of R-12 air-conditioning refrigerant as being the chemical responsible for destroying the earth's protective shield is as pathetic as the idea that the propellants (CFCs) released through spraying deodorant under our arms indirectly cause cancer to schoolchildren in Tierra del Fuego. For starters, R-12 is heavier than air and sinks. Secondly, not even normal convection currents would carry R-12 into the atmosphere to sufficient heights and in adequate volume to do any damage. It would take a sustained and prolific misuse of R-12 for at least 100 years to make any measurable impact on the ozone layer and this simply has not happened.

The result of outlawing R-12 and replacing it with an environmentally friendly alternative in car air-conditioning systems has effectively caused an overall increase in the price of automobiles. This in turn has led to increases in all society's related sector costs as a result. No doubt some enterprising economist in government got a big bonus for dreaming up that one. Not bad for a tax for which no one can be blamed. Was this the same guy or girl who dreamt up the lottery (tax on greed)?

So have some sun. It's good for you. You get Vitamin D by the bucket-load, and your intestines are lined with Vitamin D receptors, which means that calcium absorption can increase up to 20 times if these receptors are full.[384] Skin cancer will only be a concern if you a) abuse the sun over a protracted period of time while having... b) inadequate nutrition and no B17 in your diet (factors which have made skin cancer appear to be on the increase over the past few decades); or c) use sunscreens with known carcinogens in them which will permeate the skin into the bloodstream and accumulate to damage the body, creating healing trophoblastic reactions which then do not terminate (cancer).

---

[384] Barefoot Robert, *The Calcium Factor*, op. cit.

Do not burn yourself, but tan gently over a period of time. If you are fair-skinned, you must of course take a lot less sun than darker-skinned types. We looked at the need for the human body to have sunlight earlier when we learned that we have three glands behind the eyes – the hypothalamus, the pineal and the pituitary glands. Sunlight is absolutely required to stimulate these into releasing their hormone payloads for the benefit of our regular health. Many societies spend all day in the sun and do not have the chemical toxic loads we have in the industrial world and so do not suffer from the cancer scourge that is currently afflicting us. Anyone who tells you the sun is harmful in reasonable amounts is a menace.

WORKING THE BODY

Now. Back to exercise. Exercising is something we all must do, because living things DO move, and the more they move, the more alive they feel. Look at a Jack Russell puppy. It's bouncing off the walls with excitement and couldn't get into more drawers and mischief if you paid it. Inactivity is a relatively recent phenomenon with humans, ever since the abandonment of the horse and the advent of mass transport earlier in the 1900s. Many facets affecting health, like high meat and dairy consumption, drug abuse, environmental contamination and polluted food, water and air, are also quite new to us, and so are the health tragedies we are suffering as a result. It often helps to put these things in perspective. We haven't always done many of the things we do or don't do today. And with health and sickness, we are very much reaping the results of our activity or inactivity. Obesity is at an all-time high, as we examined earlier. Our convenience society, coupled with our new chemical junk diets and personal toxin fripperies, is, as they say where I'm from, doing us in. And exercise has all but gone out the window.

The key with exercise is don't overdo it, just work the muscles progressively and get cycling to raise a light sheen for a hour or so, and genteelly glow if you are a female. If you are a man, go ahead and sweat and stink all you want. Sweating's good, because the body is eliminating from the lymph massage with the exercise you are giving it. Do not use antiperspirants EVER AGAIN, as the aluminium and other compounds block up your lymph nodes, giving rise to major problems down the road when internal toxins can be driven back into the body, denied any means of escape and damage the lymph and breast.

Remember, the idea is to get everything moving both inside and outside the body.

An ideal starting exercise regimen for 16-65 year old kids is laid out below. Ensure no more than one minute's rest between the sets of any particular exercise, in order to prevent the body cooling down and to maintain the muscle stress. It is a good idea to work with the trainers available in the gyms to maximise the benefit of correct and safe techniques in exercising. But once you've got the techniques down, *"The sky's the limit, baby!"* as Ted Turner would undoubtedly say:

THE WEIGHT/CYCLING REGIMEN
15 minutes warming up with light cycling or rowing.
Barbell squats (3 sets x 15 repetitions (reps))
Bench press (3 sets x 15 reps)
Lat pull-downs (3 sets x 15 reps)
Seated rowing (3 sets x 15 reps)
Sit-ups (2 sets until muscle failure)
30 minutes light cycling to finish off, raising the sweat, sheen or glow.

NOTES:
Before embarking on an exercise regimen of any sort, it is advisable to consult your health practitioner, especially if you suffer from a serious illness.

Those over 65 should exercise OF COURSE, but the gym you join will advise on how to ease into the regimen with the minimum of difficulty.

Ensure that the weight used is enough to get your muscles failing at around the 15th repetition. The weight will then need to be increased to fail you at the 15th rep as you gain strength during the program.

Exhale as you load the muscles with weight (the positive), inhale as you release the weight (the negative).

The burn you feel in muscle exercise is the result of oxygen metabolism and is known as lactic acid. A few deep inhalations and the burn soon passes.

On your days without weights, do some light cycling for 45 minutes in the gym. I always read while I am doing this, to make the time even more productive and take my mind off what I am doing. Walking doesn't get the heart rate up enough, although walking is great exercise over the long-haul. The idea is to raise the heart rate on a consistent basis to about 75% of your maximum during aerobic exercise. Heart monitors are often provided by the gym for such monitoring.

Do the weight exercises as early in the day as your schedule allows, three times a week, such as Mondays, Wednesdays and Fridays. The intermittent days, Tuesdays, Thursdays and Sundays, should be set aside for muscle recovery. So the week will typically look as follows:

MONDAY – WEIGHT/CYCLING REGIMEN
TUESDAY – 45 MINS CYCLING OR LAP SWIMMING
WEDNESDAY – WEIGHT/CYCLING REGIMEN
THURSDAY – 45 MINS CYCLING OR LAP SWIMMING
FRIDAY – WEIGHT/CYCLING REGIMEN
SATURDAY – 45 MINS CYCLING OR LAP SWIMMING
SUNDAY – A NICE WALK! BUT OTHERWISE OFF

Seems like a lot? Probably by today's standards. Yet a few hundred years ago, your ancestors cheerfully did comparably active workouts as part of their daily chores and work and thought nothing of it. How soft and lazy we have become.

Do the above regimen for four weeks during the Natural Hygiene program. After four weeks, expand the workout under advice from your qualified gym instructor to train specific muscle groups, if this is your wish. If you continue with these core exercises however, you will see great results. "Consistency! Consistency! Consistency!" over the next few months will reap enormous benefits in both physical and mental well-being.

Ladies: Do not fear 'becoming muscular'. You have 1/100th the adrogen hormone of males and you would quite literally have to take anabolic steroids to get bulky. By exercising properly and naturally, you will tone your muscles, burn excess fat and your body will approach its lean body-weight.

BODY TYPES
Often I am asked how to put on weight by those with a lean body frame. There are three general body types, and the body likes to operate within the broad genetics offered by these categories, so you

must work within the rules and not expect results inconsistent with your body type :

Endomorphic – Very prone to putting on fat and also muscle. Often described as heavy body-types with large bones. Endomorphs can arrive at their lean body weight and demonstrate nice definition and body contouring. Often Endomorphs have a weight problem whose counter weight is the ability to lose it just as quickly with the correct regimen.

Mesomorphic – Athletic frame which will put on muscle or fat easily. Mesomorphs are the classic muscular athletic frame, which is very workable and mobile. Not as heavy-set as endomorphs.

Ectomorphic – Slender frame. Ectomorphs are typically the marathon-runner bodies. They are the slenderest of the body-types, not prone to putting on muscle or fat.

If you do the Natural Hygiene program: fruit before noon, properly combined diet, including the 'forbidden apricot kernels', 80-85% high-water content, unrefined plant dietary and have an hour in the gym tying yourselves up with all that amazing equipment, you will, as you approach the end of the fourth week, be fighting off the advances from the opposite sex (even the eighty-five year-olds, in fact, those guys are the worst), and seeing the New You rebirthing right before your dumb-founded eyes. It's a great exhilaration. You'll love it.

* * * * *

And Finally....

I cannot tell you the number of sick, depressed and drug-dependent doctors I have met. Some of them have become my fiercest critics. I was recently criticised by an establishment doctor in Australia during my March 2001 tour for promoting nutrition, disease prevention and wellness to combat a whole host of health problems. But what are his dismal efforts in healthcare producing?

> ➤ One in five Australians will suffer from a mental health problem at some stage of their life
> ➤ One in three men and one in four women are getting cancer
> ➤ One in two men and one in three women will suffer from coronary heart disease
> ➤ One in four men and one in five women will have a stroke
> ➤ One in six Australians will suffer from diabetes
> ➤ One in three will have asthma
> ➤ One in four drinks alcohol daily
> ➤ One in two has used an illicit drug
> ➤ One in six adults experiences anxiety
> ➤ Eight out of every ten adults are physically inactive, have high blood pressure or smoke cigarettes [385]

Clearly this doctor and his 'medicine' are failing spectacularly with the health of Australians. But what is his attitude? Contrition? "Oh, well, we ought to look in some new directions"? No. It is to bad-mouth, by any and all means possible, natural, common-sense measures to restore his countrymen and women to wellness. It is my view, however controversial it may be, that any healthcare practitioner or establishment doctor who gainsays and belittles proper nutrition, scientifically supported nutritional supplementation and exercise as a means of avoiding disease IS CRIMINALLY LIABLE for the above statistics in Australia and everywhere else, for that matter. They know better. It is about time the medical establishment is held to account for its brazen, flagrant abuses of citizen health and we will have more to say on this matter before this book is over.

---

[385] *Herald Sun*, 27th November 1999

Traditional medicine, as we have seen, is increasingly coming under fire as cracks appear in the flawless picture we have painted of our medicinal saviours. When *Trust Me (I'm a Doctor)* – the book and the TV series written by Dr Phil Hammond and Michael Mosley - came before the British public, the British National Health Service (NHS) and private medical practice were portrayed in a strange new, foreboding light. Dr Hammond remarks:

"In BBC2's 'Cardiac Arrest', an NHS hospital was depicted as a war zone, with staff bullying one another, humiliating patients and taking the path of least resistance in order to survive. The only way to cope was not to care. For the first time in a British TV program, nurses were portrayed as a bunch of clock-watching, bolshy witches, and the rougher side of doctors was shown... one making easily overheard remarks about a man with lung cancer ("He's got so much asbestos in him, it'll take a year to cremate him.") A bullied female doctor with an alcohol problem committed suicide. All very bleak and unsettling."[386][387]

The picture painted by most who have worked in the National Health Service is one in which overworked and inexperienced junior doctors are engaged in a daily struggle to keep their heads above crushing workloads. Some of these believe their problems started during medical school, where they were first introduced to the deeply ingrained cronyism and party culture of the medical establishment.

Two surveys, reported in *The Lancet*, discovered that heavy drinking and illicit drug use were common among second-year medical students, and that these invariably increased after graduation. [388] Of the 90 house officers studied, 60% of both sexes exceeded their safe limits. 35% of men and 10% of women reported using other drugs such as hallucinogenic mushrooms, LSD, ecstasy, amyl nitrite (the sex drug, 'poppers'), cocaine and amphetamines. As for their mental state, 21 percent of men and 45 percent of women had anxiety scores indicating possible pathological anxiety.

---

[386] Hammond, P & M Mosley *Trust Me (I'm a Doctor)*, op. cit.

[387] *Cardiac Arrest* was generally popular among doctors. One survey showed that junior doctors believed the program was an accurate portrayal of their working conditions (*British Medical Journal*, 1994, vol. 309, p.132).

[388] *Lancet*, 1996, vol. 348, pp.922-925; 1998, vol. 352, p.785

Stress too was a major factor in influencing the later mental conditions and competence of doctors when interacting with their patients. In 1991, a study of doctors who qualified in 1986 found that 58% of men and 76% of women regretted entering medicine. [389]

Dr Hammond states: *"Drinking and drug abuse are clearly coping mechanisms picked up in medical school, but it is impossible to predict which of the many heavy student drinkers will go on to develop a problem. The British Medical Association estimated that up to 13,000 practising UK doctors are addicted to drugs or alcohol. If each makes 2,000 clinical decisions a year, at a conservative estimate, that is 26 million decisions affecting patient care* [including prescribing potentially lethal drugs] *made by doctors who can't function without alcohol or other drugs."* [390]

I have never seen so many unhealthy-looking people involved with healthcare in my life. Let the truth come out, I say, for the benefit of all. And let the chips fall where they may.

* * * * *

We have covered a lot of information and travelled along a myriad of plot-lines, but ultimately, and I think, most appropriately, the answer we arrive at is the simple one. We need to educate ourselves, a day at a time, back to the basics of clean air, clean water and clean food. We need to reserve a healthy scepticism for complicated and expensive health agendas appearing to be the panacea for our longevity and good health. We need to support and encourage our doctors and health practitioners to become active in seeking the clean and simple answers that nutrition and preventative medicine have always had to offer. Oh, I know that the profits won't be anywhere near as great, but the citizen is sick of being sick – and he is awakening to the answers that will lead him back to the path of wellness. I am a great believer that the simplest and most obvious choices are generally the right ones: put the right gas in the machine, keep the machine clean and

[389] **Allen, Isobel** *Doctors and their Careers: A New Generation*, London: Policies Studies Institute, 1988
[390] Hammond, Dr Phil, op. cit.

pollution-free on the inside as well as outside, and enjoy a long and healthy life as a fitting reward for your efforts.

It serves each of us to get our own health-house in order, all the while spreading this information far and wide for the benefit of all. There is a tremendous momentum currently underway which seeks fundamental medical reform across the board – and I am all for this. It is an exciting time to be alive. There is a new 21st century healthcare system struggling to be born which will endue its followers with the 21st century longevity that should be all of ours by right. A healthcare system with nutrition and preventative medicine as its spearhead, girded also with the proven, valid and necessary procedures, which have been developed by allopathic medicine over the years.

At the present time, the health industry is torn down the middle between the orthodox and alternative. Yet there need not be an 'us and them', if the truth prevails about what the human body ultimately needs, in order to give it the optimum shot at longevity and health. And what is that truth? That the human body does its best when given clean, uncontaminated water to drink, clean, uncontaminated food to eat and clean, uncontaminated air to breathe in a poison-free and friendly environment.

Please join me in completing this mission.

Part 3

'appendices and notes'

A Guide to Nutritional Supplements

Please note that the following information is for educational purposes only and must not be construed as medical advice. A qualified health practitioner should always be sought in the matter of any illness.

B17 Laetrile/Amygdalin Tablets

These pharmaceutical grade tablets contain the active B17 ingredient derived from the kernels of apricots. Usually available in 100mg or 500mg tablets. Some people are confused with the terms Laetrile and amygdalin. These names essentially refer to the same compound – Vitamin B17 ($C_{20}H_{27}NO_{11}$) – and are, to all intents and purposes, interchangeable. These tablets are usually taken in conjunction with the apricot seeds, commencing with low dosage and working into the manufacturers' recommended intake of:

- 2-4 100mg tablets per day as a nutritional supplement for prevention (apricot seeds have been recommended by doctors in place of tablets for prevention also).
- 4-6 500mg tablets per day as a nutritional supplement for clinical cancer sufferers, taken in conjunction with enzymes and Vitamins A & E (emulsified).

Ultra Enzymes

Specific enzymes used in Metabolic Therapy include chymotrypsin (human pancreatic enzyme), pancreatin and calf thymus (animal enzymes), papain (from papayas) and bromelain (from pineapples). Ernst Krebs also states: *"The demasking effect of these enzymes against the pericellular layer of the malignant cell is something very concrete in the immunology of cancer. Now I prefer, rather than advising the use of bromelain or papaya tablets, that the individual seeking these enzymes get them directly from the fresh ripe pineapple and papaya fruit. As much as half a pineapple a day should be ingested."*[391]

---

[391] Taken from a 1974 speech presented before the Second Annual Cancer Convention at the Ambassador Hotel in Los Angeles, California.

Emulsified Vitamin A

In 1963 when Dr Contreras initiated his activities as a clinical oncologist, the use of Vitamin A as a useful agent in malignant neoplasm was considered illogical and absurd. Now Vitamin A is accepted as an agent of great use for the major epithelial cancers as well as for epidermis carcinomas, chronic leukaemia and transitional cells.

The first formal studies of the possible anti-tumour effects of Vitamin A were initiated in Germany, by investigators of Mugos Laboratories in Munich. It was a proven fact that lung cancer in Norwegian sailors was less common than in other groups, even though they smoked since childhood. Logic indicated that it had to be the opposite. After studying this phenomenon, it was discovered that they ate abundant quantities of raw fish liver, high in Vitamin A, since childhood. The logical conclusion was that high doses of such a vitamin prevented the growth of lung cancer in heavy smokers. But it was also found that high doses of Vitamin A were toxic, and could cause adverse reactions.

The main focus was to find out how to administer enough Vitamin A to observe preventive or healing effects, without injuring the liver. The solution was found by one of the investigators, when he discovered that unprocessed milk had the vitamin, and children who were breast-fed never experienced toxic effects. Nature had the solution by including Vitamin A in mother's milk in the form of micro-emulsification.

Mugos investigators proceeded to prepare a variety of emulsified concentrations, formulating their famous High Concentration A-Mulsin. One drop contains 15,000 units. They were able to administer over a million units per day in progressive doses, without producing hepatic toxicity. The explanation is that, in emulsified form, Vitamin A is absorbed directly into the lymphatic system without going through the liver in high quantities. Having solved the toxicity problem, it was possible to test the product in high doses. It was demonstrated that emulsified Vitamin A has the following effects:
  ➢ In normal doses, it protects epithelium and vision.
  ➢ In doses of 100,000 to 300,000 units per day, it works as a potent immune stimulant.

> In doses of 500,000 to 1,000,000 units per day, it works as a potent anti-tumour agent, especially in epidermis and transitional carcinomas.

Apricot Seeds/Kernels

Apricot kernels are an inexpensive, rich and natural source of Vitamin B17. They also deliver the vitamins, minerals and enzymes not found in the pharmaceutical derivative of B17.

- 7g of seeds per day for life are recommended by Dr Krebs as a nutritional supplement for those exercising cancer prevention, commencing with low intakes.
- Up to 28g of seeds per day are recommended by Dr Krebs as nutritional support for clinical cancer sufferers, commencing with low intakes.

In a minority of cases, cancer sufferers may experience nausea when taking seeds. In this event, clinics recommend that dosage is reduced and then gradually increased as tolerance is gained. Not all apricot seeds are effective. They must have the characteristic bitter taste indicating that the active B17 ingredient is present. Not to be eaten whole. May be pulped, grated or crushed.

Please note: Some cancer sufferers believe that apricot kernels alone are all that is required to fight cancer. Consultation with a qualified health practitioner familiar with Metabolic Therapy is advised for further information. Apricot kernels are usually part of the nutritional support for those exercising cancer prevention *for life* as well as cancer patients undergoing Phase 1 or Phase 2 Metabolic Therapy.

Vitamin C (Ascorbic acid)

Dr Linus Pauling, often known as the 'Father of Vitamin C' and twice awarded the Nobel Prize, declared that large intakes of up to 10g of the vitamin each day aids anti-cancer activity within the body and also assists in repairing damaged arteries and removing arterial plaque (atherosclerosis) for heart disease sufferers. Pauling was largely derided for making these declarations (yet he lived to be 94!), but today, large doses of Vitamin C are used by many practitioners for cancer patients in nutritional therapy, who believe Pauling was right and that the popular nutrient is indispensable to the body in its fight to regain health from cancer.

Several studies have suggested that Vitamin C may reduce levels of lead in the blood. Epidemiological studies have shown that people with elevated blood serum levels of Vitamin C had lower levels of blood toxicity. An examination of the data from the Third National Health and Nutrition Examination Survey, enrolling 4,213 youths aged 6 to 16 years and 15,365 adults 17 years and older from 1988 to 1994, found a correlation between low serum ascorbic acid levels and elevated blood lead levels. The authors conclude that high ascorbic acid intake may reduce blood lead levels.[392]

An analysis of the Normative Aging Study, which enrolled 747 men aged 49 to 93 years from 1991 to 1995, found that lower dietary intake of Vitamin C may increase lead levels in the blood.[393] A study of 349 African American women enrolled in the project Nutrition, Other Factors, and the Outcome of Pregnancy found that vitamin-mineral supplementation resulted in increased serum levels of ascorbic acid and decreased serum levels of lead. The authors concluded that maternal use of a vitamin supplement with ascorbic acid and Vitamin E might offer protection from lead contamination of the foetus during pregnancy.[394]

Because smoking lowers levels of ascorbic acid in the body, researchers theorised that Vitamin C supplementation may effect blood lead levels in smokers. A clinical study was performed on 75 adult men 20 to 30 years of age who smoked at least one pack of cigarettes per day, but had no clinical signs of ascorbic acid deficiency or lead toxicity. Subjects were randomly assigned to daily supplementation with placebo, 200 mg of ascorbic acid, or 1000 mg of ascorbic acid.

---

[392] **Simon JA, Hudes ES** "Relationship of Ascorbic Acid to Blood Lead Levels." *Journal of the American Medical Association,* 1999;281:2289-2293.

[393] **Cheng Y, Willett WC, Schwartz J, Sparrow D, Weiss S, Hu H** "Relation of nutrition to bone lead and blood lead levels in middle-aged to elderly men. The Normative Aging Study." *Am J Epidemiol* 1998 Jun 15;147(12):1162-1174.

[394] **West WL, Knight EM, Edwards CH, et al.** "Maternal low level lead and pregnancy outcomes." *J Nutr.* 1994 Jun;124(6 Suppl):981S-986S.

After one week of supplementation, there was an 81% decrease in blood-lead levels in the group taking 1000 mg of ascorbic acid daily.[395]

Dosage recommended by Linus Pauling for prevention is between 600mg and 3g a day – or up to 10g/day for those who have been diagnosed with cancer. High levels of Vitamin C however can cause diarrhoea and may be contra-indicated with certain chemotherapy treatments. Vitamin C is especially useful when combined in moderate amounts with Calcium d-glucarate, as formulated in the Neways product D-Toxarate (see D-Toxarate in this section).

Maximol (Neways International)

The huge rise in incidences of cancer and other degenerative diseases are primarily due to the depleted vitamin/mineral content in today's Western diet coupled with environmental/chemical toxin factors. The key nutritional ingredients invariably missing for cancer are B17, Vitamin C and the trace mineral selenium. A recent US study showed an overall drop of 50% in cancer deaths and a fall of 37% in new cancer cases, especially lung, bowel and prostate – among 1,300 volunteers taking supplements for four years. [396]

Mineral supplementation is most effective in the ionised 'liquid suspension' form, assisted by fulvic acid, where an unusually high percentage of assimilation by the body can be expected. Our bodies use minerals as raw material. These cannot be manufactured by the body, and so have to be present in the food and liquids we ingest. Sadly, as mentioned previously, our food chain is severely depleted of minerals, resulting in over 150 nutritional deficiency diseases that are now striking our societies with increasing intensity.

To combat this very real threat, mineral and vitamin supplementation, far from being a quaint health fad, is essential for everyone and can literally make the difference between life or death, especially for those with cancer. To combat this threat, Neways has formulated Maximol Solutions, probably the world's most complete liquid nutritional supplement, which contains 67 essential and trace

---

[395] **Dawson EB, Evans DR, Harris WA, Teter MC, McGanity WJ** "The effect of ascorbic acid supplementation on the blood lead levels of smokers." *J Am Coll Nutr.* 1999 Apr;18(2):166-170.

[396] *Daily Mail*, 28th July 1999, p. 31

minerals, 17 essential vitamins, 21 amino acids, three enzymes, and lactobacillus acidophilus.[397] To provide greater absorption of all these ingredients, Maximol contains nature's natural chelator, used by plants and animals for the absorption of minerals and nutrients - organic fulvic acid. It is known that fulvic acid aids in the transport and assimilation of minerals and nutrients into living cells. This may in part be due to its low molecular weight, its electrical potential, and its bio-transporting ability. Fulvic acid aids in the selective trading or supply of minerals and other nutrient stacks inside the cell. Fulvic acid is effective at neutralising a wide range of toxic material - from heavy metals and radioactive waste to petrochemicals.

Before minerals can be utilised, they must first be converted from their particular colloidal state to a micro-colloidal state. Thus, for greater bio-availability, Neways has formulated Maximol Solutions as an organic fulvic acid complexed micro-colloidal solution. In this form, Maximol provides higher percentages of easily assimilated minerals than non-ionised colloidal mineral supplements, whose particles are often too large for easy absorption.

Revenol (Neways International)
Scientists tell us that vitamins A, C, and E, as well as beta-carotene and other antioxidant bioflavonoids, are vitally important to good health. But there are antioxidant formulae around now that have many more times the power of Vitamin C and Vitamin E. The Neways product Revenol contains antioxidants that are broad-spectrum. Revenol contains antioxidants from maritime pine bark and grape seed pycnogenols extracts - up to 95% in concentration and bioavailability. Revenol also contains curcuminoids, nature's most powerful and aggressive antioxidant, which is around 150 times more powerful than Vitamin E, about 60 times more powerful than Vitamin C, and about 3 times more powerful than antioxidants from maritime pine bark and grape seed pycnogenols extract in neutralising harmful oxidation elements in our bodies. [398]

---

[397] Contents may vary by country

[398] **Majeed, Muhammed, Ph.D et al** Curcuminoids – Antioxidant Phytonutrients, Nutriscience Publishers, 121 Ethel Road West, Unit 6, Piscataway, NJ 08854 USA

Revenol also contains ginkgo biloba for the brain and circulatory system; alpha and beta carotene to increase potency; esterfied Vitamin C - a bonded form of Vitamin C that increases its power and residual retention in the body (up to 3 days); natural Vitamin E for greater absorption and effectiveness. Micro-spheres are also included which bond to the intestinal wall, allowing up to 400% more of the ingredients to be digested and absorbed.

Each tablet of Revenol supplies over 60 milligrams of curcuminoids and maritime pine bark and grape seed extract. An independent study on antioxidants has been conducted by Russian biochemists. As they announce their findings to the World Health Organization, Revenol is expected to be listed as the world's No. 1 effective antioxidant.

Cascading Revenol (Neways International)

Neways has also released an exciting, further version of Revenol, named Cascading Revenol. Oxidation elements, or free radicals as they are sometimes known, are unstable molecules hungry to scavenge additional electrons, thereby damaging healthy cells. These factors are especially dangerous for cancer sufferers. Antioxidants such as Vitamin C can help prevent the damage caused by free radicals by completing their compounds, thus rendering them inert. The problem is, after having entered the body, most antioxidant molecular structures will grab one free radical and then change into an inert state, ceasing to be of further radical-scavenging value. The additional problem is that even when an antioxidant neutralises a free radical, the process creates an off-shoot free radical that is slightly different and less potent in variety, which in turn creates another, and so on. Typical antioxidants have a linear application and thus show no ability to address this free radical cascading effect.

However Cascading Revenol's technologically advanced formulation has been designed to regenerate these scavenging molecules so that they can neutralise multiple free radicals. So, instead of only one free radical being destroyed per antioxidant molecule, each molecule is able to change structure and repeat the process again and again. Thus the value of each individual antioxidant molecule increases exponentially. Cascading Revenol's unique action is devastating to the free radical onslaught that damages cancer sufferers and in my opinion is an essential component in any nutritional support program.

Cassie-Tea (Neways International)

Cassie-Tea is a traditional health formula designed to help assist the body's efforts to eliminate toxins that accumulate in the body with age. Turkey rhubarb root supports liver and intestinal health, while sheep sorrel herb and burdock root help in the body's efforts to maintain the blood stream. Slippery Elm helps soothe irritated mucus membranes and soothe and moisten the respiratory tract.

Neways' Cassie-Tea is the same as the famous Essiac.[399] René Caisse, a Canadian nurse, treated thousands of cancer patients for sixty years using a herbal drink popular with the Ojibway Indians. In 1937 the Royal Cancer Commission of Canada conducted hearings concerning Essiac ('Caisse' backwards) and pronounced as its conclusion that the preparation had marked anti-cancer properties. Tom Mower, the president of Neways, obtained the formulation for Cassie-Tea from a source that used to mix the tea for Nurse Caisse. Cassie-Tea is an excellent supplement for those recovering with a nutritional support program.

Hawaiian Noni Juice (Neways International)

The fruit juice of *Morinda citrifolia* contains a polysaccharide-rich substance with marked anti-tumour activity, according to recent studies into the famous fruit.[400] This research, performed at the University of Hawaii, has resulted in exciting new and scientifically reputable evidence for the potential benefits of Noni fruit juice in the treatment of cancer. Neways Authentic Hawaiian Noni features all the health-enhancing benefits of the noni plant as well as raspberry and blueberry extracts – both powerful antioxidants.

Purge / Feelin' Good (Neways International)

Researchers state that the majority of people, especially those with cancer, play host to one form of parasite or another. Parasites are life-

---

[399] **Percival, J** *The Essiac Handbook,* Credence Publications, 2001 (available through www.credence.org)

[400] **Hirazumi, A & Eiichi Furusawa** "An Immunomodulatory Polysaccharide-Rich Substance from the Fruit Juice of *Morinda citrifolia* (Noni) with Antitumour Activity", Dept of Pharmacology, John A Burns School of Medicine, Hawaii, HI 96822 USA

forms that are uninvited lodgers in our acidic bodies who do not pay rent. They can range from tiny amoebae detectable only with a microscope to tapeworms many feet in length.

We inadvertently pick up parasites through our day-to-day activities and especially through eating undercooked or contaminated food. Try an experiment and put some cat food out in an isolated part of your yard for a few sunny days and then go back and examine it (don't let any pets interfere and keep away from grass and earth). You will invariably find it crawling with infestation.

Blood flukes can enter our systems through infected drinking water and take up residence in the bladder, intestines, liver, lungs, rectum and spleen, laying their eggs and breeding in humans for up to 20 years. Trichina worm larvae found in undercooked pork migrate from the intestines through the blood and lymphatic system, eventually lodging in muscles. Threadworm larvae enter skin from the soil and pass through the bloodstream to the lungs, sometimes causing pneumonia.

Eliminating parasites is effectively a three-phase program. Killing them, flushing them out and then supplementing our relieved bodies with healthy nutrients to maintain optimum health. Neways features this very effective three-phase program, employing their products Purge, Feelin' Good and Maximol Solutions respectively to execute the clean-up, leaving you bug-free and, most importantly, invigorated and strengthened to avoid re-infestation.

Cleansing Tea (Neways International)
Colon cleansing, while not a pleasant topic to address, is a subject that cannot be overlooked in the quest for extended youth, weight loss, and total health. Mucoid plaque and impacted toxic metabolites can be removed with a modified diet as well as with certain purgative agents that can assist in restoring the colon and intestines to full function. It is essential to allow the body to clean itself of detritus that has collected in the digestive system over the years, hampering the body's ability to absorb the nutrients it creaves through the intestinal lining. Cleansing Tea, with its formulation of special herbs, is great at getting it all moving again, and is an ideal adjunct to any program of wellness.

D-Toxarate (Neways International)

As we have already learned, every day we are exposed to harmful substances in our environment. The air we breathe, the food we eat, and even objects we touch are contaminated by substances that threaten our health in many ways we are only just beginning to understand. D-Toxarate is formulated with two important ingredients to help many of these substances pass through the body without harmful effects. Calcium d-glucarate, the first ingredient, can help eliminate some agents that potentially harm our cells. The second ingredient is ascorbic acid, or Vitamin C, an antioxidant with the interesting property we examined earlier- it reduces blood-lead levels.

VitaCell - Resveratrol, Maitake, Lycopene combination (Neways International)

The human body is a miraculous system of organs, with several different mechanisms for removing harmful substances from the body, repairing damaged cells or accidental mutations, replacing older cells with new cells, and removing ill or dead cells from the body. Three novel substances have recently gained attention in the scientific community for their potential anti-cancer activity: resveratrol, maitake mushroom, and lycopene. Together, these products act as antioxidants, detoxify through the enzymatic pathway, protect hormone receptors, encourage cells to go through natural differentiation and apoptosis processes, and support the immune system's efforts to police the entire system.

Osteo Solutions (Neways International)

This calcium, magnesium and Vitamin D supplement is one of my favourites, and is ideal for those seeking to bolster levels of these particular minerals and vitamins in the body for supreme health. Calcium, as we learned earlier, is a vital precursor to so many chemical reactions in the body and should be present abundantly in our diets along with *reasonable* sunlight for optimum effects.

Conflicts of Interest
An example

THE AMERICAN CANCER SOCIETY (ACS)

One of the major tools Big Cancer uses to maintain its control over the massive income derived from the disease today is the American Cancer Society (ACS), the world's most wealthy 'non-profit' organisation and the only known charity to make political contributions from its war chest. The ACS must be fixed firmly in the crosshairs of any right-minded, decent citizen who abhors the conflicts of interest polluting true medical research today. This mammoth society is the shaper of policy for cancer and interfaces with the worldwide organs of 'Big Cancer', which it influences.

The ACS, for example, encourages the US National Cancer Institute (NCI) to block funding for research and clinical trials for promising non-toxic, non-patentable alternative treatments for cancer in favour of highly toxic treatments produced by the chemical industry, which in reality have no clinical track record of efficacy in the treatment of cancer. That these drugs are compelled upon the public through the general practitioner system the public has come to trust is all the more pernicious, and a glaring example of this 'charity's' inhumanity.[401] Many families have seen cancer-struck relatives die with the classic yellow face, indicating liver shutdown through the indiscriminate prescribing of these liver carcinogens, tirelessly promoted by the American Cancer Society and its acolytes.

Patent conflicts of interest exist within the various organs of 'Big Cancer', with the ACS at its helm, which assist in aggrandising the wealth and influence accumulated and peddled by all those approved by the ACS with a vested interest in cancer. For instance, the American Cancer Society Foundation's board of trustees include corporate executives from the pharmaceutical, investment, banking and media industries. Among these are David R Bethune, president of drug company Lederle Laboratories, a division of American Cyanamid, which introduced Novatrone, an anti-cancer drug, in 1988. In 1992,

---

[401] For a fuller treatment of the scandals surrounding cancer and the highly effective, non-toxic treatments and strategies for cancer prevention, please see **Day, Phillip** *Cancer: Why We're Still Dying to Know the Truth*, Credence Publications 1999 (available from www.credence.org)

American Cyanamid announced that it would become a majority stockholder in Immunex, a cancer drug manufacturer.

Gordon Binder, CEO of Amgen, the world's most 'meteoric' biotech firm, which once wooed investors with its rocketing share price, is also on the ACS Foundation's board. Amgen's success is almost single-handedly due to its cancer drug Neupogen, which is given to chemotherapy patients to stimulate production of white blood cells, ironically depleted by the use of toxic treatments promoted by 'Big Cancer'. This is one of many examples that can be found in medicine today where one set of drugs provide a burgeoning market for others in the treatment of side-effects produced by the primary treatments.

Sumner Redstone, chaiman of the board of Viacom Inc. and Viacom International Inc., one of the world's leading mass communications media and entertainment organisations, is also on the ACSF board. Viacom has the influence necessary to dictate what gets reported and what doesn't. George Dessert is also on the ACS board. He was CEO of media monster CBS during the 70s and 80s, one of the greatest shapers of public opinion and education in America today. Diane Disney Miller, daughter of multi-millionaire Walt Disney, who ironically died of lung cancer in 1966, is also represented.

The ACS has a scandalous record when it comes to standing up for cancer prevention. In 1977 and 1978, it opposed regulation of hair colouring products containing dyes known to cause liver and breast cancer in rodents, in spite of the known human risk. In 1971, the ACS refused to testify at congressional hearings over the chemical diethylstilbestrol (DES) being used as an animal feed additive. DES had been proven to cause vaginal cancers in the teenage daughters of women treated with the drug during pregnancy. ACS would not give a reason for its refusal to participate. The ACS also blocked the Food & Drug Administration's proposed ban on saccharin in 1977 and even recommended its use by nursing mothers and babies, in spite of the clear evidence that saccharin caused cancer in rodents.

The ACS has deliberately opposed laws that would ban the addition of chemicals to the food chain that have a proven track record of causing cancer. The American Cancer Society also refused to support America's Clean Air Act, designed to ban the release of known carcinogens into the atmosphere.

In 1992, the American Cancer Society launched an aggressive marketing program with the National Cancer Institute, designed to introduce the public to the concept of 'chemo-prevention' - the highly dangerous practice of taking chemotherapy drugs to prevent cancer in supposed 'high-risk' females, who are at the time cancer-free. This program aimed to recruit 16,000 females in a five-year trial using the highly profitable Zeneca cancer drug, Tamoxifen. The women were told the drug was essentially harmless and that it could reduce their risk of contracting breast cancer. They were not however advised that Tamoxifen, described by Gary Williams, director of the American Heart Foundation, as 'a rip-roaring liver carcinogen', had been demonstrated to be a potent cancer-causing agent in rodents and able to induce human uterine cancers. [402]

---

[402] Tamoxifen is widely used today in the treatment of cancer. In May 1995, the drug was added to California's Carcinogen Identification list in compliance with Proposition 65, a law which requires the state to publish and maintain a list of all known carcinogens. Tamoxifen's dark side has been the subject of many an investigational piece. Several studies, including one reported to the FDA's Oncological Drugs Advisory Committee by the National Surgical Adjuvant Breast and Bowel Project in 1991, showed that the risk of developing life-threatening blood clots increases about sevenfold in women taking Tamoxifen. (**Sellman, Sherrill** *The Hormone Heresy Supplement*, www.ssellman.com, 1999)

What's Really Behind the EU Directive on Vitamins and Minerals?

Here in the UK and in other European countries, legislative moves are being made by various governmental agencies to control public access to vitamins and minerals. Europeans are fast becoming aware of one of those moves, in the form of the EU Directive on Food Supplements – a bill which seeks to gain control over some 300 vitamins, minerals and herbs and reclassify many of them as prescription drugs. And in the US, the Federal Trade Commission (FTC) has recently set up an initiative called Operation Cure-All. The stated aim of OCA is:

".. to use Internet both as a law enforcement tool to stop bogus claims for products and treatments touted as cures for various diseases and as a communication tool to provide consumers with good quality health information." [403]

As in Europe, the US government wishes to take control of the non-pharmaceutical health market. There is to be a crack down on fraudulent health information on the Internet. The stated aim? *To protect the consumer from possible harm.*

But is there another reason behind this overtly philanthropic move? Rufina James suffers from a serious medical condition, which is helped enormously because of her present ability to access the necessary vitamins and minerals. Without them, she would be in trouble. Ruth has taken the time thoroughly to examine the Federal Trade Commission's 'Operation Cure-All' in a broader context. Her report on the subject makes for necessary reading.

---

[403] Operation Cure All at www.ftc.gov/opa/1999/9906/opcureall.htm

The Sinister Truth Behind
Operation Cure-All

by Rufina James

www.therealessentials.com

What's really behind Operation Cure-All? Is it just the US Food and Drug Administration (FDA) and FTC taking their power too far? Or is there a deeper, more sinister purpose to this campaign?

How could a country that prides itself in its freedom of speech, freedom of choice, and freedom of information be facing such severe restrictions in health freedom and dietary supplements? Haven't the people made their will known? Didn't our government pass the Dietary Supplement Health & Education Act of 1994 to insure our right to health supplements?

Indeed, our government did. But the FDA and FTC have found ways to get around that. The laws put in place to protect us are being ignored. And what's worse is that those laws are about to be superceded, if the powers that be have their way.

A MEANS TO AN END

You see, Operation Cure-All is just a tactic, a vehicle, in a much bigger overall plan. It is a result of 'Codex Alimentarius' (meaning food code) - a set of regulations that aim to outlaw any health information in connection with vitamins and limit free access to natural therapies on a worldwide scale.

WHAT'S BEHIND CODEX?

Behind the Codex Alimentarius Commission is the United Nations and the World Health Organisation working in conjunction with the multinational pharmaceutical cartel and international banks. Its initial efforts in the US with the FDA were defeated, so it found another ally in the FTC. Now Codex, with the FTC and the pharmaceutical cartel behind it, threatens to become a trade issue, using the campaign of Operation Cure-All to advance its goals.

Codex began simply enough when the UN authorised the World Health Organisation and the Food and Agriculture Organisation to develop a universal food code. Their purpose was to 'harmonise' regulations for dietary supplements worldwide and set international safety standards for the purposes of increased trade; to standardise labelling and regulatory requirements between countries to facilitate increased international trade. Pharmaceutical interests stepped in and began exerting their influence. Instead of focusing on food safety, Codex is using its power to promote worldwide restrictions on vitamins and food supplements, severely limiting their availability and dosages.

REAL GOALS OF CODEX

To bring about international 'harmonisation.' While global harmony sounds benign, is this the real purpose of this plan? While the stated goal of Codex is to establish unilateral regulations for dietary supplements in every country, the actual goal is to outlaw health products and information on vitamins and dietary supplements, except those under their direct control in the US. These regulations would supercede domestic laws without the American people's voice or vote in the matter.

HOW CAN IT BE POSSIBLE?

Americans gasp at the thought. It goes against everything America stands for. Many believe this can't be possible. The truth is, it's not only possible, it's required by the Codex agreement.

In fact, under the terms of the Uruguay Round of GATT, which created the World Trade Organisation, the United States agreed to harmonise its domestic laws to the international standards. This includes standards for dietary supplements being developed by the United Nation's Codex Alimentarius Commission's Committee on Nutrition and Foods for Special Dietary Use.

The Uruguay Round Agreements carry explicit language clearly indicating that the US must harmonise to international standards:

"Members are fully responsible under this Agreement for the observance of all provisions.... members shall formulate and implement positive measures and mechanisms in support of the observance of the provisions.... by other than central government bodies." [WTO TBT Agreement at Article 3.5]"

In other words, the federal government must not only change federal law, but must also require state and local governments to change their laws to be in accordance with international law.

Not only that, Codex is now enforceable through the World Trade Organisation (WTO). If a country disagrees with, or refuses to follow Codex standards, the WTO applies pressure by withdrawing trade privileges and imposing sanctions. Congress has already bowed to this pressure several times and so have the governments of many countries.

While the exemption clauses USC 3512(a)(1) and (a)(2) were created supposedly to protect our laws from harmonisation to international standards, they have proven totally ineffective. The United States has already lost seven trade disputes, in spite of the exemption clauses. Due to the enormous pressures put on it by lobbyists from multinational corporations (who contribute millions to congressional campaigns), Congress bowed to pressure and changed US laws.

It appears our government is being manipulated one way or another to serve the goals of the UN, the World Health Organisation and the World Trade Organisation. Food control equals people control - and population control. Is this beginning to sound like world government and one-world order? Could this be the real goal behind Codex?

The United States, Canada, the Europeans, Japan, most of Asia, and South America have already signed agreements pledging total harmonisation of their laws including food and drug laws to these international standards in the future.

WHAT CODEX WILL BRING

What can we expect under Codex? To give you an idea, here are some important points:

> Dietary supplements could not be sold for preventive (prophylactic) or therapeutic use
> Potencies would be limited to extremely low dosages

- ➤ Only the drug companies and big phytopharmaceutical companies would have the right to produce and sell the higher potency products (at inflated prices)
- ➤ Prescriptions would be required for anything above the extremely low doses allowed (such as 35 mg for niacin)
- ➤ Common foods such as garlic and peppermint would be classified as drugs or a third category (neither food nor drugs) that only big pharmaceutical companies could regulate and sell. Any food with any therapeutic effect can be considered a drug, even benign everyday substances like water
- ➤ Codex regulations for dietary supplements would become binding (escape clauses would be eliminated)
- ➤ All new dietary supplements would be banned unless they go through Codex testing and approval
- ➤ Genetically altered food would be sold worldwide without labelling

According to John Hammell, a legislative advocate and the founder of International Advocates for Health Freedom (IAHF), here is what we have to look forward to:

"If Codex Alimentarius has its way, then herbs, vitamins, minerals, homeopathic remedies, amino acids and other natural remedies you have taken for granted most of your life will be gone. The name of the game for Codex is to shift all remedies into the prescription category so they can be controlled exclusively by the medical monopoly and its bosses, the major pharmaceutical firms. Predictably, this scenario has been denied by both the Canadian Health Food Association and the Health Protection Branch of Canada (HPB).

The Codex proposals already exist as law in Norway and Germany where the entire health food industry has literally been taken over by the drug companies. In these countries, vitamin C above 200 mg is illegal as is vitamin E above 45 IU, vitamin B1 over 2.4 mg and so on. Shering-Plough, the Norway pharmaceutical giant, now controls an echinacea tincture, which is being sold there as an over-the-counter drug at grossly inflated prices. The same is true of ginkgo and many other herbs, and only one government-

284

controlled pharmacy has the right to import supplements as medicines which they can sell to health food stores, convenience stores or pharmacies."

It is now a criminal offence in parts of Europe to sell herbs as foods. An agreement called EEC6565 equates selling herbs as foods to selling other illegal drugs. Action is being taken to accelerate other European countries into 'harmonisation' as well.

Paul Hellyer in his book, *The Evil Empire*, states:

"Codex is supported by international banks and multinational corporations, including some in Canada, and is in reality a bill of rights for these banks and the corporations they control. It will hand over our sovereign rights concerning who may or may not invest in our countries to an unelected world organisation run by big business. The treaty would make it impossible for Canadian legislators, either federal or provincial, to alter or improve environmental standards for fear of being sued by multinational corporations whether operating in Canada or not.

This will create a world without borders ruled by a virtual dictatorship of the world's most powerful central banks and multinational companies. This world is an absolute certainty if we all sit on our hands and do nothing."

This is the future the FDA and FTC are striving to bring us via Codex harmonisation. Is this a future we are going to accept or prevent?

WHY TARGET THE INTERNET?

It is no accident that the FDA and FTC are targeting Internet health sites through Operation Cure-All. We are standing in the doorway of an unprecedented revolution - the information revolution brought about by the Internet.

Now all people everywhere have the ability to learn about anything that interests them with just a few clicks. History has shown that informed, educated people change civilisations - they change the flow of thought and the flow of money. They can even change the direction of a country. When similar transitions have happened in the past, the powers that existed did not give up willingly. The Catholic Church fiercely protected its practice of selling "indulgences' as a forgiveness of sin. When the practice was abolished, the Catholic Church lost a great deal of power and money.

When the printing press was invented, books were banned and printers were imprisoned by the authorities, who feared an educated public could not be governed. In the same way, the medical monopoly (and the UN) now fears that a public educated in health and privy to the shortcomings of modern medicine cannot be controlled. Loss of control means loss of revenue and power. And they are doing everything they can to stop progress so they can contain their losses and strengthen their power.

The printing press changed the world. Can you imagine what life would be like today if the book-banners had their way? But because the printing press won, society progressed and freedom was embraced. The Internet is changing the world in an equally significant way. While the entire Internet can hardly be suppressed, the pharma-cartels and their backers are looking to protect their interests by restricting as much information as they can on the Web.

Will we, the people, win out again, or will the UN and the World Health Organisation agenda and the pharmaceutical cartel change the course of history and take us back to the 'dark ages' of medicine?

The *Food For Thought* Dietary Regimen

➤ Eat properly constituted, organic, whole, living food, a high percentage consumed in its natural state. Excellent recipes are provided in our companion guide, *Food For Thought*.
➤ The ideal balance is: 80% alkali/20% acidic ash foods. Closer attention to this area reveals that most diets today comprise 90% acid/10% alkali. Not a good state of affairs.
➤ Try to limit meat components to no more than 10% of the total diet. Also, reduce dairy intake. Eliminate both if sick.
➤ Fish, deep and cold caught, is good, excepting those listed below.
➤ Hydrate the body (4 pints of clean, fresh water a day).
➤ Detoxify (eat fruit before noon on an empty stomach). A full account of what to do can be found in *Health Wars*.
➤ Reduce meat and dairy intake (eliminate if sick).
➤ A basic supplement program (see '*Food For Thought*').
➤ Exercise (to get everything moving!).
➤ Rest.
➤ Reduce environmental toxicity (dangerous jobs, using toxic chemicals, radiation, etc.).
➤ Use safe personal care products.
➤ Use safe household products.

FOODS TO AVOID

➤ Pork products (bacon, sausage, hot-dogs, luncheon meat, ham, etc.) With today's intensive farming methods especially, these products are high in nitrites, and are known homotoxins, which can cause high blood urea. They can also help form dikitopiprazines – a metabolic chemical by-product, which has been linked to brain tumours and leukaemia.[404]
➤ Scavenger creatures (inc. ALL shellfish and other carrion-eaters – see Leviticus 11 in the Bible). Carrion-eaters, pork and shellfish in particular, concentrate toxins of other

---

[404] **Day, Phillip** *Food for Thought*, Credence Publications, 2nd Ed., 2002; "Adverse influence of pork consumption on human health", *Biologic Therapy*, Vol. 1, No. 2, 1983

animals in their tissues, which we then consume to our detriment. The same goes for the elimination organs of commercially raised animals, such as liver and kidney, which can be high in drug and pesticide residues.

> Aspartame/saccharin, artificial sweeteners. These are known mental impairment problems and cancer risks.
> Refined sugar/flour/rice. Restricted amounts of wholegrain bread are OK. Use only wholegrain rice. No sugars should be consumed other than those contained naturally in whole foods.
> Hydrogenated & partially hydrogenated fats (margarine).
> Junk (processed) food, including fizzy sodas and other soft drinks containing sugar, artificial sweeteners or phosphoric acid, which are drunk out of aluminium cans.
> Fat-free foods. Essential fats are essential!
> Olestra, canola, soy, etc. Avoid fake or synthetic fats. Soy, in its unfermented state (meat and milk substitute products), disrupts the hormone (endocrine) system, blocks the absorption of calcium and magnesium, and acts like estrogen in the body. Small usage of fermented soy products (soy sauce and miso) is OK.
> Polluted water (chlorinated or fluoridated – see *Health Wars* section, entitled 'Water Under the Bridge').
> Caffeine products.
> Excessive intake of alcohol products.
> Excess salt. It's better to spice food with ground kelp to maintain a healthy iodine intake.

THE FOUR PILLARS OF MENTAL HEALTH
> Eliminating allergies
> Maintaining blood sugar balance
> Avoiding toxins and pollution
> Ingesting optimum nutrition[405]

For a full analysis of 'food as it should be', see *Food For Thought*, the food recipe companion to this book and others in the Credence stable (see 'Other Books by Credence').

---

[405] Day, Phillip, *The Mind Game*, op. cit.

Supermarket Smarts

Below is a list of the main products available at any supermarket (this list is from an English store). Bolded items can be purchased with the appropriate comments listed. When considering the validity of this list, keep in mind the food your ancestors would have consumed three hundred years ago. Also imagine the diets of those peoples who do not suffer from the degenerative and toxin diseases afflicting the Western world today.

ITEM	COMMENTS	
Birthday Cakes	No	Processed food
Cakes	No	Processed food
Flan and Pastry	No	Processed food
Rolls	No	Processed food
Speciality Bakery	No	Processed food
Bread	**Wholegrain, sparingly**	
Cream Cakes and Desserts	No	Processed food
In Store Bakery	No	Processed food
Savoury Morning Goods	No	Processed food
Sweet Morning Goods	No	Processed food
Alcopops	No	
Bitters and Ales	No	
Cider	No	
Light Spirits	No	
Rum	No	
Whisky	No	
Beer	No	
Brandy	No	
Gin	No	
Liqueurs	No	
Vodka	No	
Fresh Pasta, Sauces and Soup	No	Processed food
Pies, Quiche and Savoury	No	Processed food
Ready Meals and Pizza	No	Processed food
Meat Free	No	Processed food
Prep Meats, Fish and Poultry	No	Processed food
Sandwiches, Sushi and Snacks	No	Processed food
Butter and Margarine	**Real butter, sparingly**	
Cream	No	
Home Cooking	No	Processed food

Organic	**Yes, be selective**	
Cheese	No	Processed food
Eggs	**free range, sparingly**	
Milk	No	Processed food
Yogurts and Dairy Desserts	No	Processed food
Bacon	No	Processed food
Chicken	**only organic, sparingly**	
Fish	**deep-sea cold fish, sparingly**	
Offal	No	
Prep Meats, Fish and Poultry	No	Processed food
Speciality Meat and Poultry	No	Processed food
Beef	N o	Processed food
Cooked and Continental Meat	No	Processed food
Lamb	No	Processed food
Pork	No	Processed food
Sausage	No	Processed food
Turkey	No	Processed food
Frozen Desserts	No	Processed food
Frozen Meat Cuts	No	Processed food
Frozen Natural Fish	No	Processed food
Frozen Pies and Savouries	No	Processed food
Frozen Potato Products	No	Processed food
Frozen Ready Meals	No	Processed food
Large Tub Ice Cream	No	Processed food
Frozen Fish Products	No	Processed food
Frozen Meat Products	No	Processed food
Frozen Natural Vegetables	No	Processed food
Frozen Pizza and Bread	No	Processed food
Frozen Poultry	No	Processed food
Frozen Peas, corn, mixed veg	No	Processed food
Apples	No	possibly contaminated
Berries and Rhubarb	No	possibly contaminated
Cucumbers and Peppers	No	possibly contaminated
Grapes	No	possibly contaminated
Luxury and Exotic Vegetables	No	possibly contaminated
Organic Fruit	**organic only**	
Other Salad	No	possibly contaminated
Potatoes	No	possibly contaminated
Salads, Dressings and Dips	No	processed food
Tomatoes and Fresh Herbs	No	possibly contaminated
Bananas and Melons	No	possibly contaminated
Citrus	No	possibly contaminated
Exotic Fruit	No	possibly contaminated
Lettuce	No	possibly contaminated

Mushrooms, Onion and Garlic	No	possibly contaminated
Organic Vegetables	**main source is organic**	
Pears	No	possibly contaminated
Prepared Fruit, Veg and Salad	No	possibly contaminated
Stone Fruit	No	possibly contaminated
Traditional Vegetables	No	possibly contaminated
Baked Beans and Pasta	No	possibly contaminated
Breakfast Cereal	No	processed food
Cooking Sauces	No	processed food
Desserts and Baking Mixes	No	processed food
Ethnic and Kosher	No	processed food
Gravy and Pour Over Sauces	No	processed food
Meat and Fish	No	processed food
Oils	**cold press organic only**	
Pasta	**wholewheat pasta only**	
Rice and Pulses	**organic only**	
Savoury and Sweet Spreads	No	processed food
Soup	No	processed food
Sugar	No	processed food
Vegetables	No	processed food
Baking Aids	No	processed food
Canned Fruit	No	processed food
Custard	No	processed food
Dried Fruit and Cooking Nuts	**organic only**	
Flour and Suet	**organic flour only**	
Herbs and Spices	**organic only**	
Mincemeat, Milk and Cream	No	processed food
Organic sundries	**so long as they are!**	
Pickles and Condiments	No	processed food
Sauces, Vinegars and Dressings	No	processed food
Snack Meals	No	processed food
Stuffing and Breadcrumbs	No	processed food
Tomato Puree and Pizza	No	processed food
Baby Food and Care	No	processed food
Haircare	non-toxic versions are not avail here	
Male Grooming	non-toxic versions are not avail here	
Personal Grooming	non-toxic versions are not avail here	
Bathroom	non-toxic versions are not avail here	
Healthcare	no unnecessary drugs	
Oral Hygiene	non-toxic versions are not avail here	
Skincare	non-toxic versions are not avail here	
Cleaning Products	non-toxic versions are not avail here	
Gifts	**yes please...**	
Laundry Products	non-toxic versions are not avail here	

Foils, Wraps and Bin Liners	non-toxic versions are not avail here
Household Sundries	non-toxic versions are not avail here
Tissues and Towels	**non-scented**
Chilled Fruit Juice	Possibly contaminated
Filter and Ground Coffee	No
Milk Based Drinks	No — processed food
Soda Stream	No
Squash	No — processed food
Water	**uncontaminated only**
Coffee Whiteners	No — processed food
Fizzy Drinks	No — processed food
Longlife Fruit Juice	No... ask why it has a long life...
Mixers	No — processed food
Single Drinks	No — processed food
Tea	sparingly
Boxed Chocolates and Sweets	No — processed food
Chocolate Biscuit Bars	No — processed food
Crisps	No — processed food
Everyday Treats	No — processed food
Kids Biscuits	No — processed food
Savoury Nibbles	No — processed food
Snacks	No — processed food
Sweets	No — processed food
Chocolate Bars	No — processed food
Crackers and Crispbreads	No — processed food
Everyday Biscuits	No — processed food
Healthy Biscuits	No — processed food
Popcorn and Nuts	No — processed food
Single Packets of Chocolate and Sweets	No — processed food
Special Treats	No — processed food
Cigarettes and Cigars	No, sorry...
Champagne and Sparking Wine	**every now and then...**
Rose Wine	**every now and then...**
Wine Accessories	No — processed food
Red Wine	**every now and then...**
White Wine	**every now and then...**

Small amounts of the above 'No's' are not going to land you in court. The purpose of this illustration is to make the point that our food supply, in the main, is processed, often contaminated with pesticides, and devoid of the 'whole foods' once eaten by our ancestors. Our emphasis should be on these 'whole foods', organically grown, which should comprise 80-90% of our diet. 80% of our diet should be water-based foods, such as fruits and vegetables. **Organic** meat, fish or dairy products should not comprise more than 5-10% of the total food we consume.

Testimonies

Dear Credence,

I have twice been diagnosed as having prostate cancer, and twice overcome the condition.

On the 8th October 1998 and with a PSA of 22.7 was diagnosed as having prostate cancer. Within a few days I had changed my lifestyle and my way of thinking, I became a semi-vegetarian, eliminated fats and sugar from my diet and wherever possible all artificial flavourings, colourings, E numbers and chemicals. I also developed a daily protocol of vitamin and herbal supplements. Three months later my PSA dropped to 1.3 and a biopsy reported that no malignancy was found.

A few months later and with a PSA of 9 was again diagnosed as having prostate cancer. This time my original healing program appeared not to have any affect and after trying numerous other 'alternative' treatments my PSA rapidly rose to 25.2. At this time – November 1999 – by chance came upon a book written by Phillip Day and titled *Cancer, Why We're Still Dying To Know The Truth*, wherein it described the benefits of apricot kernels. I immediately ordered a two-pound pack of kernels and commenced daily to consume forty apricot kernels and half of a fresh pineapple. Then in May 2000 my PSA dropped to 0.7 and a subsequent biopsy again reported no malignancy found.

Today my PSA is a steady 0.5 and I firmly believe that this success is entirely due to the consumption of the apricot kernels and now continue to take 10 daily as a maintenance dose.

Yours sincerely
Roger S (UK)

Dear Credence,

Thanks for your message. Our cat's name is Eric. For the record, here is his full story:

Eric is a neutered domestic shorthair red tabby, prone to dozy inactivity(!). He was diagnosed with feline lymphoma in November 1999 after a biopsy. The vet could feel a lump the size of a walnut on his bowel; this prompted the operation to determine malignancy. He suffered chemotherapy in two forms: a half tablet every other day, injected cancer drug every fortnight requiring general anaesthetic, and a steroid pill every day. By June his facial fur had thinned out, he was hardly alive, though not yet dramatically underweight, and by July all of his whiskers had fallen out.

We got hold of Phillip Day's book *Cancer: Why We're Still Dying to Know the Truth* and within a week Alison was treating Eric with 4 apricot seeds a day, ground up into organic food, mainly chicken breast or natural smoked fish, Neways Maximol in Evian water, and a third of a Revenol antioxidant tablet. We stopped the chemotherapy, thinking that he simply could not get any worse. The vet was doubtful of any benefit the apricot seeds could provide, but she had heard of their use. To confound medical science, Eric steadily improved.

Within a week he was much better. Within a month he was fatter, brighter and livelier than ever before. His fur started to grow back, as did his whiskers. His stools had been the yardstick by which we judged his condition and these remained healthy. After nearly two months of no chemotherapy we took him to the vet; the vet did not know precisely what we had been doing and we now had to admit we had stopped giving him the chemotherapy tablets. She was astounded, and reluctantly admitted, after a blood test under anaesthetic, that he was back to normal and that she could feel no lump at all.

Eric now has a maintenance dose of two seeds per day, still eats only organic food and drinks only Evian water (Evian is one of the few bottled waters with no fluoride content). He also takes Maximol and Revenol. The only bad news is that he now suffers pneumonia, brought on by the chemotherapy; he is treated with the homeopathic remedy echinacea. Otherwise, he is alert, keen, frisky (more than we're used to and extremely irritating late at night!) and by far a healthier cat than we have ever known. This is without question, a testament to the discoveries made by Ernest Krebs, and all thanks to Phillip Day's tireless researches. We intend to submit a report of this to the Royal Veterinary College, demanding further clinical trials. With animals, there is no placebo effect, no psychology, only results. Thank you, Phillip Day, for all you have done.

Your sincerely
Alison Dalby and Jonathan Downs
And Eric!

Dear Credence,

We lived in South Africa and my brother Athol was employed in the building industry for all his working life. He often worked directly with asbestos. The workmen were not given any warnings, nor were they issued with any protective clothing. He had no idea that asbestos was a deadly substance. In June 1997, my beloved brother was diagnosed with malignant mesothelioma, (a rare form of cancer of the lining of the chest caused by asbestos dust). He fought this disease with the only treatment he was offered, i.e. surgery, radiotherapy and chemotherapy. Sadly this treatment was of no help to him and in fact only exacerbated his suffering, and caused severe deterioration in his condition. He gradually became weaker and weaker until he died on 5th August 1998.

Some months after Athol's death, I developed a persistent cough that I successfully ignored. Then early in 2001 I began to experience difficulties in climbing stairs. My reaction to this was that I had become unfit and thought that I should try and exercise more. This only made the problem worse and by June of 2001 I began to feel decidedly unwell. Eventually I decided a visit to the doctor was necessary, and after a series of tests, biopsies, etc. I was finally diagnosed in early September as having malignant mesothelioma, the very same disease that had taken my brother three years earlier. This was devastating news for my whole family. When my brother, Athol, was diagnosed with the same disease we understood that this dreadful form of cancer was very rare. It seemed impossible that it could strike both a brother and a sister, but it did. It appeared that I had breathed in the asbestos dust from his clothing. My world was turned upside-down and suddenly all those things that seemed important were not important anymore.

My immediate decision was that I would not follow the same route as my brother had done, since clearly this would only hasten my death. In any case, conventional medicine could only offer me 'palliative chemotherapy', but no hope of any survival. I sent a panic e-mail to a nutritionist in South Africa for advice, as my own common sense told me that nutrition would be the best way forward. She e-mailed back with three instructions:

> Get onto the Hallelujah Diet. (This is a diet consisting of 85% raw fruit and vegetables, carrot juice, Barley Green, and of course eliminating five foods that are known problems for cancer patients: meat, dairy, salt, sugar and white flour, as well as eliminating all processed food from the diet).
> Try to get to the Oasis of Hope Hospital in Mexico.
> Spend as much time with God as possible.

Well, nos. 1 & 3 were no problem, but I initially rejected no. 2. I soon began to realise that nos. 1 & 3 were not enough as my health continued to decline. But God was not going to allow me to ignore the possibility of going to The Oasis of Hope Hospital in Mexico and He kept prompting me until I could no longer ignore this. Being a single Mum with two young children to support, I had nothing like the finances available to go there, so I said to God, "OK I'm listening now, if I am meant to go to Mexico I know that You will provide", and I put my trust TOTALLY in Him and went ahead and made the necessary arrangements.

In all this time I was becoming weaker and weaker and it appeared that the cancer had metastasised to the liver. But God is ever faithful and the money was provided in miraculous ways. After overcoming many obstacles, including visa difficulties, and finally British Airways' initial refusal to grant me clearance for the flight because of my state of health, my 13-year-old daughter, Auriol and I finally arrived at the Oasis of Hope hospital in Tijuana, Mexico.

It was quite the most amazing experience I have ever had in my life. I knew from the moment I walked through the doors that I was in the right place. God's love permeates this remarkable hospital where everywhere you look there are colourful banners with Bible texts and wise sayings that help to create a positive attitude. Here I was not just a sick body but a person with a mind and a soul. In this hospital, they regard Jesus Christ as the Medical Director and with that one you just cannot go wrong. (There cannot be many places where your doctor will pray with you and hug you each time you meet and where they give all the glory to God.) I met so many wonderful people and forged many strong friendships that I know will last for eternity. I was immediately started on the treatment of B17 administered intravenously as well as chelation therapy, oxygen therapy and shark cartilage enemas. Of course, the nutrition program was all important too.

I came back home very much stronger, the fluid on my lung had stabilised, and so had the tumour. The two cancer spots on my liver had completely disappeared. I brought home with me 6 months' supply of the B17 that I would administer myself daily through a permanently inserted catheter in my chest, as well as other treatments with instructions to return in 6 months for a check-up and further supplies. I came home with real HOPE and knew that God was looking after me and I felt that I now had a future that I would not have had if it had been left to conventional medicine.

God again miraculously provided for the return trip in May 2002 where the doctors described my condition as 'remarkable' and I praise God for that. I am enjoying a quality of life that I could not have wished for had I not taken this step of faith and although I owe my life to B17, the ultimate glory must go to God who has masterminded all this.

I think of my brother Athol daily and feel a great sadness that we did not know about this treatment at the time he was so ill, because had we known he would have been spared a great deal of suffering and would most probably still be alive today.

Anne Rycroft

In November 2001, five-year-old Laura Boomsma was diagnosed with a large Wilms' tumour on her right kidney. She underwent pre-operative chemotherapy in December which saw her hair fall out. She became very sick and stopped eating. During this period, Laura's father attended a Phillip Day cancer seminar in Brisbane and learned that there were considerable dangers to human health with certain conventional cancer treatments.

Laura's parents decided to stop all chemotherapy treatment immediately and Laura began a full nutritional program, including Vitamin B17. After about one month of B17 treatment, Laura was feeling much better and a scan confirmed that Laura's tumour had shrunk right down in size. In January, the hospital surgically removed the tumour and insisted on 12 sessions of post-operative chemotherapy. Laura's parents objected and said they wanted to seek alternative treatment overseas. The hospital, believing them to be 'unfit' parents, sought legal means to take Laura from them and forcibly medicate her with chemotherapy. Laura's father said he would go to jail before the authorities took Laura from them. The Campaign for Truth in Medicine became involved.

In conjunction with the Boomsma's legal team, CTM assisted in drawing up the affidavits that would be presented in court. The sheer weight of evidence contained in the affidavit against chemotherapy was enough to force the hospital to back down before the case was heard in the Queensland Supreme Court, setting a world precedent.

Free to leave Australia without having their passports seized, Laura and her father duly travelled to the UK where Laura received non-toxic, immune-boosting treatments for her condition. At the time of writing, Laura is doing very well. Said father Aaron Boomsma:

"I am just so grateful to Phillip and the mission at Credence. The change in Laura since beginning the alternative treatment has been incredible."

The following letter was posted to Credence head office. Mary had attended a talk in Dianella, Perth, Australia, on the subject of cancer and Vitamin B17, presented by the founder of Credence Publications, Phillip Day. Phillip's presentation was based upon the information contained in his book, Cancer: Why We're Still Dying to Know the Truth.

I came out to Australia last July having been diagnosed with two malignant tumours in my left breast. I had already signed a form agreeing to an operation for mastectomy and removal of all my lymph glands. My daughter and son-in-law had insisted on my cancelling my appointment at the Royal United Hospital, Bath, UK, where I was told there was no other option.

My daughter also insisted that I came out to Australia where I saw two cancer specialists, who, after examining me and reading the medical file I'd brought from the RUH, declared a lumpectomy and removal of two lymph glands was all that was necessary. However, we decided to try radiation therapy – no surgery and no drugs.

I had just finished the 1st phase, when we went to Dianella, Perth, to hear Phillip Day speaking about cancer. We were so profoundly impressed by his splendid talk on cancer and Vitamin B17 metabolic therapy, that we brought his books, read them carefully and decided to go 'all out' on his anti-cancer diet. We all three felt so much better in health and were surprised at how energetic we felt. I still attended Bethesda Hospital for blood tests, and we were absolutely delighted to get reports of the malignant cells diminishing. Then, finally, a report that I was in full remission. There was no need to attend for any more blood tests.

So now, 10 months later, I am returning to my home in Wiltshire and will continue my apricot kernels and diet as a safe-guard against any possible recurrence of cancer. I also wish to join the Campaign for Truth in Medicine and will deal with this as soon as possible after my arrival home in UK.

The very worried and depressed person who spoke to Phillip at that Perth meeting is now a radiant, energetic 84-year-old. He has transformed my life and those of my daughter Linda and son-in-law, Henry.

Yours very sincerely,

Mary

Dear Credence

Re: Vitamin B17

I was diagnosed with cancer at the base of my tongue in March 1998. I underwent an extensive course of radio & chemotherapy and for a few months this seemed to have been successful. In the summer of 2000 however, a scan revealed that not only was the cancer still there but it had extended. Surgery would involve not only removal of my larynx but the most part of my tongue. As I was not prepared to accept that, conventional medicine had nothing further to offer.

I started a course of Metabolic Therapy at the Dove Clinic in November 2000. Quite soon I started to feel better and regain weight. Shortly before Christmas I coughed up several pieces of what my E.N.T. consultant confirmed was dead tumour. She confirmed that my tumour had definitely reduced in size and this could only be due to the treatment I had had. So, within 3 months with the B17 therapy my tumour has reduced in size. I have put on nearly a stone and feel better than I have felt for a long time.

Elizabeth Owen (Mrs)

Dear Phillip

A brief résumé of my history of Non Hodgkin's Lymphoma and the eventual discovery of B17.

My first occurrence of the disease happened in 1987 and after a parotid operation and radiotherapy all appeared to go well. I had annual checkups and blood tests and nothing untoward was discovered. In the latter part of 1996 I had discomfort in my back and stomach which reached a peak with excruciating pain in April 1997. My doctor and I both thought it may be an ulcer, however after an endoscopy nothing was found and a CT scan showed a tumour in my abdomen and a biopsy showed that the disease had returned. I then had 15 treatments of chemotherapy, CVP and CHOPS. The tumour reduced in size and a biopsy of my bone marrow showed no signs of the disease.

In September 1999 during a normal visit to my oncologists she informed me that the tumour was active again and suggested further chemotherapy. I did not like the possible side-effects, weakening of heart muscles, liver and kidney and definitely the immune system. My wife and I were always against poisoning the body, and my oncologist knew this. But, by this time we had found out about alternative methods of treating the cancer though reading magazines and the Internet. We were prepared to go to Mexico. Fortunately only a few weeks before, after purchasing your book *Cancer: Why We're Still Dying to Know the Truth*, we found out about B17 and a doctor who prescribed the treatment. Two phone calls later - one to the publishers for the doctor's telephone number and one to the doctor himself - two weeks later I was receiving treatment with B17 and Vitamin C.

I had pain in my back and stomach again, although not so intense this time, probably because the cancer was in the early stages. The day after I started my treatment the pain subsided. I will say here, that prior to starting on the treatment I could and did easily drop off to sleep after eating a sandwich or a meal, and driving the car for an hour left me tired for the rest of the day. Within two days the 200-mile round trip to the doctor's clinic was taken in my stride and I have never had so much energy in the previous ten years.

On my initial blood test with the doctor my red cells were stacked up together like a bunch of coins and my white cells were small and appeared to have given up the ghost. Now the red cells are bright, and although there is still some bunching, there are many freely wandering through my system, the white cells are now more numerous and are healthy and vibrant. My blood has been sent to a laboratory for further tests to ascertain if the cancer has gone, I feel it has, my original oncologist thinks it "spontaneous remission". I have recommended my new doctor to friends and some have taken up his offer of treatment. I cannot thank him enough. Of course I am receiving treatment with other supplements to build up my immune system but to think that the B17 has cured my lymphoma without side-effects is phenomenal.

Sincerely
Richard Courtier

Dear Jan (Neways distributor)
As you know when I was diagnosed as having prostate cancer last April the P.S.A count was 99 and after going on a dairy-free diet and taking Maximol and Revenol and then taking the apricot kernels, I had a blood test 1st August and the P.S.A count was down to 19.

I have just had another blood test and I and the doctor were amazed to find that the P.S.A count had dramatically dropped to 2.3, yes that is 2 point 3 and I feel very well.

I do not know whether it is the tablets I am taking, or the dairy-free diet or the Maximol and Revenol and kernels that are having the good effect, but I have my own ideas and I will certainly carry on taking the minerals and the nuts in future.

Thank you for your help and advice, with all good wishes to you and your family for Christmas and the New Year,

Yours sincerely
Tom M, Cheshire, UK

Dear Phillip

I was diagnosed as having breast cancer in November 1998. Since then, I have had a full mastectomy and reconstruction of my left breast; a capsulotomy (to soften the reconstruction); 6 monthly sessions of chemotherapy using a cocktail of three drugs; 25 days radiotherapy; 14 further weekly sessions of chemotherapy.

In February 2000, I had been given two sessions of the drug Taxotere. I ended up neutropenic (no immune system) and in hospital for a week, in isolation to begin with as any germs could have been fatal for me. 12 weekly sessions of the drug Taxol then followed, ending in August. After all that, my cancer was still here!

In March 2000, I bought *Cancer – Why We're Still Dying to Know the Truth*. I read the first 20 or so pages and put it in a drawer. It frightened me because it was going against the "establishment", I suppose. I had been accepting everything that the doctors and oncologists had been telling me. In fact, I even asked my oncologist about Vitamin B17 and he said that it was just a load of "quackery" and that was it! Embarrassingly so, I accepted what he said.

Anyway, in July, my husband asked to read the book. The chemotherapy I was on at the time had shown some improvement, but certainly nothing radical. By the end of August, nothing had really changed since the beginning of the year when I'd started the second lot of chemo.

My husband Russell really got into the book and was very keen to take it further. Anyway, to cut a long story short, we ended up going to the Stella Maris Clinic in Mexico for three weeks in November.

I cried all the way to the airport. I have remained so positive throughout all of my treatment, but this was something different. I was having to go to Mexico for treatment – what on earth was it going to be like? What was the doctor going to be like, was it going to be clean, was it going to be "dangerous"?

Well, we arrived at San Diego, and were taken the next day to the Stella Maris Clinic. As soon as we stepped into the clinic, all my doubts and fears were gone. It was such a lovely atmosphere; Dr Alvarez and his team were wonderful.

I spent three weeks having Metabolic Therapy. A typical day consisted of breakfast with supplements; IV Vitamin C, DMSO and Vitamin B17; fruit juice and supplements; coffee enema; lymphatic massage; and lunch and supplements.

We had lectures by Dr Alvarez explaining the theory behind his treatment program; lectures by a nutritionist; and educational videos about how the immune system works and how to prepare good wholesome food for yourself.

All the food was made from scratch. There were no additives, preservatives or colourings, just loads of soups, vegetables, salads, millet, rice, nuts and dried fruit and it all tasted absolutely gorgeous! I didn't want to come home!

When we arrived home, the kitchen was completely turned upside down. I am now healing myself through supplements, juicing, and very healthy food – loads of vegetables, salads and juice. I give myself a coffee enema everyday to rid my body of toxins and I feel great!

My hair is growing quickly, my skin feels fresh and my nails are all returning back to normal! Of course, I have my downs, everybody does, but I give myself the time to come out of them and end up feeling better each time. At this very moment, I feel as though I could rule the world! And things continue to get better ☺

Sarah H, Southampton, UK

Dear Credence

Reading your book, *World Without AIDS*, was like a breath of fresh, mountain air. I have been an AIDS dissenter since 1991 and have experienced the complete denial by elected officials, other bureaucrats, and my friends and family who can't seem to break their romance with the medical/pharmaceutical establishment. Your thorough work puts into easy to understand language a subject matter that others have so far made quite complicated, which has resulted in lay people not having much understanding or interest in the AIDS debate. People who read this book should be prepared to be shunned by the denizens [inhabitants] of ignorance, greed, and nobility who will chastise and condemn you for your 'foolishness' and 'audacity'. But truth sets you free - and you get an extra helping in this book! Thank you, Steven and Phillip for an outstanding effort and let the AIDS bastions of lies, deceit, and murders begin their much-welcomed demise.

Bill Bissell, 'AIDS truth' campaigner and former substance abuse centre manager

Dear All

I am sending you this as a gift. I hope you will accept my invitation to join me in helping ourselves as well as others.

In February of 1986 I received the devastating news that I was HIV positive. The nurse advised me to get in touch with the local support organization for the support I would need because the next cold I would catch could be my last.

I started going to a support group of 13 men who had received the same sad diagnosis. The talk was how to prepare to die. I had, 3 years earlier, bid my last early farewell to my brother, who was 13 months my junior. I was not about to put my parents through a similar hell. I stopped going to the support group and curtailed the activities that had brought me to this sad conclusion. I am now the only surviving member of that group.

I started listening to self-healing tapes and stopped spending as much time in bars and at activities that were considered risky. I focused on living and surviving and winning.

New drugs promising survival and life extension came along and the panic and fear had people clamoring to have access to them, taking no consideration for what the side effects might be.

As the numbers of people and friends taking AZT climbed, so did the numbers of people and friends joining the statistics of deaths related to AIDS.

In 1990 I was introduced to Images, now Neways. Neways provided nutritional supplements that supported and encouraged immune response and well-being. I started right off taking Life Enhancer, VMM and Emperor's Formula. Within a month I was noticing more vitality and energy.

It was also at this time that I began seeing a doctor for HIV tracking and monitoring. I was invited to participate in many drug studies that included AZT, ddI, 3TC and D4T. I declined the invitations. By then I had already witnessed the ill-effects of AZT and felt an inner prompting to avoid the testing and trials. Instead I tried to focus on eating better and generally taking care of myself.

At this time my life hit a brick wall of emotional, spiritual, physical and legal trials. I escaped into the labyrinth of alcohol and drug abuse. My health declined and so did my CD4 (T-cell) count. I had gone into a deep depression because of events in my life and used cocaine and alcohol to escape the pain. The drug abuse placed my immune system under a compromise that it had never before experienced and it was reflected in the existing tests. I relented to the doctor's request and started taking 3TC and D4T. Some time later they added Nelfinavir to the mix, but I continued to refuse AZT.

About this same time Neways introduced the antioxidant formula Revenol. Because of costs and not a lot of cash I went to using Life Enhancer, VMM and Revenol. Margie Aliprandi and Melissa Timmerman were very helpful in that they understood the personal trials I was experiencing and they paid for the supplements and brought them to my home. Their love and concern helped me to wake up and pull myself out of where I'd allowed myself to go.

Shortly after I added Revenol to the mix, my T-cell count began to climb and has held ever since. My lifestyle in the past 4 years has undergone extreme change. I experienced a life-changing spiritual experience while performing the role of Ebenezer Scrooge in "A Christmas Carol". I was aware of something happening within and when I was on my knees, pleading with the Spirit of Christmas Yet to Come, the words "I am not the man I was! I will not be the man I must have been!" rang in my heart and shook the fibres of my soul.

Since that day I have left behind the gay lifestyle. I have gone through the steps required for rejoining my church and I have married. In the last year, since my wedding, my health has been on a steady improve with some setbacks but nothing serious. As a result of reading *World Without AIDS* and meeting with Phillip Day, I decided to start my own trial in October 2000 and I stopped taking the 3TC, D4T and Nelfinavir. At this writing, January 2001, I am enjoying increased vitality, which is a good thing as I am performing in a very athletic version of "Joseph and the Amazing Technicolor Dreamcoat." My wife Tammy and I are enjoying great health and a very active lifestyle.

Take the Credence AIDS tour at www.credence.org. Join me in beating this.

Scott Morgan, Salt Lake City

Dear Sirs,

I have just finished reading your book, *World Without AIDS*, and I must tell you that I am quite impressed. I would not have thought before that the ideas expressed in your book could be realistic. After 22 years in senior scientific marketing positions of international research pharmaceutical companies, I am now living in South Africa, and at the forefront of the AIDS discussion.

As a matter of fact, I was approached by a German microbiology professor, who has developed an immune barrier system for use during sexual intercourse. He asked me to help him with finding sponsors for his systems. Via personal contacts, I approached several companies, including Boehringer Ingelheim, Bristol Meyers-Squibb, Roche, MSD, SmithKline Beecham and others in South Africa, checking their interest in marketing such products. From all companies I received a negative response. There is no interest in the 'prevention' of AIDS. The companies are allocating research money only to their 'treatment' programmes. After reading your book, I believe I understand their motives! With best regards.

Karl J. Stahl, PhD.Org.Chem.

Dear Credence

I was diagnosed HIV+ more than 3 years ago and since then, I have felt I have been on a journey towards hell. Tests, clinic appointments, doctors, more tests, depression, fear of getting ill, fear of death, are only some of the factors that almost drove me to insanity. It is very difficult for me to translate into words what I have felt for the past 3 years. Nobody told me that the hepatitis vaccination could cause an HIV+ response.

In truth I was just waiting for AIDS to come and get me. Every simple illness (flu, fever, etc.) made me believe that this was the beginning of the onset of AIDS. I spend several months crying like a child. I lost my sense of humour, my spontaneity towards other people, and I built a wall around me to protect myself from the external world to cover the shame.

Eventually, a good friend of mine told me about a book called *World Without AIDS*. It took me 4 months to find the courage to buy it. Indeed, since my diagnosis I never found the courage to read anything related to HIV/AIDS because I knew it could have discouraged and depressed me. Thank God *World Without AIDS* was a completely different book. For the first time, clear and honest information about HIV and AIDS was available for the public to access. I read the book in one sitting. By the time I had finished, I felt confused, and angry and disappointed in the media, the government and the scientists. How could they allow such a lie to exist? How can money ever be more important than human life?

Just reading the book made me feel completely different. I felt I had a new life; I felt I had been born again. I immediately became conscious of my eating habits and introduced minerals, vitamins, antioxidants into my diet. I chose not to waste any more time going to the clinic and getting my blood checked out. I chose to live!! I felt like I was truly living in a world without AIDS. Some of my friends did not agree with my choice (although they offered support), but they were relieved to see me happy and energetic. One of them told me: "I have never seen you so... well!!" And indeed I am. I am well and healthy and I have every intention of being so for many years to come.

Thank you for giving my life back.

Vincenzo M, London

Dear Credence

Recently, we alerted you to the case of Baby Garfield, an 18 month old boy from New York caught up in the system of mandatory newborn HIV screening recently initiated in that state. After allegedly testing positive at birth (the actual test was missing from his medical records), and following a series of inconsistent lab work and other questionable tests and recommendations, his mother sought a second opinion about the AIDS drug treatments prescribed for her healthy son.

A few days later, under orders from the Department of Social Services, Baby Garfield was taken from his home by seven police officers. He was placed in foster care and put on an aggressive regimen of mandatory AIDS medication. His parents were allowed to see their child only one hour a week while awaiting a hearing to establish long-term arrangements for his custody.

When the parents found Alive & Well, Garfield had been in a foster home for more than a month and the custody hearing was just a few weeks away. In record time, helped by your donations and good wishes, we pulled together a legal defense team led by Alive & Well's pro bono attorney Denis Sheils of Philadelphia, PA. Although Denis is one of the best and busiest attorneys in the country, he gave his time--including weekends--to the effort to return Baby Garfield to his parents.

A coincidental interview with a national news program brought myself and my family to New York for the custody hearing. I am happy to report that the day after the hearing, Garfield was back in his mother's arms. The victory was resounding as the state has decided not to appeal the judge's decision. Outside the courtroom, after a round of hugs and tears of relief, I shared your e-mail messages with the family. It was a great honor to present them with all the good wishes and promises of donations from across the country and around the world. Help and concern came from as far away as Australia, Canada, England, and Iceland. Thank you!

Christine Maggiore, USA,
Director of the AIDS action group, 'Alive & Well'

TESTIMONIES FROM DR MATTHIAS RATH'S
Why Animals Don't Get Heart Attacks, but People Do

Dear Dr Rath,

In August 1990, at the age of 20, I was diagnosed with viral cardiomyopathy. My doctors informed me that my only hope for survival would be a heart transplant. In November 1990, I was transported to the hospital for heart transplant surgery.

As part of my post-operative treatment, I go into the hospital for an annual heart catheterisation. Up until January 1995, my heart caths were fine. In January 1995, I had a heart catheterisation and my cardiologist found four blockages; three (coronary artery) vessels were approximately 90% occluded (blocked) and the fourth vessel was approximately 60% occluded. I had also gained 100 pounds since the transplant and my cardiologist was furious. I was instructed to begin a low-fat diet immediately.

In May 1995, I was introduced to your cardiovascular vitamin program. I had lost 30 pounds on my low-fat diet and began with the nutrition you recommended.

The results were phenomenal!! This cath showed that the three occlusions previously at approximately 90% were reduced by approximately 50% and the fourth occlusion previously at approximately 60% had no obstruction at all. The other exciting news was that I had lost an additional 50 pounds for a total of 80 pounds. All of this occurred in 6 months. This regimen dramatically improved my life!

Sincerely, **JB**

Dear Dr Rath

I am an eighty-five year old woman. Ten years ago I was diagnosed with angina pectoris. I was told by my doctor that two major arteries were 95% blocked. The doctor prescribed nitroglycerin tablets to relieve the painful condition induced by stress. I have been taking three nitroglycerin tablets a day for chest pains for 10 years.

Last December I started on the cardiovascular vitamin program you recommended. After two months I was almost completely off nitroglycerin, and now take a nitroglycerin tablet only occasionally.

Sincerely, **RA**

Dear Dr Rath

In July I complained of chest pain and pain in my left arm. During a treadmill exercise of about 9 minutes, I had pain in my chest and numbness in my left arm. I was given nitroglycerin and the pain went away immediately. The following day I was admitted to the hospital for an angiogram.

The result of the angiogram indicated that my left main coronary artery was 75% blocked and that I would need a double by-pass. In the meantime, I started on the vitamin program you recommended. I tripled the dosage, while continuing to take the doctor's prescribed medication. The heart surgeon called me for the open-heart surgery. When the cardiologists set up a thallium treadmill test, he was amazed at the results – they were normal, with no chest pain or shortness of breath. He told me I could postpone the surgery indefinitely and come back in six months.

Just last week the doctor looked at my laboratory records and said: "This is amazing!" He went across the hall to see the cardiologist to make sure the report was correct.

Thank you again, Dr Rath. I think this is the beginning of the end for heart disease.

Sincerely, **JK**

Dear Dr Rath

I have been following the cardiovascular vitamin program for five months. In the meantime my doctor reduced my blood pressure medication by half so I can honestly say I am taking half the medication I was five months ago. I am maintaining a blood pressure average of 120/78. Thrilled? You'd better believe it! Next goal: no medication at all. Thank you again.

Sincerely, **LM**

Dear Dr Rath

I am a 53 year old man and my blood pressure was controlled by blood pressure medication. I had been taking blood pressure medication of various types for 10 years.

After 4 months on your cardiovascular vitamin program, I went off all blood pressure medication, while my blood pressure was checked every two weeks. My blood pressure has now been normal for 6 weeks, only with the supplement program you recommended. I had noticed some angina prior to this program, and those symptoms have all been eliminated.

Sincerely, **JL**

Entrenched Scientific Error
it can happen... and it does
(Virus-Hunting Disasters)

For those of us who cannot come to terms with the possibility that the medical establishment could have been wrong about many serious diseases for so long, a quick trawl through medical history serves as a salutary wake-up call. History is replete with flashes of medical inspiration, which have proven to be nothing more than *an incorrect course followed with the maximum of precision*. This is the classic definition of entrenched scientific error. The chief flaw comes when a new public health emergency is centrally organised with little room for wider debate or correction.

The first president of the United States, George Washington, was bled to death in 1797 by some of the most well-educated medical practitioners of his day. No doubt, had you been at the august president's deathbed raising a fuss as they incised his wrists, these learned professionals would have angrily turned on you: *"We know what we're doing. We're DOCTORS!"* It must be noted that the men who killed George Washington were extremely intelligent. They were among the most experienced practitioners of their day – they were highly educated. And they were wrong.

King Charles II of England's doctors were also wrong. When His Majesty fell into a swoon in 1685 (possibly suffering a stroke), he was attended by fourteen of the nation's most well-educated and skilled physicians. His treatment is recorded thus:

> *"...the king was bled to the extent of a pint from a vein in his right arm. Next his shoulder was cut into and the incised area was supped to suck out an additional eight ounces of blood. An emetic and a purgative were administered followed by a second purgative followed by an enema containing antimony, sacred bitters, rock salt, mallow leaves, violets, beetroot, camomile flowers, fennel seed, linseed, cinnamon, cardamom seed, saphron, cochineal and aloes. The king's scalp was shaved and a blister raised. A sneezing powder of hellebore was administered. A plaster of Burgundy pitch and pigeon dung was applied to the feet. Medicaments included melon seeds, manna, slippery elm, black cherry water, lime flowers, lily of the valley, peony, lavender and dissolved pearls. As he grew worse, forty drops of extract of human skull were administered followed by a rallying dose of Raleigh's antidote. Finally bezoar stone was given."* [406]

---

[406] **Buckman, Dr Robert & Karl Sabbagh** *Magic or Medicine?* Pan Books, 1993 Dr Buckman explains that a bezoar was held by legend to be the crystallized tears of a deer which had been

Curiously His Majesty's strength seemed to wane after all these heroic interventions and as the end of his life seemed imminent, his doctors tried a last ditch attempt by forcing more Raleigh's mixture, pearl julep and ammonia down the dying king's throat. Further treatment was rendered more difficult by the king's death." [407]

Hopefully posterity will not judge us too harshly with the barbaric treatments dispensed by the orthodoxy to cancer and other patients today – treatments which have as much in common with sound medicinal practice today as pigeon dung had for King Charles II's welfare then.

Included below is a brief study of a number of other very costly and incorrect medical courses.

SCURVY

Scurvy had traditionally been a fatal scourge to seafarers. Between 1497 and 1499, veteran Portuguese explorer Vasco da Gama lost over a hundred men to the disease on one voyage alone. And according to naval records, between 1600 and 1800 over one million British sailors died of scurvy. Yet for hundreds of years the cure for this gum-rotting, organ-destroying disease was well known to peoples credited by the West with limited medical intelligence.

In the winter of 1534/5, French explorer Jacques Cartier found himself stranded when his ship became trapped in the ice in a tributary of the St Lawrence River in Canada. Soon his crew began dying of scurvy. Out of one hundred and ten men, twenty-five had already perished of the disease and many others were so sick they were not expected to recover.

Believing that the condition was caused either by bad vapours lurking in the hold of his ship or some malignant cause to do with the 'sea airs' (a common belief at that time), Cartier was astonished when help came from an unexpected direction. Some friendly local Indians showed Cartier how to boil pine needles and bark from the white pine, later found to be rich in Vitamin C.[408] His sailors swiftly recovered after drinking the prepared beverage. Upon his return, Cartier enthusiastically reported this miraculous cure to medical authorities. But Cartier's observations were dismissed as "witchdoctors' curses of ignorant savages" and the authorities did nothing about the information they were given, except to log it into their records.

On a lengthy voyage to Brazil, Sir Richard Hawkins, the famous British Elizabethan admiral, faced scurvy among his crew and discovered that eating

---

bitten by a snake. In fact most bezoars used in therapy were gallstones found in the stomachs of goats. See also **Silverman, W A** *Controlled Clinical Trials*, "The Optimistic Bias Favouring Medical Attention", Elsevier Science, New York, 1991

[407] Noted by H W Haggard and quoted in **Silverman, W A** *Human Experimentation*, Oxford Medical Publications, Oxford, 1985

[408] Interestingly, the main ingredients in the pine needles and bark offered to Cartier's sailors by the Indians are contained in a number of beneficial antioxidant products available today.

oranges and lemons cured the condition very quickly. However, despite reporting this phenomenon to the British Admiralty and to any physicians who would listen, this valuable information was again ignored by the medical establishment.

Deaths from scurvy became so numerous that by the 18th century more British sailors were dying from ascorbic acid deficiency than were being killed in combat. In 1740, British admiral George A Anson set sail to circumnavigate the globe in his flagship *Centurion*. Originally starting with six ships and almost 2,000 men, *Centurion* was the only ship that eventually returned. Anson reported that scurvy alone had killed over 1,000 of his men.

The great embarrassment this event caused in British Admiralty circles prompted Scottish naval surgeon John Lind to seek a cure for the dreaded disease. On 20th May 1747, Lind began an experiment which dramatically demonstrated that fresh greens and plenty of fruits eaten by scurvy sufferers produced stunning recoveries. Later experiments clearly showed that those who ate a balanced diet, fortified with these vegetable and fruit elements, did not contract scurvy.

Yet what was the reaction of the establishment? Once again, the British Admiralty and numerous other physicians, who were attempting to solve the same problem (and at the same time earn both grants and fame), barely acknowledged Lind's findings. It took 48 more years and thousands more scurvy deaths before his diet advice finally became official Navy quartermaster policy. Ironically, after implementing this simple measure, the British, who became known as 'limeys' because of their new nutrition procedure, soon gained strategic ascendancy on the world's seas. After 1800, British sailors never contracted scurvy. The naval might of Britain's enemies however continued to be decimated by it. Author Edward Griffin surmises that the founding of the British Empire in large measure *"was the direct result of overcoming scientific prejudice against vitamin therapy."*[409]

One would have thought that scurvy ended there. But that was not the case. As the obsession with virus and microbe hunting began to grip developing medicine during the late nineteenth century, it was easier to blame a bacterium than to isolate the elusive vitamin. Scientists became distracted. Suddenly a simple nutritional deficiency no longer seemed the plausible and complete answer to scurvy. It had to be something more complicated, more scientific. Whilst there were indeed some blessings which arose from increased scientific knowledge, there were also the attendant pitfalls. The new milk-pasteurisation techniques for instance unwittingly destroyed the milk's ascorbic acid content, leading to hundreds of fresh scurvy cases among children each year.

Professor C P Stewart of Edinburgh University remarks:

---

[409] Griffin, G Edward, *World Without Cancer*, op. cit. p.54

"One factor which undoubtedly held up the development of the concept of deficiency diseases was the discovery of bacteria in the nineteenth century and the consequent preoccupation of scientists and doctors with positive infective agents in disease. So strong was the impetus provided by bacteriology that many diseases which we now know to be due to nutritional or endocrine deficiencies were, as late as 1910, thought to be 'toxemias'." [410]

By the 1930s, purified Vitamin C had been successfully isolated and scurvy was officially declared vanquished. For the correct cure to reach this status in Europe, all it had taken to conquer scurvy was 400 years of following an incorrect course, many, many thousands of deaths, and finally the realisation that the answer did indeed lie in a simple diet of fruit.

BERIBERI

Though more well known as a disease of the Orient, beriberi put in a fearsome appearance after the French Revolution. Professor Peter Duesberg explains:

"Though it has primarily plagued Asia throughout history, beriberi appeared with a vengeance in the West after the French Revolution, when the French population rejected the dark bread of peasantry in favour of the royal milled white bread, from which the thiamin [Vitamin B1] had been unknowingly removed. Bread processing soon swept throughout Europe and the United States, and beriberi followed closely." [411]

A Japanese doctor and later Surgeon General to their navy, Dr Kanehiro Takaki, was appalled at the attrition beriberi was wreaking among his sailors. He began by experimenting with their diets and soon found that he could cure and prevent the disease completely. He reported his results to his superiors, and the military acted without delay, changing the official diet of the Japanese Navy. The Japanese beriberi epidemic was eradicated in 1885.

Takaki enthusiastically spread the word, even having his findings written up in the British medical journal *Lancet*. However, instead of the British medical establishment acknowledging beriberi as a chronic metabolic deficiency disease brought on by the missing food factor thiamin, Takaki's research and results were ignored. Once again, it was the height of the bacteria-hunting craze, and Robert Koch had only just isolated the bacillus for tuberculosis, bringing the promise of ending the rampage of other global killers through the lens of microbiology. Even in Takaki's own country, the

---

[410] **Stewart, CP** and D Guthrie, *Lind's Treatise on Scurvy*, Edinburgh University Press, 1953 pp. 408-409

[411] **Duesberg, Peter H**, *Inventing the AIDS Virus*, Regnery Press, 1996. See also **Williams, R R** *Towards the Conquest of Beriberi*, Harvard University Press, 1961

virus hunters began sniping at him, insisting that the beriberi outbreak had merely been cured by improving the sailors' sanitary conditions and stamping out 'a beriberi micro-organism'.

Christian Eijkman, a Dutch army physician, also observed beriberi among Dutch soldiers in Java in the late 1800s. He noticed that the soldiers were getting sick while the natives were spared the illness. Nevertheless, his microbe hunting background led him to believe that there was an infectious cause to the disease. Yet while investigating microbes as the cause of beriberi, Eijkman's experiments consistently failed to meet Koch's Postulates. He could not produce any guilty agent common to all his patients. Frustrated, he tried to transmit the disease to chickens using the blood from beriberi victims. At first nothing happened. Then the chickens began to get sick from a syndrome quite similar to beriberi. Further experimentation revealed that the birds were succumbing to sickness because they were eating polished (de-husked) rice. Eijkman realised that the Dutch all ate polished rice, while the local population did not.

Eijkman's findings though were not met with the approbation he expected. His colleagues, busy hunting down protozoa, bacteria, viruses and fungi for beriberi, were openly contemptuous of his nutrition theory. Between 1890 and 1911, while thousands died across the world from the disease, the medical research establishment remained largely fixated with the notion of an infectious beriberi.

Bacteriologist Robert Koch himself got to grips with his own failure to provide the causative microbial agent and graciously published his negative results, prompting a search for the answer in new arenas. Sadly, this did not stop the more enthusiastic virus hunters from recommending that patients with beriberi suffer the necessary treatments for the 'deadly microbe'. Those treatments included quinine, arsenic, strychnine and an awesomely agonising death.

Vitamin B1 (thiamin) was finally isolated in 1911 and again in 1926. Today the vitamin is always added back into bread after the refining process and as a result beriberi has all but disappeared. Robert Williams, one of the scientists who pioneered the isolation of Vitamin B1, later commented on the tragic blindness that had caused so many needless deaths.

> "Because of [the work of Pasteur and Koch] and other dramatic successes bacteriology had advanced, within twenty years after its birth, to become the chief cornerstone of medical education. All young physicians were so imbued with the idea of infection as the cause of disease that it presently came to be accepted as almost axiomatic that disease could have no other cause. This preoccupation of physicians with infection as a cause of disease was doubtless responsible for many digressions from attention to food as the causal

factor of beriberi. " [412]

PELLAGRA
(Trouble in the South)

Pellagra was a fatal disease that affected the poor. Noted originally in the 18th century as a European condition that appeared to be linked to corn diets among the impoverished, pellagra's symptoms were as exotic as they were fatal. Named 'pellagra' (the Italian for 'rough skin'), sufferers of this disease were affected by dermatitis, inflammations of the mucous membranes, chronic diarrhoea and mental problems, including depression, irritability, anxiety, confusion, migraine headaches, delusions and hallucinations.

Most European doctors working in the eighteenth and early 19th century had correctly noted two things about pellagra. Firstly, that it only occurred within groups that were poor. Secondly, that it was linked in some way to corn diets, which had become popular among the poor as a cheap and convenient staple diet. Some theorised that a fungus growing on corn produced a poison that caused pellagra. Others surmised that corn was not nutritious enough, and that pellagra was some kind of nutritional deficiency disease.

Many doctors being trained around the end of the 1800s were specialising in the new medical science - microbiology. And so inevitably, new disease syndromes were analysed as microbiological illnesses. For instance, Titius, a prominent German bacteriologist, pronounced pellagra infectious, even though he had never been to the afflicted areas and had a cursory knowledge of the condition. Other doctors began treating pellagra as infectious, and so the remedies of the day employed against infection were used to appalling effect - quinine, arsenic and strychnine.

The Italian researcher Ceni claimed that a fungus growing on mouldy corn was responsible for releasing poison into the patient, thus causing the disease. Ceni's work inspired others to come up with their own proprietary bacteria, which then created a new problem: the sheer volume of papers being written on these new 'infectious agents' for pellagra were consuming prodigious amounts of time to study and refute, thus preventing any possibility that closed minds could be opened to other potential causal factors. The European microbe-hunting bonanza continued, and a cure for pellagra remained as remote as ever.

And then in 1902, an isolated first case was noticed in Georgia, USA. Then in 1906, a rash of pellagra cases occurred in Alabama in a hospital for the insane. Eighty-eight patients contracted the condition and most subsequently died. Soon cases were appearing everywhere, even in some major metropolitan areas of the United States.

Convinced that they were facing a grave new public health threat, the Public Health Service of the US government swung into action. It set up a

---

[412] Williams, R R, op. cit.

pellagra institute in South Carolina and appointed Claude Lavinder to head up the research. Lavinder was convinced that pellagra was microbe-driven, but became frustrated when his experiments failed to produce a spread of the disease in animals. In 1909, a national conference on pellagra was convened, again in South Carolina. Once again, pellagra's links with corn diets and poverty were reiterated. The prevailing mood of the conference was that pellagra was either airborne or infectious in nature. The following year, John D Long replaced Lavinder as head of the PHS's pellagra lab. Long's theories on pellagra were influenced by the well-known British doctor, Louis Sambon, who also believed pellagra to be infectious.

With no evidence to back his claim, Sambon declared to the press in 1910 that pellagra, like malaria, was transmitted by insects. Now flies were apparently picking up the deadly pellagra 'microbe' from horses, who then transferred it to blackbirds, who then flew to other areas, where more insects became infected and then spread the pellagra 'microbe' to humans. Sambon had of course failed to consider the significance that, unlike malaria, pellagra was not spreading outside its declared risk groups like other insect-driven diseases.

But Sambon was considered a genius and he did have the advantage of the full weight of the medical establishment behind him. In 1912, the Department of Agriculture even sent a special team to South Carolina to study the role of insects in the transmission of pellagra. Newspapers began fanning the flames of fear, and soon those who had been diagnosed with the disease found themselves social and community outcasts. Researcher E W Etheridge gives us a picture of what it was like living under the shadow of pellagra in the early 1900s - a picture all too reminiscent of the hype and public fear that would later surround AIDS:

> *"So great was the horror of the disease that a diagnosis of pellagra was synonymous with a sentence of social ostracism. A severe case of eczema was enough to start a stampede in a community, and 'pellagrins' sometimes covered their hands with gloves and salve, hoping to conceal their condition.*

> *Many hospitals refused admission to pellagra patients. One in Atlanta did so on the grounds that it was an incurable disease. At another hospital in the same city, student nurses went on strike when they were required to attend to pellagrins. Physicians and nurses at Johns Hopkins Hospital in Baltimore were forbidden even to discuss the pellagra cases that might be there. Fear of the disease spread to schools and hotels too....*

> *Tennessee began to isolate all its pellagra patients. The state board of health declared pellagra to be a transmissable disease and required physicians to report all cases.... Exhibits on pellagra were*

prepared for the public, creating fear of the disease along with interest in it... There was pressure for a quarantine in Kentucky, and pellagra patients at the Western Kentucky Asylum of the Insane were isolated...

Isolation did not prevent the spread of pellagra, but only heightened the panic over it." [413]

The turn in the disease came in 1914. Two important things happened that year. Britain declared war on Germany, and the United States Public Health Service appointed the unknown Dr Joseph Goldberger as head of its pellagra team. By this time, a quarter of a million people had perished from the pellagra epidemic in the United States.

Goldberger arrived in the South and, although a bacteriologist by profession, immediately began noticing obvious indications that pellagra was not infectious. He saw that even when pellagrins were kept in close confinement, their doctors and nurses did not contract the condition. He also noticed the different diets shared by the two groups. The poor ate the staple diet of corn, while the more affluent doctors, nurses and other hospital staff ate meat and vegetables. Dr Goldberger then set about following the *correct course with the maximum of precision*. He changed the diets of the pellagrins and was able to rid the disease entirely from hospitals, prisons, asylums and orphanages, demonstrating that the occurrence of pellagra was related to a deficiency of fresh green material in the diet. Goldberger approached this problem by the use of brewer's yeast, which would completely prevent and cure pellagra. Further studies years later would show that the factor in brewer's yeast that was most active in the curative effect was niacin Vitamin B3.

What happened next amazed even the stoic Goldberger. The *New York Times* published the story of Goldberger's success with pellagra, explaining his hypothesis concerning poor diet and nutritional deficiency. As a result, Goldberger began to draw intense criticism, most notably from the medical establishment and their bacteria hunters. They accused Goldberger of propagating a dangerous and reckless philosophy in the light of so lethal a disease. A doctor at one medical conference drew considerable applause when he described the newspaper publicity on Goldberger's work as 'pernicious', expecting people to believe that such a lethal epidemic was solely the result of poor diet. [414]

Goldberger continued to receive major criticism from his peers, culminating in the most vicious attacks in 1916. Finally becoming exasperated, Goldberger, his wife and 14 workers decided to perform a series of rather

---

[413] **Etheridge, E W** *The Butterfly Caste: A Social History of Pellagra in the South*, Greenwood Publishing Co, 1972. p.11
[414] Ibid.

extreme experiments for the benefit of the log-jammed medical establishment. They injected themselves with samples of blood, mucus, faeces other bodily fluids from the pellagrins. None of them contracted pellagra. The medical establishment was less than impressed and the attacks continued. As a result, Goldberger's dietary recommendations to end pellagra were completely ignored for the next twenty years, resulting in hundreds of thousands of further needless deaths. Many pellagrins who developed the mental anguishes associated with the condition were pronounced insane and shut away in asylums. Here they were subjected to electric shock treatment, powerful sedative drugs and prefrontal lobotomies in the hopes of rendering them controllable.

Goldberger continued trying to break the establishment's intransigence on pellagra up until his death in 1929. His work was continued by his faithful colleague, Dr W Henry Sebrell. Cases of pellagra were still being reported up to the onset of World War 2 in 1939, even in spite of the fact that Vitamin B3 (niacin) had been isolated as the missing pellagra factor in the mid-1930s.

Soon after the end of World War II, it was finally admitted by the European and American medical establishments that pellagra had, all along, been a chronic metabolic deficiency disease brought on by an absence of green material in the common diet.

NEUROSYPHILIS
(Playing Medical Mind Games)
Neurosyphilis was supposedly identified along with syphilis, a genuinely infectious venereal disease, in the first few decades of the 20th century. Apparently, neurosyphilis was the result of the syphilis bacterium invading the central nervous system and the brain (sometimes years after the original infection), thus causing dementia and insanity. Today syphilis is still identified with insanity, and yet neurosyphilis and its accompanying dementias were subsequently found to be caused, not by the syphilis microbe at all, but by the toxic mercury and arsenic treatments used before 1950 in an attempt to stem the disease. It was only following the introduction of penicillin to treat syphilis in the 1950s that the mercury and arsenic treatments disappeared, and with it, neurosyphilis. It later became apparent that doctors had been confusing the long-term poisonous effects of their mercury and arsenic treatments with the syphilis itself.

Other false virus and microbe trails resulting in needless deaths and millions of wasted dollars include the hunt for non-existent microbes for Legionnaire's Disease (later found to be pneumonia), pernicious anaemia (later found to be a Vitamin B12 cyanocobalamin and B9 folic acid deficiency) and the most serious of them all, cancer (pancreatic enzyme and nutritional deficiencies, exacerbated by damaging environmental factors).[415]

---

[415] **Day, Phillip** *Cancer: Why We're Still Dying to Know the Truth*, op. cit.

SMON (Subacute Myelo-Optico-Neuropathy)
(Trouble in the Orient)

The virus misdiagnosis disaster that most clearly prefigures AIDS is surely the SMON fiasco of the 1960 - 1970s. In 1959, patients in Japan began falling ill from a combination of intestinal problems, internal bleeding, diarrhoea and a mysterious nerve disorder which paralysed limbs. As Japanese doctors began to notice the rising statistics, they recognised the spectre of a new syndrome. Almost immediately, it was assumed the syndrome was infectious – even its sudden appearance was enough to convince many that a new virus was on the loose. Infection clusters broke out around villages and towns. One family member would succumb, followed by another within several weeks. Hospital staff too were not immune from the new epidemic – even doctors and medical workers became sick from the illness.

Yet there was striking evidence that SMON did not display symptoms indicative of an infectious disease. It was not spreading exponentially into the population, nor was it infecting both sexes equally – the classic infection pattern. The new syndrome favoured middle-aged women, was less common among men and was virtually non-existent among children, who are usually the first to succumb to any volatile infection. Neither did those suffering from SMON demonstrate any tell-tale signs of rash or fever, indicating that their body was fighting off an infectious micro-organism. These factors alone should have started the alarm bells ringing. Sadly they did not.

By 1964, with the Olympics looming, the SMON syndrome remained very much at large. The media had whipped Japan into national hysteria. Japanese politicians, formerly delighted with the idea of hosting the world's tourists at the long-awaited Olympic Games, ended up dreading the famous event, imagining in their worst fears an uncontrollable plague devastating the Games. Grant money was speedily allocated, an SMON commission convened, and Japanese virus hunters got to work in search of the guilty microbe.

After three years, no virus had been isolated and SMON was still killing the Japanese public. During the fruitless investigation however, one research team discovered that about half the SMON patients had been previously prescribed a diarrhoea-fighting drug known as Entero-vioform. The other half had received a compound marketed under the name Emaform. Both drugs were routinely prescribed for problems of the digestive tract, the early symptom of SMON, and for the first time, suspicion arose that maybe the two drugs had something to do with the disease. But after studying the evidence, the SMON commission remained intent on a viral explanation for the disease, and summarily dismissed the medication-linked theories, citing the improbability that two different drugs could cause the same illness.

By 1969, the Japanese government had become thoroughly unnerved by the medical establishment's continued failure to come up with any explanation or cure for SMON. A new SMON Research Commission was convened, an entity which was to become the largest and most well-funded medical commission ever devoted to a single disease in Japan. Dr Reisaku Kono, Japan's leading virologist, was chosen to chair the commission, sending a strong message to medical institutions world-wide that the centralised SMON research program was to remain dominated by the virus establishment. Yet by 1970, after twelve hard years of virus-centred research into SMON, researchers were still yielding the same dismal results. No virus behind SMON, and no relief in sight for the victims. To make matters worse, the death toll from the disease continued to rise, two thousand Japanese victims alone being claimed by SMON in 1969.

But one pharmacologist was on to something. Dr H Beppu had also noticed the Entero-vioform-Emaform connection with SMON victims. Beppu realised that both compounds were different brand names for the same substance, the Ciba-Geigy drug, clioquinol. Beppu conducted experiments where he fed the green clioquinol to mice, expecting to see the nerve damage disorders typical of SMON manifest in his rodents. The mice merely died, exposing the drug's extreme toxicity. Clioquinol had been marketed for years on the assumption that it was not absorbed by the body, but remained in the intestinal tract to kill germs. But SMON's victims produced a green coating on their tongues and produced green urine, symptoms that quite remarkably went unnoticed until nation-wide data on the disease was gathered. These green discharges were later isolated and tested to reveal an altered form of clioquinol in the patient's body. For the very first time, even the élite within the medical establishment were compelled to consider the unthinkable: that SMON was being caused by clioquinol consumption, not by a virus.

Doctors at the hard end of the crisis became horrified as the truth leaked out. They had been prescribing Entero-vioform and Emaform to patients with intestinal complaints for years and had been in the habit of innocently but arbitrarily increasing the doses of clioquinol as more diarrhoea and abdominal cramps manifested in the sufferer. Once Beppu had established the SMON-clioquinol connection, other seemingly irrelevant information began to make sense. For instance, SMON's tendency to make its presence felt in hospitals, family groupings, medical workers and in summertime all reflected the pattern of Japan's chronic clioquinol consumption. Cases of SMON were also found to have risen and fallen with the sales of clioquinol. That Japan suffered more cruelly from the syndrome than other countries in which clioquinol was available has been put down to Japan's well-known, traditional over-consumption of pharmaceutical drugs in general.

On 8th September 1970, the Japanese government banned sales of clioquinol. That same month SMON cases dropped to below twenty. The following year saw only 36 cases. Three more were reported in 1972, and one in 1973. At last, this tragedy had run its course, and SMON could now be entered into the medical history books, archived under 'widespread needless death'.

317

Ironically, the fight over whether SMON had been the result of clioquinol or a mystery virus was to prevail for many more years in spite of the clear evidence, the virus hunting establishment refusing to consider that they had been wrong. Or was it that it was refusing to consider that SMON was actually that most despicable of syndromes, a classic iatrogenic illness – a disease brought on by the very medication prescribed by doctors to treat it? The concept of iatrogenic diseases is rarely considered because it understandably horrifies many doctors who in almost all cases have the care and well-being of their patient at heart.

For this reason, very few doctors outside Japan are aware of SMON, let alone the cause of the disaster that claimed so many lives. A bad mistake is rarely discussed by the guilty and so the lessons of SMON went unheeded. Today, the virus still dominates medical research and, as we have discovered, this fact alone led to the myopic research mindset which paved the way for the widespread, needless deaths in AIDS.

'HIV'/AIDS

One of the greatest scandals in medicine today surrounds the classification of AIDS as an infectious disease. The supposed pathogen, human immunodeficiency virus (HIV), despite much fanfare and fear-mongering, has never been isolated according to any recognised and appropriate scientific procedure. And so, from a scientific standpoint, HIV can be deemed not to exist. In the 16 years since Dr Robert Gallo's 'discovery' of HIV (for which he was later convicted of science fraud), no empirical proof of the existence of HIV has ever been furnished to the scientific establishment. Cash rewards for 'The Missing Virus' remain uncollected, INCLUDING MINE OF £5,000, for a properly isolated HI virus, according to all the normal rules.

All the evidence shows that immune suppression ('AIDS') in the First World is primarily brought on by long-term recreational or pharmaceutical drug toxicity AND IS NOT INFECTIOUS OR SEXUALLY TRANSMITTED. Third World or 'African' 'AIDS' is nothing more than the cynical reclassification of diseases that have always killed Africans: dysentery, cholera, malnutrition, TB, malaria and parasitic infections, brought on by the frequently contaminated water supplies Africans other nations are forced to tolerate. Africans are almost always classified as 'AIDS carriers' through the arbitrary visual-only Bangui definition.

In the First World, AIDS is hardly less scandalous. Many unwitting victims are drawn into the AIDS nightmare by inadvertently triggering a 'positive' on one of two main tests given to patients today. The ELISA (Enzyme-Linked Immuno-Absorbent Assay) and Western Blot tests are designed to highlight the presence of the supposed HIV, not by identifying the virus itself, but by identifying the presence of antibodies in the blood, allegedly unique to, and stimulated by the virus. The only real difference between the two tests is that the ELISA is supposed to measure antibody

318

activity as a whole, whereas the Western Blot measures reactions to separate proteins supposedly making up the virus. As a result of this claim, the Western Blot method is deemed by most in the AIDS industry to be more specific than the ELISA test, and will often be used to confirm a positive ELISA test. [416] But as we shall discover, all the diagnostic methods employed by the recognised laboratories are far from specific.

Researcher Christine Maggiore, herself a victim of these fraudulent tests, states the major problem as follows:

"Both tests are non-specific to HIV antibodies and are highly inaccurate. Non-specific means that these tests respond to a great number of non-HIV antibodies, microbes, bacteria and other conditions that are often found in the blood of normal, healthy people. A reaction to any one of these other antibodies and conditions will result in an HIV positive diagnosis. A simple illness like a cold or the flu can cause a positive reading on an HIV test. A flu shot or other vaccine can also create positive results. Having or having had herpes or hepatitis may produce a positive test, as can a vaccination for hepatitis B. Exposure to diseases such as tuberculosis and malaria commonly cause false positive results, as do the presence of tape worms and other parasites. Conditions such as alcoholism, liver disease and blood that is highly oxidated through drug use may be interpreted as the presence of HIV antibodies. Pregnancy and prior pregnancy can also cause a positive result."[417]

The triggering of an HIV positive will lead invariably to prescriptions for the deadly cell toxins AZT, ddI and other 'HIV' drugs, which have an appalling history of causing the very immune deficiencies they were supposedly designed to prevent. South African barrister Anthony Brink remarks:

"In truth, AZT makes you feel like you're dying. That's because on AZT you are. How can a deadly cell toxin conceivably make you feel better as it finishes you, by stopping your cells from dividing, by ending this vital process that distinguishes living things from dead things? Not for nothing does AZT come with a skull and cross-bones label when packaged for laboratory use."[418]

And indeed that is the case. With a skull and cross-bones on the outer label and a reminder to wear *suitable protective clothing when handling,* the inner contents of the AZT packaging include the following side-effects advisory notice:

---

[416] **Lake, Douglas** *The Biology Project* University of Arizona School of Medicine.

[417] **Maggiore, Christine**, *What if Everything You Thought You Knew About AIDS Was Wrong*, Alive and Well, Studio City, CA 90604, USA

[418] **Brink, Anthony,** *AZT and Heavenly Remedies,* Rethinking AIDS Homepage: www.rethinkingaids.com

WHOLE BODY: abdominal pain, back pain, body odour, chest pain, chills, edema of the lip, fever, flu symptoms, hyperalgesia.

CARDIOVASCULAR: syncope, vasodilation.

GASTROINTESTINAL: bleeding gums, constipation, diarrhoea, dysphagia, edema of the tongue, eructation, flatulence, mouth ulcer, rectal haemorrhage.

HAEMIC AND LYMPHATIC: lymphadenopathy.

MUSCULOSKELETAL: arthralgia, muscle spasm, tremor, twitch.

NERVOUS: anxiety, confusion, depression, dizziness, emotional lability, loss of mental acuity, nervousness, paresthesia, somnolence, vertigo.

RESPIRATORY: cough, dyspnea, epistaxis, hoarseness, pharyngitis, rhinitis, sinusitis.

SKIN: rash, sweat, urticaria.

SPECIAL SENSES: amblyopia, hearing loss, photophobia, taste perversion.

UROGENITAL: dysuria, polyuria, urinary frequency, urinary hesitancy.

I spent eight years in Los Angeles and San Francisco working among homosexuals deemed HIV positive by the medical establishment. In all cases, their plight could be laid at the door of either recreational or pharmaceutical drug terrorism. Their sure and ready remedy was to cease the drug abuse and move towards wellness with a properly constructed regimen of sound nutrition and supplementation.

Our full report is contained in *World Without AIDS*, the result of 15 years' research into this tragically misunderstood realm of medical error. The further tragedy is that expectant mothers are now required to take an 'HIV' test, resulting in more than a few cases being deemed positive simply because of the antibody load picked up by these tests. The resultant medication is as catastrophic to the baby as it is to the mother. For this reason, we issue the following advisory to all pregnant mothers around the world:

HEALTH WARNING TO EXPECTANT MOTHERS

If you have recently become pregnant, you may be recommended to take an HIV test as part of a standardised ante-natal care package.[419] This test is highly inaccurate and remains scientifically unproven. It should be refused on the following grounds.

1) All manufacturers of these tests include the following or similar disclaimer with their test kits: "At present, there is no recognised standard for

---

[419] Refer to "Review of antenatal testing services", NHS Regional Office, London, UK Dept of Health." Recommending the HIV test became UK national policy in July 1999, and is now mandatory in some US states.

establishing the presence or absence of antibodies to HIV-1 and HIV- 2 in human blood."[420]

2) The reason for this disclaimer is because the AIDS test does not measure the presence of a virus.[421] The AIDS test has been designed to detect levels of antibody activity in the blood. Antibody activity in the blood stream is a normal occurrence in humans, but is being misinterpreted by the AIDS test as indicative of the presence of HIV.

3) As a result of this misinterpretation, healthy individuals are being wrongly diagnosed as HIV positive. Since this information has come to light, in excess of 60 different medical conditions have been recorded that can give rise to a false HIV positive reading. These separate conditions include flu, flu vaccination, malaria, tetanus vaccination, Hepatitis A and B, Hepatitis vaccinations, alcohol and drug use, recent viral infections and even pregnancy.[422] Receiving a spurious but wholly devastating diagnosis of HIV positive will prompt your doctor to recommend a course of anti-HIV drugs. Known as protease inhibitors or anti-retrovirals, these drugs are highly toxic. They have the well-documented capacity to harm the mother, and also to severely deform and even kill the unborn child.[423]

The current levels of spending on AIDS drugs in the Western World are phenomenal. So too are the profits enjoyed by the AIDS drug manufacturers. As a result, the information contained in this advisory is largely being ignored by the medical establishment. Sadly, this is not an unexpected reaction. The pursuit of profit at the expense of health, the wilful employment of flawed medical procedures, the administration of dangerously toxic drugs to expectant mothers, the disregard for the plight of thousands upon thousands of wrongly diagnosed people, and a refusal by the medical establishment to listen to sound contrary evidence or to admit medical negligence - all are the hallmarks of that once-respected drug thalidomide. Do not allow either yourself or your child to face the possibility of becoming another heartbreaking medical statistic. For more information on AIDS, please obtain a copy of *World Without AIDS*, available through Credence Publications.

---

[420] The above disclaimer is included in all Abbott 'AXSYM' AIDS tests, the world's leading supplier of AIDS test kits.

[421] Monetary rewards offered to leading organisations within the scientific community by concerned organisations for reasonable evidence that HIV exists remain uncollected.

[422] Johnson, Christine, *Continuum Magazine*, September 1996. Maggiore, Christine. *What if Everything You Knew about AIDS was Wrong?* An Alive and Well Publication, April 2000. Ransom & Day, *World Without AIDS*. Credence Publications, July 2000. www.credence.org

[423] Kumar et al, Journal of Acquired Immune Deficiency Syndromes, 7; 1034-9, 1994. JAMA Journal of American Medical Association, Jan 5th 2000, Incidence of liver damage. *World Without AIDS*. AZT and enlarged craniums in infants. Refer to www.virusmyth.com for a more comprehensive list of scientific references which catalogue the damage caused by AIDS drugs.

Vaccine Fillers

In addition to the viral and bacterial contaminants that are part of vaccines, the following is a list of vaccine fillers:

aluminum hydroxide
aluminum phosphate
ammonium sulphate
amphotericin B
animal tissues: pig blood, horse blood, rabbit brain,
dog kidney, monkey kidney,
chick embryo, chicken egg, duck egg
calf (bovine) serum
betapropiolactone
foetal bovine serum
formaldehyde
formalin
gelatin
glycerol
human diploid cells (originating from human aborted foetal tissue)
hydrolized gelatin
monosodium glutamate (MSG)
neomycin
neomycin sulphate
phenol red indicator
phenoxyethanol (antifreeze)
potassium diphosphate
potassium monophosphate
polymyxin B
polysorbate 20
polysorbate 80
porcine (pig) pancreatic hydrolysate of casein
residual MRC5 proteins
sorbitol
sucrose
thimerosal (49.6% mercury)
tri(n)butylphosphate,
VERO cells, a continuous line of monkey kidney cells
washed sheep red blood cells

An Unbeatable Offer?

PRESS RELEASE- 29th January 2001

THE FOLLOWING OFFER is made to US-licensed medical doctors who routinely administer childhood vaccinations and to pharmaceutical company CEOs worldwide.

Jock Doubleday, president of the California non-profit corporation Natural Woman, Natural Man, Inc., hereby offers $20,000.00 (U.S.) to the first medical doctor or pharmaceutical company CEO who publicly drinks a mixture of standard vaccine additive ingredients in the same amount as a six-year-old child is recommended to receive under the year-2000 guidelines of the U.S. Centers for Disease Control and Prevention.

The mixture will not contain viruses or bacteria dead or alive, but will contain standard vaccine additive ingredients in their usual forms and proportions. The mixture will include, but will not be limited to: thimerosal (a mercury derivative), ethylene glycol (antifreeze), phenol (a disinfectant dye), benzethonium chloride (a disinfectant), formaldehyde (a preservative and disinfectant), and aluminium.

The mixture will be prepared by Jock Doubleday, three medical professionals that he names, and three medical professionals that the participant names. The mixture will be body weight calibrated.

The participant agrees, and any and all agents and associates of the participant agree, to indemnify and hold harmless in perpetuity any and all persons, organizations, or entities associated with the event for any harm caused, or alleged to be caused, directly or indirectly, to the participant or indirectly to the participant's heirs, relations, employers, employees, colleagues, associates, or other persons, organizations, or entities claiming association with, or representation of, the participant, by the participant's participation in the event.

Because the participant is either a professional caregiver who routinely administers childhood vaccinations, or a pharmaceutical company CEO whose business is, in part, the sale of childhood vaccines, it is understood by all parties that the participant considers all vaccine additive ingredients to be safe and that the participant considers any mixture containing these ingredients to be safe.

The event will be held within six months of the participant's written agreement to the above and further elaborated terms. This offer, dated January 29, 2001, has no expiration date unless superceded by a similar offer of higher remuneration. Contact Jock Doubleday at jockdoubleday@aol.com.

Why Are the Nations Dying?

Degenerative diseases are taking hold of industrialised nations like never before. The following excerpted US Senate document warned of the health holocaust to come.

Senate Document No. 264, 1936.

74th Congress, 2nd Session

"Our physical well-being is more directly dependent upon minerals we take into our systems than upon calories or vitamins, or upon precise proportions of starch, protein or carbohydrates we consume... Do you know that most of us today are suffering from certain dangerous diet deficiencies which cannot be remedied until depleted soils from which our food comes are brought into proper mineral balance?

The alarming fact is that foods (fruits, vegetables and grains), now being raised on millions of acres of land that no longer contain enough of certain minerals, are starving us - no matter how much of them we eat. No man of today can eat enough fruits and vegetables to supply his system with the minerals he requires for perfect health because his stomach isn't big enough to hold them.

The truth is, our foods vary enormously in value, and some of them aren't worth eating as food... Our physical well-being is more directly dependent upon the minerals we take into our systems than upon calories or vitamins or upon the precise proportions of starch, protein or carbohydrates we consume.

This talk about minerals is novel and quite startling. In fact, a realization of the importance of minerals in food is so new that the text books on nutritional dietetics contain very little about it. Nevertheless, it is something that concerns all of us, and the further we delve into it the more startling it becomes.

You'd think, wouldn't you, that a carrot is a carrot - that one is about as good as another as far as nourishment is concerned? But it isn't; one carrot may look and taste like another and yet be lacking in the particular mineral element which our system requires and which carrots are supposed to contain.

Laboratory test prove that the fruits, the vegetables, the grains, the eggs, and even the milk and the meats of today are not what they were a few generations ago (which doubtless explains why our forefathers thrived on a selection of foods that would starve us!)

No man today can eat enough fruits and vegetables to supply his stomach with the mineral salts he requires for perfect health, because his stomach isn't big enough to hold them! And we are turning into big stomachs.

No longer does a balanced and fully nourishing diet consist merely of so many calories or certain vitamins or fixed proportion of starches, proteins and carbohydrates. We know that our diets must contain in addition something like a score of minerals salts.

It is bad news to learn from our leading authorities that 99% of the American people are deficient in these minerals [this was in 1936!], **and that a marked deficiency in any one of the more important minerals actually results in disease. Any upset of the balance, any considerable lack or one or another element, however microscopic the body requirement may be, and we sicken, suffer, shorten our lives.**

We know that vitamins are complex chemical substances which are indispensable to nutrition, and that each of them is of importance for normal function of some special structure in the body. Disorder and disease result from any vitamin deficiency. **It is not commonly realized, however, that vitamins control the body's appropriation of minerals, and in the absence of minerals they have no function to perform. Lacking vitamins, the system can make some use of minerals, but lacking minerals, vitamins are useless. Certainly our physical well-being is more directly dependent upon the minerals we take into our systems than upon calories of vitamins or upon the precise proportions of starch, protein of carbohydrates we consume.**

This discovery is one of the latest and most important contributions of science to the problem of human health."

Common Alkali Ash Foods

(Help to control acid in your internal environment)

Almonds
Apples
Apricots
Avocados
Bananas
Beans, dried
Beet greens
Beet
Blackberries
Broccoli
Brussels sprouts
Cabbage
Carrots
Cauliflower
Celery
Chard leaves
Cherries, sour
Cucumbers
Dates, dried
Figs, dried
Grapefruit
Grapes
Green beans
Green peas
Lemons
Lettuce

Milk, goat*
Millet
Molasses
Mushrooms
Muskmelons
Onions
Oranges (small portions)
Parsnips
Peaches
Pears
Pineapple (small portions)
Potatoes, sweet
Potatoes, white
Radishes
Raisins
Raspberries
Rutabagas
Sauerkraut
Soy beans, green
Spinach, raw
Strawberries
Tangerines
Tomatoes
Watercress
Watermelon

* Recommended for infants only when mother's milk is not available.
Note: Some of the above foods may seem acidic, but in reality leave an alkali ash in the system.

Convert your diet to 80% alkali ash/ 20% acid ash foods. Ensure that your diet is predominant high-water content foods that are fresh and organic. Supplementation with trace minerals and vitamins is also advised.

Common Acid Ash Foods

Bacon
Barley grain
Beef
Blueberries
Bran, wheat
Bran, oat
Bread, white
Bread, whole wheat
Butter
Carob
Cheese
Chicken
Cod
Corn
Corned beef
Crackers, soda
Cranberries
Currants
Eggs
Flour, white
Flour, whole wheat
Haddock
Lamb
Lentils, dried
Lobster
Milk, cow's ^

Macaroni
Oatmeal
Oysters
Peanut butter
Peanuts
Peas, dried
Pike
Plums ^
Pork
Prunes ^
Rice, brown
Rice, white
Salmon
Sardines
Sausage
Scallops
Shrimp
Spaghetti
Squash, winter
Sunflower seeds
Turkey
Veal
Walnuts
Wheat germ
Yoghurt

^ These foods leave an alkaline ash but have an acidifying effect on the body.

NEUTRAL ASH FOODS THAT HAVE AN ACIDIFYING EFFECT

Corn oil   Corn syrup   Olive oil   Refined sugar

Contacts! Contacts! Contacts!

If you wish to purchase more copies of this book or find out where you may obtain any of Credence's other book and tape products, please use the contact details below. Credence has local sales offices in a number of countries. Please see our website at www.credence.org for further details on how to contact them:

> UK Orders: (01622) 832386
> UK Fax: (01622) 833314
> www.credence.org
> e-mail: sales@credence.org

HEALTH REVIEW MAGAZINE
What other book entitles you to a free magazine subscription and regular e-mail updates completely free? If you have not received these and have purchased this book, contact us on the above numbers.

Credence Publications
PO Box 3
TONBRIDGE
Kent TN12 9ZY
England
sales@credence.org

ECLUB BULLETINS
Twice each month, the Campaign for Truth in Medicine sends out the EClub Internet bulletin to thousands of subscribers worldwide. This highly informative e-mail newsletter is available FREE to customers who have purchased this book or who have requested EClub. This online bulletin contains the latest news and research on cancer, heart disease, mental health and other vital health topics. DO NOT BE WITHOUT THIS GREAT RESOURCE! If you wish to subscribe, log on to the Campaign site at www.campaignfortruth.com and click the 'Join CTM' tab to complete your free application.

THE CANCER PREVENTION COALITION

The *Cancer Prevention Coalition* (CPC), with its STATEMENT OF PURPOSE, "Stop Cancer Before It Starts", opened its national office in Chicago, Illinois in July 1994. Chaired by Samuel S. Epstein, M.D. emeritus Professor of environmental medicine at the University of Illinois School of Public Health, Chicago.

Dr. Epstein is an internationally recognized authority on cancer prevention and on avoidable causes of cancer. These include unknowing exposures to industrial carcinogens in air, water, the workplace and consumer products - food, cosmetics and toiletries, and household products including pesticides - and carcinogenic prescription drugs. He has published some 260 peer-reviewed articles, and authored or co-authored 10 books including: the prize winning 1978 **The Politics of Cancer**; the 1995 **Safe Shopper's Bible**; the 1998 **Breast Cancer Prevention Program**; and the 1998 **The Politics of Cancer, Revisited**.

Dr. Epstein's honours are numerous, including the 1998 Right Livelihood Award (the alternative Nobel Prize) for his international contributions to cancer prevention, and the 1999 Project Censored Award (the alternative Pulitzer Prize for investigative journalism) for an article critiquing the American Cancer Society.

The CPC is a unique nationwide coalition of leading independent experts in cancer prevention and public health, together with citizen activists and representatives of organized labour, public interest, environmental and women's health groups. The primary goal of CPC is to reverse escalating cancer rates in the U.S. and internationally, through a comprehensive strategy of outreach, public education, advocacy and public policy initiatives to establish prevention as the foremost cancer policy.

The CPC has Local and Regional Offices in the U.S., and also international Offices in Canada, Australia, Japan, Korea, Mexico, Singapore and the United Kingdom. For more information, including membership application, please visit www.preventcancer.com.

Other Book Titles by Credence

Scared Sick of Cancer? Don't Be. Get the Facts... and then get on with your life !

CANCER: WHY WE'RE STILL DYING TO KNOW THE TRUTH

by Phillip Day

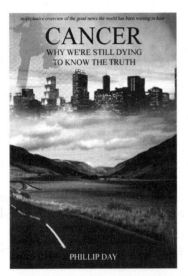

For more information on the truth behind cancer and Metabolic Therapy, our world-famous book, *Cancer: Why We're Still Dying to Know the Truth* is the excellent starting point. This overview title exposes the ongoing establishment cover-up over the failure of traditional cancer treatments and explains Metabolic Therapy (Vitamins B17/A&E/enzymes), the controversial treatment for cancer and its prevention. This book further details the amazing track record of nutrition and its role within the simple, combined protocol of Metabolic Therapy. Whether you have cancer, or are exercising prevention for you and your family, PLEASE get educated on this vital issue today.

Title: *Cancer: Why We're Still Dying to Know the Truth*
by Phillip Day
First published in April 1999 by Credence Publications
Available at www.credence.org

B17 METABOLIC THERAPY IN THE PREVENTION AND CONTROL OF CANCER
- a technical manual -
compiled by Phillip Day

From the desks of some of the world's leading cancer scientists comes the empirical proof of Vitamin B17 and its co-factors in the treatment and prevention of cancer. These explosive findings have been the cause of the real cancer war, where vested interests have moved to vilify and denigrate nutrition in order to protect their highly lucrative cancer incomes.

B17 METABOLIC THERAPY

in the prevention and control of CANCER

a technical manual

compiled by
PHILLIP DAY

> ➤ Find out why 18 'primitive' cultures do not get cancer in their isolated state.
> ➤ What three nutritional components have been found vital in the prevention and the treatment of cancer?
> ➤ What can you do to change your diet in ways which will give you maximum protection from cancer and other associated ailments?
> ➤ Why do animals not get cancer in the wild, yet succumb to it when 'domesticated' by humans?
> ➤ Discover the amazing research of Professor John Beard of Edinburgh University and American Biochemist Ernst T Krebs Jr which shows what cancer actually is. Remove your fear of this disease forever.
> ➤ Why are huge budgets continually spent on 'fighting the war against cancer' when this information has been in the public domain for 50 years?
> ➤ Examine the actual technical theses and trials carried out by doctors and scientists that validate this amazingly simple protocol.

> Find out what you can do today to join the global movement to eradicate cancer from the 21st century!

Phillip Day: *"Now comes the empirical information for doctors, scientists and laymen alike, which can be used at a local, state or global level to eradicate cancer and its heartache from the human race forever. Each of us has a chance today to be great – to remove far from us the greed, entrenched error and ignorance that has allowed cancer to flourish like an evil bloom in our midst. In a sense, cancer will remain around only as long as it takes humankind to achieve that rare level of maturity, when he will treasure his own well-being and that of his friends and loved ones above the tempting lure of wealth, prestige and renown."*

Title: *B17 Metabolic Therapy – A Technical Manual*
by Phillip Day
First published in 2002 by Credence Publications
Available at www.credence.org

GREAT NEWS ON CANCER IN THE 21ST CENTURY
by Steven Ransom

THERE IS TIME!

A cancer diagnosis calls for decisions – decisions that because of circumstances, are so often made in haste. *Great News on Cancer in the 21st Century* is the first book that tells us there is time to consider the options! Within these pages is everything you need to know about taking the next step.

Did you know for instance that vested interests in the cancer industry will be having a direct impact on the advice you are receiving from your doctor? Why aren't we being told about the validated, non-

332

conventional treatments that are saving and enhancing lives daily? Instead, we are offered profitable chemotherapy and radiation treatments that damage the immune system – sometimes irreparably. Get informed on the dangers associated with these treatments – including the facts and figures they don't tell you! Learn how to interpret the misleading information for yourself.

Cancer mis-diagnosis is on the increase. Are you making life-changing decisions without a second opinion? Breast cancer screening/mammography, for example. How dangerous is it? Find out about the simple breast self-examination procedures that are just as effective and pose no danger to women's health, and discover the great news that will lift the current fear associated with breast cancer. Read the powerful testimonies of people who are being helped tremendously with various non-conventional treatments - stories of doctors unable to believe the disappearance of supposedly incurable cancers! This summary represents just a fraction of the wealth of information you will uncover in *Great News on Cancer in the 21st Century*.

"Excellent and well researched. Congratulations! I will certainly be directing all my cancer patients to your book." **Dr Bill Reeder**

"Informative and empowering. This book should be required reading for anyone who values his or her health." **John J Moelaert** - author of *The Cancer Conspiracy*

"Dear Steve, thank God you wrote this book! Thank you, thank you, thank you!" **Edie Matthews**

"Dear Steve, I must blame you for a sleepless night. Just brilliant! I have been immersing myself in all of this information for a while now, but never have I found it written so well!" **Ledonna James**

Title: *Great News on Cancer in the 21st Century*
by Steven Ransom
Published by Credence Publications 2002
Available at www.credence.org

THE MIND GAME
by Phillip Day

Every new year brings incredible new inventions, new advances in technologies, new medicines, further discoveries in physics, chemistry and the other sciences. There are also new political challenges and military threats. News channels such as ABC, CNN, the BBC and Sky report 24 hours a day on the problems besetting this complicated, restless and fretting planet. Credence Research monitors this prodigious output; our publications division prepares reports and publishes books on these subjects. Our lecturers travel and host public meetings around the world to share this vital information.

But *The Mind Game*, it must be said, has been my most extraordinary and challenging project to date. I believe, after you have finished reading this book, that you also will agree that there are no greater or more important issues facing us as a civilisation than those under discussion in these pages. I speak to thousands of citizens a year during the course of my own touring. Almost to a man, woman or child, my audiences are worried about the world around them. They are at present known as the Silent Majority.

Author and researcher Bruce Wiseman writes: *"Outside our windows, the peaceful streets of years past now harbour violence. In some neighbourhoods, gunfire pierces the night. Police helicopters fly overhead, scanning yards and alleys for runaway criminals.*

We worry about our children. Once-quiet schools are now hothouses of drug-trafficking, promiscuity, and vice unimaginable in days gone by. We hear of an ever declining literacy rate, dwindling test scores, and of graduates who can't even find their home city on a map. We wonder how they will ever make it in the adult world.

In our homes, at our jobs, on our television screens, we see that the once-clear line between right and wrong has become grey and hazy. Virtue is held up to ridicule. The honest man is viewed as a fool. Criminal behaviour is now excused under the banner of 'irresistible impulse' and 'diminished capacity'.

Hardly anyone would argue with the statement that <u>something</u> has been eating at the moral fabric for decades now.... No one questions that there is a palpable, destructive force. In the United States, for example, people are at each other's throats over it. Liberals blame it on conservative policies, right wingers rebuke the left. Many in the religious community have held the entertainment industry accountable." [424]

THE SILENT MAJORITY

The Silent Majority of the public sees these things, yet has remained silent up to now. These are ordinary, decent citizens who have grown exasperated with the ineffectiveness and corruption of their political system. Many have registered their protests by refusing to vote. Others are frustrated at the media for eschewing its collective responsibility to evaluate the social problems we really face. Most people, as we will learn later, have not the slightest idea which ends the press really serves. Dumbfounded, we look on as our newspapers, TV and cinemas feed us a steady, putrid fare of sex, violence, money and the shenanigans of the famous, instead of promoting the common-sense approaches that could heal our nations, restore our health services and stabilise our societies.

PSYCHIATRY

Psychiatry is one science in particular that comes under scrutiny in my book. At first glance, most would not even acknowledge the incredible changes psychiatric and psychological theories have had on our world. Yet we shall see that they have permeated our courts, our police, our hospitals, our movies and TV, our schoolyards, our governments and even our homes. Who would consider for one moment that psychiatry could have played such a fundamental role in

---

[424] Wiseman, Bruce, *Psychiatry – The Ultimate Betrayal*, Freedom Publishing, Los Angeles: 1995, pp.5,6

the development of politics, education, entertainment, war and medicine?

OFF THE RAILS?

Many have concluded that mankind itself must be going insane. Indeed, we are told, at no other time in human history has a greater segment of society been diagnosed 'mentally ill' than today. Our nations' governments, schools and courts appreciate this, which is why they are veritably aswarm with armies of politically correct legislators, administrators and the inevitable battalions of psychologists, psychiatrists and other 'mental health' experts. One could expect that with such an impressive arsenal of professional expertise on call, victory itself would be assured. Who would possibly consider for a moment, in their right mind, that these might conceivably be the very same armies responsible for all the chaos?

THOMAS SZASZ

Dr Thomas Szasz is an interesting individual. He is Professor of Psychiatry Emeritus at the State University of New York at Syracuse and Lifetime Fellow of the American Psychiatric Association. Although reaching the pinnacle of his profession, Dr Szasz has repeatedly denounced psychiatry as *"...probably the single most destructive force that has affected American society within the last fifty years."* An author of 23 books, including *The Myth of Mental Illness*, described by *Science* magazine as *"bold and often brilliant"*, the Hungarian-born specialist has covered, in his writings, every type of abuse carried out by his profession. Szasz pronounces psychiatry guilty, not only of gross abuses of power and human rights over its patients, <u>but also for the far-reaching, deleterious effects its philosophies have had on society throughout the world</u>:

"Psychiatry is a part of the general liberal ethos.... Everybody is a victim, everybody has special rights, no responsibilities. This psychiatric view has so completely infiltrated [global thinking], *people don't even think of it as psychiatry."* [425]

---

[425] Citizen's Commission of Human Rights (CCHR) Interview with Dr Thomas Szasz, 17th September 1993

THE *MIND GAME* MISSION

This book traces the origins of psychiatry - this 'science of the mind' - and lays bare the startling and unsettling history of the Trojan Horse that has taken up residence in our midst. Part 1 of my book deals with psychiatry itself, while Part 2 examines the major 'mental disorders' from their true and vital standpoint. And it is here that the good news about our predicament is truly seen. Is there really such a thing as 'mental disease', or is the reality for us and our societies altogether more straightforward and, most importantly, manageable?

There is great news here for those concerned about Alzheimer's, Parkinson's, ADD/ADHD, schizophrenia, anorexia, multiple sclerosis and a host of other disorders. For the millions who wrestle with these problems and issues daily, help is at hand. My task in the pages to follow is to report to you the leading research on these issues from the mouths of the specialists themselves, so the reader may make up their own mind on how to proceed from here.

For those unsettled and perplexed by the predicaments of the modern world and why seemingly nothing is being done about them, the journey we will shortly take will explain the nature of Wiseman's *"palpable, destructive force"*, and how it has gained so much power over us. More to the point, my new book will discuss measures whereby the public may retake control over much of what has been given up or taken away. If you are sympathetic to the mission of this book, then take heart, for there are millions of people who think the same way you do. I believe, if we are to pass on to our children a future world that contains any legacy at all of decency, honesty and a moral compass, then we must discuss and resolve the answers to the ultimate question that faces our world today:

"What on Earth is Going On?"

Title: *The Mind Game*
by Phillip Day
Published by Credence Publications 2002
Available at www.credence.org

TOXIC BITE

by Bill Kellner-Read

Most people go to the dentist at some point in their lives, and many go regularly. But who really questions what happens when we are in the dentist's chair? Can we be sure that we are receiving the best, long-term treatment for such an important and necessary part of our body?

Finally there's a new book that demystifies dentistry and lets you take control of your own dental health. *Toxic Bite*, by British dentist Bill Kellner-Read, gets to the bottom of some startling questions:

➢ Could your gum disease be responsible for heart disease or stroke?
➢ What products are we using every day that contribute to wider toxic illnesses?
➢ And what about those extractions? Do we really need that tooth pulled?
➢ Should we really be extracting children's teeth for orthodontic correction?
➢ What are the longer-term consequences of having less teeth in our mouth?
➢ What about the other correctional work being carried out today?
➢ Is there a link between nutrition and gum disease?

You might not have toothache. But what about back-ache, neck-ache, jaw-ache, migraine or those constant blinding headaches? It may well be an underlying dental problem that is contributing to wider systemic disease, chronic pain and discomfort in your body.

For the best in toxin-free tooth, mouth and body care, read *Toxic Bite* - the latest addition to the Credence roster of top-selling healthcare titles.

Title: *Toxic Bite*
by Bill Kellner-Read
First published in 2002 by Credence Publications
Available at www.credence.org

FOOD FOR THOUGHT
compiled by Phillip Day

Need a guide on where to go with your food? What better way to embrace the dietary concepts laid down in *The Mind Game, Cancer: Why We're Still Dying to Know the Truth* and *Health Wars* than to obtain a copy of our official recipe book.

This delightful guide takes you through the main concepts of acid/alkali, Vitamin B17 dishes, the proper combining of foods, the problems with meat and dairy in excessive amounts, fruit consumption techniques, smart foods, a host of detox menus, 5-10% meat and dairy recipes, snacks, pro-active sickness dieting, children's dishes and proper supplementation. Whether you are suffering or just want to make a change for your extended future, sensible nutrition comes to life in *Food For Thought*, bringing you the most delicious foods that WON'T KILL YOU!

Title: *Food for Thought*
Compiled by Phillip Day
First published in August 2001 by Credence Publications
Available at www.credence.org

PLAGUE, PESTILENCE AND THE PURSUIT OF POWER

by Steven Ransom

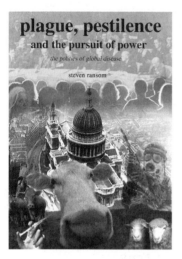

plague, pestilence
and the pursuit of power
the politics of global disease
steven ransom

Almost every day, it seems, we are hearing reports of some 'highly infectious' disease breaking out somewhere across the world - the recent flu pandemics, AIDS decimating Africa, tuberculosis on the rise again, measles, and meningitis on the increase. And in the animal kingdom, we've seen Bovine Spongiform Encephalopathy (BSE), poultry flu, swine fever, more BSE and now foot and mouth, wreaking havoc across our countryside. One could be forgiven for thinking that we are quite literally surrounded by virulent illness. But not everything is as it seems – not by a long way.

In this book, we discover that these so-called 'epidemics' are NOT the deadly illnesses we have been led to believe by our respective governments, national papers and news programs. With all the above-mentioned illnesses, the facts being disseminated have been grossly misleading, accompanied, in many instances, by a deliberate intent to scare and deceive. Welcome to the shocking world of the politically manufactured epidemic - the 'psycho-plague'.

The formula is quite simple. Using the mainstream media as their chosen vehicle for change, powerful vested interests are deliberately instigating national and international fearsome headlines. Through these channels, the problem – the epidemic – the psycho-plague, is manufactured. A crisis has now been firmly embedded into the mind of the populace. **"We must have a solution!"** we cry. Lo and behold, a governmental/corporate solution is speedily proffered.

In reality, the epidemic needing 'swift state intervention' has been nothing more than a Trojan Horse either for creating immense profit for various pharmaceutical industries or, as we shall discover, for ushering in unsavoury, global super-state ideology. Throughout this whole process, we are being taught what to think about health and disease, but not how.

In examining the facts laid out before us, we soon realise that our battle is not so much against pathological disease, as against corrupt and self-serving desires, birthed in the minds of man. This book contains the supporting evidence to make this case. You are invited to consider the evidence for yourself.

But this book also maps out a positive way forward. For, in discovering the true nature and causes of these 'epidemics', a longer lasting remedy can now be planned for the future.

Plague, Pestilence and the Pursuit of Power is dedicated to those who want to find out what really goes on behind the closed doors of Big Business and Big Government and to those who wish to see truth reign in conventional science and medicine.

Title: *Plague, Pestilence and the Pursuit of Power*
by Steven Ransom
First published in June 2001 by Credence Publications
Available at www.credence.org

WORLD WITHOUT AIDS

by Steven Ransom & Phillip Day

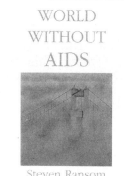

World Without AIDS dismantles one of the world's greatest fears and lays bare the deceit, fraudulent science and needless fearmongering that lie at the heart of this supposed global epidemic. Over ten years in the making, this impeccably researched book gives an eye-opening account of what vested interests can get away with, given a trusting public, an almost limitless supply of money and scant scruples. It also explains the non-existence of HIV, the bankruptcy of the HIV test, the real causes of immune suppression, the AIDS-devastating-Africa myth and the appalling dangers of the establishment-approved medications prescribed to those who have been written off as 'HIV positive'.

Title: *World Without AIDS*
by Steven Ransom and Phillip Day
First published in June 2000 by Credence Publications
Available through credence.org

All titles can also be obtained from the distributor whose details are in the *Contacts!* section of this book.

THE CAMPAIGN FOR
TRUTH IN MEDICINE
"a force for change"

WHAT IS CTM?

Campaign for Truth in Medicine is a worldwide organisation dedicated to pressing for change in areas of science and medicine where entrenched scientific error, ignorance or vested interests are costing lives. Its ranks comprise doctors, scientists, researchers, bio-chemists, politicians, industry executives and countless members of the world public, all of whom have made one observation in common. They  have recognised that, in certain key areas of global disease, drug treatments and overall healthcare philosophy, the medical, chemical and political establishments are pursuing the wrong course with the maximum of precision, even when their own legitimate and erudite scientific research has illustrated the dangers of pursuing these courses.

CTM BACKS ITS PEOPLE'S CHARTER

CTM's People's Charter catalogues these key problem areas - for example AIDS, cancer, the mental health concerns discussed in this book, heart disease and vaccinations - all where the preponderance of evidence demonstrates severe cause for concern over deadly errors in basic science, resulting in needless loss of life. CTM's charter also highlights industry's every-day use of potentially harmful contaminants and biohazards, such as toothpaste's sodium fluoride, shampoo's sodium lauryl sulphate and cosmetic's propylene glycol, which have long been linked to long-term serious health risks and death. CTM's purpose is to present this damning evidence to its members, to the public at large and to the establishments and individuals involved in these errors, in order to press for immediate

343

change and cessation of their use for the benefit of humanity. The People's Charter is periodically amended to reflect current issues and new areas of concern.

CTM STANDS FOR TRUTH
For decades members of the public and a significant proportion of their medical and scientific professionals have become increasingly angry and frustrated at what they see as establishment indifference and even downright hostility towards much-needed changes in healthcare, especially in areas where the proven solution is substantially less profitable than the current status quo.

PROMOTING THE TRUTH
CTM believes in promoting the truth in these matters, thereby exposing those morally bankrupt and compromised politicians, corporations and individuals responsible. This method of action is viewed as a top priority. CTM is dedicated to pushing for immediate change, in order that immediate relief from many of the diseases and their causes, currently afflicting us, may be implemented, the remedies for which, in certain cases, have been a matter of existing scientific knowledge for decades.

The Journal of the American Medical Association (JAMA) implicitly reports that western healthcare, along with its drugs, treatments and hospitals, is now the third leading cause of death in the United States, next to heart disease and cancer. If we examine this astonishing fact, also highlighted by US consumer advocate Ralph Nader in the early 1990's, we come to realise that the Western healthcare paradigm is adopted by almost all developed nations and many other developing countries around the world. Thus this tragic statistic of iatrogenic death can be fairly considered to be global in application.

This would be serious enough on its own, yet the true extent of this orthodox medical catastrophe is unfortunately far more devastating. Western medical establishments are in possession of key life-saving information that can immediately and drastically reduce current and future global incidences of cancer, heart disease, AIDS and other treatable, non-fatal conditions. But in almost all cases these institutions have chosen neither to adopt these measures, train their healthcare practitioners in these practices, nor publicise the latter to a generally trusting world populace. Thus these government personnel and their associated medical luminaries, who have wilfully kept this life-saving information from their doctors and the public, may justifiably be exposed for becoming the leading cause of death across the planet today.

CTM STANDS FOR DIRECT ACTION
CTM believes that, in certain cases, legitimate direct action is warranted against these institutions and individuals to halt their wilful and harmful actions and hold them to account. In these circumstances, CTM calls upon its membership to organise and act in a unified, lawful and mature fashion to bring these matters to the attention of the mass communications media, government leaders and heads of state through demonstrations and other appropriate action. CTM is dedicated to being part of the people's movement in this regard; a powerful and irresistible force for change, compelling vital reform TODAY for a safer and healthier world for our children and children's children.

CTM IS FREE FROM VESTED INTEREST FUNDING
Through its network of worldwide professional contacts, CTM has constant access to well-researched information on key health issues. CTM brings its members highly readable and jargon-free information, such as that contained in this book.

CTM HAS ALL THE NECESSARY CONTACTS
...at local and central government/corporate level, responsible for particular health legislation and legislative change. Names, addresses, contact details and relevant template letters are supplied with all CTM newsletters.

CTM IS A HEALTH ADVOCACY ORGANISATION
with purpose and direction. It is a conduit through which the individual minority voice can become a powerful and respected, collective majority voice for change.

WHAT YOU CAN DO NOW

CTM invites you to visit its web-site to learn more about how you can join this worldwide movement FOR FREE and receive regular bulletins and further information on these fascinating subjects as they develop. Be part of a different future. One that celebrates life!

Campaign for Truth in Medicine
PO Box 3
Tonbridge
Kent
TN12 9ZY UK
e-mail: info@campaignfortruth.com
www.campaignfortruth.com

Index

Assimilation cycle, 231
Asthma, 135, 136, 260
Ataxia, 192
Atherosclerosis, 54, 57, 60, 61, 69, 70,
135, 138, 148, 151
Auckland, 39
Auschwitz, 181
Australia, 10, 13, 17, 33, 38, 39, 42, 71,
156, 160, 260, 305, 329
AZT, 21, 302, 319, 321

B

Bacteria, 32, 34, 95, 123, 137, 214, 234,
310, 319, 323
Barefoot, Robert, 248, 249, 255
Basel, Switzerland, 60
Beard, John, 84, 85, 86, 88, 128
Bedwetting, 136
Bell's palsy, 227
Bengal, 14, 15
Bentonite, 214
Benzaldehyde, 87
Berglas, Dr Alexander, 12
Beriberi, 35, 227, 311
Beta carotene, 60, 272
Beta-blockers, 65
Beta-glucosidase, 87
Bible, The, 287
Biliary tract, 123
Binzel, Philip, 90, 91, 150
Bioflavonoids, 60, 272
Biosphere, 17
Bladder, 126, 128, 235, 275
Blood flukes, 275
BMA (British Medical Association),
22, 262
BMJ (British Medical Journal), 38, 69,
70, 261
Bonaparte, Napoleon, 30
Boomsma, Laura, 296, 297
Bouziane, N R, 92
Bovine Spongiform Encephalopathy
(BSE), 340
Brain, 8, 47, 48, 57, 59, 72, 74, 122,
123, 129, 161, 162, 177, 179, 183, 192,
210, 238, 272, 322
Braverman, Albert, 81

British Army, 12
British Broadcasting Corporation
(BBC), 334
British Columbia, Canada, 101, 102
Bromelain, 93, 267
Bronchitis, 32
Bubonic plague, 33
Burk, Dean, 89, 105, 106
Burkitt, Dean, 149, 150
Burton, Dan, 187
Butane, 214

C

Cairns, John, 80
Caisse, René, 93, 274
Calcium, 93, 141, 248, 249, 250, 251,
255, 271, 276, 288
Calf thymus, 93, 267
California, 37, 50, 59, 81, 89, 98, 105,
127, 131, 133, 148, 168, 178, 253, 279,
323
Campaign for Truth in Medicine
(CTM), 297, 328, 343
Canada, 39, 92, 102, 124, 126, 274,
305, 308, 329
Canadian Dental Association, 102
Cancer, 8, 9, 10, 11, 12, 13, 15, 21, 22,
30, 32, 35, 36, 37, 38, 39, 42, 46, 49,
51, 52, 53, 54, 65, 71, 76, 77, 78, 79, 80,
81, 82, 83, 84, 85, 86, 87, 88, 89, 90,
91, 92, 93, 94, 105, 106, 107, 108, 109,
113, 123, 124, 127, 128, 136, 145, 149,
150, 151, 152, 158, 160, 161, 163, 165,
167, 168, 169, 174, 194, 195, 196, 200,
205, 209, 212, 213, 216, 217, 222, 226,
227, 234, 237, 238, 242, 248, 254, 255,
256, 260, 261, 267, 268, 269, 270, 271,
273, 274, 276, 277, 278, 279, 288, 293,
298, 299, 300, 315, 328, 329, 330, 331,
332, 343, 344, 357
Cancer Prevention Coalition, 79, 197,
216, 217, 329
Candida albicans, 34
Cannon, Geoffrey, 201, 204
Canola oil, 288
Carbolic acid, 191

348

Carcinogens, 127, 128, 194, 196, 205, 213, 217, 255, 277, 279, 329
Carnitine, 61, 66
Carnivore, 145, 146
Carotid artery, 51, 70
Cartier, Jacques, 55, 56, 308
Casein, 139
Cassel, Ingri, 142
Cassie-Tea, 273, 274
Castration, 157
Catabolism, 235
CDC (Centers for Disease Control), 22, 97, 104, 184
Cell respiration, 119, 163, 213, 216, 249
Cellulite, 122
CFCs (Chlorofluorocarbons), 254, 255
Charcoal, 111
Charterhouse, 357
Chemotherapy, 37, 76, 78, 80, 81, 90, 271, 278, 279, 293, 294, 296, 297, 298, 300
Chicago, Illinois, 79, 88, 109, 197, 216, 329
Chicken pox, 191
Chile, 254
Chirac, Jacques, 25
Chlorine, 96, 111, 254
Cholera, 23, 24, 95, 184, 318
Cholesterol, 46, 57, 58, 60, 61, 62, 64, 65, 70, 249
Cholestyramine, 64
Christchurch, New Zealand, 39
Christian Brothers, 81
Chronic Fatigue Syndrome, 183
Chymotrypsin, 85, 88, 93, 123, 150, 267
CIA (Central Intelligence Agency), 24, 25
Cisplatin, 81
Citrus, 86
CMA (Chemical Manufacturers' Association), 194
CNN, 7, 27
Cocaine, 261, 302
Coenzyme Q10, 64
Coffee, 10, 50, 93, 118, 125, 199, 300, 301
Cohen, Samuel, 128
Colitis, 13, 123, 149

Collagen, 55, 56, 57, 59, 74, 214, 215
Colloidal minerals, 93, 272
Committee for Freedom-of-Choice in Cancer, 89
Committee for Freedom-of-Choice in Cancer Therapy, 89
Committee on the Safety of Medicines, 190
Condoms, 26, 27
Coney, Sandra, 156, 162
Confectionary, 199, 200
Constipation, 107, 121, 149, 152
Contreras, Ernesto, 92
Contreras, Francisco, 92
Corpus luteum, 161, 162, 166, 180
Cosmetics, 87, 194, 196, 209, 213, 215, 216, 217, 329
Cowpox, 173, 174, 175
Credence Publications, 3, 23, 37, 93, 94, 181, 227, 277, 321
Crime, 13, 117
Crohn's disease, 123, 227, 234
Curcuminoids, 272, 273
Cyanocobalamin, 90
Cycling, 256, 257

D

Daly City, California, 133
Day, Phillip, 296, 297, 330, 331, 332, 333, 334, 337, 339, 342
Dean, H Trendley, 98
Delaney Clause, 126, 127
Delinquency, 13, 15
Denmark, 45
Dental fluorosis, 102, 106, 107, 113, 114
Dentistry, 338
Depo-Provera, 159
DES (Diethylstilbestrol), 278
Dextrose, 118
Diabetes, 8, 10, 13, 31, 37, 70, 124, 125, 135, 141, 145, 149, 227, 260
Diamond, Harvey, 95, 134, 139, 145, 148, 230, 235
Diethanolamine (DEA), 212
Dikitopiprazines, 287
Diosgenin, 169
Disney, Walt, 278

E

F

Formic acid, 130
Free radicals, 69, 120, 234, 273
French, Roger, 34
Fructose, 118
Fulvic acid, 271, 272

G

Gall bladder, 47
Gallo, Robert, 191
Gastritis, 32
General Medical Council, 22
Georgians, 16, 172
Gey, Professor, 60
Ginko Biloba, 272
Glaciers, 14
Glucose, 118, 119, 203, 238
Glutamate, 129, 203, 322
Glutamic acid, 122
Gluten, 138
Glycerin, 215
Goat's cheese, 14
Grand Rapids, Michigan, 99
Gray, Alan S, 101, 102
Greenpeace, 168
Greer, Germaine, 156
Griffin, G Edward, 89, 90, 191, 309
Grigorski, Leon, 185
Guidetti, Etore, 93

H

Hammond, Phil, 261, 262
Hanover, Germany, 91
Harrison, Rosalind, 157, 158
Hawaii, 31, 274
Hawaiian noni, 93, 274
Hayes, Jr., Arthur Hull, 131
Hazleton Laboratories, 195
hCG (human Chorionic
Gonadotrophin), 180, 181
Headaches, 338
Healing, 47, 57, 58, 63, 77, 78, 85, 93,
108, 123, 128, 150, 165, 210, 230, 234,
236, 255, 268, 293, 301
Health Wars, 287, 288, 339

Heart disease, 8, 9, 10, 13, 15, 30, 31,
32, 37, 39, 42, 46, 49, 51, 52, 53, 54,
55, 56, 57, 58, 59, 60, 61, 62, 63, 65,
69, 70, 73, 74, 135, 140, 145, 149, 151,
163, 200, 222, 226, 227, 237, 242, 260,
328, 338, 343, 344
Hepatitis A, 191
Hexafluorosilicic acid, 103
High blood pressure, 13, 59, 65, 70, 74,
169, 260
Himmler, Heinrich, 181
Hippocrates, 53
Hirsutism, 160
HIV (Human immunodeficiency
virus), 21, 22, 184, 301, 302, 303, 304,
318, 319, 320, 321
Hodgkin's disease, 83
Holmquist, Kathryn, 186
Hooper Bay, Alaska, 109
Hopis, 17
HRT (hormone replacement therapy),
71, 73, 155, 157, 159, 160, 161, 163, 164,
165
Hunzas, 10, 12, 13, 14, 16, 83, 86, 251
Hydrazine sulphate, 93
Hydrocyanic acid, 79, 86, 87
Hydrogen cyanide, 87
Hydrogenated fats, 288
Hyperactivity, 122
Hypothalamus, 162, 256
Hysterectomy, 73, 157, 163, 164

I

Iatrogenic death, 40, 45, 46, 344
IMF (International Monetary Fund),
23
Immune system, 181, 183
India, 13, 26, 101, 172, 173, 181
Insects, 313
Insulin, 124, 125, 141
Internet, 280, 285, 286
Intestines, 123, 139, 145, 231, 234, 255,
275
Intracellular fluids, 249, 250
Ionised calcium, 248, 249, 250, 251,
271, 272
Irish Republic, 186

MCL (Maximum contaminant level), 112
MD Anderson Comprehensive Cancer Center, 83
Medved, Michael, 223
Memorial Sloan-Kettering (MSK), 81
Mengele, Josef, 181
Menstruation, 161, 162, 163
Mercola, Joseph, 38, 39, 40, 45, 120, 124, 125, 131, 184, 187
Mercury, 104, 191
Mesomorphs, 259
Metabolic diseases, 35, 36, 227
Metabolic therapy, 269, 330
Metabolism, 55, 61, 167, 257
Metabolites, 119, 121, 123, 130, 153, 233, 236, 275
Methanol, 129
Mexican wild yam, 169
Mexico, 92, 180, 298, 300, 329
Micro-emulsification, 268
Middletown, Maryland, 110
Milk, 288
Miller, Diane Disney, 278
Mineral oil, 216
MMR (Measles, mumps and Rubella), 186, 187, 188, 189, 190, 191
Monethanolamine (MEA), 213
Monsanto, 129, 136, 195
Monte, Woodrow C, 130, 131
Montreal, Canada, 92
Morinda citrifolia, 274
Mosley, Michael, 261
Mosley, Michael, 261
Moss, Ralph, 81
Mount St Helen's, 254
Mouthwashes, 213
Mower, Tom, 217, 274
Moyers, Bill, 194, 196
MSDS (Material safety data sheet), 212
Mucoid plaque, 233, 234, 275
Mugos Laboratories, 268
Multiple Chemical Sensitivity, 197
Mundy, George R, 250
Muskegon, Michigan, 99

Nader, Ralph, 39, 44
Nagel, Janet, 97, 110, 111
Naismith, Donald, 202
NAO (National Audit Office), 67
National Academy of Sciences, 63, 64, 109, 215
National Cancer Institute (NCI), 88, 89
National Institute of Occupational Safety and Health, 209
Natural Hygiene, 32, 70, 93, 150, 226, 228, 230, 231, 237, 241, 242, 253, 259
Navarro, Manuel, 92
NBC, 184
NCI (National Cancer Institute), 79, 89, 105, 106, 108, 196, 213, 277, 279
Nechilli Eskimos, 12
Nelson, Ethel R, 145
Neurons, 129
Neurotransmitters, 129
Nevada, 86
New Jersey, USA, 98, 109, 113, 114, 171
New York, 308, 314, 336
New Zealand, 17, 38, 87, 205
Neways International, 217
Newburgh, New York, 100, 101
NHS (National Health Service), 42, 222, 261, 320
Nicotinic acid (B3), 61
NIEHS (National Institute for Environmental Health Services), 127
Nieper, Hans, 91
NIH (National Institutes of Health), 22, 160
Nippon Dental College, 108
Nitriloside, 86, 87, 88, 91
Nitrosamines, 212, 213
Nixon, Alan C, 80
Nobel Prize, 112, 248, 269, 329
Norplant, 159
NTP (National Toxicology Program), 106, 109, 127
Nutrasweet, 128

N

O

O'Leary, Paula, 47
Obesity, 67, 224, 256

353

P

Q

R

S

T

About the Author

Phillip Day was born in England in 1960. He was educated at the leading British education establishments Selwyn and Charterhouse, and throughout his 20's had a successful entrepreneurial career founding businesses in sales and marketing. With a firm grounding in business and the ways of the media, Phillip's research career began after he became interested in wars going on in the realms of health and politics over issues that were being deliberately withheld or misreported to the public.

His research into AIDS and cancer, as two examples of the medical establishment's entrenched scientific error and brazen profiteering to society's great cost, culminated in two books that have captured the public's imagination around the world: *Cancer: Why We're Still Dying to Know the Truth* and *World Without AIDS*. Phillip's 2002 release is *The Mind Game*, a round-up of research on mental disorders and the aberrant philosophies of psychiatry. The information expounded upon in his books - information deliberately not promoted by governments and their medical establishments - forms the basis of the promotional and educational work in which Phillip's research and investigational units are engaged.

Today Phillip's schedule takes him all over the world, lecturing on the subjects of entrenched scientific error and the little-known groundbreaking research doctors and biochemists have made to break the back of diseases for the benefit of everyone. His goal is to educate the public directly on these issues, a task both the medical establishment and mainstream mass communications media have failed to address to their great shame, due to deep-rooted vested interests and ulterior agendas.

Phillip heads up Credence, a publishing and research organisation now based in twelve countries around the world, which collates the work provided by researchers around the globe. Credence's intention is to work with the establishments and organisations concerned to resolve these life-threatening issues, and to provide the necessary information for citizens to make their own informed choices in these vital matters.

Phillip Day currently lives in Kent, England.

357